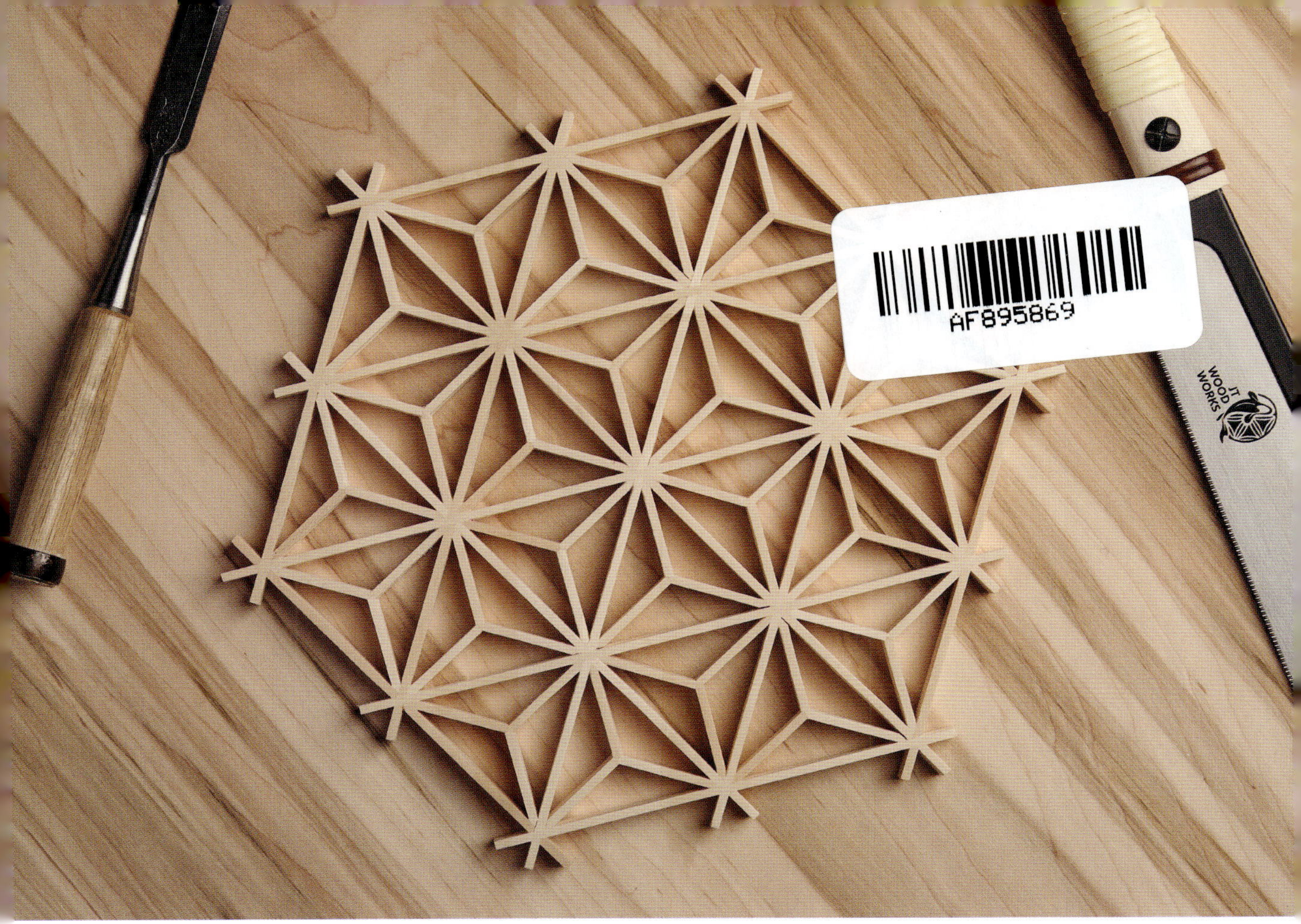

AF895869

Kumiko

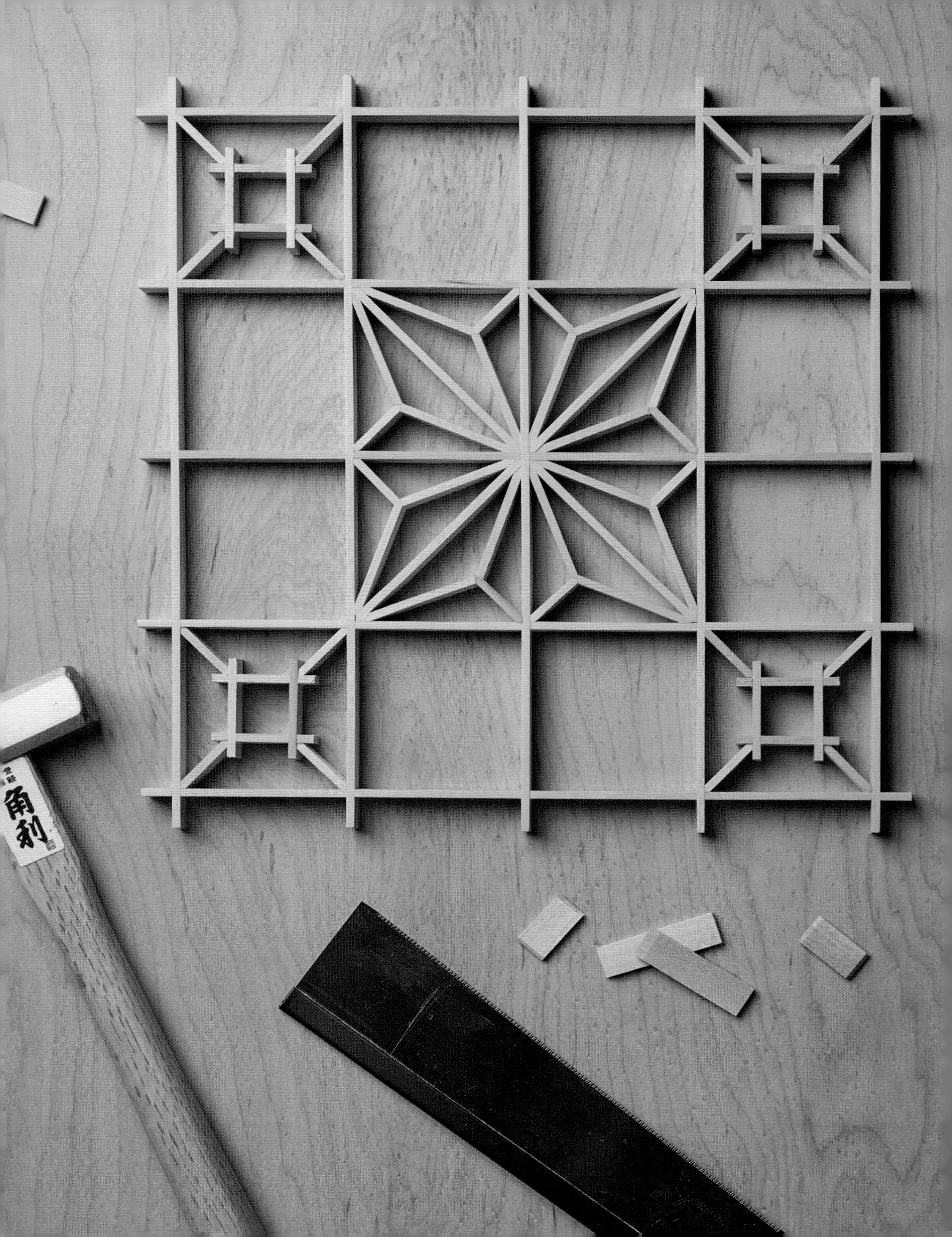
角利

Kumiko

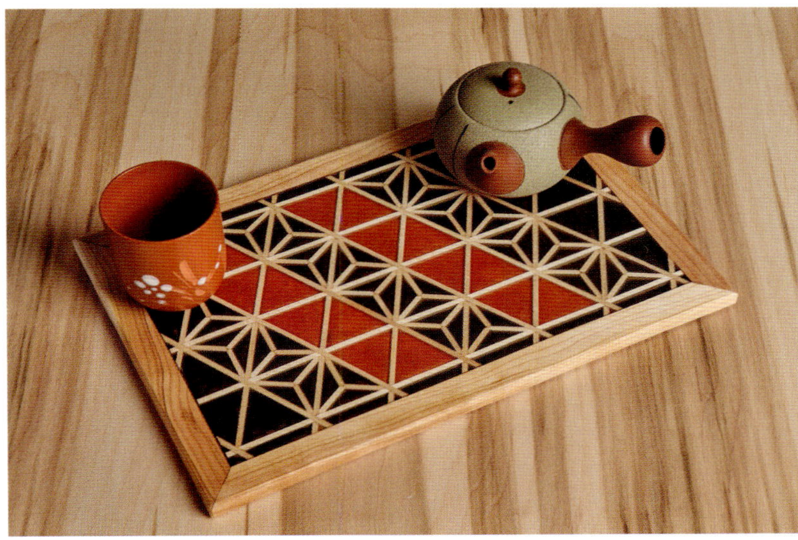

Japanese Joinery Projects with a Modern Twist

Johnny Tromboukis

HERBERT PRESS
LONDON • OXFORD • NEW YORK • NEW DELHI • SYDNEY

HERBERT PRESS
Bloomsbury Publishing Plc
50 Bedford Square, London, WC1B 3DP, UK
Bloomsbury Publishing Ireland Limited,
29 Earlsfort Terrace, Dublin 2, D02 AY28, Ireland

BLOOMSBURY, HERBERT PRESS and the Herbert Press logo are trademarks of Bloomsbury Publishing Plc

First published in Great Britain 2026

Copyright © John Tromboukis, 2026
All project images © Audrey Marie Bufalini, 2026

John Tromboukis has asserted their right under the Copyright, Designs and Patents Act, 1988, to be identified as Author of this work

All rights reserved. No part of this publication may be: i) reproduced or transmitted in any form, electronic or mechanical, including photocopying, recording or by means of any information storage or retrieval system without prior permission in writing from the publishers; or ii) used or reproduced in any way for the training, development or operation of artificial intelligence (AI) technologies, including generative AI technologies. The rights holders expressly reserve this publication from the text and data mining exception as per Article 4(3) of the Digital Single Market Directive (EU) 2019/790

Bloomsbury Publishing Plc does not have any control over, or responsibility for, any third-party websites referred to or in this book. All internet addresses given in this book were correct at the time of going to press. The author and publisher regret any inconvenience caused if addresses have changed or sites have ceased to exist, but can accept no responsibility for any such changes

A catalogue record for this book is available from the British Library

Library of Congress Cataloguing-in-Publication data has been applied for

ISBN: PB: 978-1-78994-382-5; eBook: 978-1-78994-395-5

2 4 6 8 10 9 7 5 3 1

Page layout design by Jerry Goldie Graphic Design
Printed and bound in China by RR Donnelley APS

MIX
Paper | Supporting responsible forestry
FSC www.fsc.org FSC® C144853

To find out more about our authors and books visit www.bloomsbury.com and sign up for our newsletters
For product safety related questions contact productsafety@bloomsbury.com

This book is dedicated to my parents, grandparents, and brother.
Thank you for your generous support and encouragement over the years.
I love you all.

Many tools demonstrated in this book are specialist tools I've designed and produced. Because these are not generally available, you can purchase them from my website (www.jtwoodworks.com) or download plans to build them yourself. The book also includes general guidance for working without these specialty tools, though they are recommended to streamline and facilitate your kumiko work.

Contents

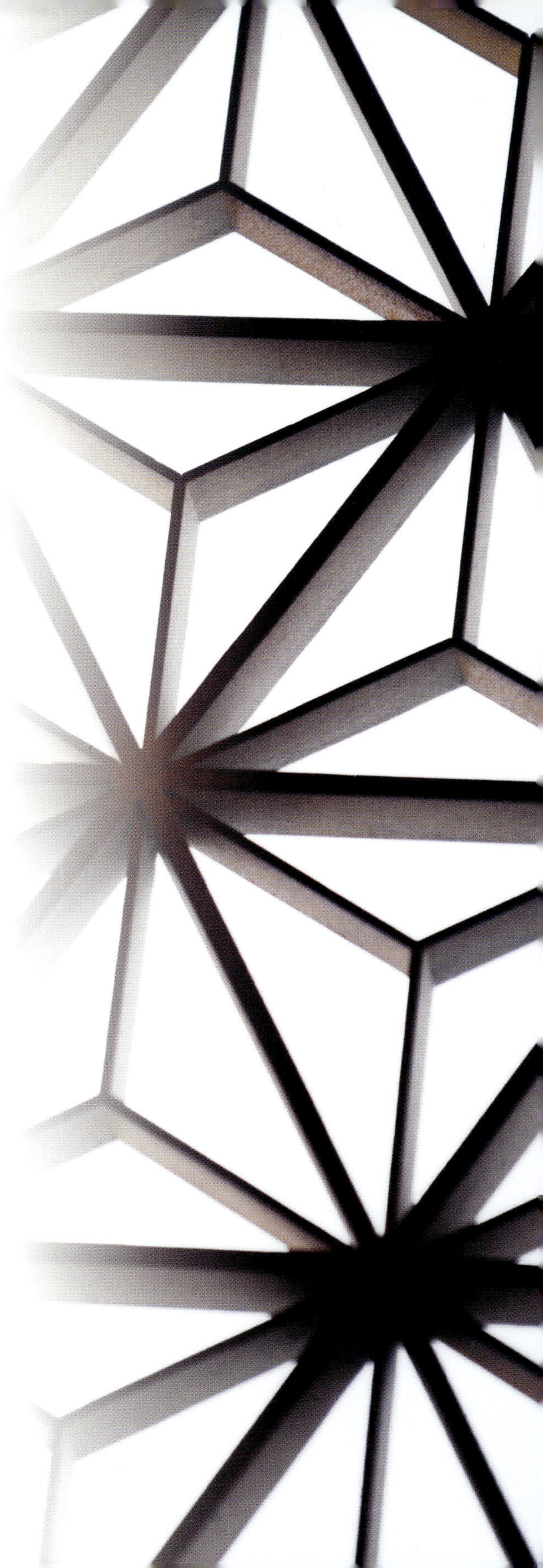

Introduction

Woodworking is more than just a craft, it is an art form that connects us to history, culture, and the natural world. Among the many traditions of woodworking, few are as captivating and intricate as kumiko (組子).

Kumiko is a traditional Japanese woodworking technique that dates back to the Asuka period (538–710 CE), with its origins closely tied to the construction of Buddhist temples. This intricate craft involves the assembly of wooden pieces without the need of nails or glue, relying instead on precise joinery to create geometric patterns. Initially, kumiko was used in the creation of shoji (障子) screens, which are sliding panels that serve as room dividers in traditional Japanese homes. Over time, the technique evolved, incorporating more complex designs and expanding its application to furniture, decorative panels, and architectural elements. The artistry of kumiko reflects the Japanese aesthetic principles of simplicity, harmony, and attention to detail, making it a revered craft that has been passed down through generations of artisans.

Culturally, kumiko holds significant value as a symbol of Japanese craftsmanship and the enduring connection between nature and human creativity. The patterns used in kumiko often draw inspiration from nature, such as flowers, waves, and animals, embodying the Japanese philosophy of finding beauty in the natural world. Additionally, kumiko represents the concept of monozukuri (ものづくり), a term that encapsulates the spirit of meticulous craftsmanship and innovation in Japanese culture. It is a philosophy that emphasizes skill, dedication, and the pursuit of perfection in the creation of high-quality goods. In modern times, kumiko has gained international recognition, not only as a traditional art form but also as a source of inspiration for contemporary design. Its delicate and timeless appeal continues to captivate people worldwide, bridging the gap between historical tradition and modern artistry.

▶ **The Former Tanaka Family Residence blends sukiya-style elegance with intricate kumiko latticework.** Photo by John S Lander/LightRocket via Getty Images.

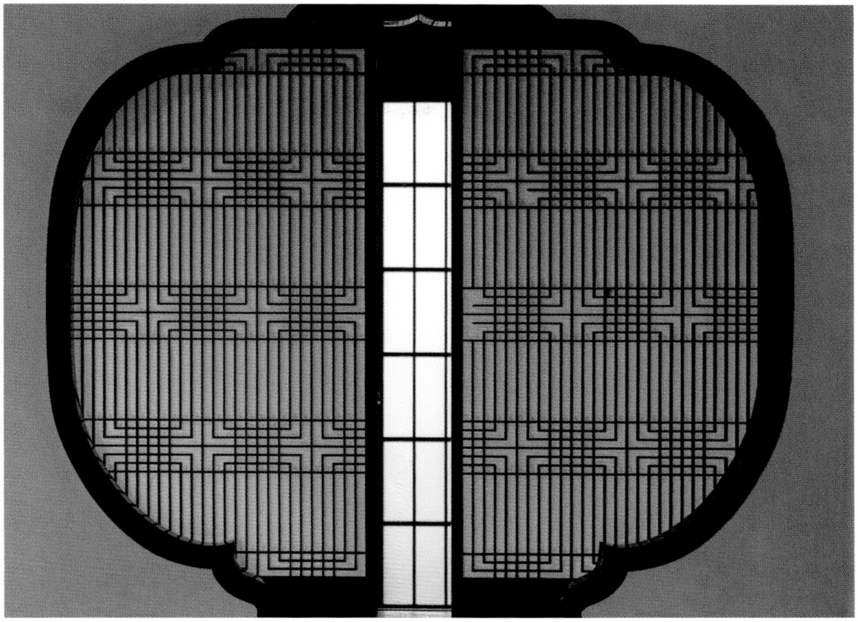

This book is an invitation to explore the world of kumiko, whether you are a curious beginner or an experienced woodworker seeking to expand your skills. Within these pages, you will discover the rich history and cultural significance of kumiko, as well as its enduring relevance in modern woodworking. In addition, you will learn how to create these stunning patterns yourself, step by step, and incorporate them into your own projects.

The journey begins with an introduction to the essential tools, materials, and techniques that form the foundation of kumiko. From there, you will progress through a series of carefully designed lessons, starting with simple patterns and gradually advancing to more complex projects. Each chapter builds on the last, ensuring that you develop both the skills and the confidence to tackle increasingly intricate work. Along the way, you'll find detailed instructions, clear illustrations, and practical tips to guide you through every cut, fit, and assembly.

Kumiko is a meditative process, a celebration of craftsmanship, and a bridge between the past and the present. By the time you reach the final pages, you'll not only have mastered the core principles of kumiko but also gained the inspiration to incorporate it into your own unique creations. As you embark on this journey, remember that every cut, every fit, and every pattern you create connects you to an art form that has stood the test of time. Let's begin.

OVERLEAF
Erinji Temple Garden, a timeless expression of Japanese design. Photo by John S Lander/LightRocket via Getty Images.

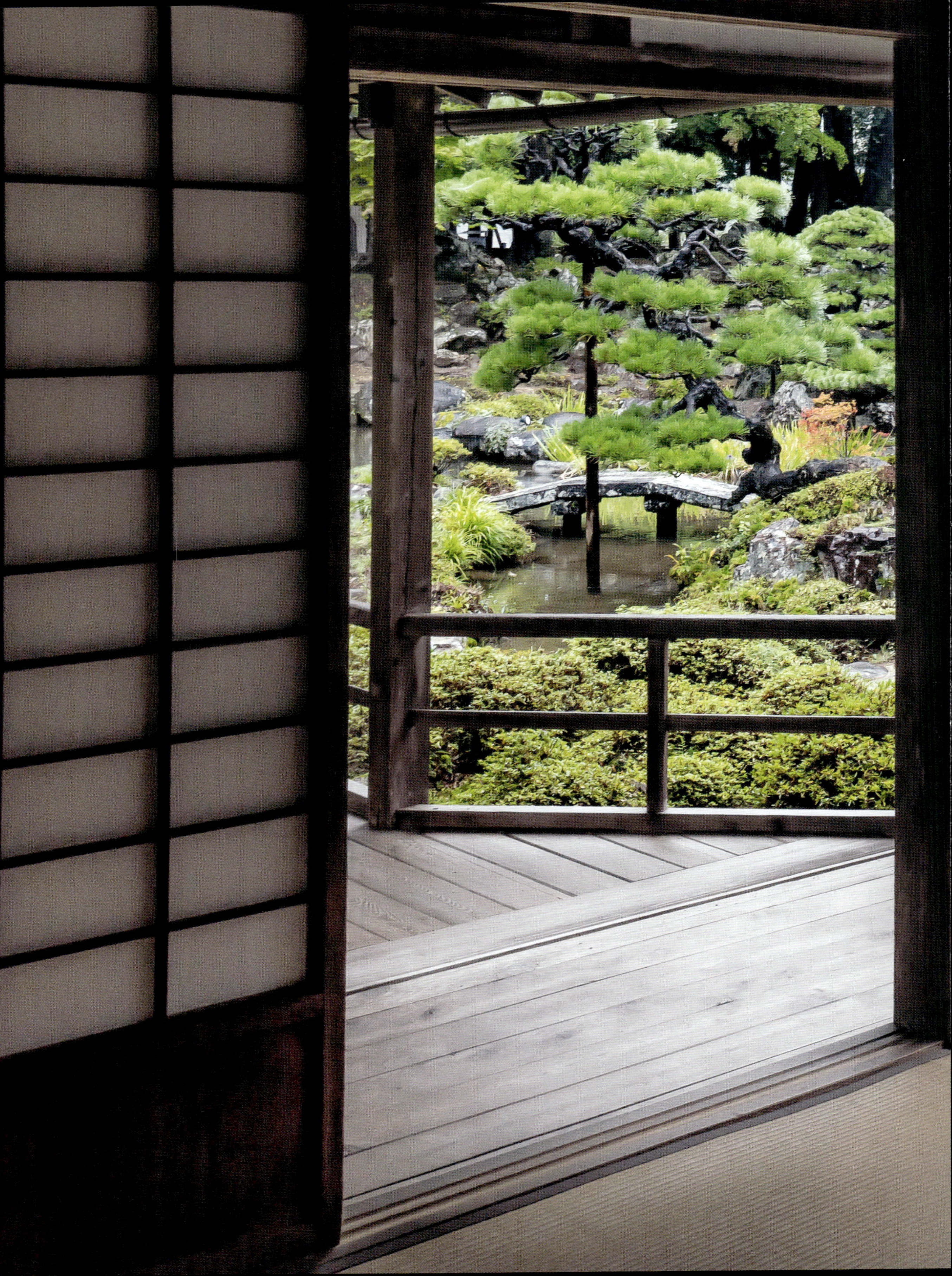

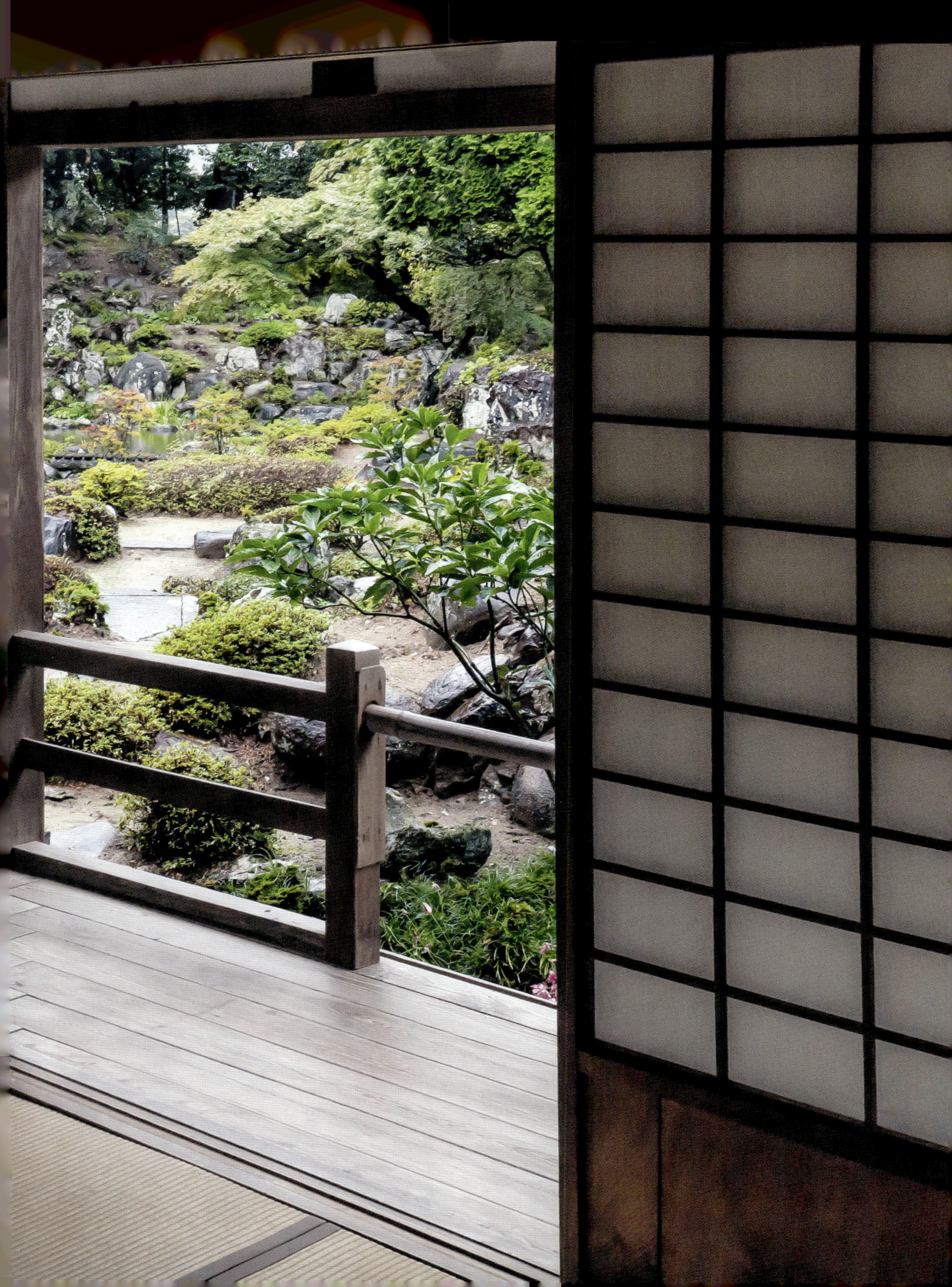

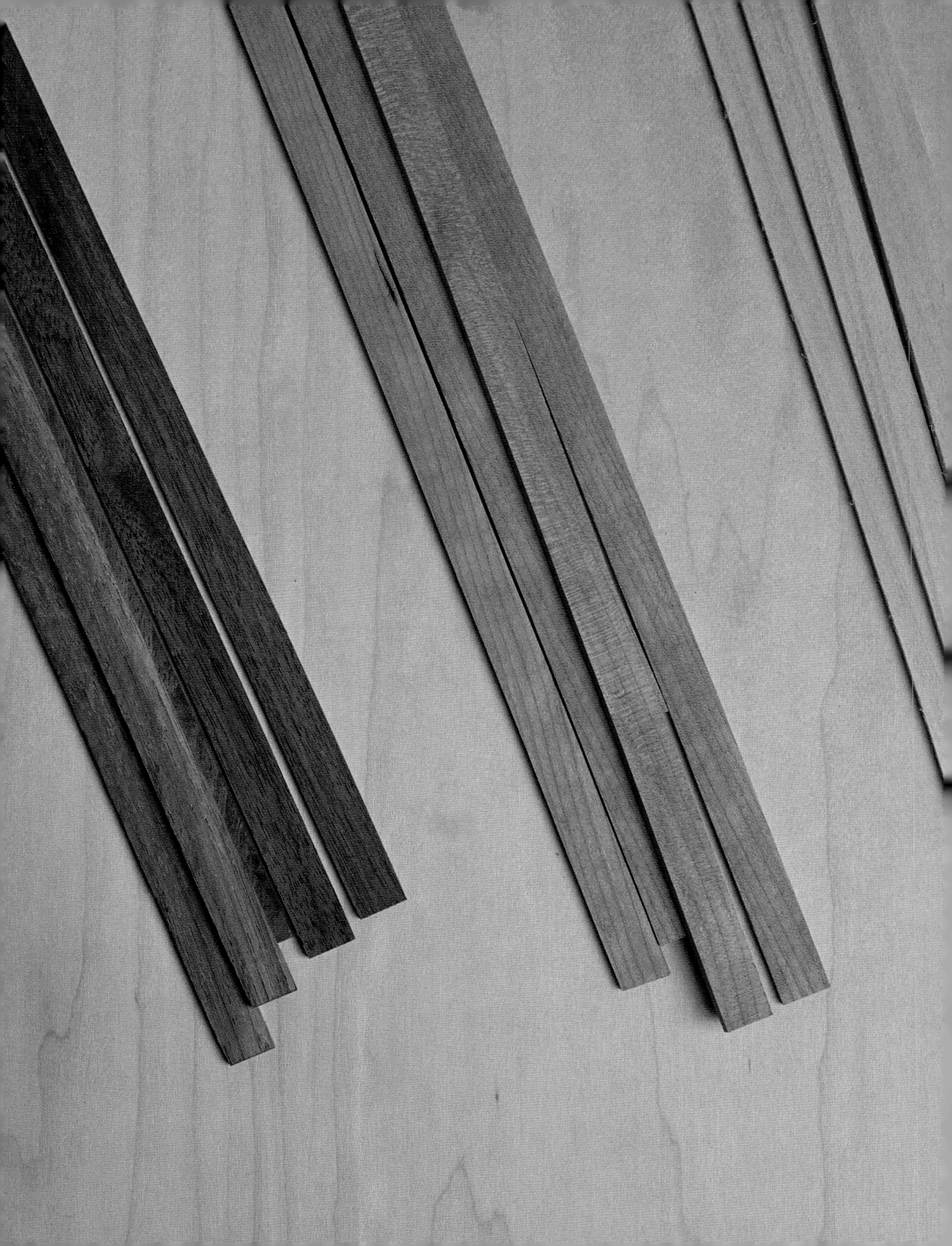

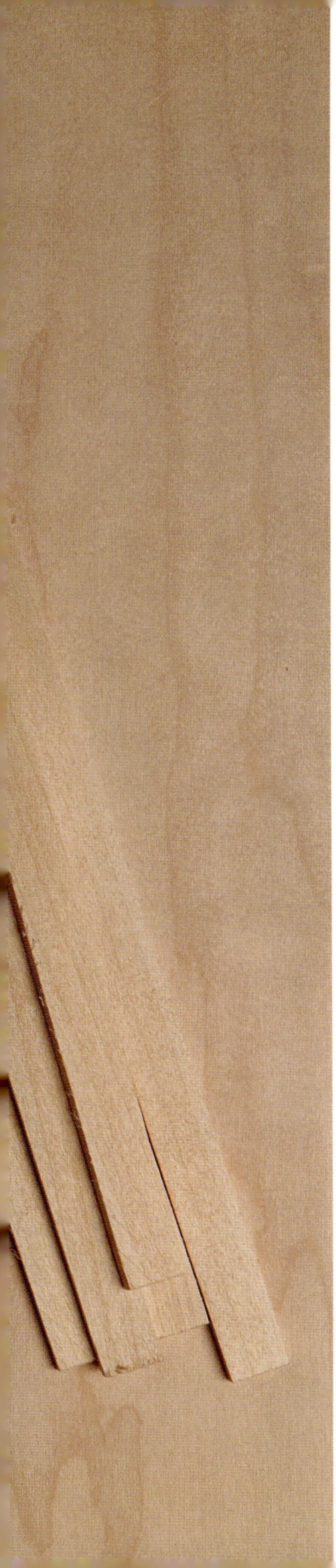

Chapter 1

Tools and Materials for Kumiko

It is essential to familiarize yourself with the tools and materials that bring this delicate art form to life. To create kumiko, precision is key, and achieving that precision starts with the first step. The foundation of kumiko lies in thin, finely milled wooden strips typically made from soft yet stable woods.

Kumiko traditionally uses straight-grained, lightweight woods like hinoki (檜 — Japanese cypress) or sugi (杉 — Japanese cedar), though other fine-grained woods like basswood (also known as lime or limewood) are also suitable. These materials are chosen for their workability and ability to hold fine details. Additionally, you may choose to add a variety of tones in your projects. Feel free to include different hardwoods to emphasize certain areas. Walnut and cherry are great options but keep in mind that hardwoods are generally more difficult to work with. As with all fine woodworking, patience and attention to detail are just as important as the tools themselves.

◀ From left to right: walnut, cherry, and basswood.

Traditional hand tools are essential for this craft, including a dozuki saw (胴付鋸) for precise cuts, chisels for refining joints, and a kanna (鉋) (a Japanese hand plane) for achieving ultra-smooth surfaces. Additionally, specialized jigs help ensure consistent measurements and repeatability.

Although the tools needed to start your kumiko journey are mainly simple and common hand tools, specialty tools can help make some processes easier. There will be a variety of tools shown within this book, and some of them are specialty tools that I've developed. These tools can be purchased from my website (www.jtwoodworks.com) and some are offered in downloadable plans so you can build your own.

Chisel and Plane (Nomi — のみ and Kanna — 鉋)

A chisel is a vital tool allowing for precise, clean cuts and the fine detail needed for making kumiko. Its sharpness and control are essential for crafting the intricate, small pieces and tight joints that define kumiko. Many types of bench chisels (Japanese or Western style) will work just fine. The important thing is that it's sharp. Alternatively, a small hand plane can be used for similar tasks. One excellent option is the kiwa kanna (際鉋), a specialized edge plane. Its skewed blade creates a shearing action that typically results in a smoother cut. These planes are compact and come in both right- and left-handed versions, allowing you to work comfortably.

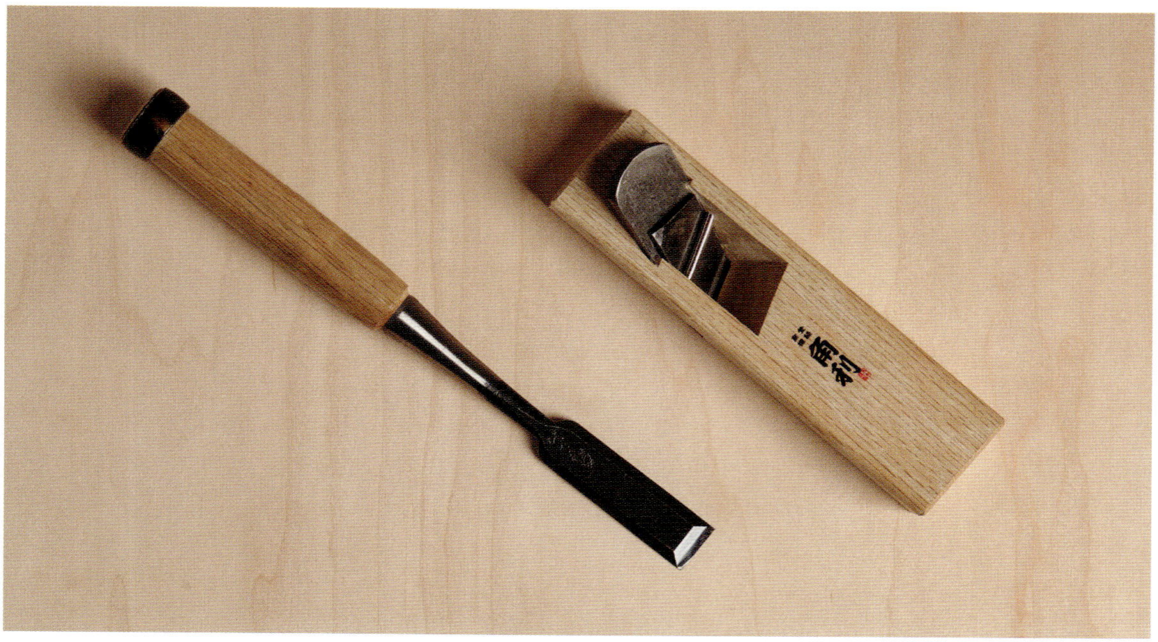

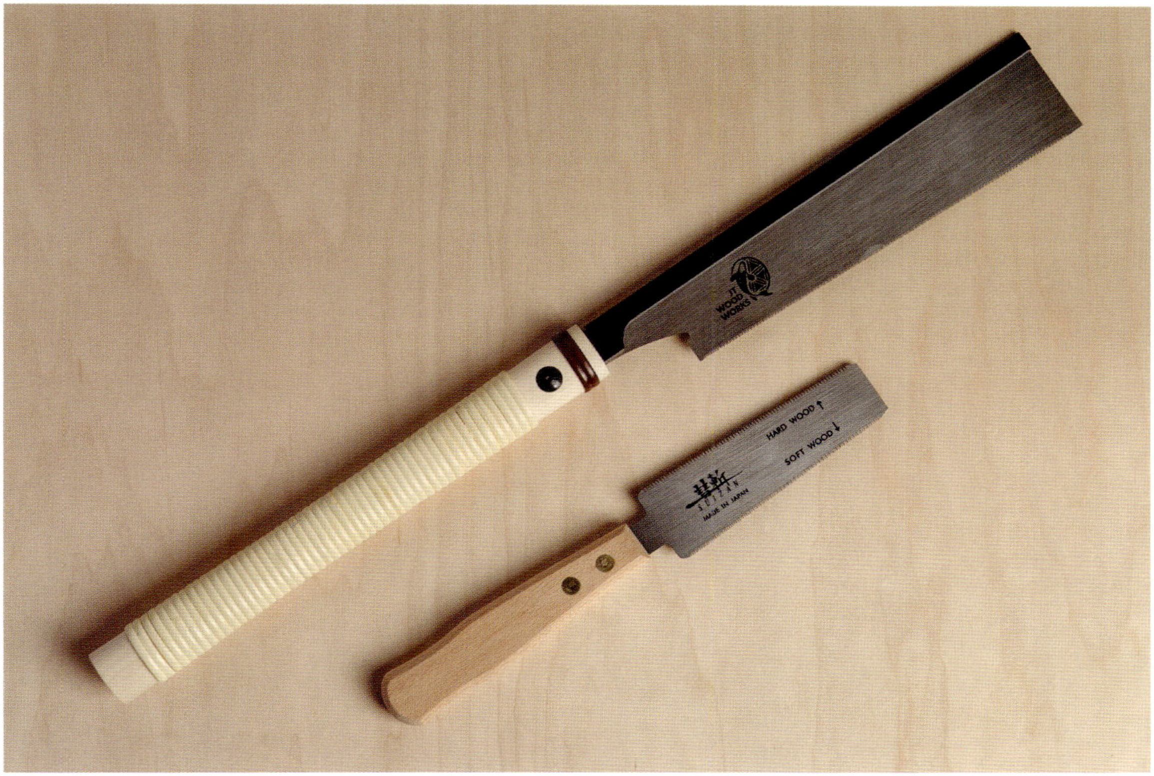

▲ Dozuki saw (top) and flush trim saw (bottom).

Saw (Nokogiri — 鋸)

A dozuki (胴付き) saw is essential due to its fine, thin blade and precise cutting ability. Its razor-sharp teeth and pull-stroke design enable clean and accurate cuts in delicate wooden strips. These saws often feature inexpensive replaceable blades which eliminate the need for sharpening. A small flush trim saw is also handy when trimming kumiko panels to their final size.

Kumiko Jigs

Kumiko patterns are assembled with many small pieces of wood cut to specific lengths with precise angles on their ends. To achieve accurate and repeatable results, a jig is used. "Jig" is a broad term used to describe a tool that helps you achieve a specific task. Kumiko jigs are crucial for creating consistent and precise angles on kumiko pieces. They act as guides to ensure uniformity and accuracy, allowing you to replicate intricate pieces and designs. You can make these jigs yourself, or you can purchase them on my website (www.jtwoodworks.com). They're specialty tools, and ones you won't often find available elsewhere.

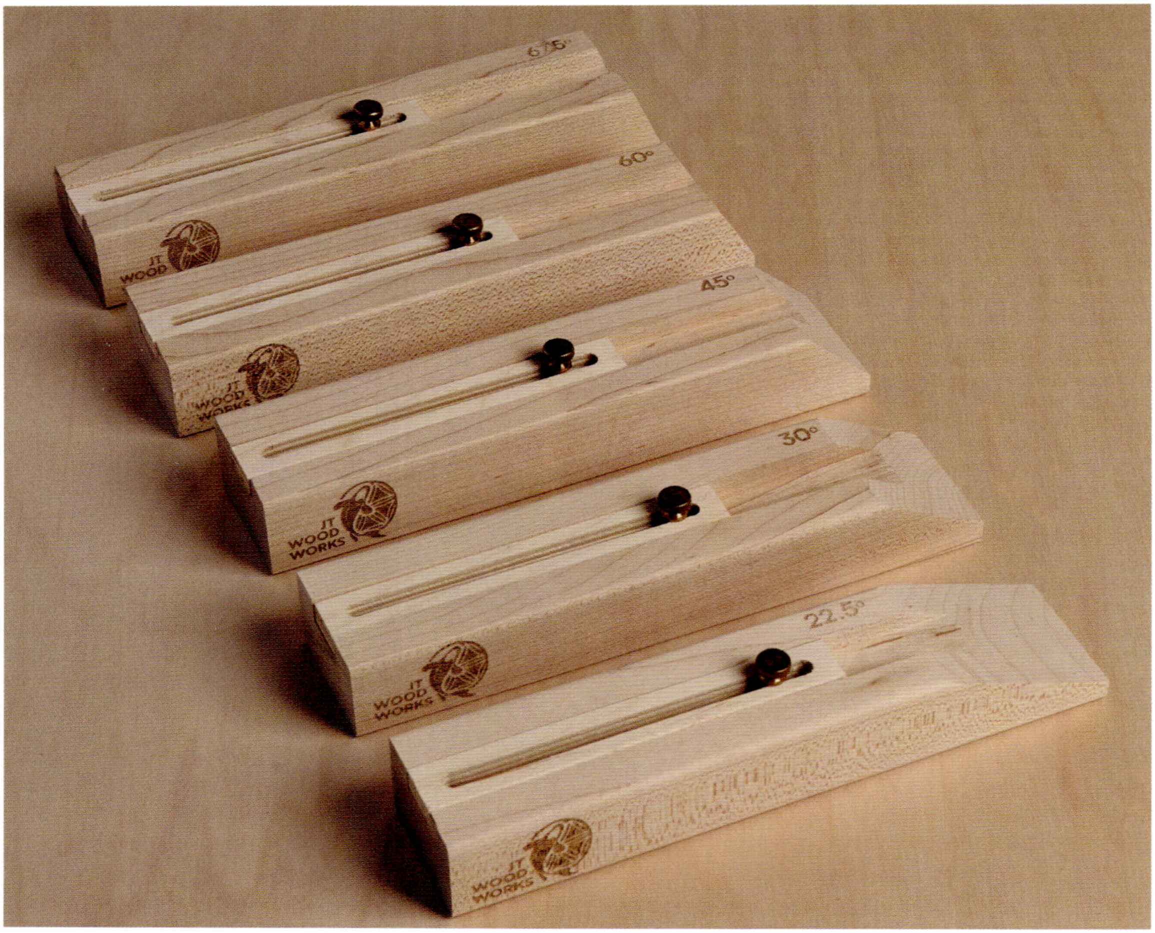

▲ The main angles needed to make most kumiko patterns.

Table Saw and Kumiko Table Saw Sled

The foundation of kumiko is the jigumi (地組) — the gridwork on which all the patterns are built. The joints needed to assemble the grid can be cut by hand, but using that method can make it difficult to maintain accurate spacing in the grid and tight-fitting joints, especially when it comes to hexagonal grids. The pairing of a table saw and sled can greatly speed up the preparation of parts while maintaining exceptional accuracy. Their ability to cut consistent and repeatable joints makes them especially valuable when working with larger projects. The precision of the table saw and kumiko sled ensures uniformity across every piece.

For this work, a reliable table saw (such as a cabinet-style or contractor-grade table saw) is recommended; one that runs smoothly, holds its settings, and produces clean, accurate cuts.

The quality of the saw itself plays a major role in the consistency and ease of building kumiko. As with all power tools, however, safety should always come first. Take care to keep your hands clear of the blade and remain focused during every cut.

The sled shown here has multiple functions and features adjustable registration keys (see the Glossary on page 172 for an explanation of the importance of registration keys). These are explored in detail in future chapters; however, briefly put, they allow you to cut a variety of grids with different spacing and thicknesses of wood.

▼ JT Woodworks kumiko table saw sled.

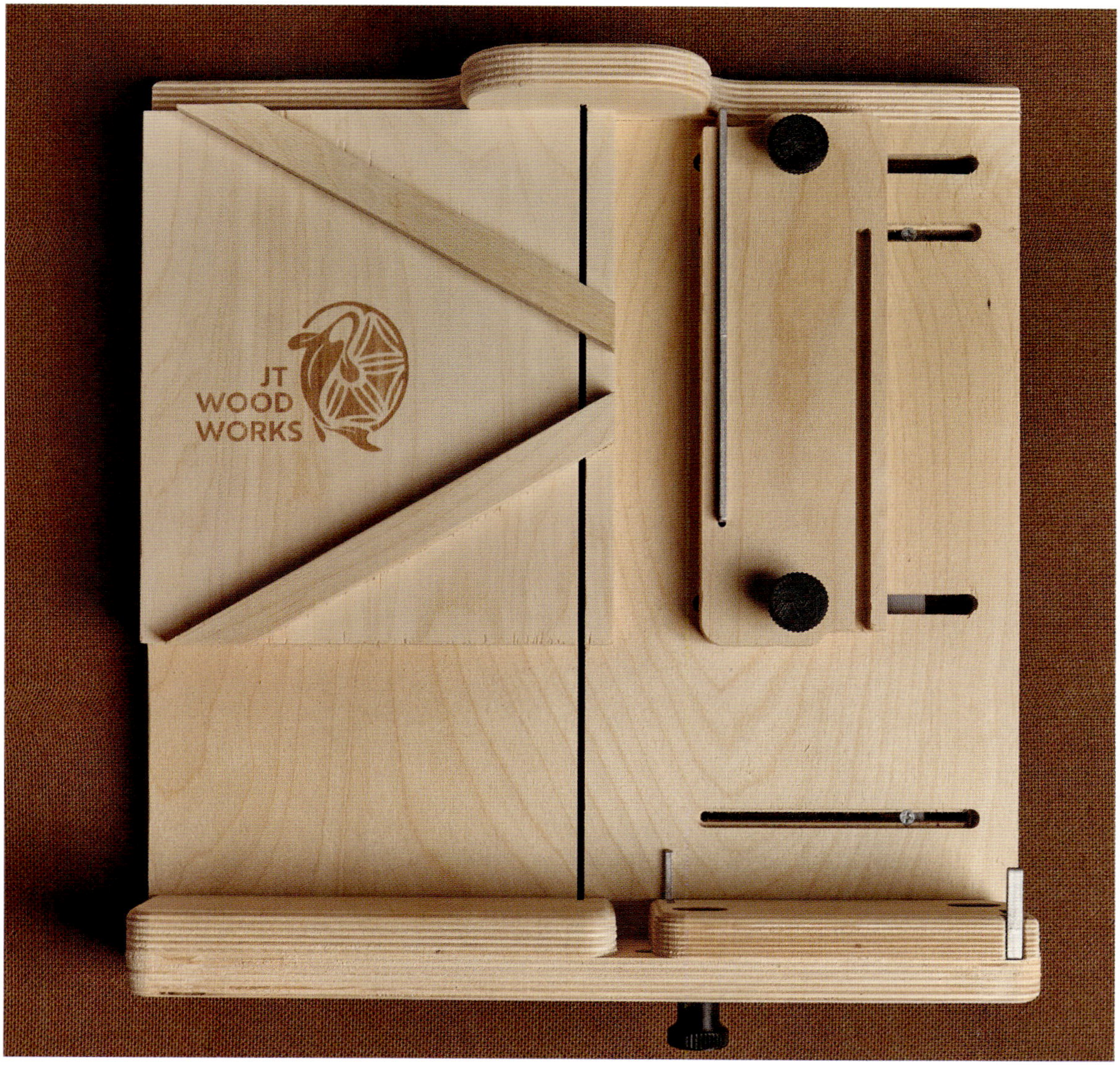

Sharpening, Gluing, and Sanding

Sharp tools are critical in all woodworking, but they are especially vital for kumiko, where you might need to take ultra-thin shavings to achieve a perfect fit. A sharp chisel is indispensable for this level of precision. Keeping your tools sharp is a skill in itself, and while there are many methods to explore, the best approach is to invest in quality sharpening stones and then practice consistently. Sharpening is a deep topic, but mastering it will elevate your kumiko work to the next level.

Glue isn't traditionally required in kumiko, as the precisely cut joinery is designed to hold everything together through friction and tension. However, using a small amount of glue can be beneficial for reinforcing delicate pieces, especially in applications where the panel may be handled frequently or exposed to movement. It's a matter of preference and practicality, rather than necessity. Standard woodworking glue like PVA works perfectly. Since only a small amount is needed, a little goes a long way. You can apply it precisely into the joints using a toothpick or small brush.

Some adhesives are specialized for certain aspects of kumiko. Nori glue (糊) or double-sided tape is used when adhering shoji paper. This process is shown on page 93.

Shoji paper is a traditional Japanese translucent paper made primarily from natural fibers like kozo (mulberry — 楮), mitsumata (三椏), and gampi (雁皮). It's lightweight yet durable, allowing soft, diffused light to

▼◀ Examples of sharpening stones. Coarse stone (optional) 200–600 grit; medium stone 1000–1500 grit; fine stone 4000 grit or finer.

▼ Nori glue and double-sided tape.

▶ Various designs of shoji paper.

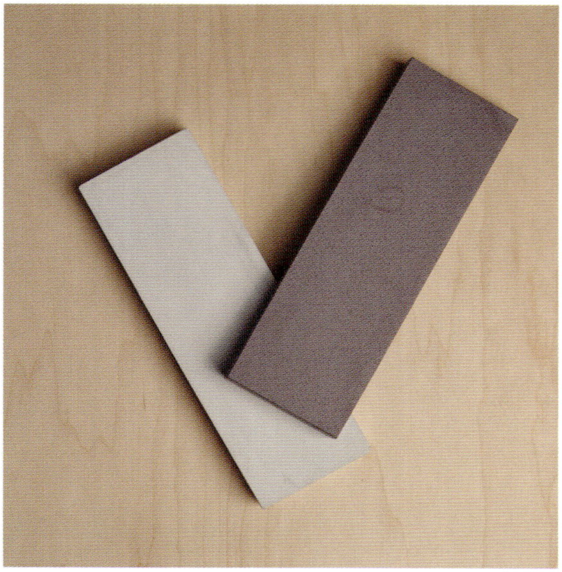

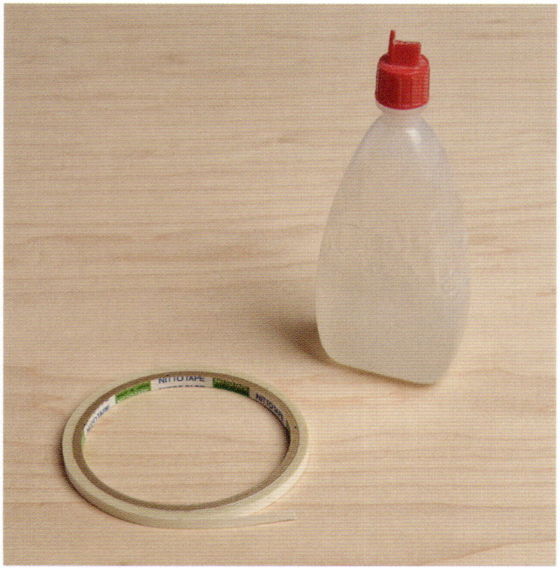

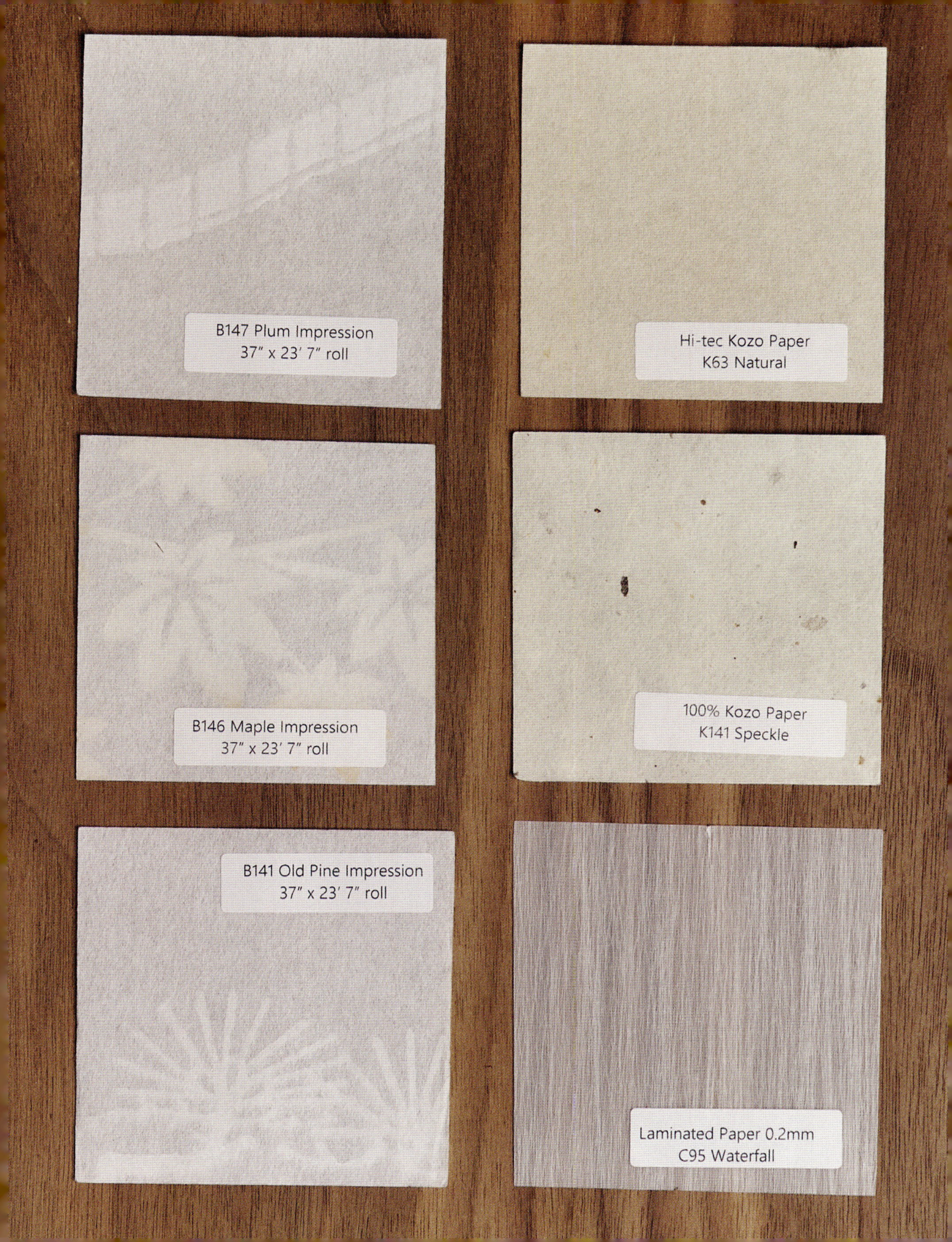
B147 Plum Impression
37″ x 23′ 7″ roll
Hi-tec Kozo Paper
K63 Natural
B146 Maple Impression
37″ x 23′ 7″ roll
100% Kozo Paper
K141 Speckle
B141 Old Pine Impression
37″ x 23′ 7″ roll
Laminated Paper 0.2mm
C95 Waterfall

pass through while maintaining privacy. Traditionally, shoji paper is used in sliding doors, windows, and room dividers (shoji — 障子) in Japanese homes, creating a serene and harmonious atmosphere. Shoji paper comes in a wide variety of styles, not just in material but in design as well. Some papers have a natural, earthy character, often showing small specks from the pulping process. Others are decorated with subtle patterns, like leaves or floral motifs, which add a gentle elegance. For more practical needs, there are also laminated and synthetic options that offer greater durability, especially in humid or high-traffic environments.

Once your panel is complete, sanding it is an important final step. After pressing all the pieces into place, you might notice slight, unflattering height variations. Sanding is essential for smoothing these areas and flattening your panel. You can use a sanding block, sandpaper adhered to a flat surface, or a random orbital sander on a low-speed setting. Begin with a fine grit, such as 220, since soft wood sands easily, then progress to higher grits to achieve a smooth finish. Even on a low setting, a sander can be aggressive when it comes to sanding kumiko. Use caution when using this method.

Ha-ganna

This is a specialized tool and is not required to get started but it is an important part of the story. This hand plane is called a ha-ganna (葉鉋, also referred to as a kumiko kanna — 組子用鉋) and it is used to trim kumiko pieces to an exact length while cutting the needed angles on the ends at the same time. The blades are V-shaped. Sharpening them, setting them, and tuning them to work just right takes patience and a certain feel that comes with many years of experience, but once they're dialed in, they cut beautifully, effortlessly, and precisely. The ha-ganna is still used today and is the preferred method for Japanese kumiko makers. These specialized tools come in different angles and have become difficult to find. If you ever find one, or decide to make one, spend time with it; it will teach you something different to any modern tool.

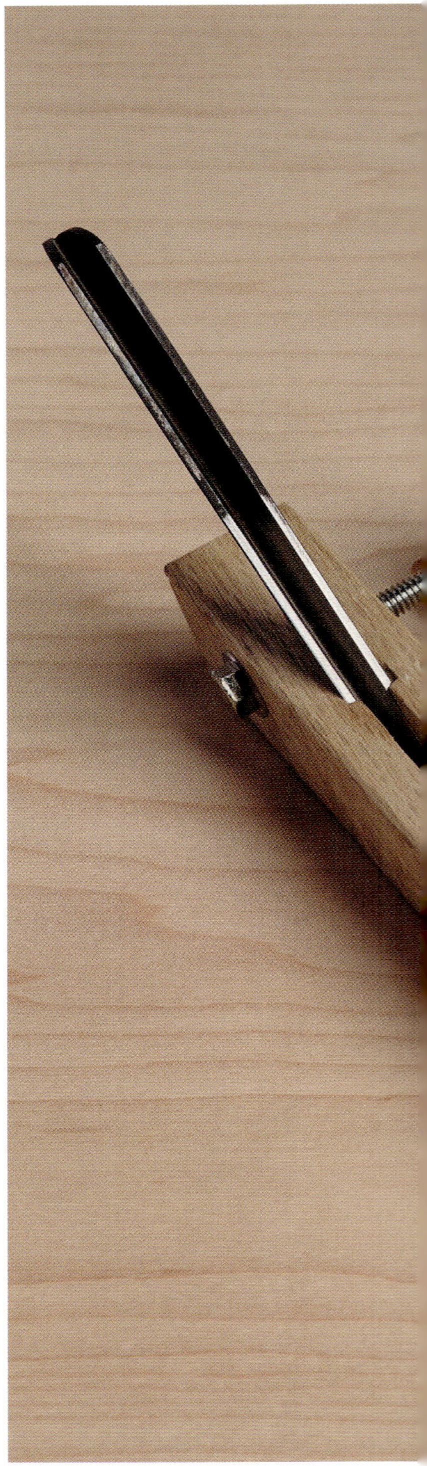

▶ 60° ha-ganna (left) and 30° ha-ganna (right)

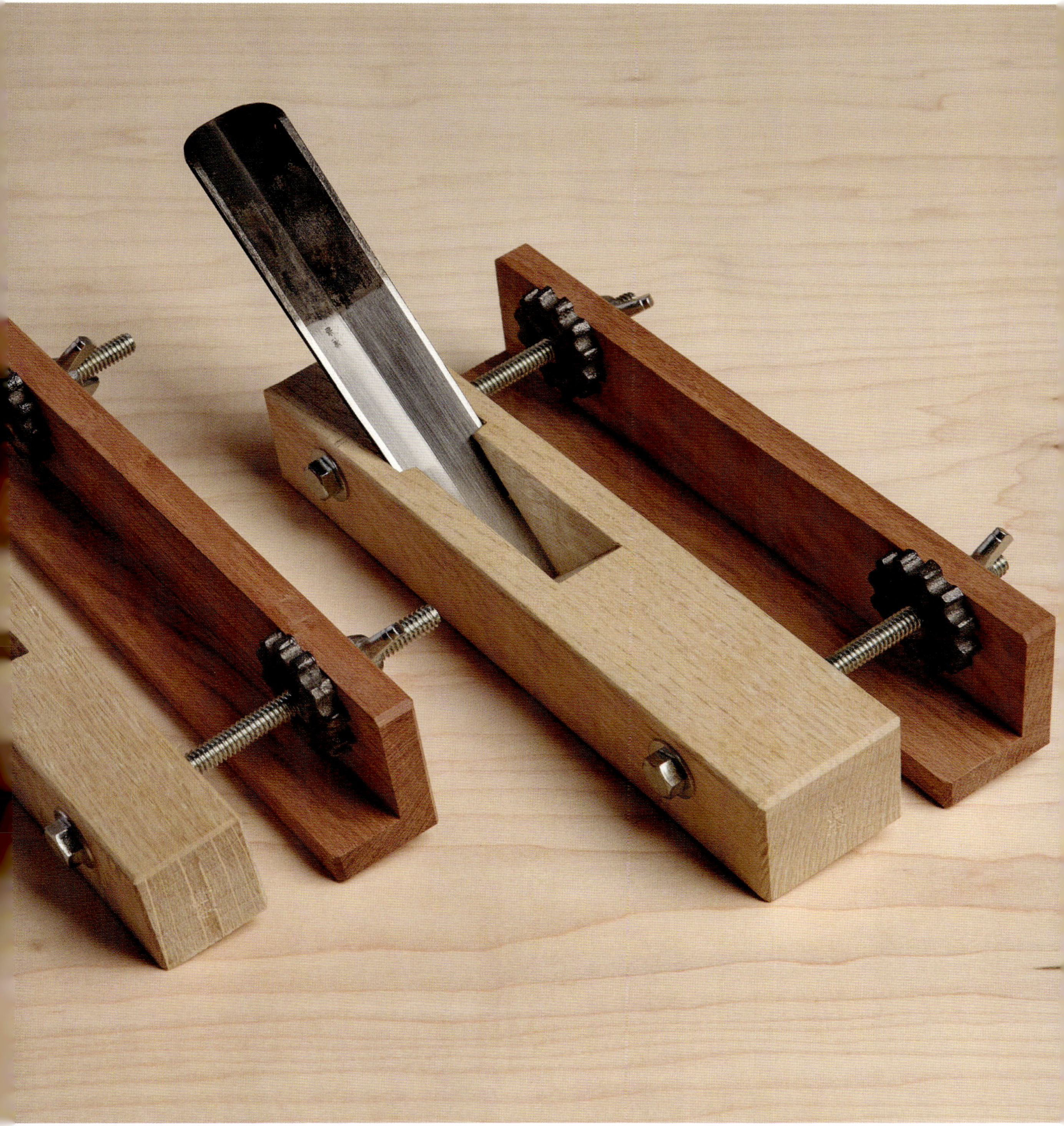

OVERLEAF Shoji windows show how paper, wood, and simple joinery create the soft light that is central to Japanese design.
Photo by John S Lander/LightRocket via Getty Images.

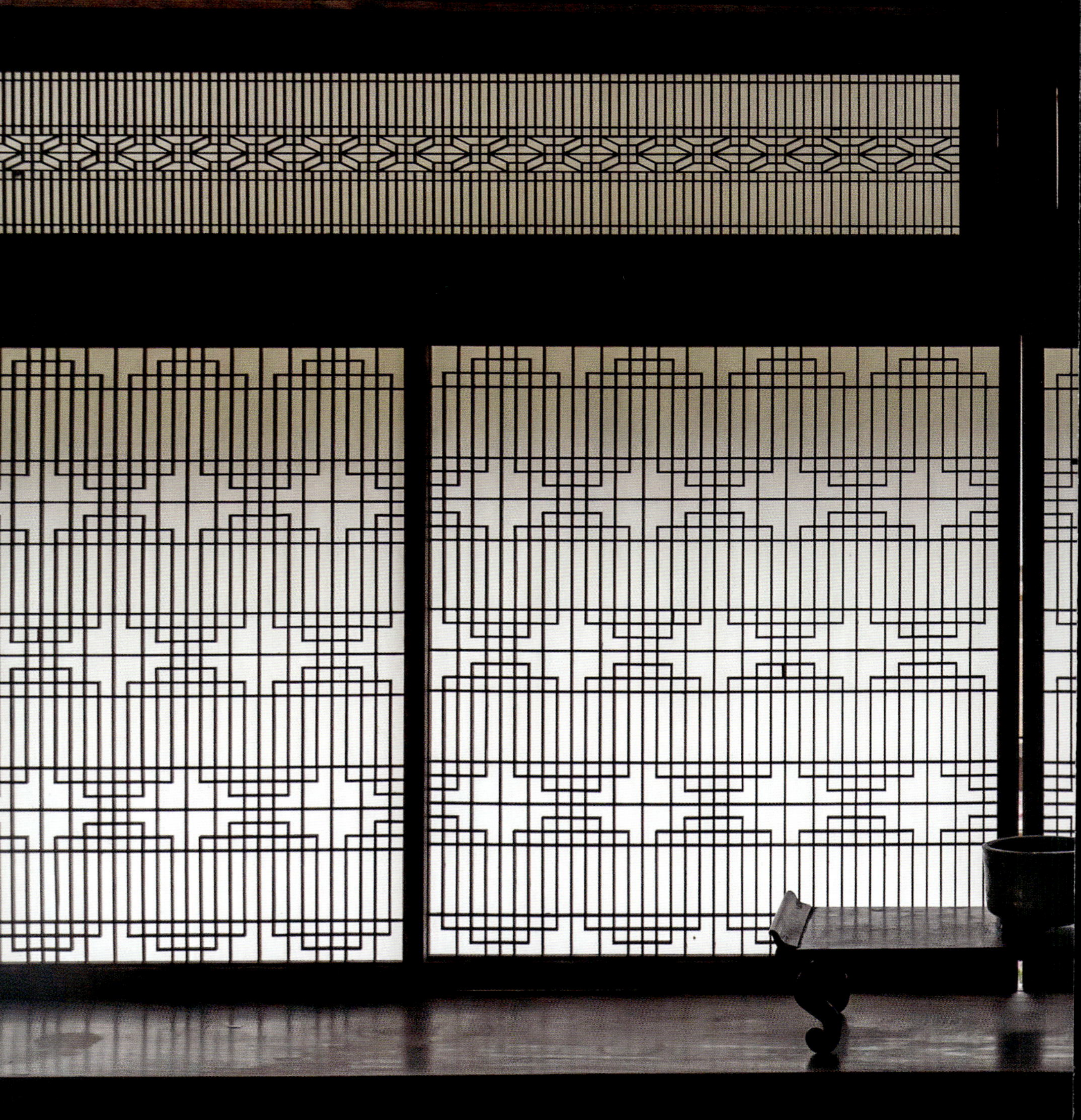

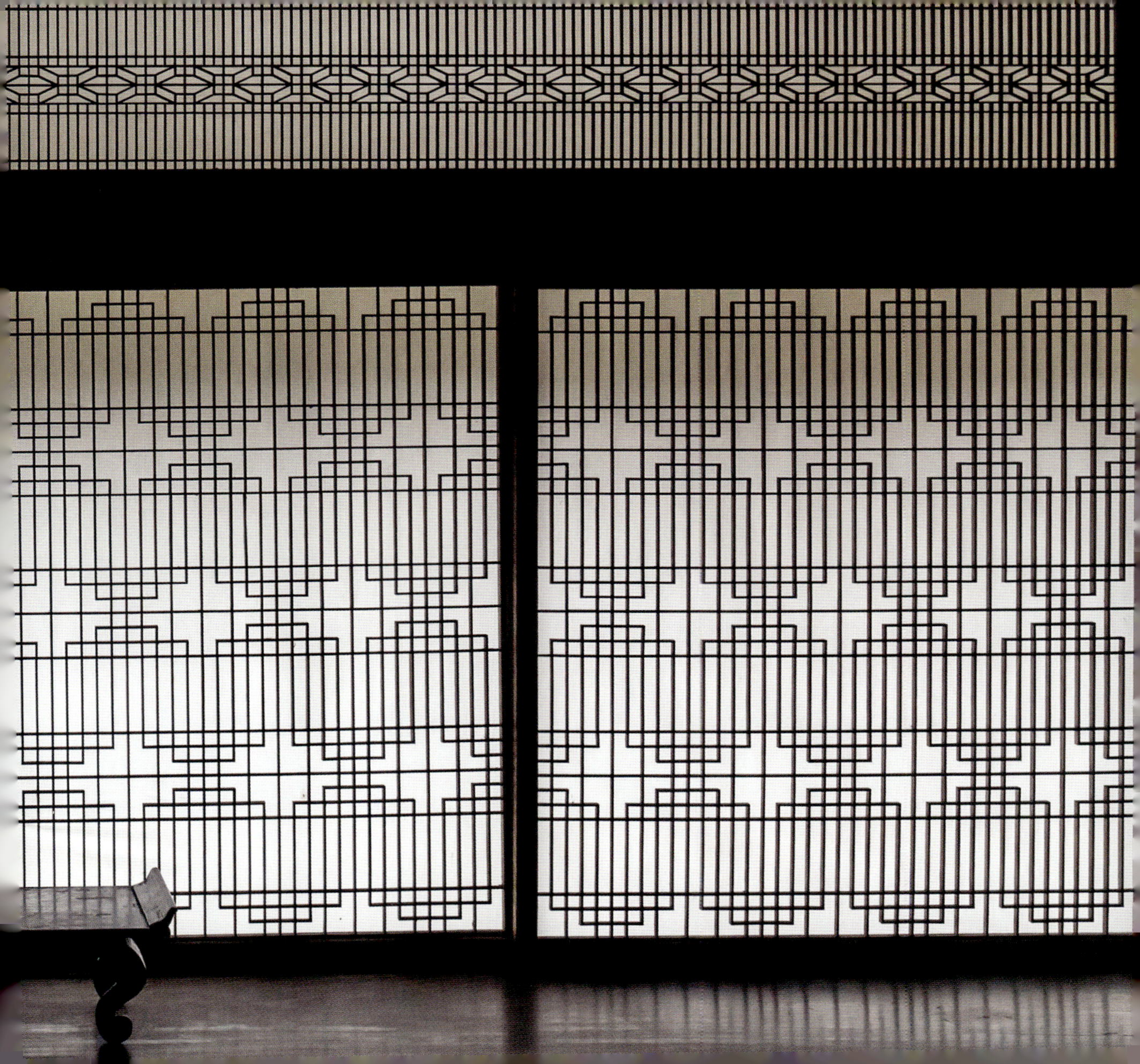

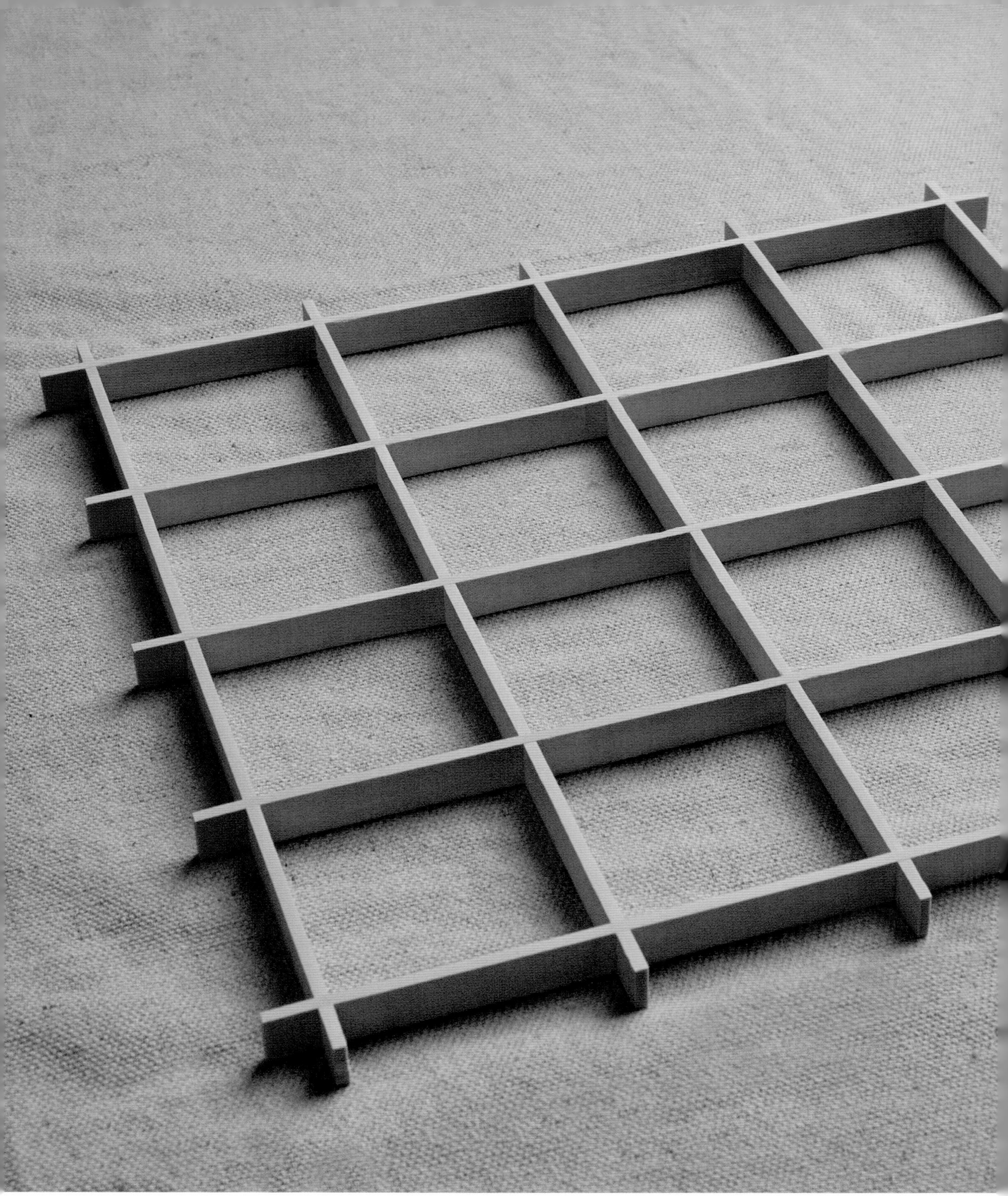

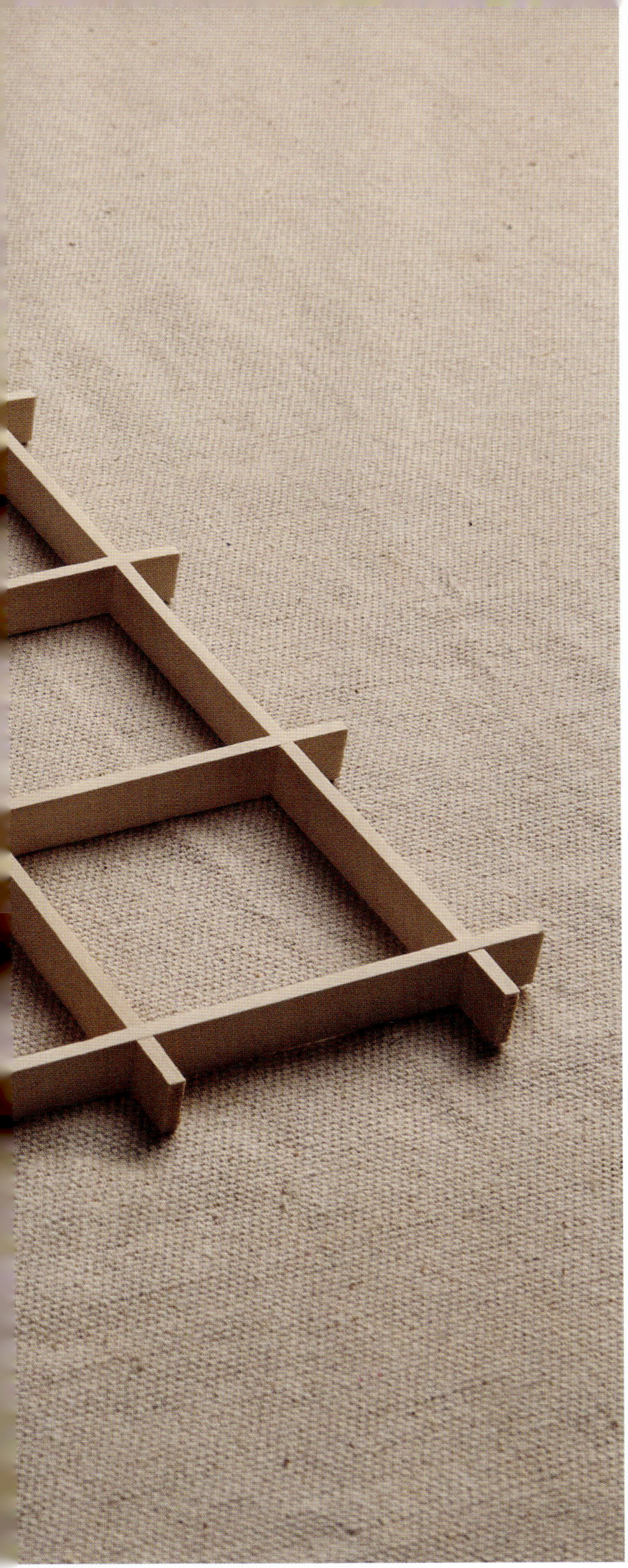

Chapter 2

Making Square Grids

The jigumi (framework or grid) is the foundation of all kumiko patterns. A square grid is the simplest type of kumiko grid to make as each intersection of the grid features a half-lap joint, and both the vertical and horizontal strips are identical. Using strips measuring ½ in x ⅛ in (12.7 mm x 3.2 mm) and a pitch of 2½ in (64 mm) is a great place to start. The pitch refers to the distance between the inside faces of neighboring, parallel strips.

Please note millimeter measurements throughout are rounded to the nearest 0.1 mm for simplicity. Please see the conversion table on page 175 for the precise conversions.

◀ These strips used here measure ½ in x ⅛ in x 11⅝ in (13 mm x 3 mm x 295 mm). The pitch is 2½ in (64 mm) resulting in a 4 x 4 grid.

Cutting Square Grids by Hand

Kumiko invites us to slow down, to trust in a few simple tools and the steadiness of our own hands. To cut this joinery you need little more than a sharp saw, a chisel, and the familiar companions of layout. But the true heart of the process is the cutting guide — the small, steadfast fixture that holds each strip with precision (**A**).

Build yours from something stable, like MDF or a hardwood that won't expand or contract with changes in humidity. The dimensions shown in the illustration offer a reliable starting point, yet feel free to adjust them if your work shifts toward a larger or smaller scale. Aside from the angle, every measurement is simply a suggestion. Leave a small gap, about ¼ in (6.4 mm) between the side support and the end stop. That little breath of space lets sawdust escape rather than gather, keeping your layout and cuts clean.

When shaping the side support, mill it to exactly half the depth of your kumiko strips. If your strips are ½ in (12.7 mm) deep, then the support should be ¼ in (6.4 mm). This becomes your reference plane that tells the saw where each joint will end.

90° CUTTING GUIDE

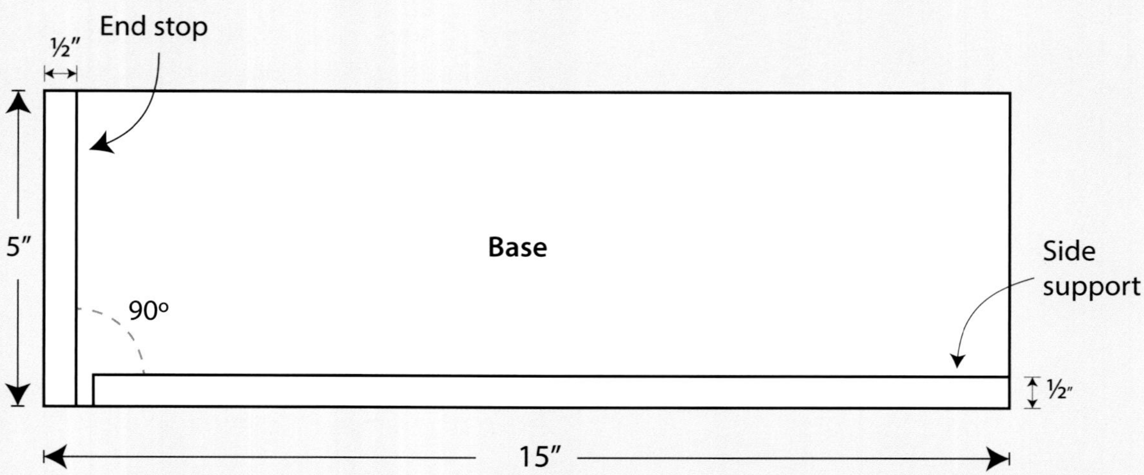

A

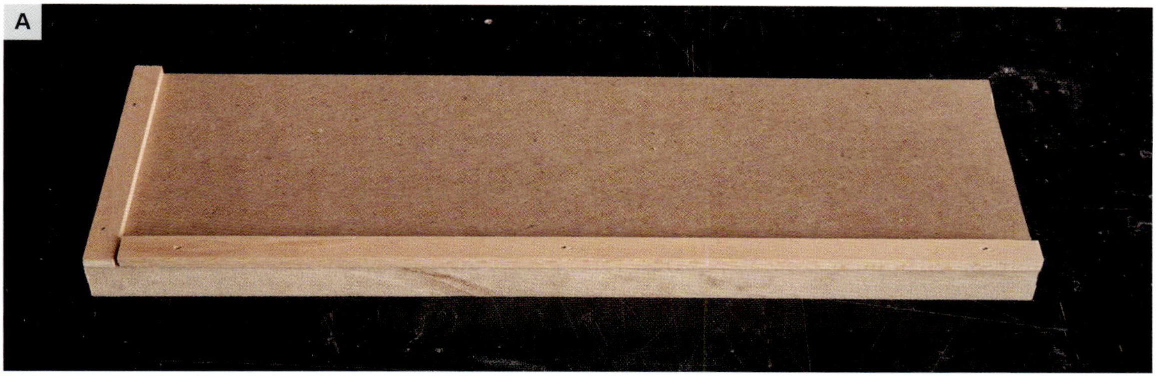

Setup

1. Set your strips into the guide so they rest cleanly against both the end stop and the side support. Accuracy begins with this alignment. It's best to work in small bundles, no more than six to eight strips at a time. Beyond that, you risk drifting slightly out of square, which can cause the pieces to fit poorly.

B

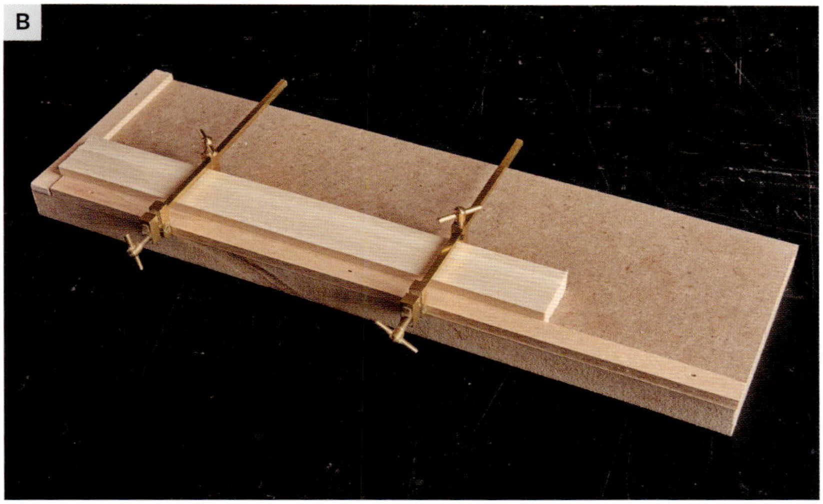

2. Hold the strips firmly with small clamps (**B**). Alternatively, create a gentle pressure system by fastening a thin ¼ in (6.4 mm) strip to the base so it presses the kumiko gently against the side support (**C**). It creates consistent pressure, just enough to keep everything settled and true while you cut.

C

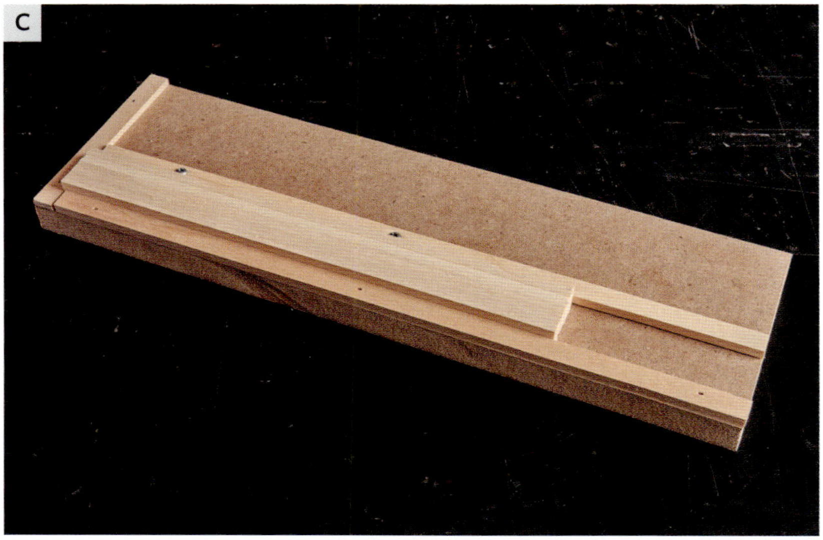

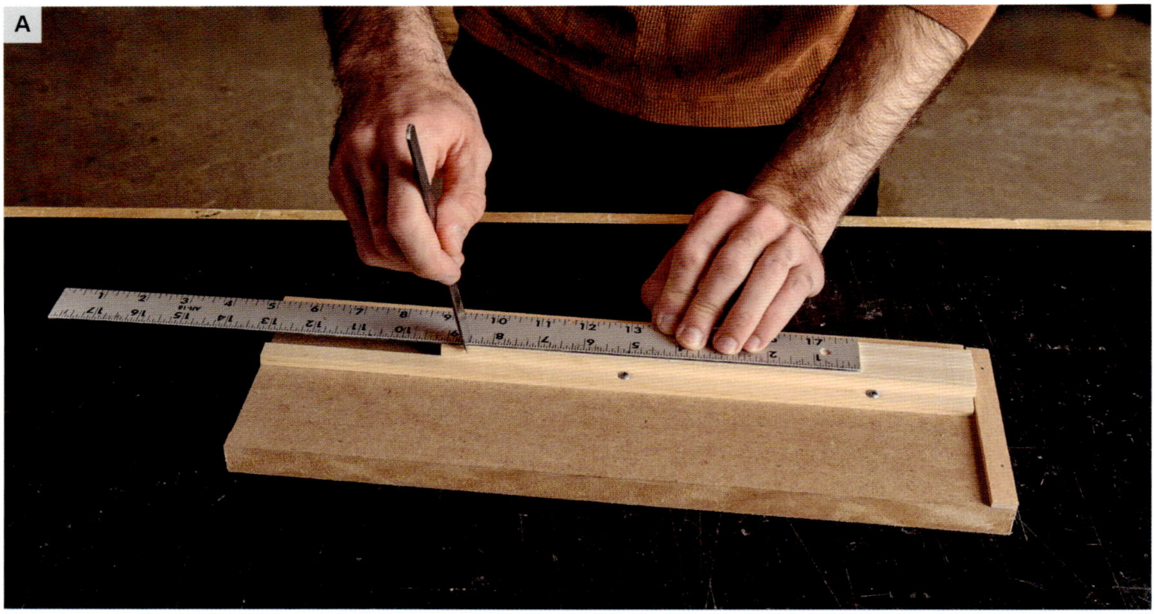

Lay out the joints

Accurate layout is the beginning of every successful kumiko panel. The grid you create here becomes the foundation for all that follows. When the grid is square and the spacing even, the infill pieces seem to find their places naturally, fitting cleanly, aligning gracefully, and allowing the final pattern to come together with a sense of balance and harmony.

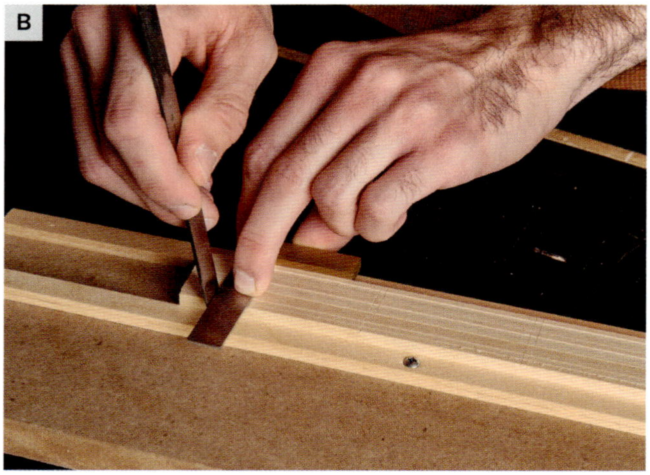

1. With a ruler in hand, measure ½ in (12.7 mm) in from the end support (**A**). Then, using a square, draw a clean line across the bundle with a marking knife (**B**). This first line becomes the reference point for everything that follows.

2. From that first line, measure ⅛ in (3.2 mm) and strike a second mark. This small distance reflects the thickness of the kumiko itself and defines the boundary of the first joint.

3. Next, from that boundary line, measure 2½ in (64 mm) and mark across the bundle once more. This becomes the starting point for your second joint.

4. Carry on in the same steady rhythm: mark the joint width, then the spacing, repeating as many times as needed for the grid you've imagined. For a four-section grid you'll lay out three joints on six strips. Measure and mark each line with care. Accuracy here quiets a thousand small problems later. You may find it helpful to extend those lines down the faces of the strips so there is a visible guide to help keep every joint edge square, honest, and true.

Cut the joints

1. With a sharp dozuki, begin cutting on the inside of the marked lines, always staying on the waste side (**C**). Let the saw track true and keep each cut square. Work with intention and stop exactly at the halfway point of the strip, no further.

2. Once all the cuts are made, bring in a narrow chisel to free the waste (**D**). The side support can act as a guide here, helping you maintain square, even cuts across every piece.

Assemble the grid

Assembling the pieces is simple. If you choose to use glue, apply a thin layer to the inside of each joint with a small brush or toothpick, just enough to hold without excess squeezing out (**E**). For more on gluing and full assembly, see pages 30 and 31.

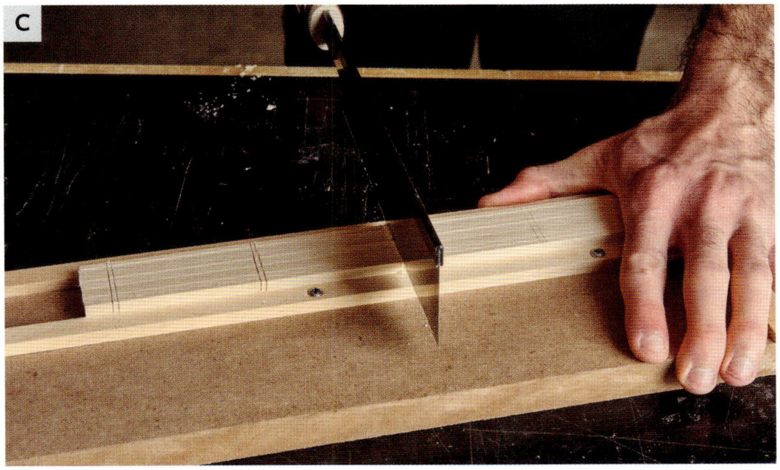

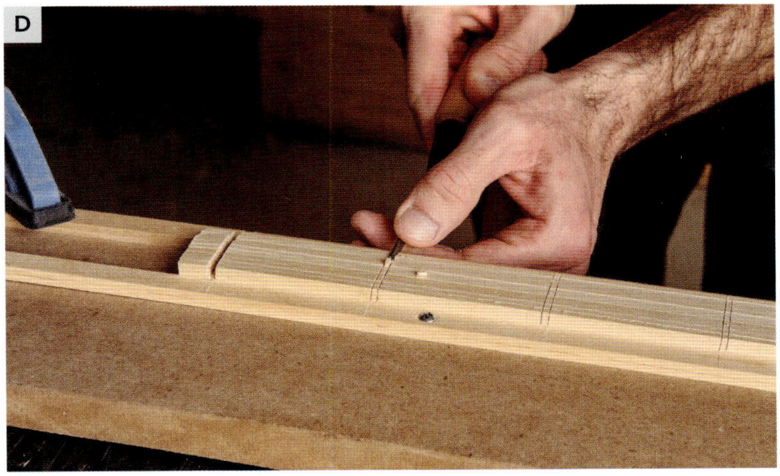

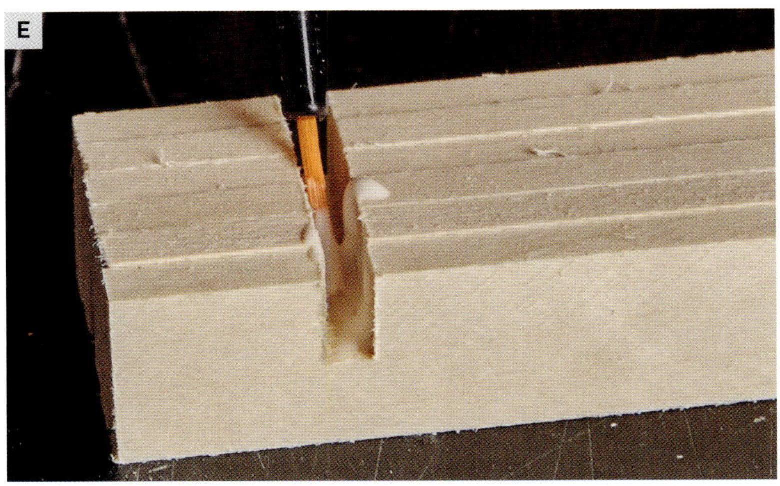

Cutting Square Grids with a Table Saw and Kumiko Sled

Setup

1. Install a blade with a kerf that matches the thickness of your kumiko strips (**A**). For example, when using ⅛ in (3.2 mm) thick strips, install a blade with a thickness of ⅛ in (3.2 mm). For best results, ensure the strip thickness, blade kerf, and registration key are all the same dimension.

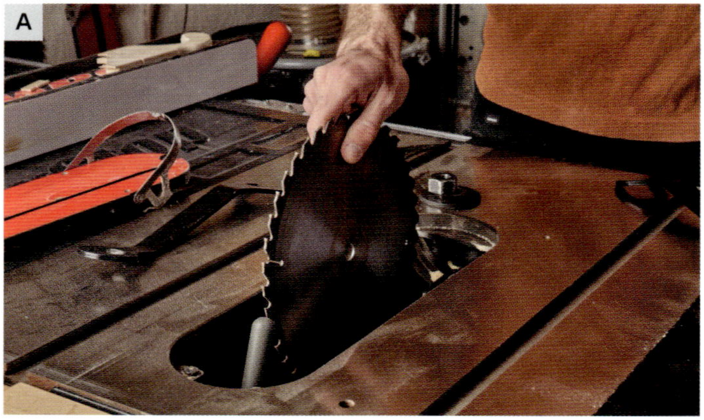

2. Raise the blade height to ¼ in (6.4 mm) above the sled's top surface, which is half the width of the ½ in (12.7 mm) strips. Two ⅛ in (3.2 mm) strips can be used as a height gauge (**B**).

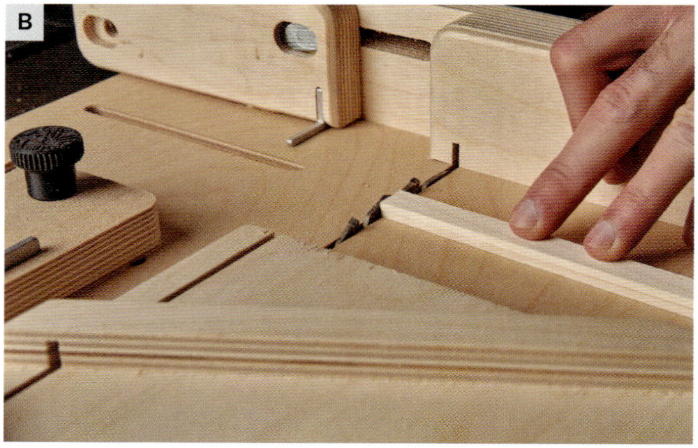

3. Make a test cut ½ in (12.7 mm) in from one end of two strips and fit them together perpendicular to each other to check the joint. The top faces of both strips should be flush when assembled (**C**). Adjust the blade height if needed to achieve this alignment.

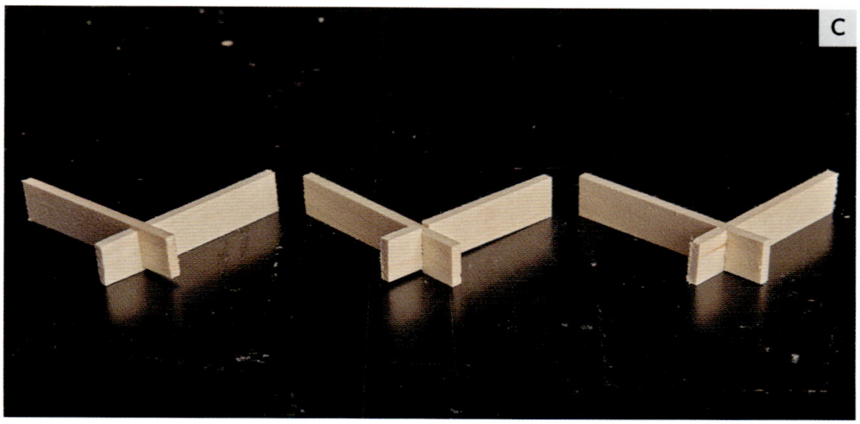

◀ From left to right, cuts are too shallow, too deep, just right.

Cut the joints

1. Loosen the knob and set the registration key to your desired grid spacing. Tighten the knob to lock it in position. The distance between the inside edge of the blade's teeth and the near edge of the registration key will determine the spacing between each half-lap joint and thus, the size of the grid squares. Refer to the Glossary on page 172 for more details on half-lap joints.

2. Make your first cut and place it over the registration key (**D**), ensuring the strips are flat on the sled's base and fence (the straight edge).

3. Place your second cut over the registration key to make your next cut (**E**). Repeat these steps for the length of your strips or for the amount of joints needed to make your desired grid. Multiple strips can be cut at once to speed up the process.

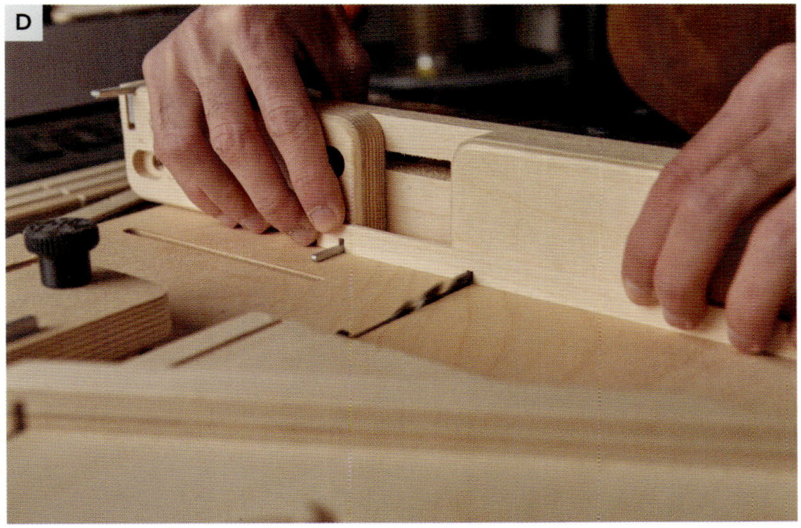

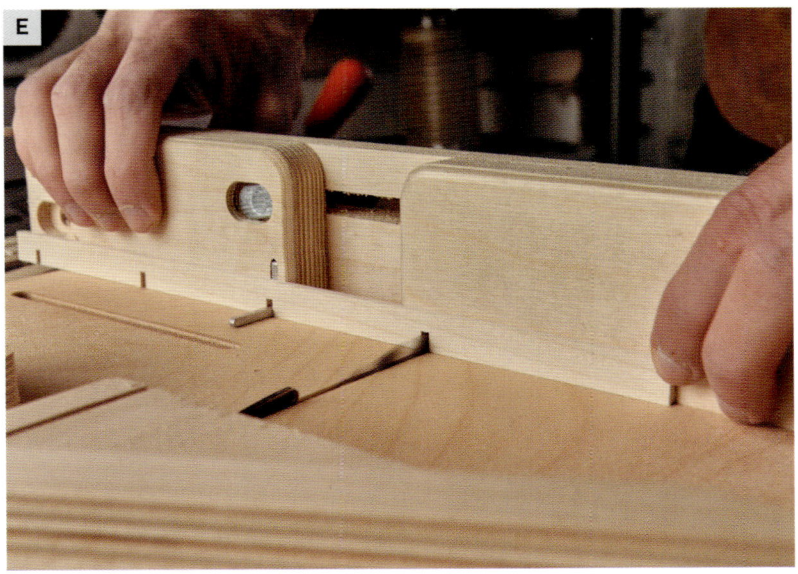

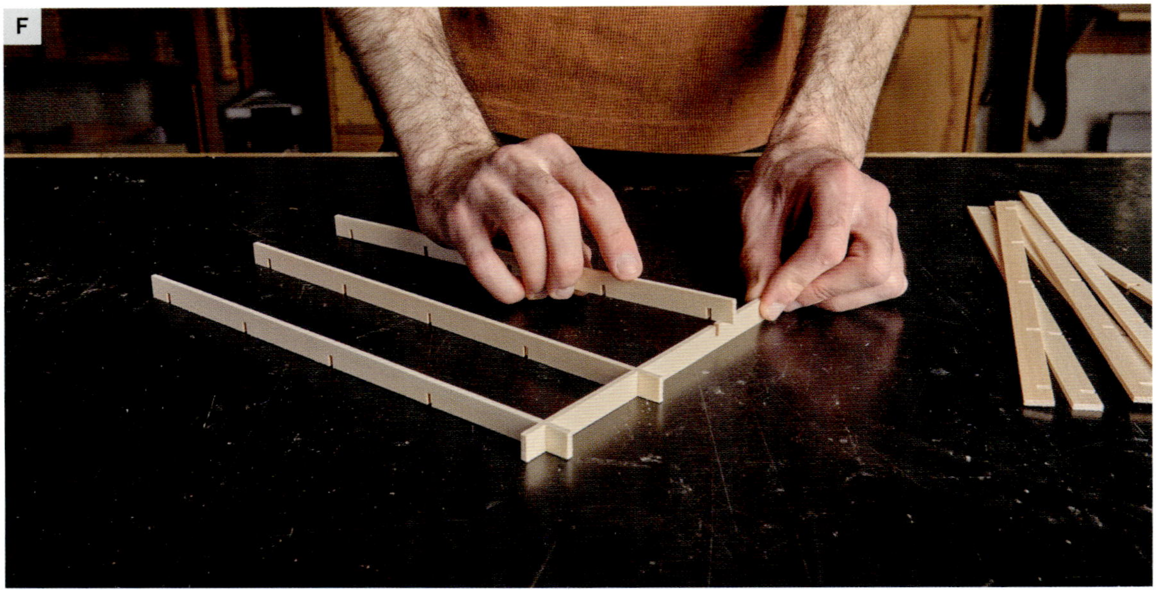

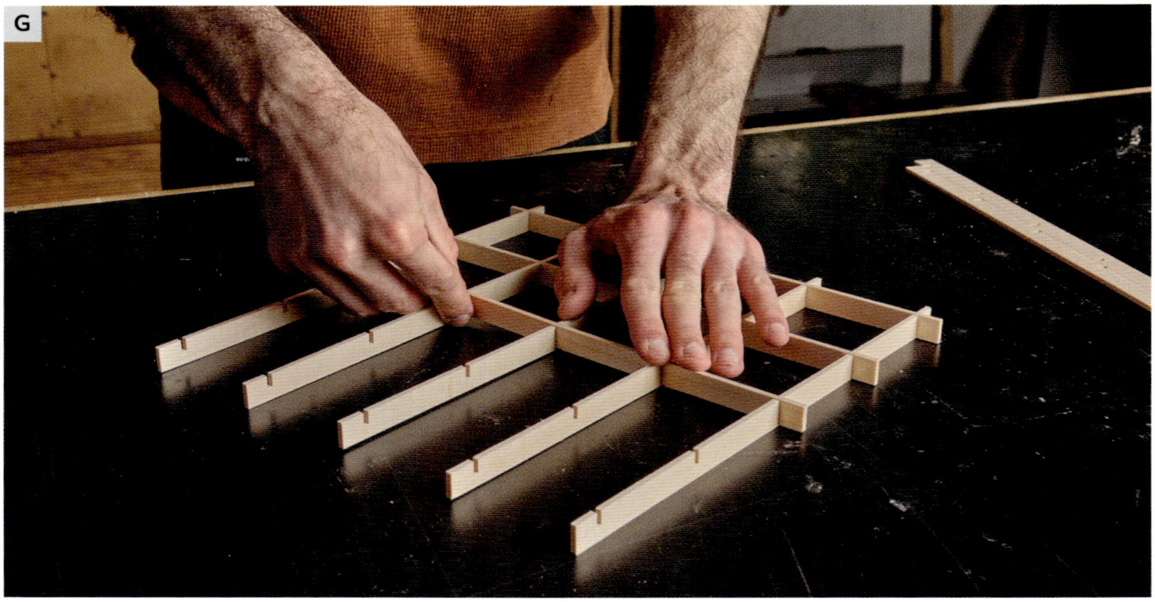

Assemble the grid

1. Begin by inserting all the horizontal strips into one vertical strip (**F**).

2. Now flip the panel over and insert the remaining vertical strips to complete the grid (**G**).

H

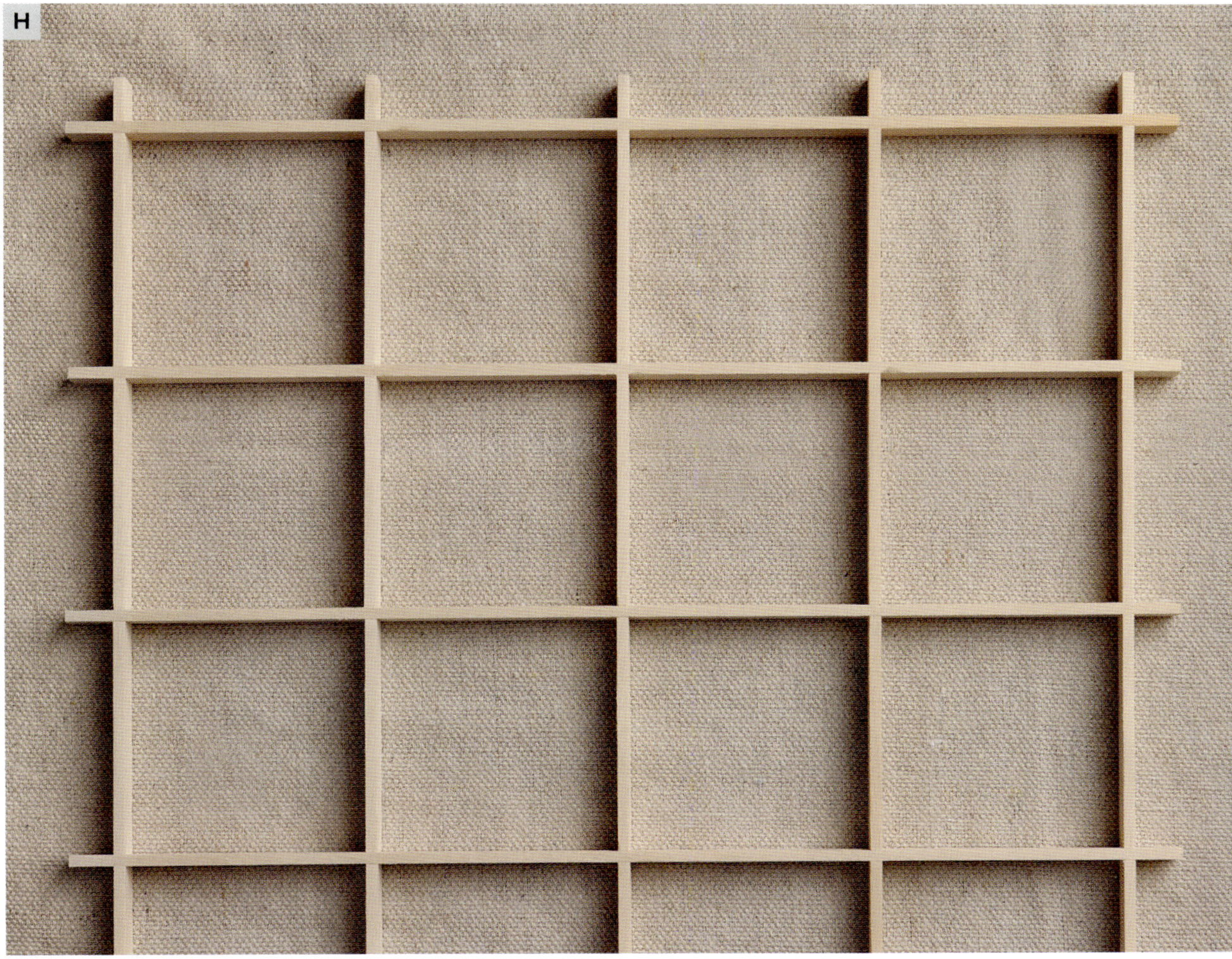

While traditional kumiko grids are held together by precise joinery alone, applying a small amount of glue at each joint can strengthen the panel, especially for larger grids or pieces that will be moved or handled frequently. Use a fine-tip applicator or brush to apply glue sparingly into the half laps before assembly, being careful not to overapply and risk squeeze-out that could affect the clean appearance of the pattern. This technique can be used with all the grid types covered in this book: square, diamond, and hexagonal (**H**).

These are the fundamental steps for creating a square kumiko panel. To explore creative variations, experiment with adjusting the grid spacing to incorporate a mix of squares and rectangles.

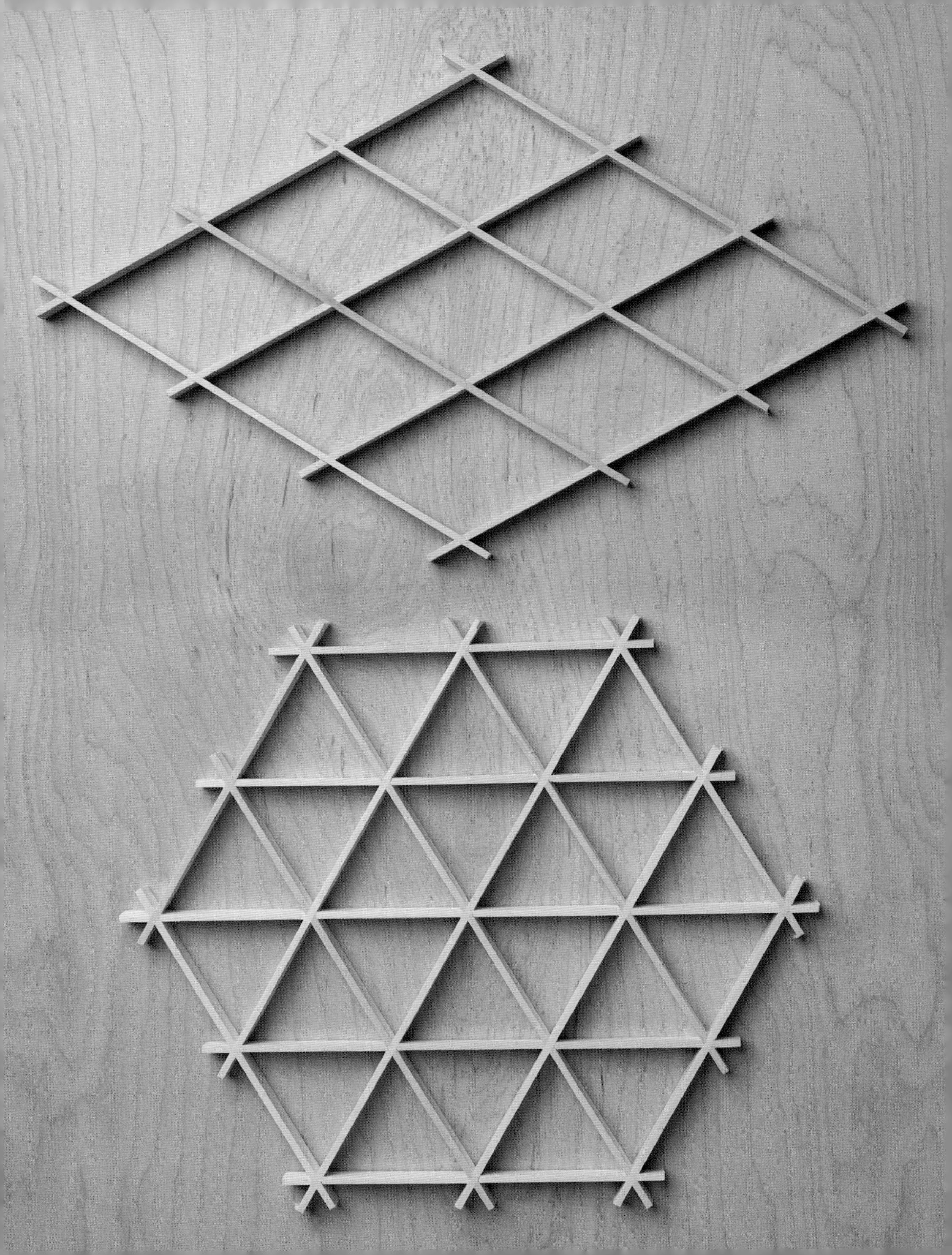

Chapter 3

Making Diamond and Hexagonal Grids

Diamond grids are built much like square grids, but with angled cuts to form rhombus-shaped openings as opposed to square openings. They follow the same basic process, with just a slight adjustment in angles. The steps are exactly the same as in the previous chapter but cut the joints at a 60° angle to the strips' faces.

◀ These strips measure ½ in x ⅛ in x 9 in (12.7 mm x 3.2 mm x 229 mm). The pitch is 2½ in (64 mm).

Cutting Diamond Grids by Hand

A cutting guide similar to the one used in the previous chapter serves here, with one important change: the end stop sits at a 60° angle to the side support (**A**). This angled end stop can be positioned on either end of the guide. Choose the orientation that feels most comfortable for your hands and workflow. You need one to create diamond grids and either setup shown will allow you to do so, though both guides will be required later in this chapter to construct the hexagonal grid.

Before placing the strips into the guide, cut a 60° angle on each end (**B**). You can use a kumiko jig to pair the ends of the strips for these

60° CUTTING GUIDE

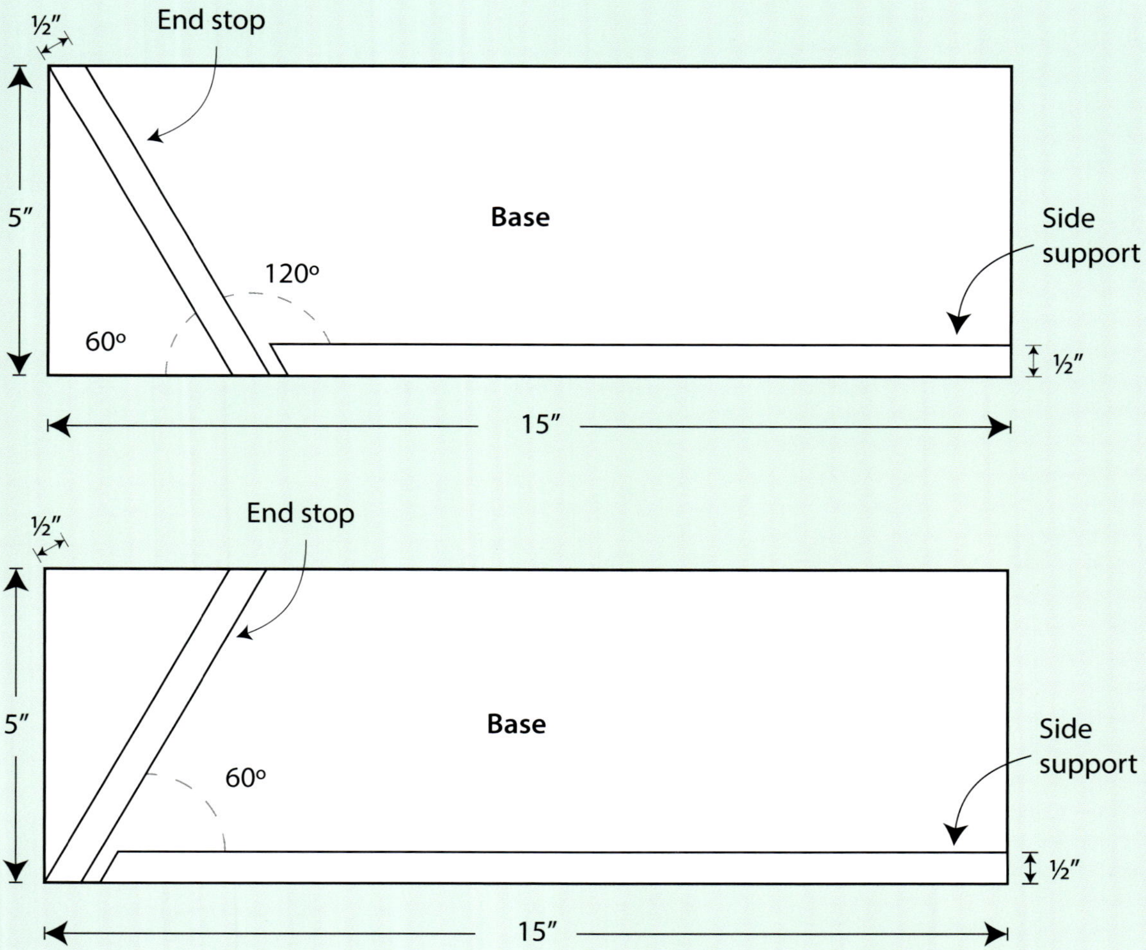

angles, ensuring consistency. These angled ends allow the strips to sit neatly against the angled end stop, making layout and measurement more precise and helping the grid come together cleanly.

From this point, the process closely follows the hand-cutting steps used for square grids in the previous chapter.

A

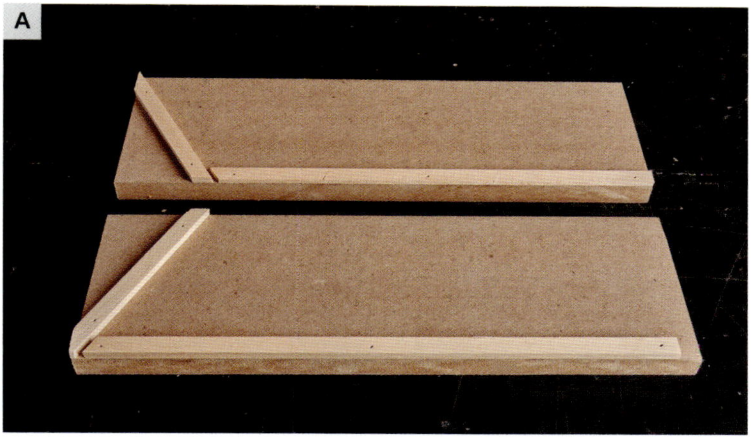

Adapting the process

What follows is an overview of how those steps are adapted to create a diamond grid, highlighting the adjustments needed for the angled cuts and the unique geometry of the pattern.

1. Place the strips in the guide so they sit flush against both the end stop and the side support (**C**). You can secure a strip to the base, gently pressing the kumiko strips against the side support for a steady hold. Clamps are another option, though they can get in the way when making cuts at an angle, so a simple base stop often works best.

B

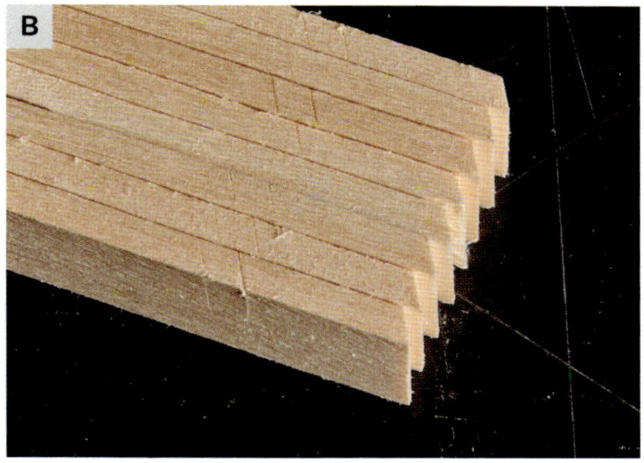

▲ A 60° angle is cut on the ends of all the strips.

POSITIONING THE STRIPS

C

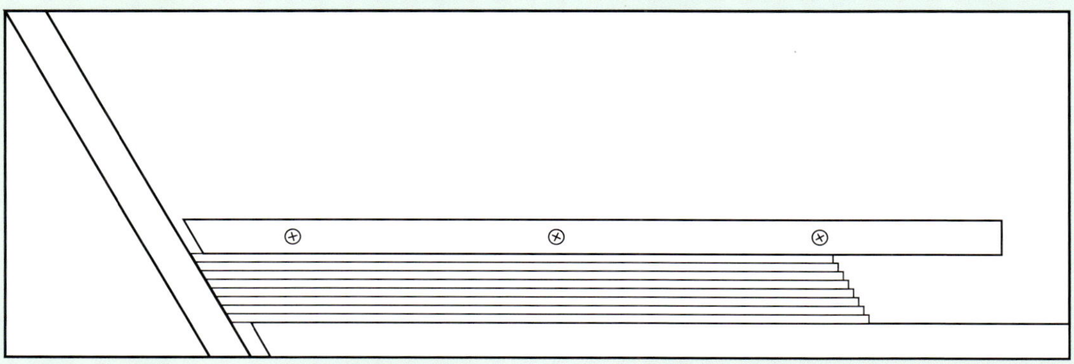

2. With a ruler, measure ½ in (12.7 mm) from the end stop. Using a marking knife and a bevel gauge set to 60°, draw a clean line across all the strips (**D**). This line will serve as the first reference for your angled cuts.

3. From that first line, measure ⅛ in (3.2 mm) and mark a second line. This distance corresponds to the thickness of the kumiko strip and establishes the boundary of the first joint.

4. Next, measure 2½ in (64 mm) from that line and mark across the strips again. This marks the starting point for the second joint. Continue in the same manner, measuring and marking each joint and spacing until the full diamond grid is laid out (**E**).

D

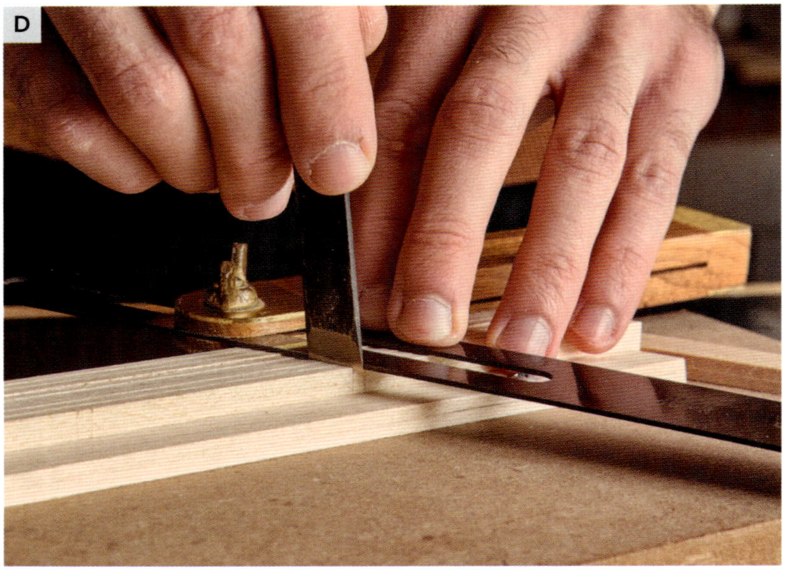

5. Take a sharp dozuki saw and cut just inside each marked line, being careful to stay on the waste side (**F**). Keep the cuts square and stop when you reach the halfway point of the kumiko strips.

E

MARKING 60° REFERENCE LINES

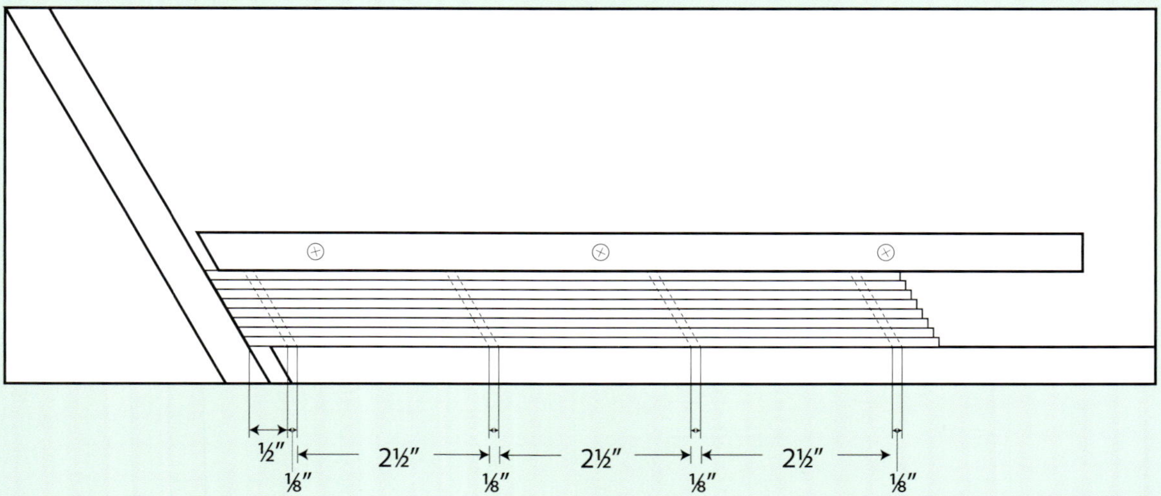

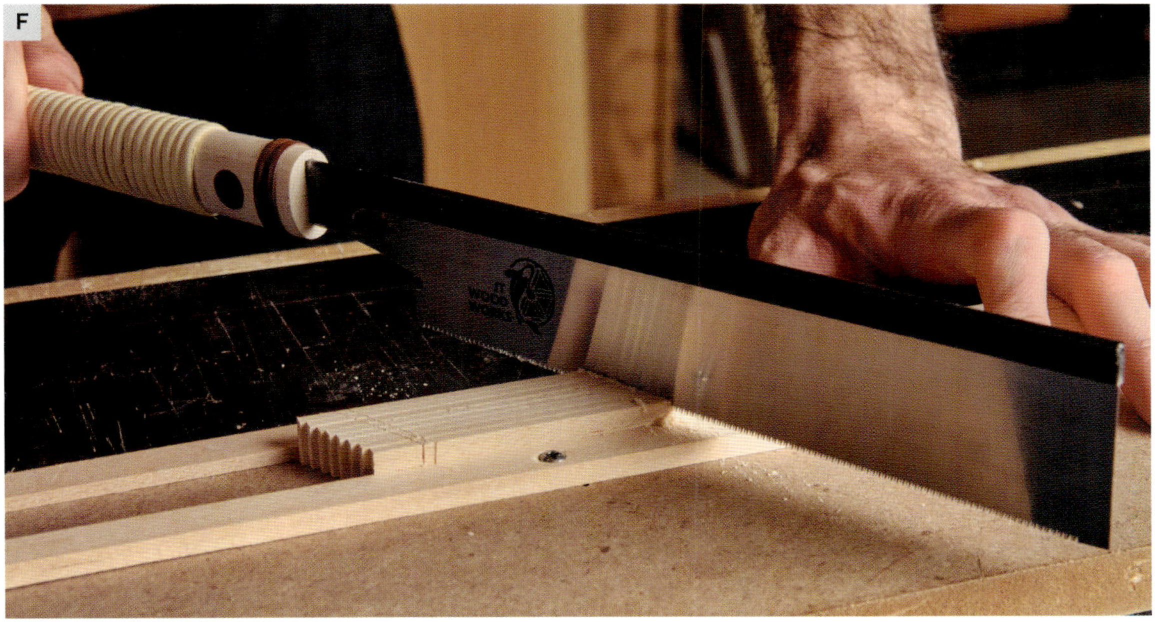

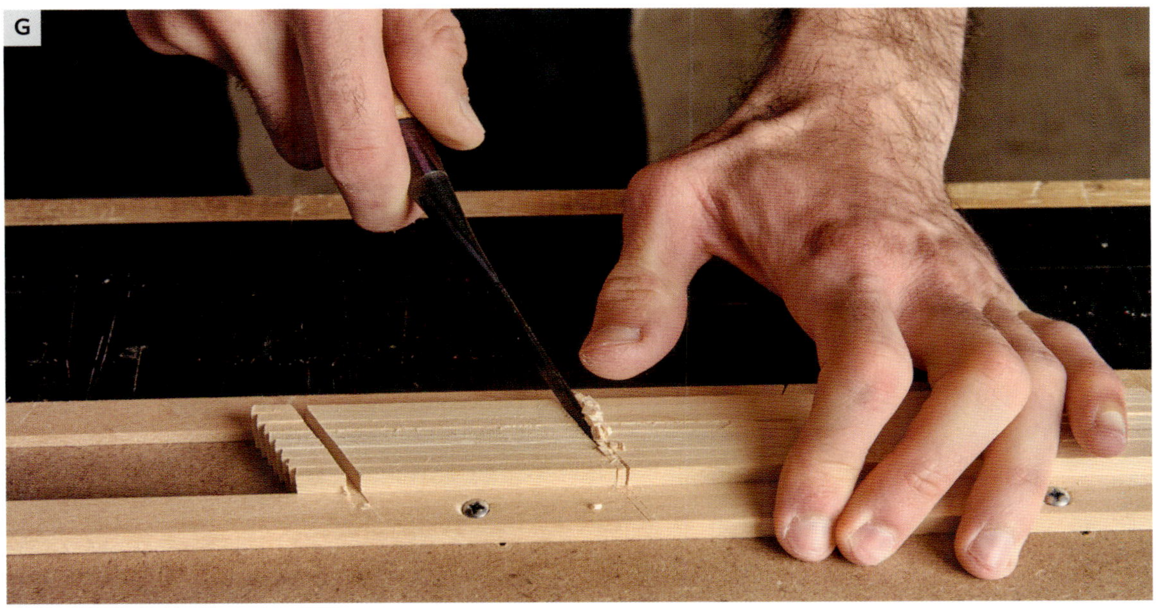

6. Once all the cuts are complete, use a narrow chisel to remove the waste material, clearing the joints so the pieces fit cleanly (**G**).

7. Assembling these pieces into a diamond grid is simple and follows the same steps as assembling the square grid (see page 30). If you decide to use glue, apply a thin layer to the inside of each joint with a small brush, just enough to hold without excess.

Cutting Diamond Grids with a Table Saw and Kumiko Sled

If you are using a table saw and kumiko sled, make the cuts for the joints using one of the angled fences on the sled (**A–B**). Which one you choose isn't important, but consistency is. Use the same fence for all of the joints (**C**).

Additionally, an infill piece can be added to divide each rhombus into two equilateral triangles. This piece is cut to a point on both ends using a 60° kumiko jig, allowing it to fit cleanly between opposing corners of the rhombus (**D**). How to use a kumiko jig is explained on page 54. By doing this, each segment now mimics the structure of a hexagonal grid, making it possible to incorporate the same infill patterns introduced on pages 68 to 74.

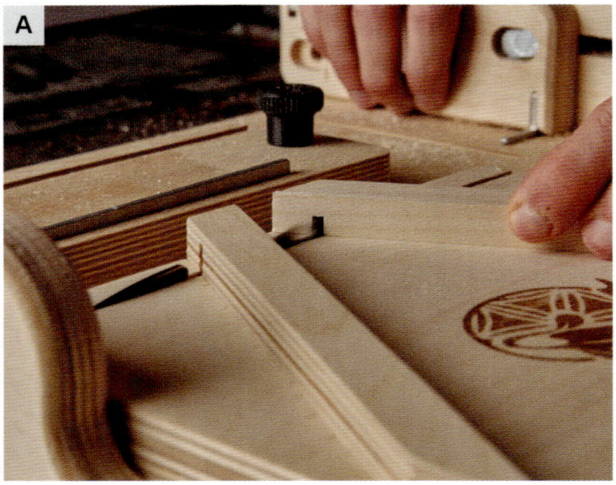
A

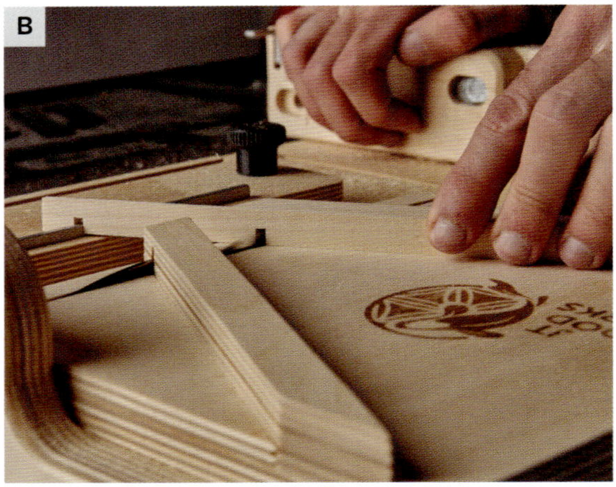
B

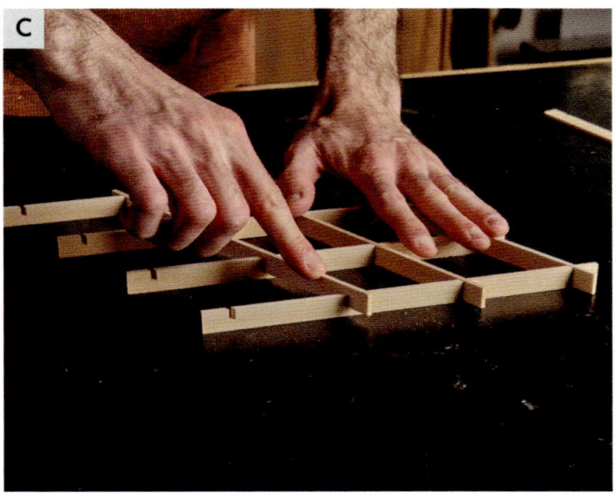
C

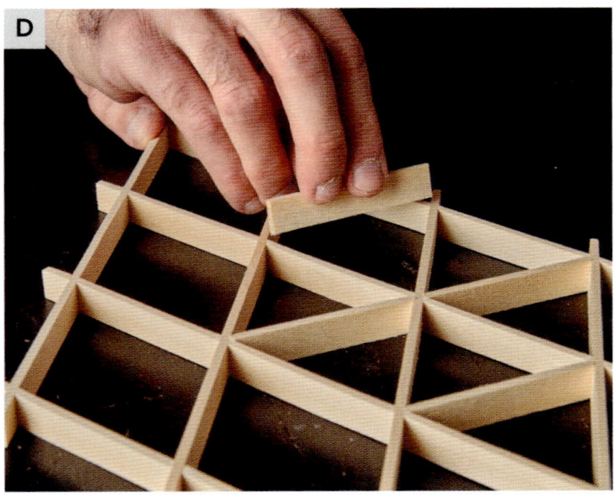
D

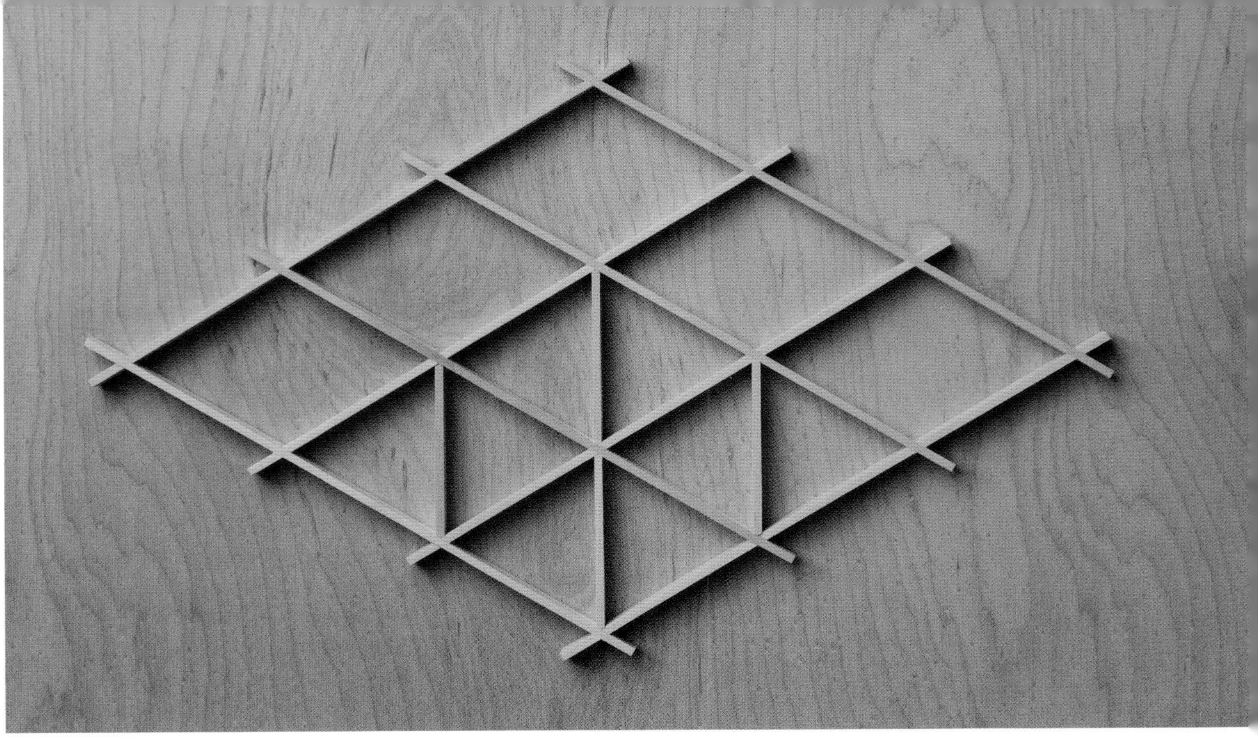

Hexagonal Grid (Mitsukude)

Hexagonal grids are the more complex kumiko grid. Instead of two layers of intersecting strips, like the previous grids, they require three strips to join at each intersection. Based on their complexity, it may take some practice to achieve hexagonal grids that fit together properly. There are two different types of pieces required to make this grid. They will be referred to as A- and B-pieces. At each intersection of the grid, there are two A-pieces and one B-piece. While preparing the strips to make this grid, plan accordingly to ensure you have enough pieces. It's always a good idea to cut extra pieces in case some are damaged or miscut.

The strips used here measure ½ in x ⅛ in (12.7 mm x 3.2 mm) with varying lengths. The pitch is 2¼ in (57 mm). Their lengths are 6½ in, 9 in, and 11¾ in (165 mm, 229 mm, and 298 mm). For each length, two A-pieces and one B-piece will be cut.

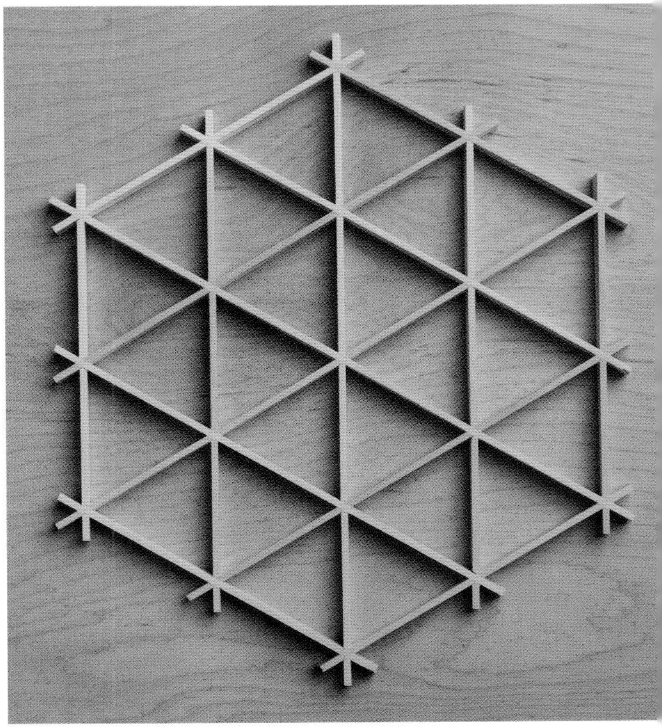

▲ Mitsukude (三つ組手)

STRUCTURE OF HEXAGONAL GRID: A- AND B-PIECES

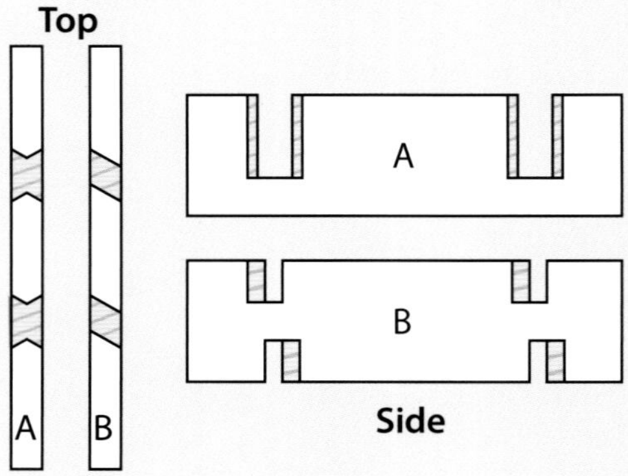

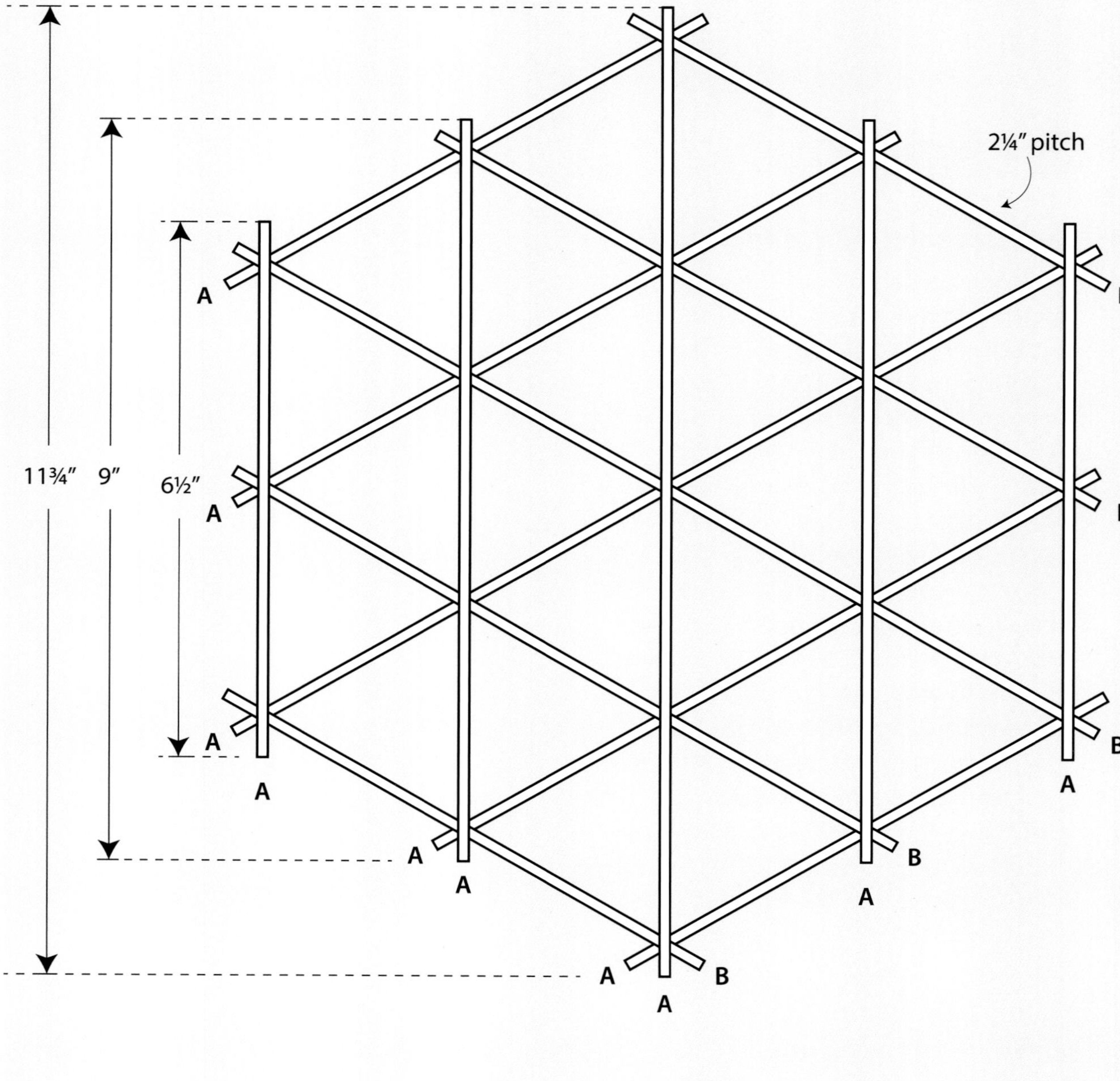

Cutting Hexagonal Grids by Hand

Achieving pieces that fit together cleanly requires close attention to detail. A mark or cut that's off by even a fraction of a millimeter can lead to an uneven or misshapen panel. As you work through the following steps, move slowly and focus on accuracy. Keep extra strips on hand so you can practice as needed. You may not get it right the first or even the second or third time, but with patience and repetition the geometry will begin to click, and you will arrive at beautiful results.

To cut these pieces by hand, you'll need two 60° cutting guides. For clarity, they'll be referred to as the right-hand and left-hand guides. The A-pieces require cuts made with both guides, while the B-pieces are shaped using only one. Work with calm intention, and the pieces will come together as they should.

USING LEFT- AND RIGHT-HAND 60° GUIDES

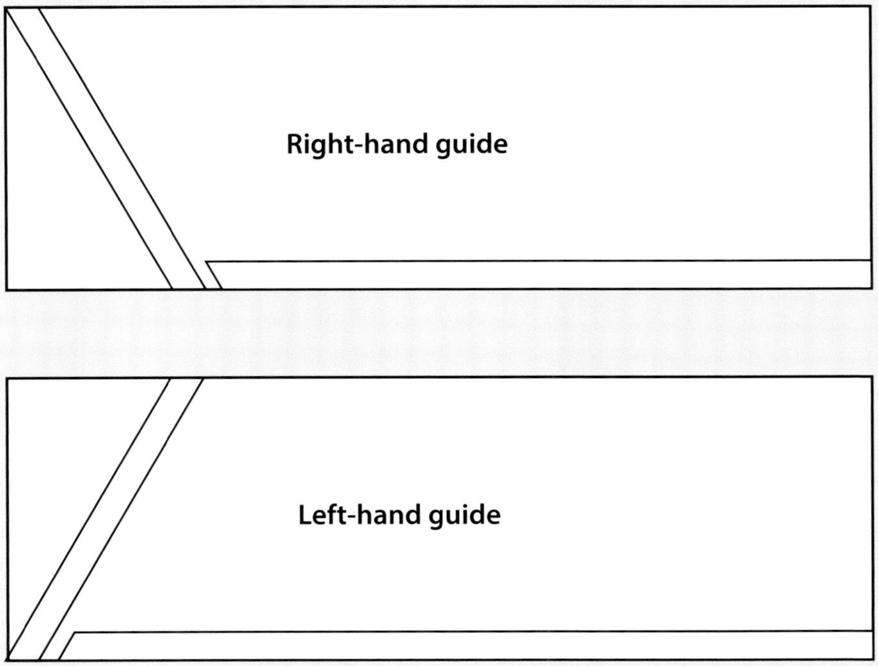

Cutting the A-pieces

Setup

1. Before placing the strips in the cutting guide, cut a centered point on one end of each piece using the 60° kumiko jig (**A**). This angled point helps the strips nest cleanly against the end stop of the guide, making the measuring and marking that follow much easier and more accurate.

A

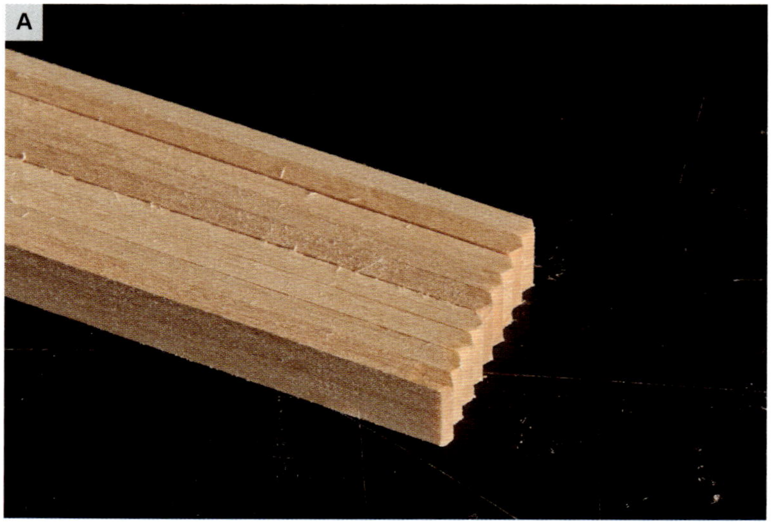

2. Place the strips in the left-hand guide, making sure they sit firmly against both the end stop and the side support. Secure one strip to the base to press the bundle gently against the side support (**B**). Clamps can be used, but they often interfere with the angled cuts.

B

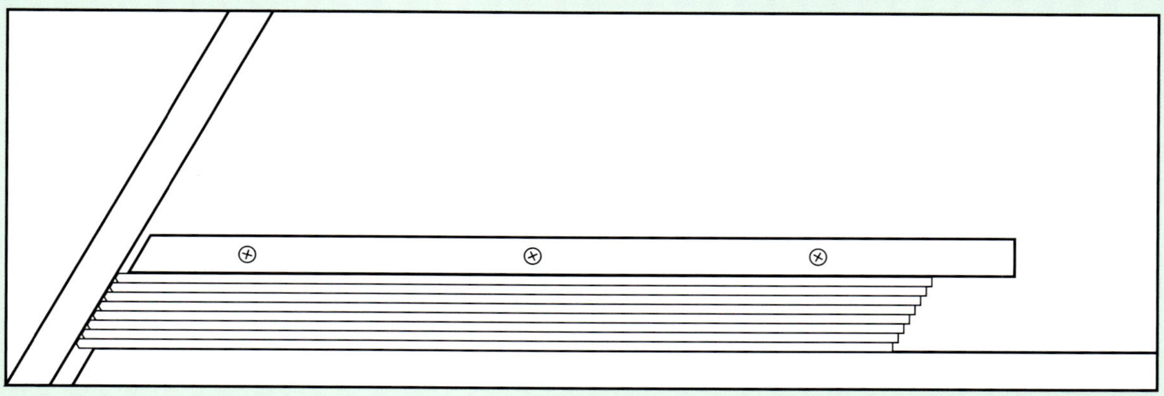

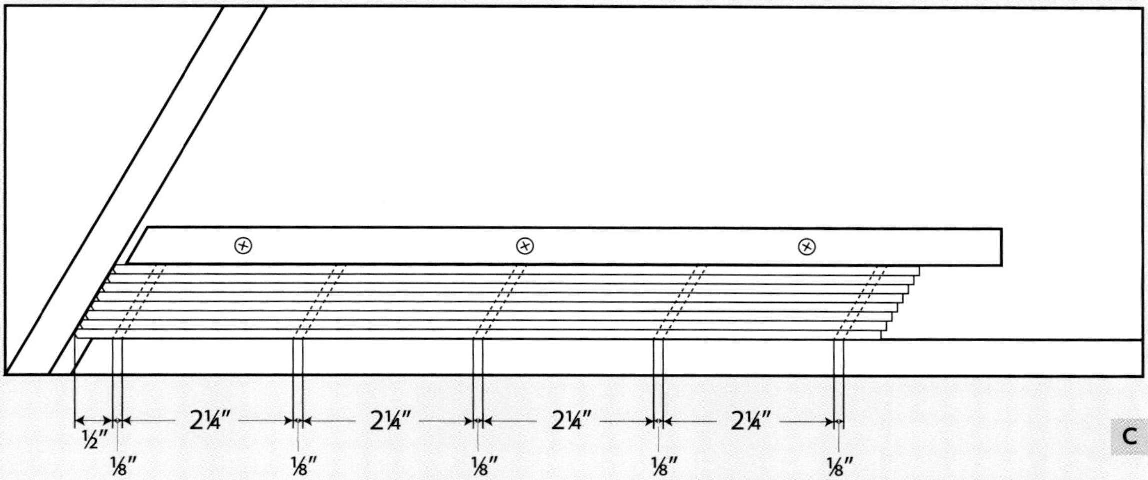

C

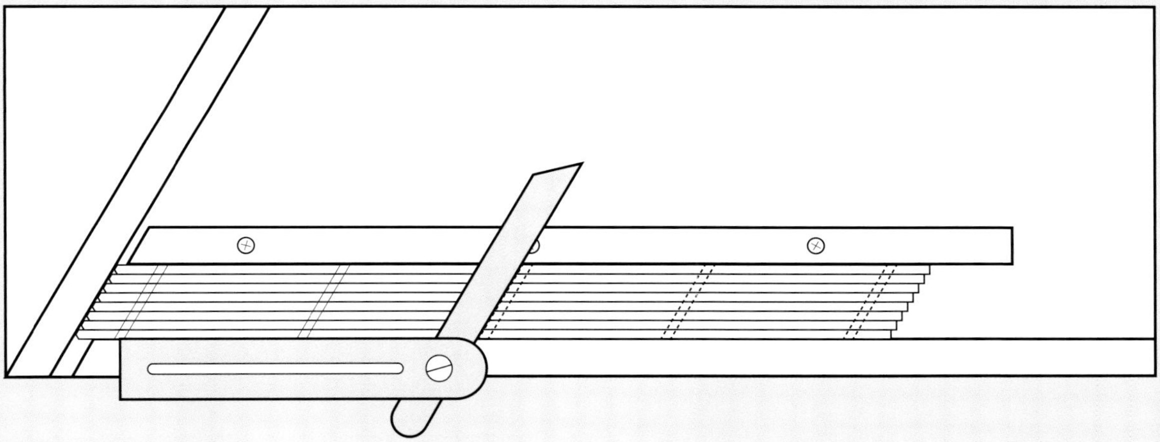

D

Lay out the joints

The first set of layout instructions is the same for both the A- and B-pieces. Each type of piece has its own requirements which will be explained later. These instructions cover the first set of layout lines and the second set will be made after the cuts are completed. Work with one group of pieces at a time. Finish all the A-pieces first, then move on to the B-pieces.

1. Begin by laying out the joints just like on the diamond grid pieces. Using a ruler and marking knife, make your tick marks on the strip closest to you. Start with a mark ½ in (12.7 mm) in from the end stop, then make a second mark ⅛ in (3.2 mm) beyond it. These two lines establish the boundary of the first joint.
2. Continue marking the strip with a 2¼ in (57 mm) spacing, followed by another ⅛ in (3.2 mm) line, repeating this pattern for the full length of the strip or for as many joints as your project requires (**C**).
3. Set your bevel gauge to 60°. You can use the cutting guide itself as a reliable reference to set the angle accurately. Use the bevel gauge to transfer each mark across all the strips, keeping the lines consistent and accurate (**D**).

Cut the joints (A)

1. The joints on the A-pieces are cut to two-thirds the width of the strip. For a ½ in (12.7 mm) strip, this works out to approximately 11⁄32 in (8.7 mm) (**A**).

2. Place your saw on the correct side of the first layout line and cut down to the measurement shown. If it helps, add a small reference mark on the side of the strips so you know exactly where to stop.

3. Repeat this process for all the required cuts, but don't remove the waste just yet (**B**). Leaving it in place will be helpful in the steps that follow.

4. Remove the strips from the cutting jig and place them into the right-hand cutting guide. Make sure the ends are fully seated against both the end stop and the side support. Secure a strip to the base, pressing it firmly against the kumiko strips as you tighten it in place (**C**).

5. To mark the next set of cuts, you won't need the ruler. Instead, mark by connecting the reference points shown here: the intersection of the strip's centerline and the previous cut. Draw a line between those points on the strip closest to you and the strip furthest away from you (**D**). Repeat this process for each earlier cut.

A

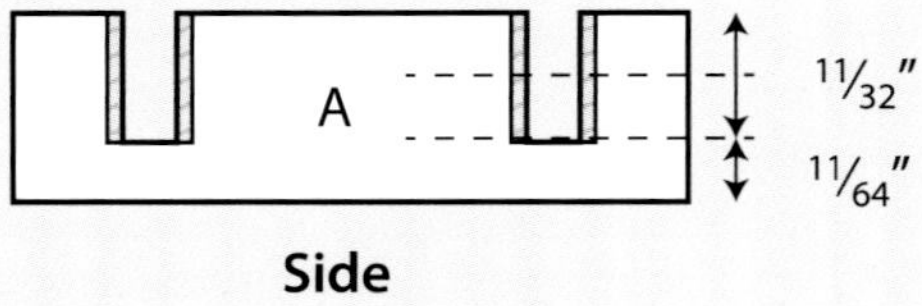

B

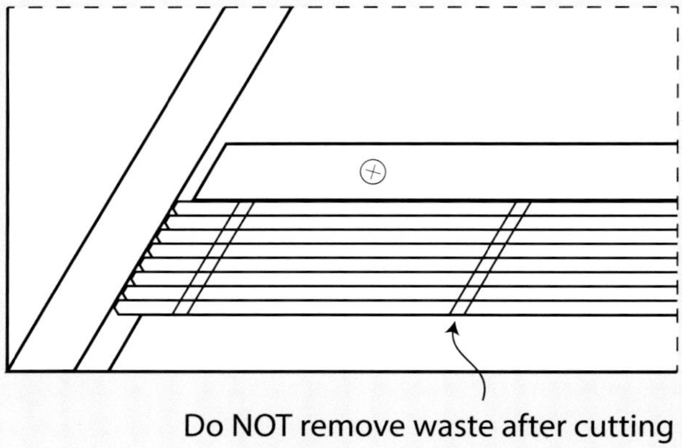

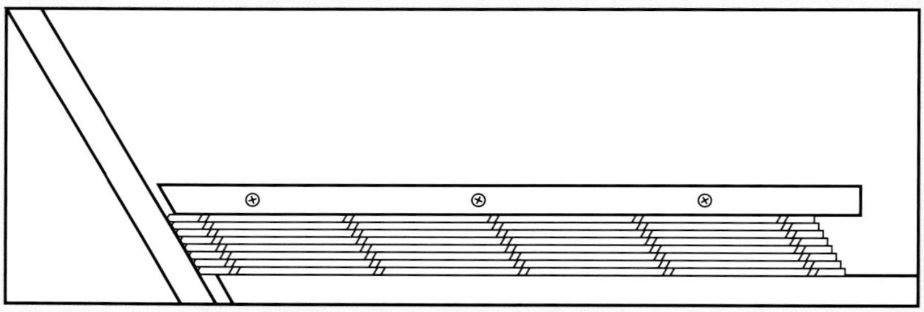

C

D

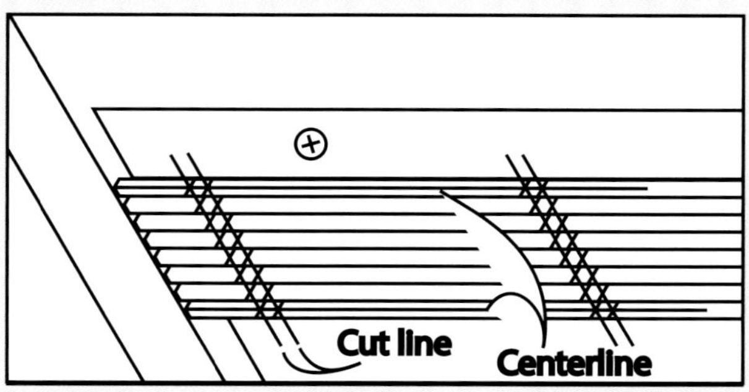

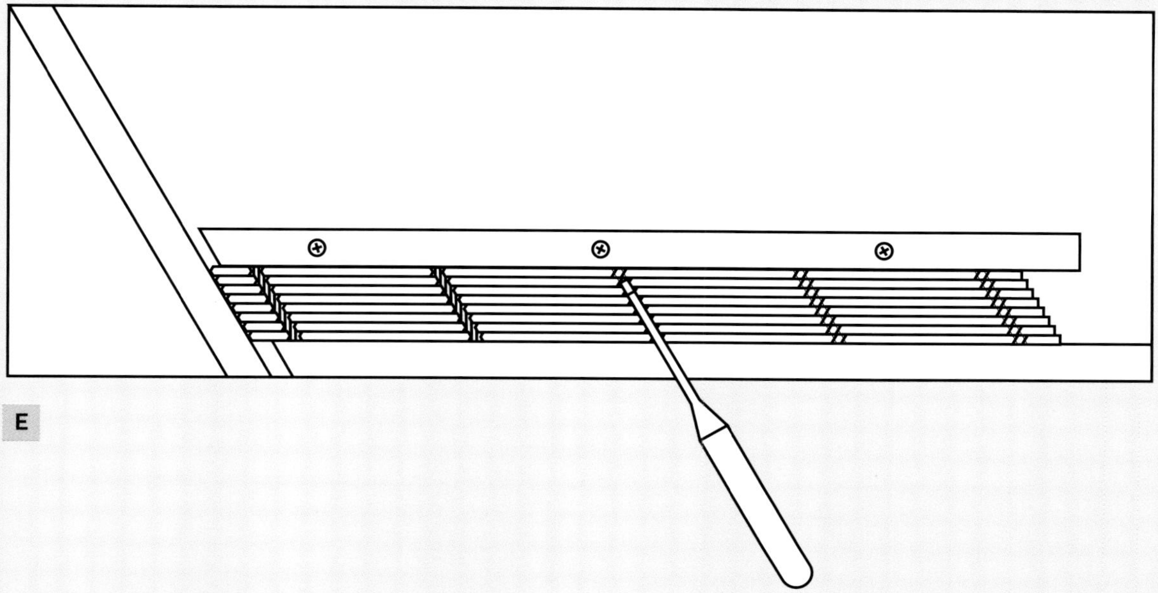

E

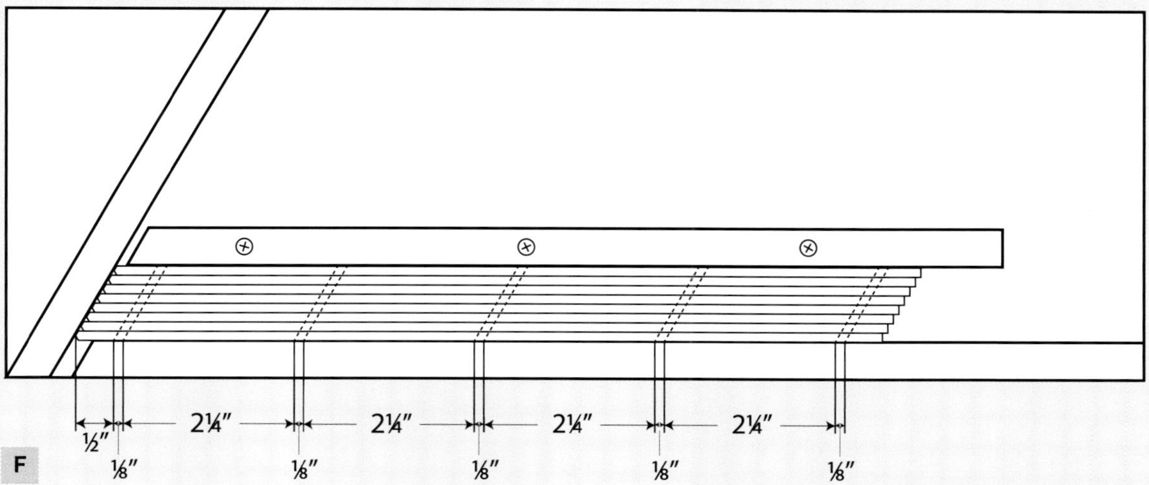

F

6. From here, make the cuts as you normally would. Keeping the waste material in place helps guide the saw and prevents it from drifting into the open joint.

7. Once all the cuts are complete, use a narrow chisel to clean out and remove the waste from each joint (**E**).

Cut the joints (B)

1. For the B-pieces, you'll only need one cutting guide. It doesn't matter which one you choose, just be sure to use the same guide for both parts of the process so your angles stay consistent.

2. Follow the same steps as before to secure the strips in the cutting guide and take your time laying out the joints with the same level of care and accuracy (**F**).

G

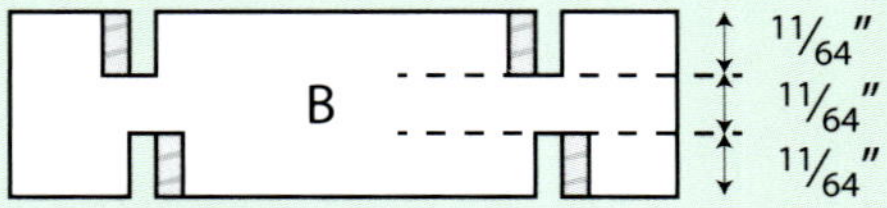

Side

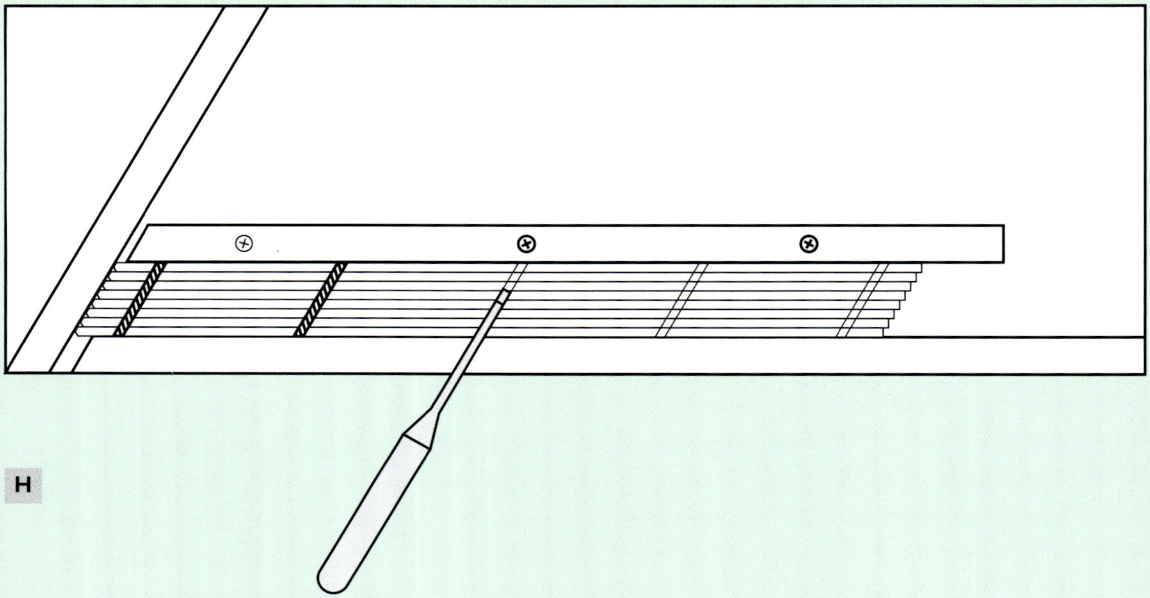

H

3. The joints on the B-pieces are one-third the width of the strip and cut on both edges. For a ½ in (12.7 mm) strip, this comes to 11⁄64 in (4.4 mm) (**G**).

4. Cut along the marked areas as usual, then use a narrow chisel to remove the waste material (**H**).

5. Remove the strips from the cutting guide and rotate them so the cut joints face downward, resting against the base. Secure them as before to keep them steady and repeat the same process of marking, cutting, and chiseling to clear the joints on this new face of the strips.

Assemble the grid

Assembling this grid can be intricate. Follow the instructions on pages 50 and 51 to fit the pieces together correctly and use glue if you wish to secure the joints.

Cutting Hexagonal Grids with a Table Saw and Kumiko Sled

Cutting the A-pieces

Setup

1. Install a blade that matches the thickness of strips you will use. In this case, we'll use $\frac{1}{8}$ in (3.2 mm) strips, so a blade with a $\frac{1}{8}$ in (3.2 mm) kerf thickness is used. For best results, the thickness of the strips, blade kerf, and registration key should be the same.

2. Adjust the blade height to cut two-thirds the width of the strip. For a $\frac{1}{2}$ in (12.7 mm) strip, this measurement is $\frac{11}{32}$ in (8.7 mm).

Cut the joints

1. The first joint needs to be accurately cut twice at opposing angles. To ensure accuracy, align it with the end of the fence. This gives a reference point for the second set of cuts.

   A small piece of wood can be helpful to properly align the strip with the edge of the fence (**A**).

2. After making the first cut, place that notch over the registration key and make your second cut. Repeat this process for all your joints. Ensure your strip is flat against the base and fence while making each cut.

   The first image (**B**) shows the first cut being made on the strip; the second image (**C**) shows subsequent cuts.

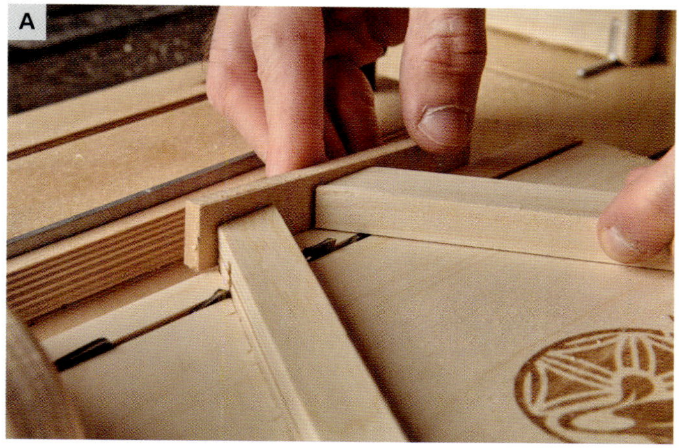
A

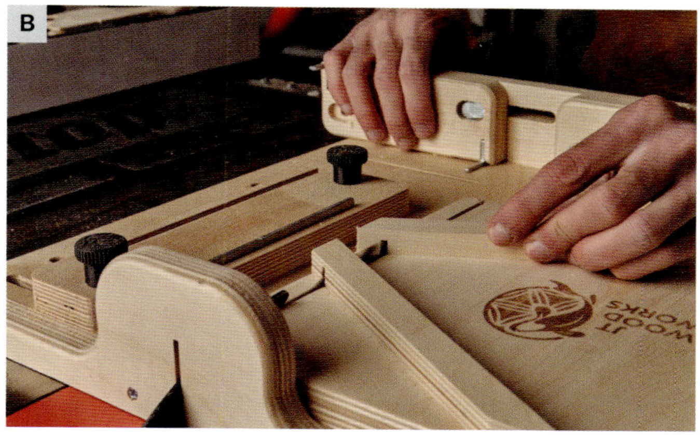
B

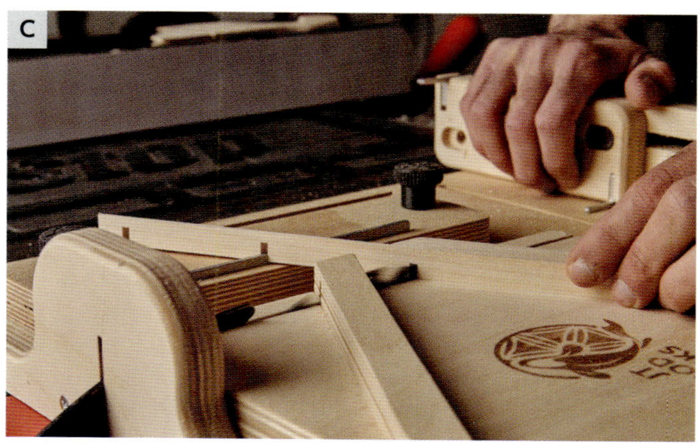
C

Cut the opposing angles

1. The second set of cuts is similar to the first but made using the other 60° fence. Align your strip to the end of the fence like before and make your first cut. Repeat the same steps as before at this new angle (**D**).

2. The most important thing is that the joints create a point exactly in the center of the strip's thickness. A good way to ensure this is: before making each cut, make sure the corner of the notch created by the first cut is aligned precisely with the center of the blade.

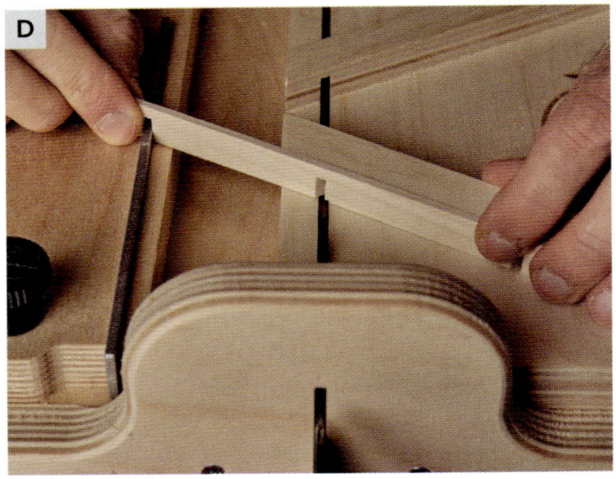
D

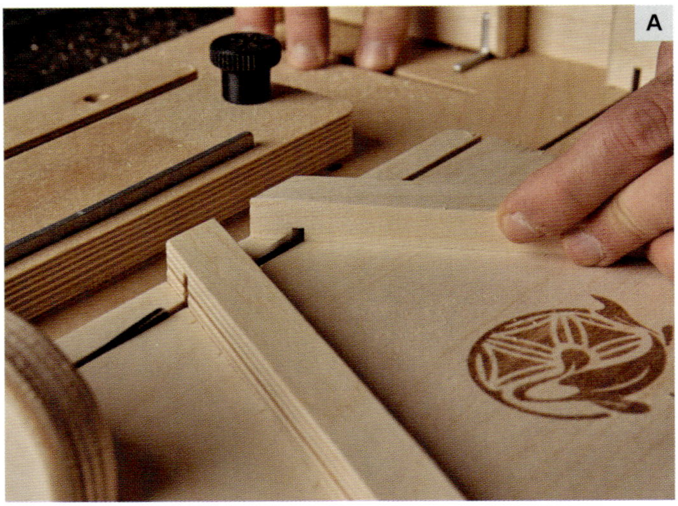
A

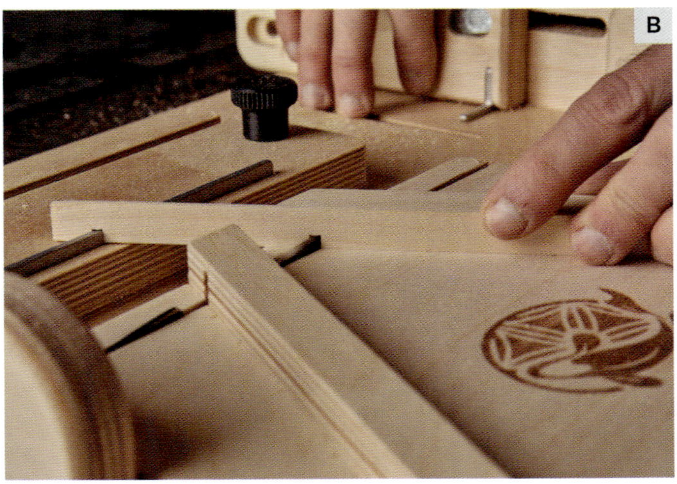
B

Cutting the B-pieces

Setup

1. Lower the blade height to cut one-third of the width of the strip. This measurement is $^{11}/_{64}$ in (4.4 mm).

2. Align the end of the strip with the end of the fence, as you did with the A-pieces, and make your first cut. Assemble this B-piece with one of the A-pieces and make sure the top surfaces are flush. Adjust the blade height as needed (**A**).

Cut the joints

1. After making the first cut, place that joint over the registration key and make your second cut, repeating this process for all your joints (**B**).

2. Ensure your strip is flat against the base and fence while making each cut.

Cut the opposing angles

The second set of cuts is similar to the first but made on the strip's opposite edge and using the same fence on the sled. Align your strip to the end of the fence like before and make your first cut. Repeat the same steps as before on this new edge (**C–E**).

These joints may appear staggered from the side view, however, because of their angles, the center of the joints are in line with each other (see the Hexagonal Grid on page 39).

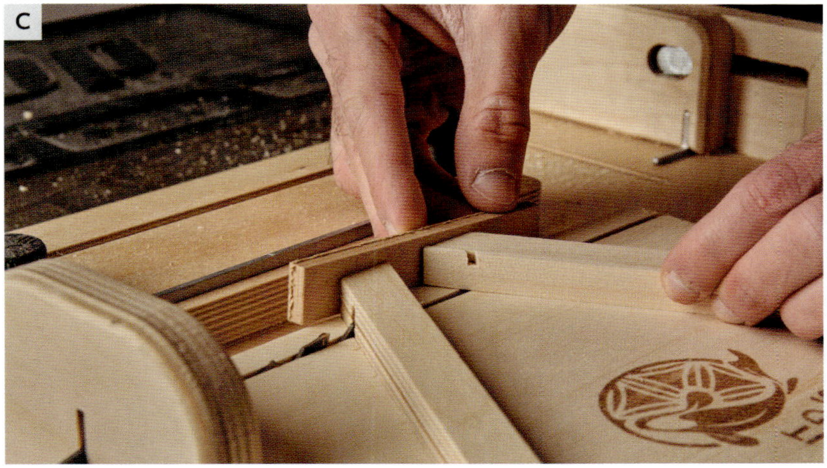
C

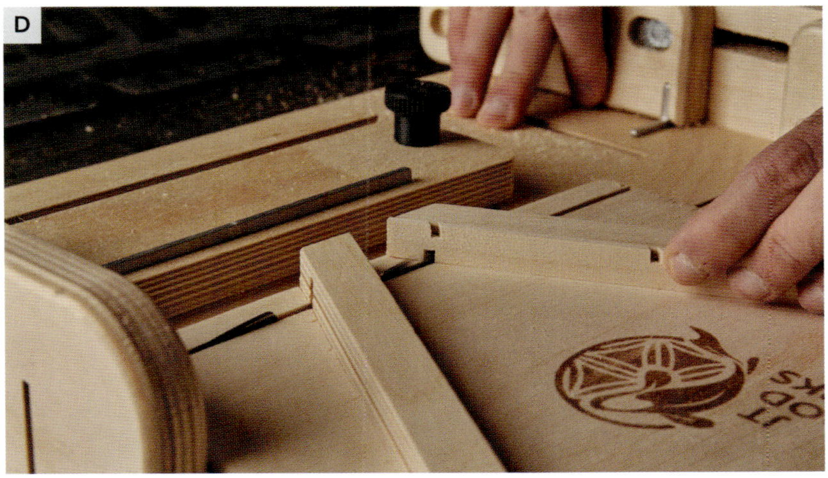
D

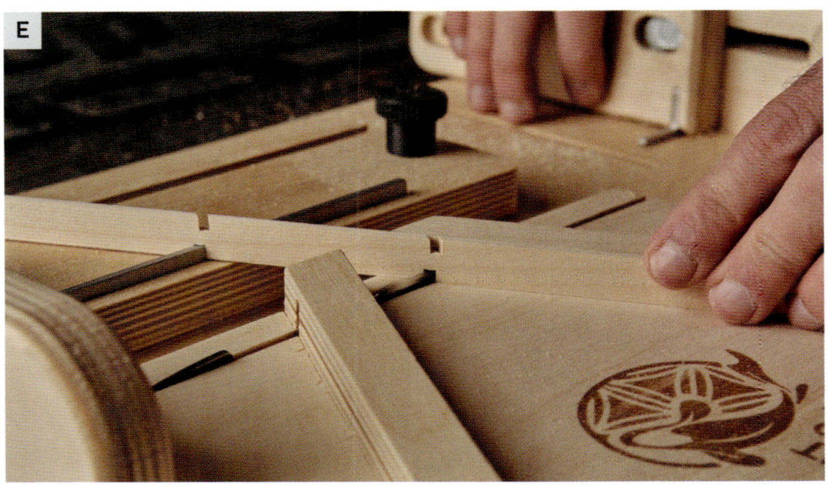
E

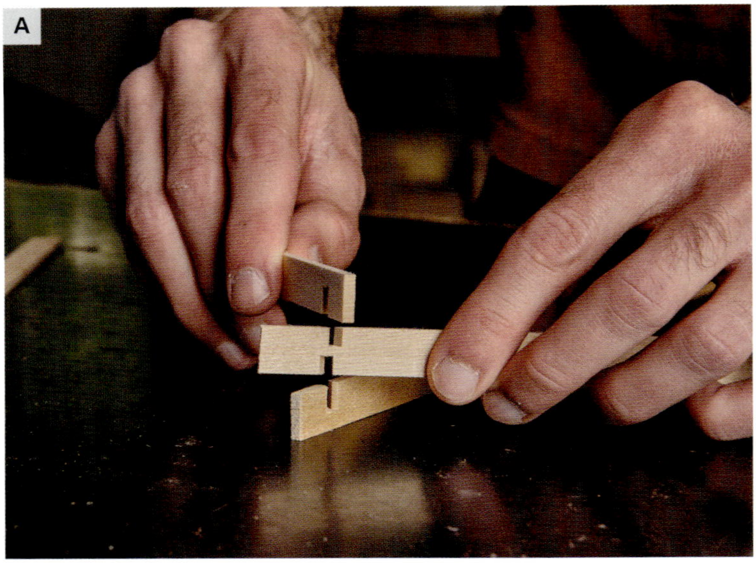

Assembling the grid

1. The grid is assembled with an A-piece on the bottom, then insert a B-piece, followed by another A-piece on top (**A**).

2. Begin by inserting all of your B-pieces into the notches of a single A-piece. Align each joint carefully. The longer strips intersect on their center joints followed by the shorter strips moving outward, staggering the joints (**B**).

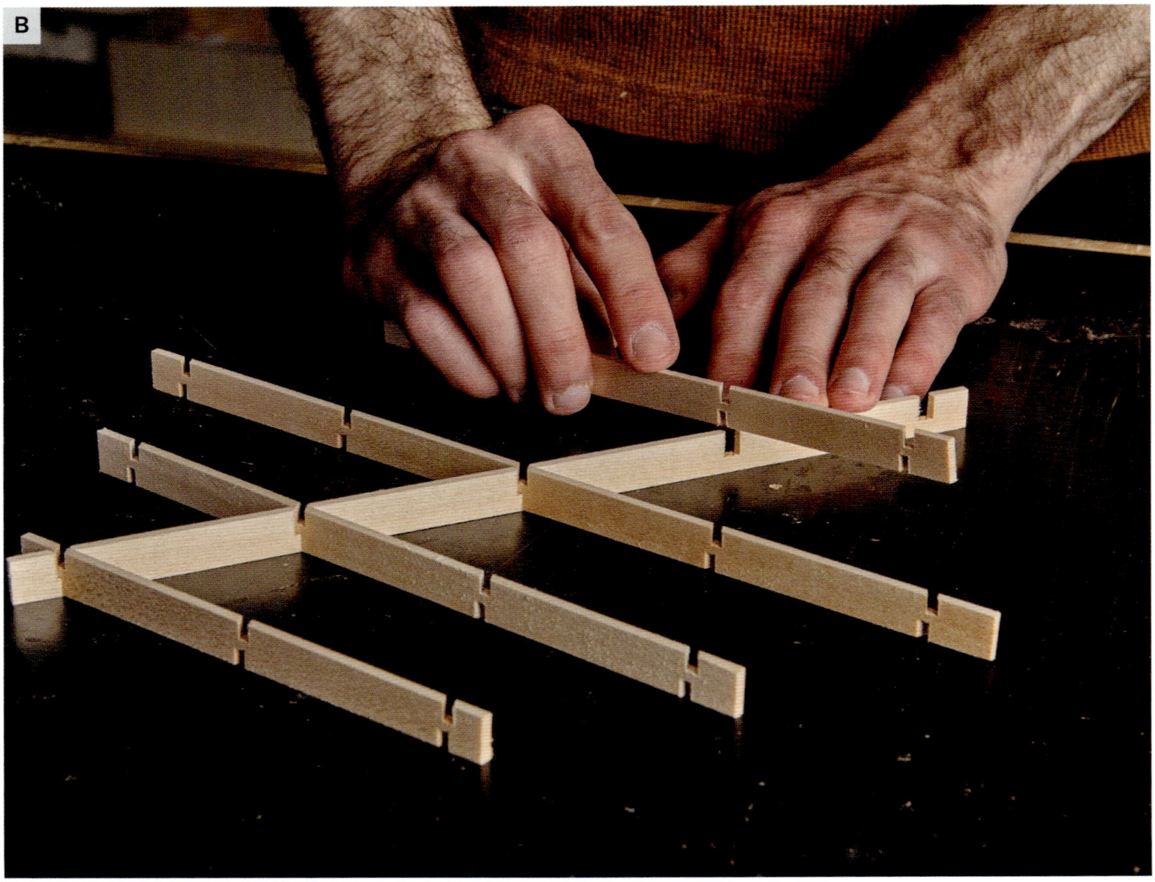

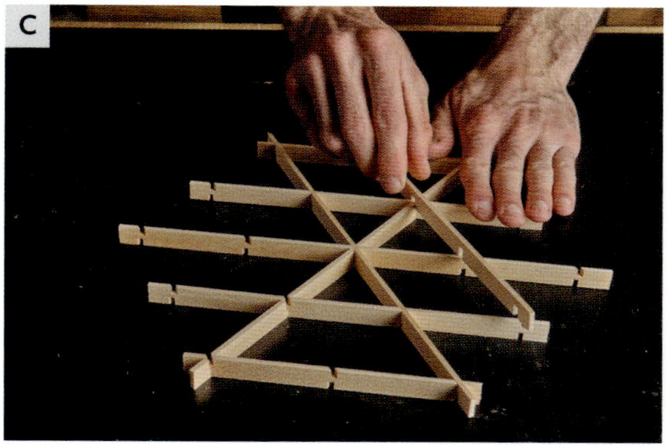

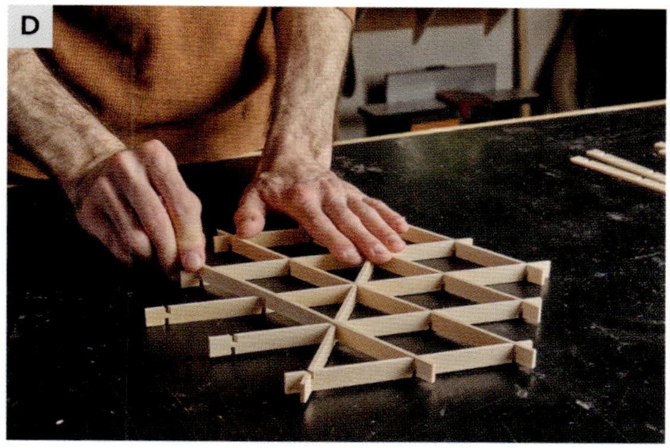

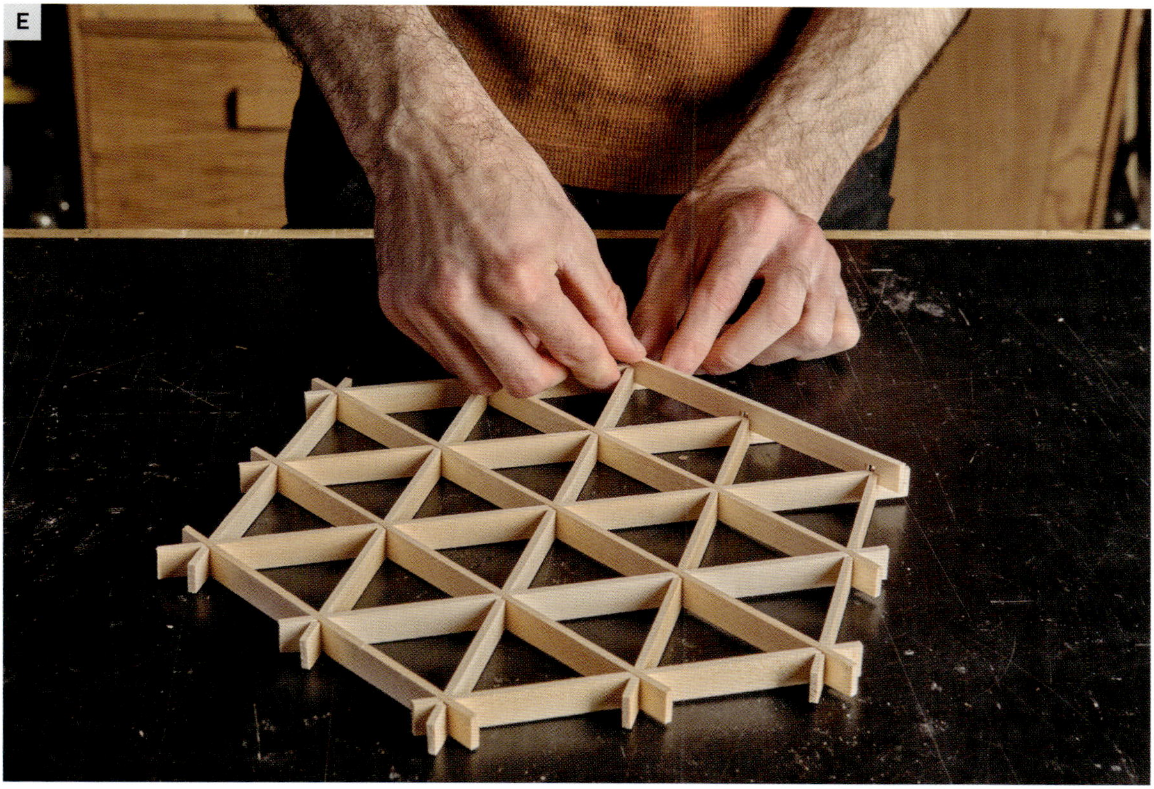

3. Next, place additional A-pieces into the top notches of the inserted B-pieces, continuing the pattern (**C–D**). Work gently and evenly to avoid stressing the joints as the structure begins to take shape.

4. Once that side is complete, carefully flip the entire panel over. Fill in the remaining A-pieces by inserting them into the exposed notches to complete the grid (**E**). If the joints are a bit tight, get the piece started and place a scrap block on top. Use light taps with a hammer to make sure all joints are fully engaged and the overall grid lies flat.

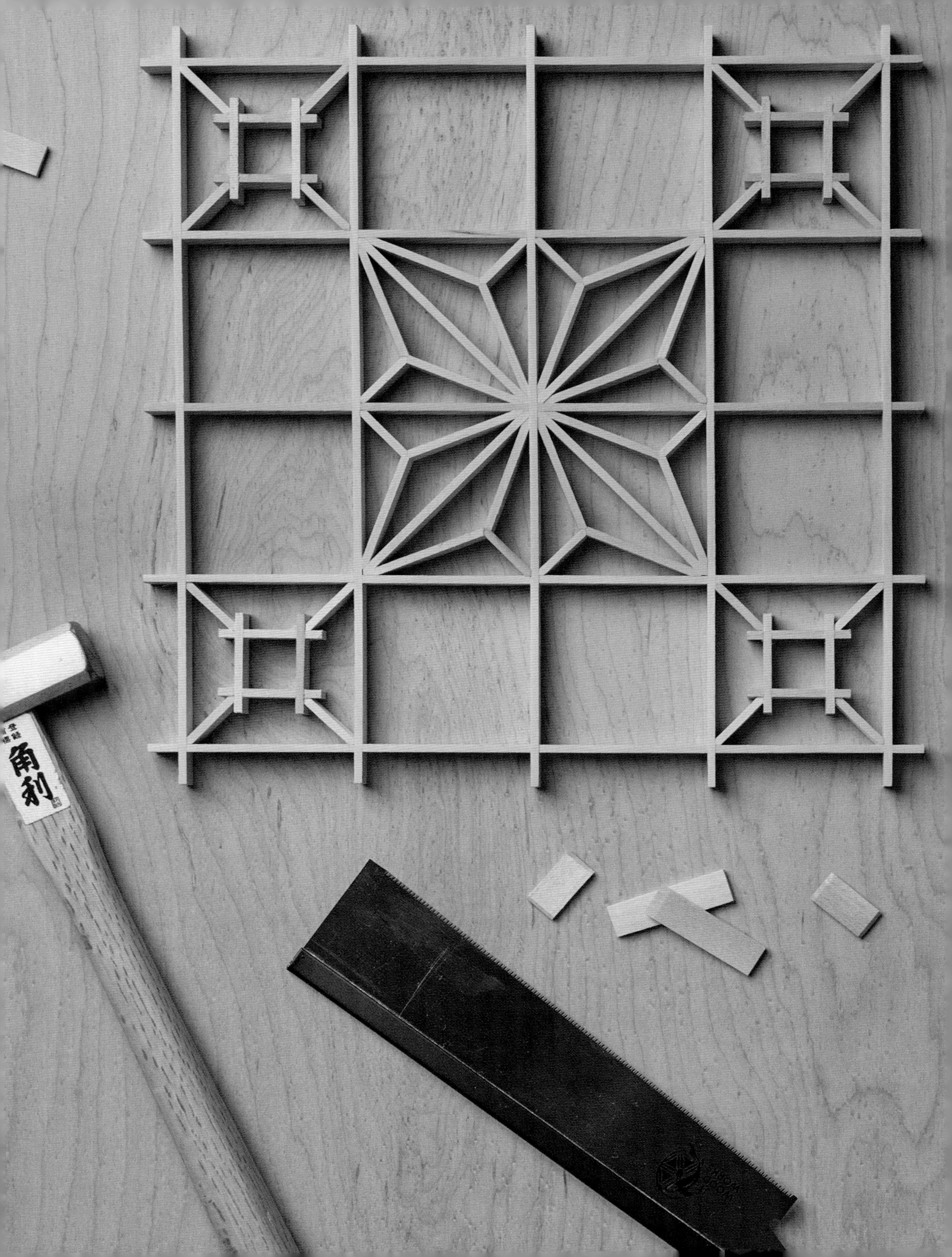
角利

Chapter 4

Making Square Kumiko Patterns

There are hundreds of different kumiko patterns, with asa-no-ha being the most popular. There are also variations of asa-no-ha that can be made in a square or hexagonal grid. The square version is called kaku asa-no-ha, sometimes shortened to kaku-asa. The word asa-no-ha (麻の葉) translates to hemp leaf. This pattern is so popular that it extends past the world of woodworking and is often seen on fabrics, weaving, paper manufacturing, and dyeing. The hemp plant grows quickly and straight, and in ancient Japan, this pattern was often put on children's clothing in the belief that it would help with their growth and development.

Although it may be the most popular, there are many more patterns than the beautiful asa-no-ha. This chapter will also cover how to make the yotsuba-izutsu-tsugi (四つ葉井筒継ぎ) pattern as well.

Before diving into the patterns, let's begin with an understanding of how to use kumiko jigs.

◀ Kaku asa-no-ha in the center with elements of yotsuba-izutsu-tsugi in the corners.

Using Kumiko Jigs

Many kumiko patterns need pieces cut with various angles on them. The steps to cut a piece for kumiko are the same whichever angle you need. Here are some helpful tips to keep in mind while cutting your pieces.

- When cutting the ends of the pieces, the ½ in (12.7 mm) face will always be on the base of the groove of the kumiko jigs and I recommend using either a ½ in (12.7 mm) or ¾ in (19.1 mm) chisel. A block plane can also be used. Either way, make sure your tool is sharp enough to produce great results.
- To use the jigs, loosen the screw and slide the sliding stop block to your desired position and tighten the screw to secure it. Place the jig in a vise or clamp it to a sturdy surface when cutting the bevels. If using a vise, it's a good idea to angle the jig slightly upward for ease of use.
- Place the piece to be cut against the groove's wall, toward the direction the tool will be cutting. For example, if you're using a chisel, align the piece against the further wall. If using a Japanese plane that cuts on the pull stroke, align the strip against the wall closer to you.
- There are two key points to keep in mind when cutting your pieces. First, make sure your piece stays flat against the wall and base of the groove.
- Second, as you're cutting, if using a chisel, try to keep the tool flat on the reference face of the jig. It's okay to lift it up to take multiple small passes (in fact, this is encouraged) but try not to lift the rear of the chisel, forcing the tip toward the jig where it would be cutting into the jig itself.
- To make the cutting easier, it's helpful to skew the tool downward. If you're having difficulties cutting, try sharpening your chisel or plane iron. A sharp tool makes a big difference.

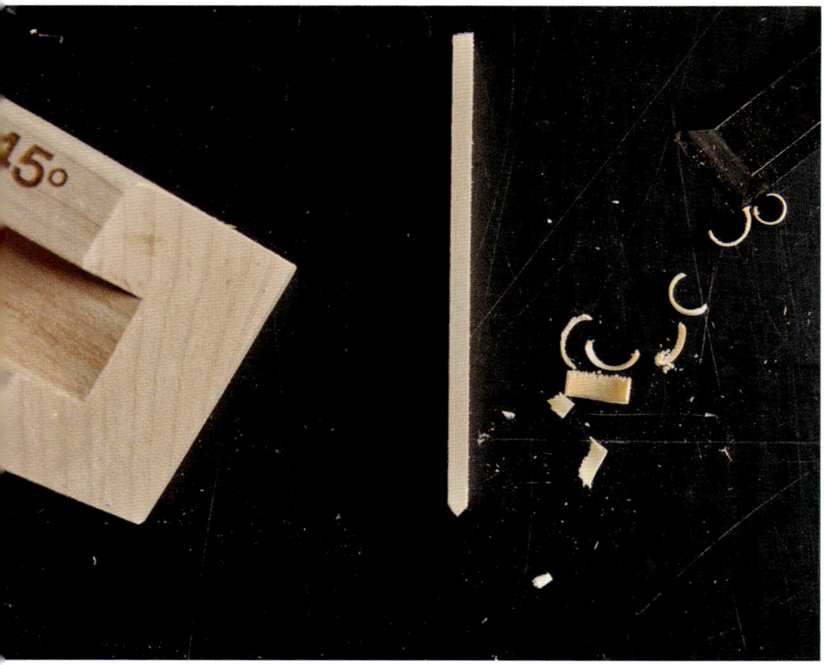

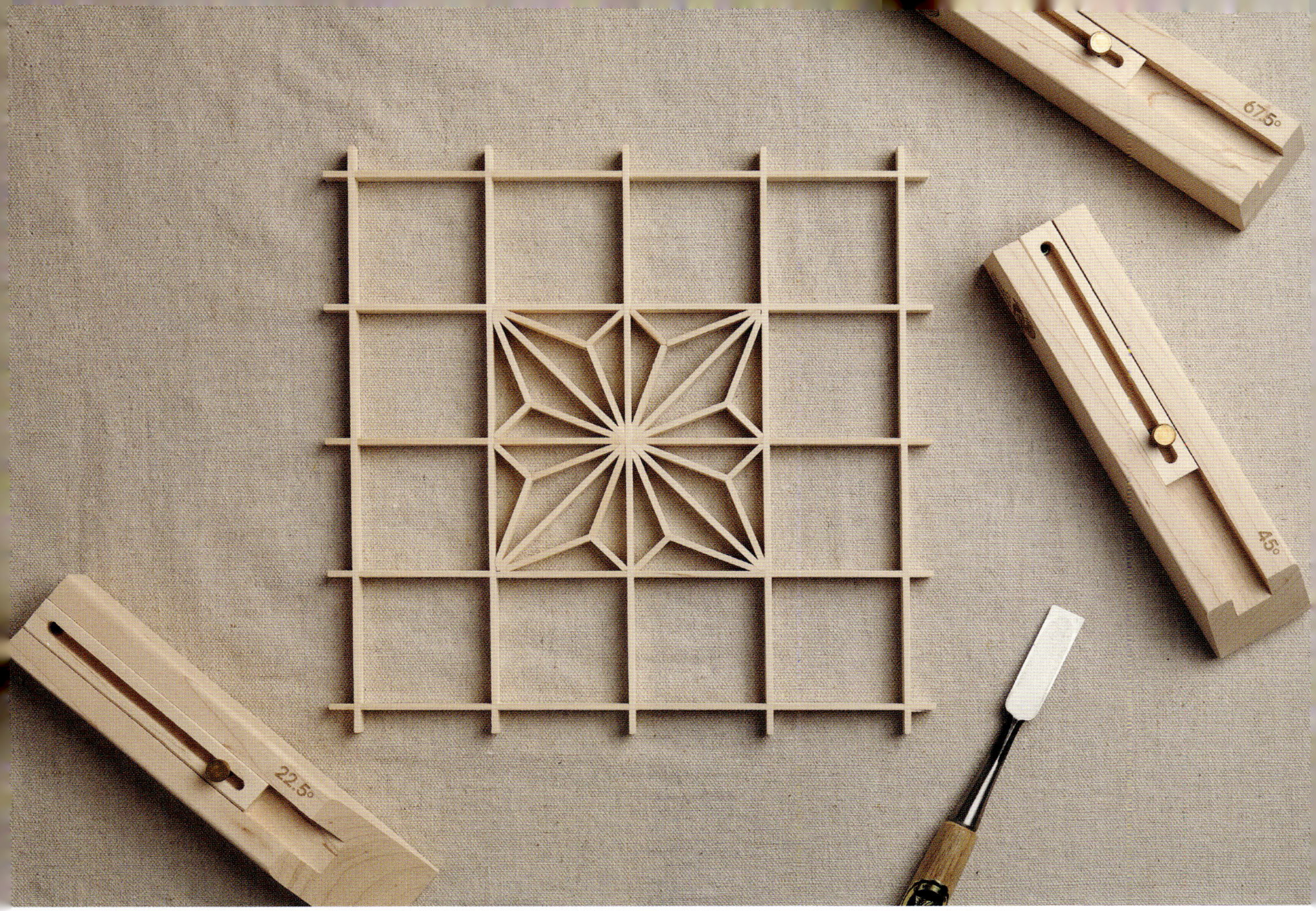

Square Patterns

Kaku Asa-no-ha (角麻の葉)

The jigs needed to make this pattern are 22.5°, 45°, and 67.5°. These angles evenly divide a 90° angle of the grid, and when the pieces are cut with these angles on their ends, they rest in the grid perfectly. It's important these angles are accurate to achieve the proper balance and appearance on the pattern.

Follow the steps on pages 24 to 31 to make a square jigumi to use for this pattern. You can make this as large as you'd like to include multiple kaku asa-no-ha patterns. Don't forget to glue the grid together. There are four different ways to make this pattern. The method shown here is called genkotsu type 1 and is the simplest.

STRUCTURE OF KAKU ASA-NO-HA

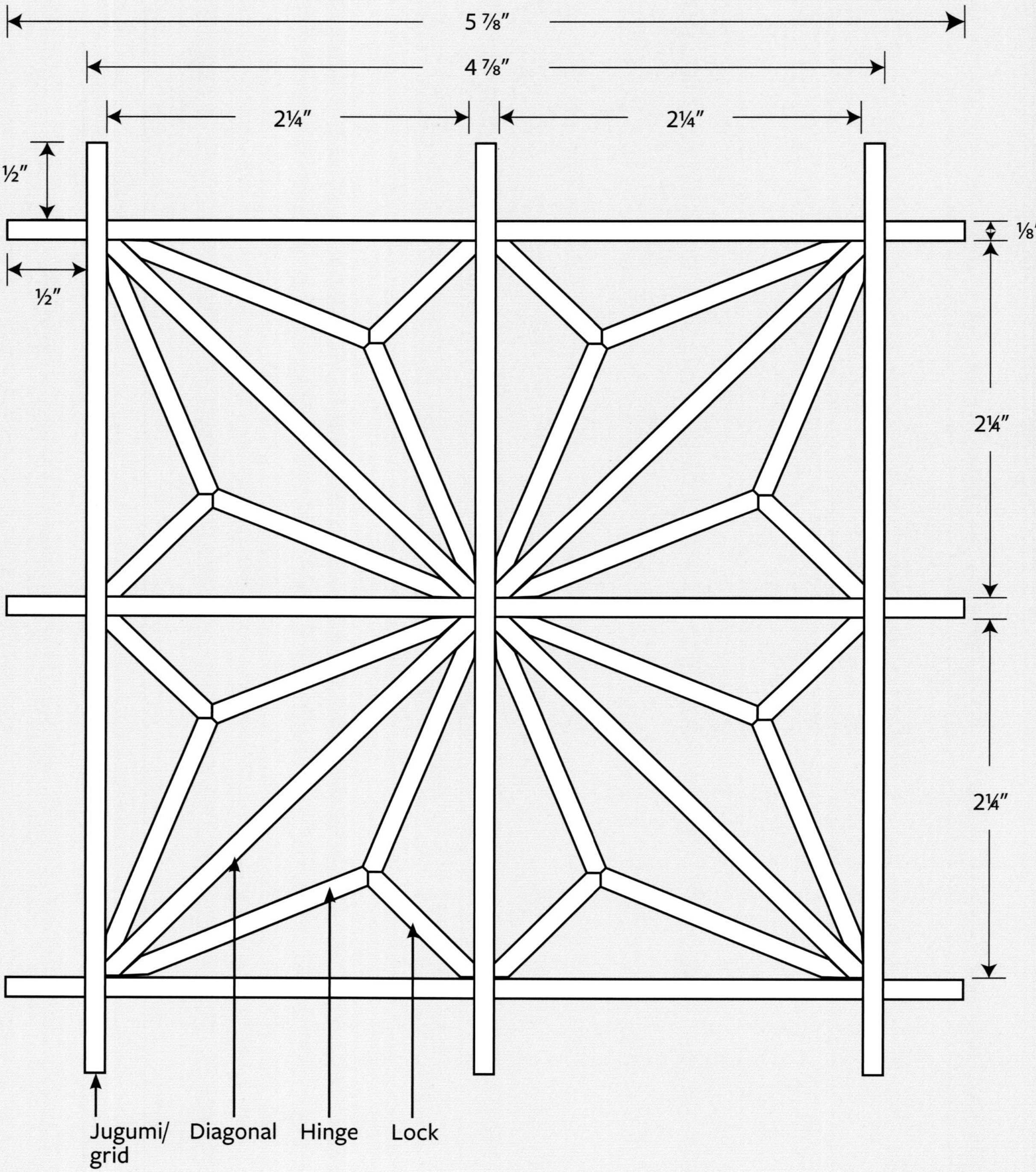

A

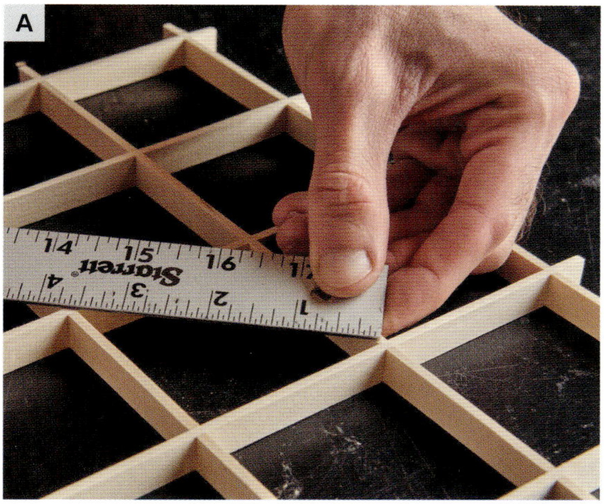

B

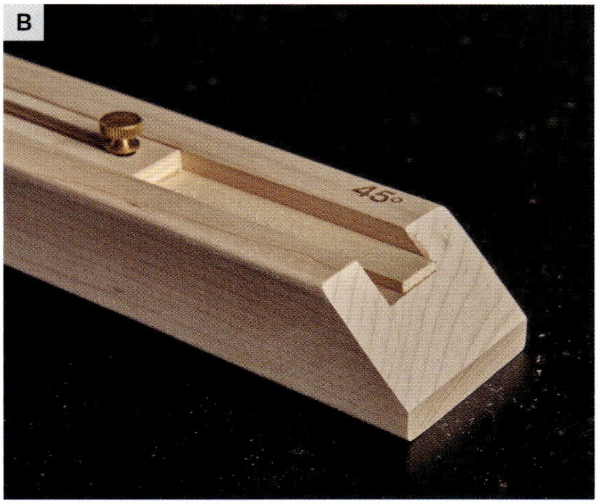

C

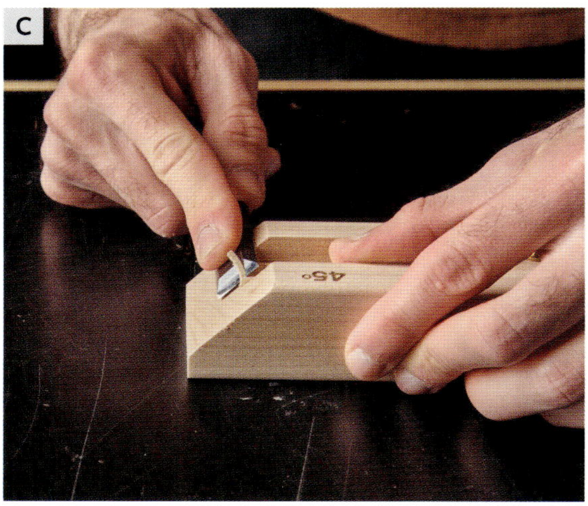

Diagonals

1. Measure the length needed for the four central diagonal pieces (**A**) and cut pieces to be slightly oversized by about ¼ in (6.4 mm) to ensure you have enough extra material to pare down to the final size using the jigs. It's a good idea to cut a few extras to account for mistakes.

2. Now adjust the 45° jig's sliding stop block to where the center of the piece slightly passes the angled area of the jig (**B**). The corner of the upper side should protrude the angled portion of the jig to be sheared at 45°.

3. Cut the angle with your chisel or plane (see page 54) (**C**).

4. Flip over the piece to the opposite face and cut this end to achieve a point on the end of the piece (**D**). This point makes a 90° angle that will fit into the 90° angle of the grid (**E**).

D

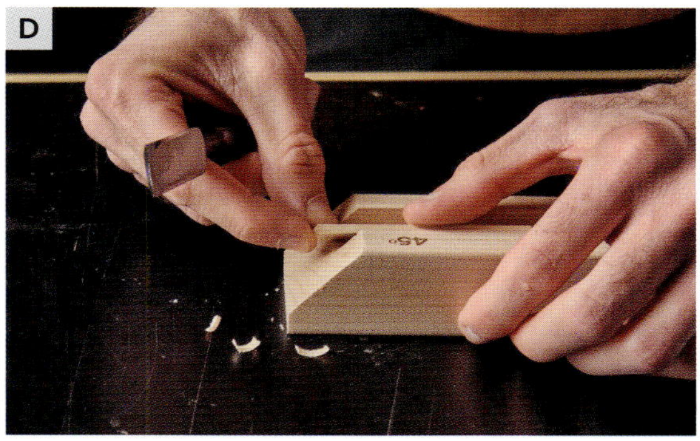

E

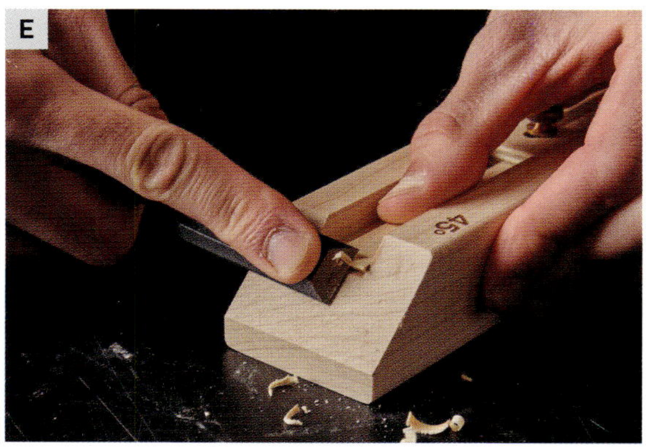

F

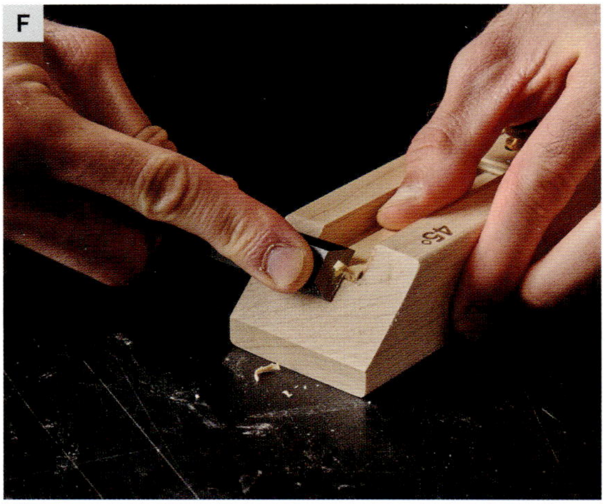

G

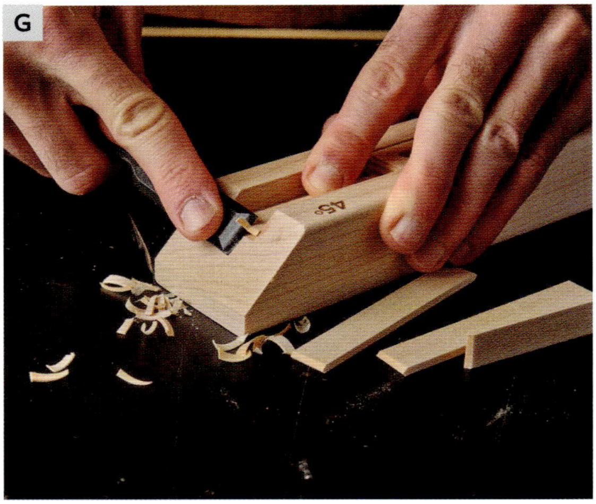

H

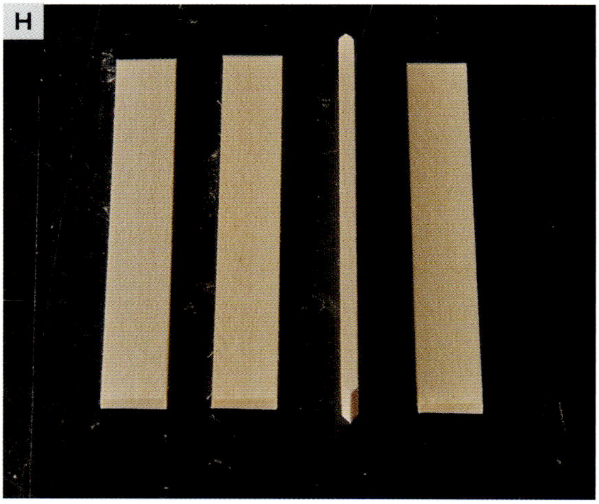

I

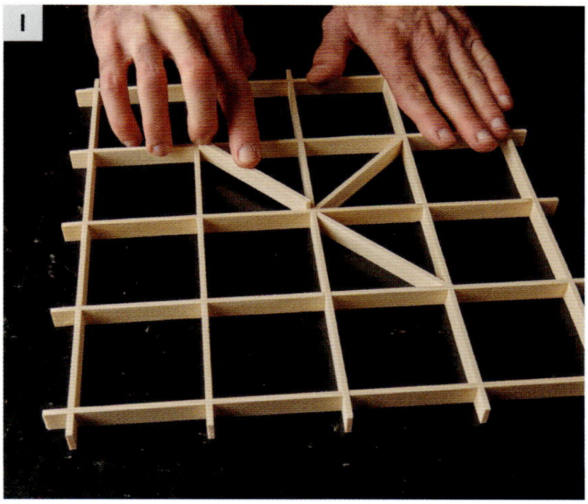

5. Do not move the stop block yet! Cut one end of all the pieces now before moving the jig's stop block (**F**).

6. Now flip the piece end for end and cut the opposite end to a point (**G**).

7. Cut only one piece for now. That piece should now be too long to fit in the grid (**H**). Move the stop block in slightly (toward the angle) and shorten your piece bit by bit until you have achieved a snug friction fit.

8. Cut the remaining pieces at this same setting and insert them into the grid, spanning from the center of the pattern toward its outer corners (**I**).

Hinges

These can be the most complex pieces; however, with a firm understanding and a bit of patience, you can achieve a nice, snug fit.

Marking

1. Place a ruler at a 45° angle on top of the grid that spans from one open corner of the pattern to the other, perpendicular to a diagonal piece. Measure the distance between the diagonal piece and the opposing corner (**A**). The center of this measurement is where the end of the hinge pieces will meet and intersect with the locking piece.

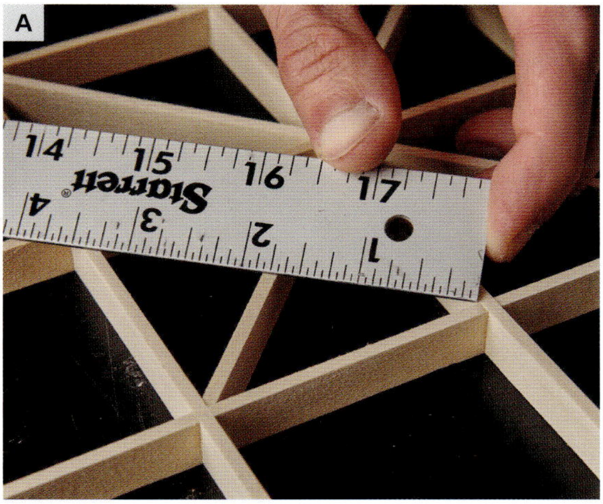

2. Place a strip from the corner of the triangle created by the diagonal piece and mark the opposite end just past the center measurement (**B**).

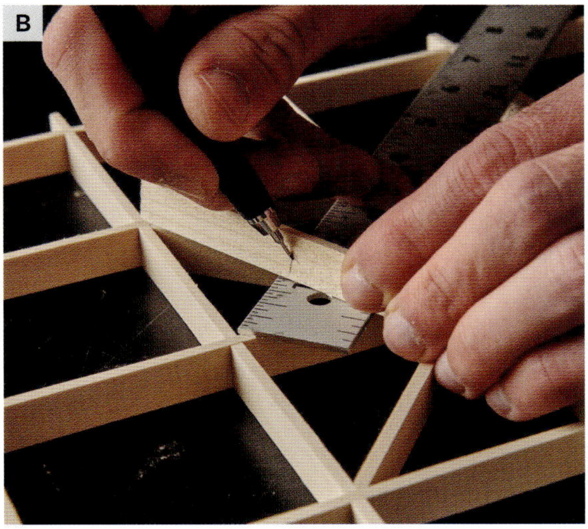

3. Cut the 16 pieces needed for the kaku asa-no-ha pattern at this length. It's a good idea to cut six to ten extras to account for any mistakes you make along the way.

Cutting

1. Start with the 22.5° jig, cutting a point on one end of each piece just like the diagonal pieces in Step 1 on page 57. This is the end that will fit in the corner of the grid and diagonal pieces (**C–D**).

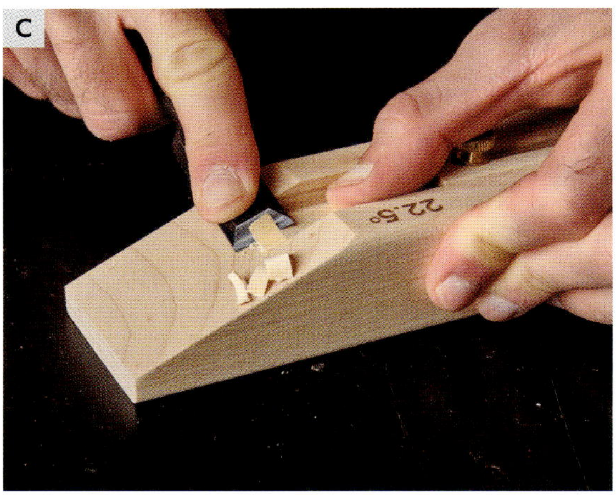

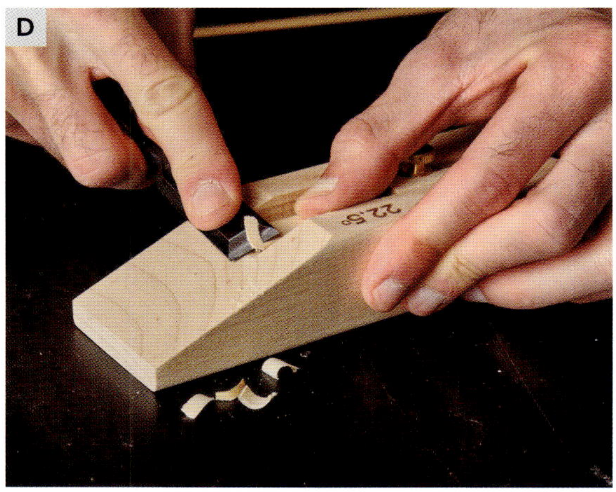

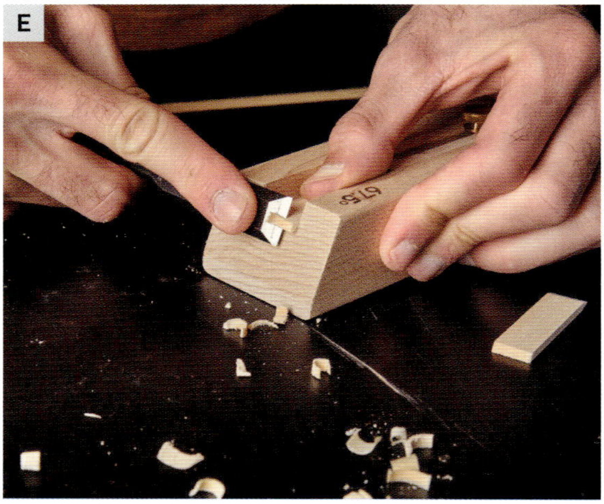

E

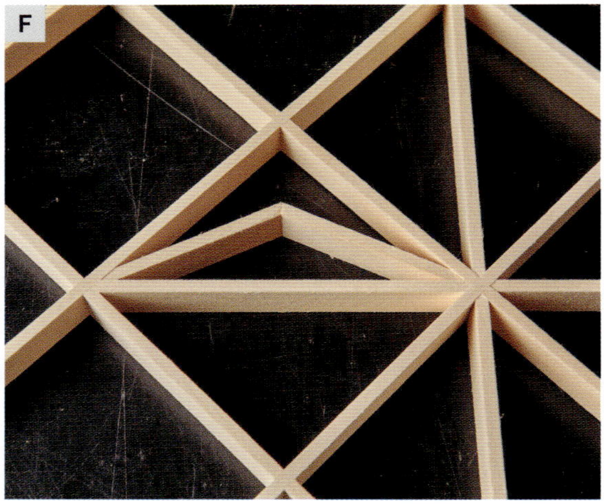
F

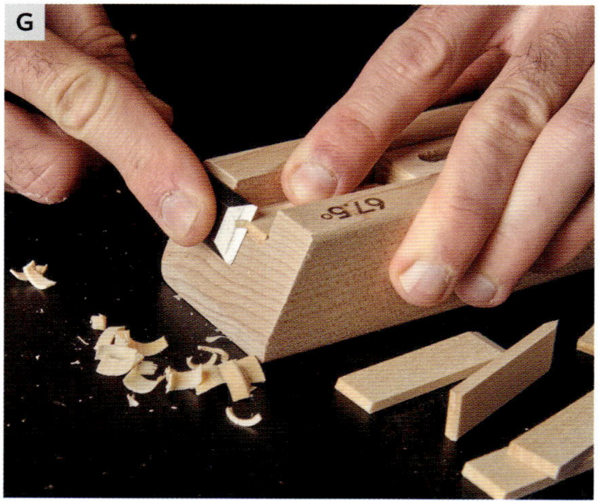

G

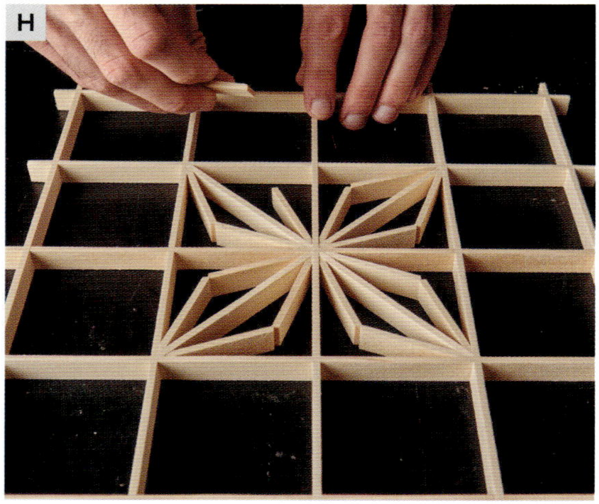
H

2. The opposite ends of these pieces need a 67.5° cut. Cut the ends just like before but don't flip it in the jig to create a centered point on the end. Cut only one face (**E**).

3. Cut two pieces and test them in the pattern. Ideally there should not be a gap between the 67.5° bevels and 22.5° corners (**F**). Adjust the stop block on the 67.5° jig to slightly change the piece's length to achieve no gaps. Once you accomplish this for one set of pieces, cut the rest at this same setting of the jig.

4. There is still one more cut needed on these pieces and for that you need to move the stop block on your 67.5° jig forward the tiniest amount. Here you have to remove two-thirds of the pointed end of the bevel you just cut to create an asymmetrical point. This might take some trial and error so start by taking off less material than needed and sneaking up on the fit (**G**).

5. The point of the bevel should be offset from the center of the strip by one-third of its thickness.

6. Two pieces fit into place with the one-third, the smaller face of the bevels, meeting each other (**H**).

Locking piece

1. There are eight pieces required for this step as well as the 45º jig. Measure from the hinge pieces to the corner of the grid and cut them slightly oversized. These pieces are cut in the same way as the first diagonal pieces on page 57.

2. Cut a 45º point on one end of all pieces. Then sneak up on a snug fit on the opposite end, cut at the same angle (**A**).

3. If there are inconsistencies across your panel or if some pieces were cut too tight and forced the grid out of square, they would compound and affect this step, causing some or all of these short locking pieces to be slightly different lengths. If you run into this, begin with the smallest piece first and adjust your jig for each piece (**B**).

A

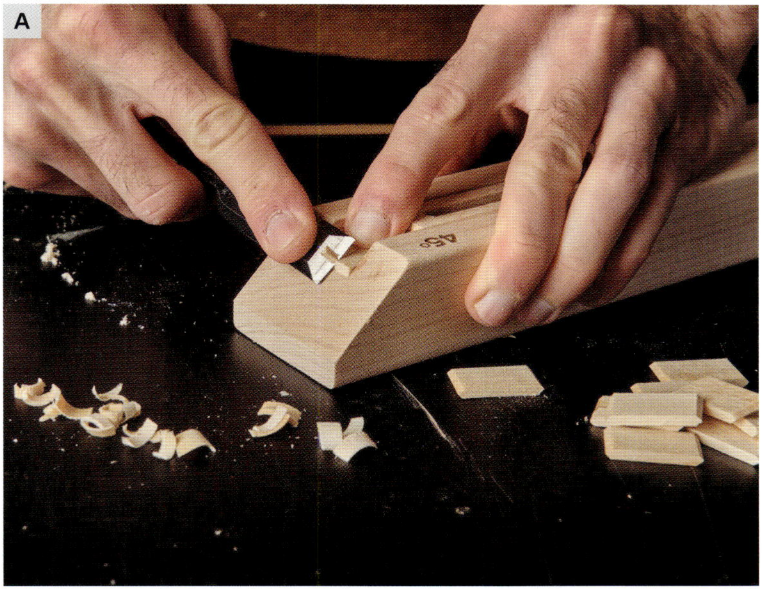

B

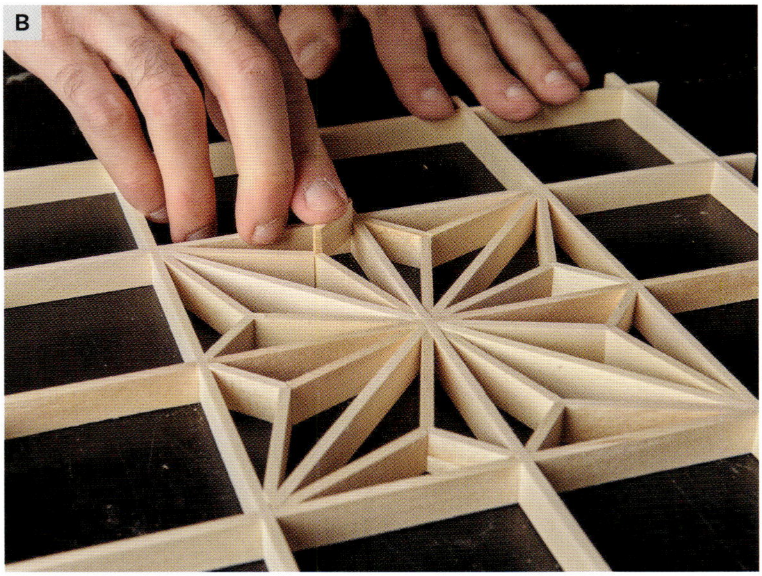

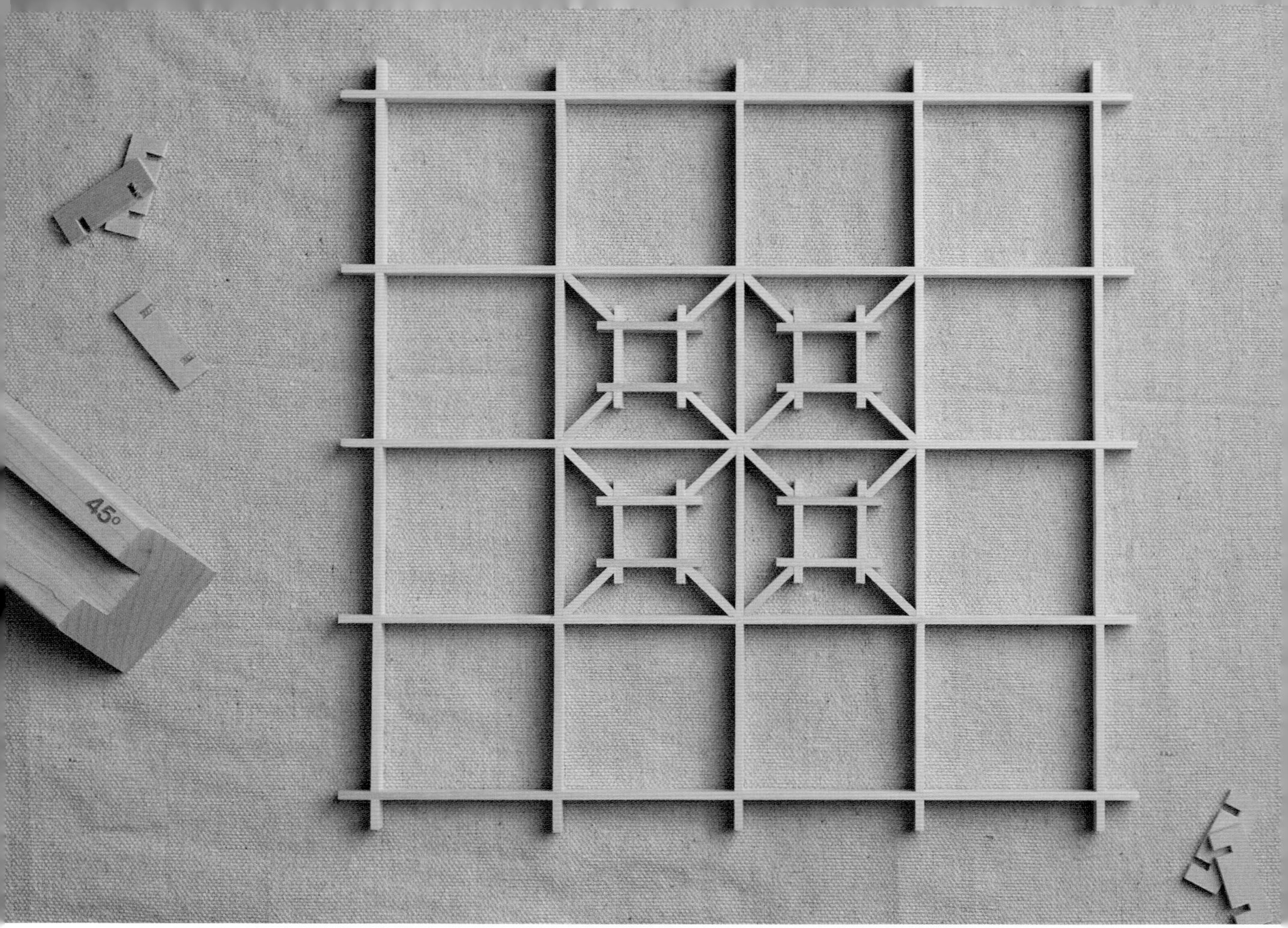

Yotsuba Izutsu-Tsugi (四つ葉井筒継ぎ)

Yotsuba in Japanese means "four leaf," izutsu is a term for a well curb, and tsugi simply means joint. Rather than a direct translation of "four-leaf well-curb joint" (which doesn't make sense in English), let's look at it as a pattern that pulls elements from nature and elements found in a garden. There are several types of izutsu-tsugi patterns with the above being one of the simplest. The internal square pieces are identical to each other, and the locking pieces are all the same as well.

The relationship between the internal square and the square of the grid it occupies is a crucial ratio in order to achieve a balanced and visually pleasing design. This balance is a personal preference, so feel free to play around with the dimensions of these pieces. A good ratio to start with is 3:1. For example, if the main grid has a pitch of 2¼ in (57 mm) then use a pitch of ¾ in (19.1 mm) for the internal squares.

STRUCTURE OF YOTSUBA IZUTSU-TSUGI

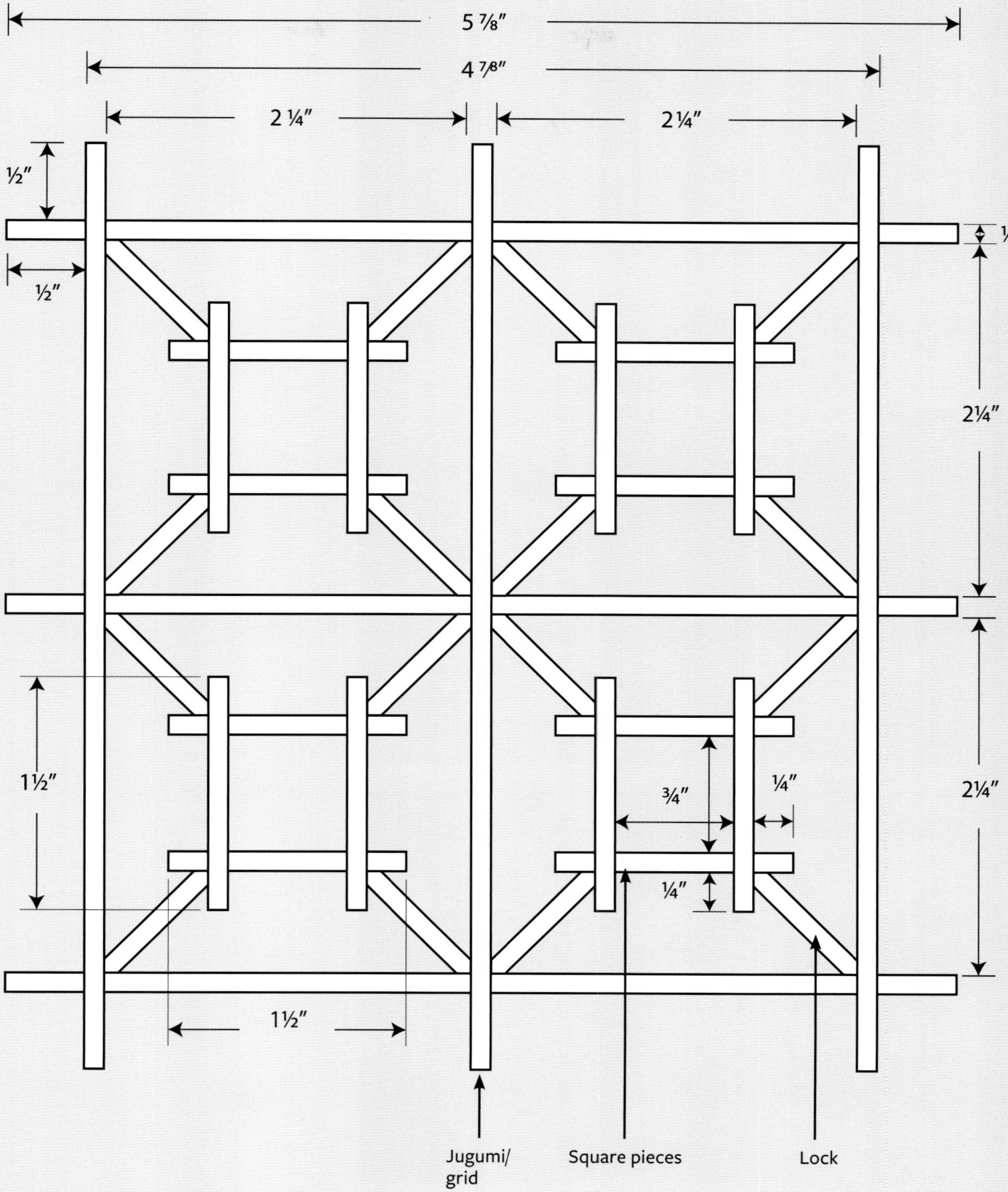

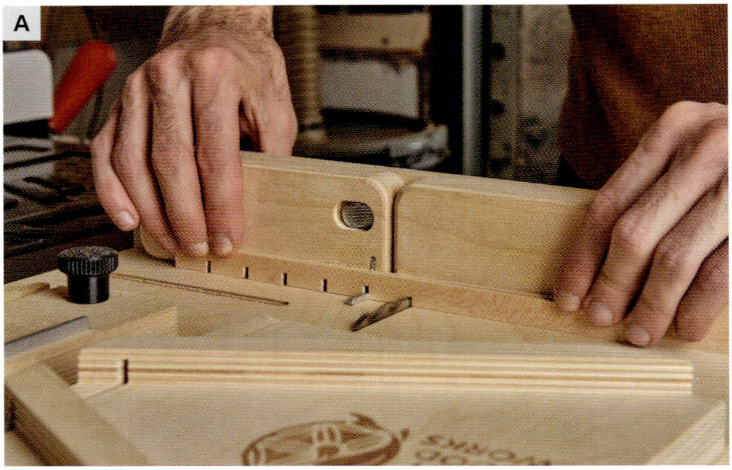
A

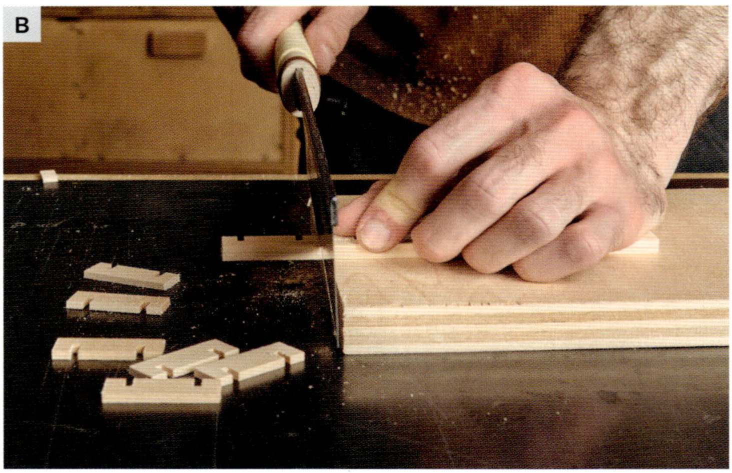
B

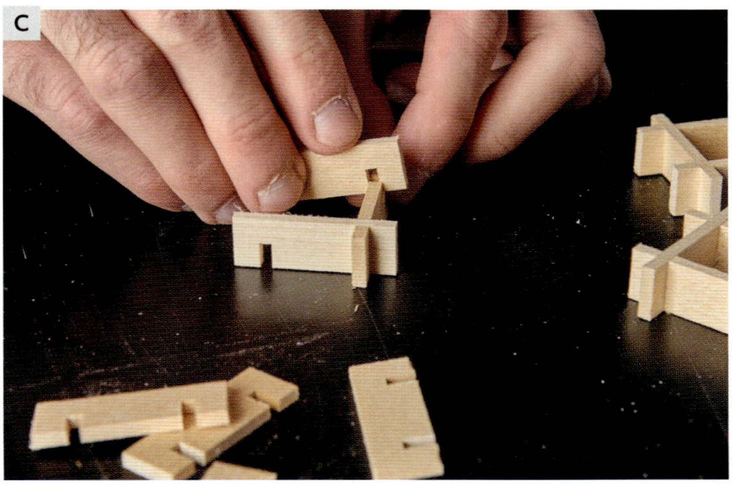
C

Internal square

1. Begin by cutting the joints for the internal square pieces just like the joints for the grid using the table saw sled or by hand. Since these parts are small, you may find it's easier and safer when using the table saw sled method to cut the joints along a longer strip first (**A**). After the joints are complete, trim the pieces down into shorter sections to their final size for easier handling and accurate fitting.

2. With the joints complete, use a dozuki saw to carefully cut each of the 16 pieces free (**B**).

3. Assemble the small squares in the same way that you built the main grid (**C**).

Locking piece

1. There are 16 pieces required for this step as well as the 45° jig. These pieces are cut in the same way as the diagonal piece for the kaku asa-no-ha pattern (see page 57) (**A**).

2. The four pieces for each portion of this pattern are identical, so when trimming to size, work with four at a time until they fit snugly in place. Then trim the remaining pieces to the same size to complete the rest of the pattern (**B**).

A

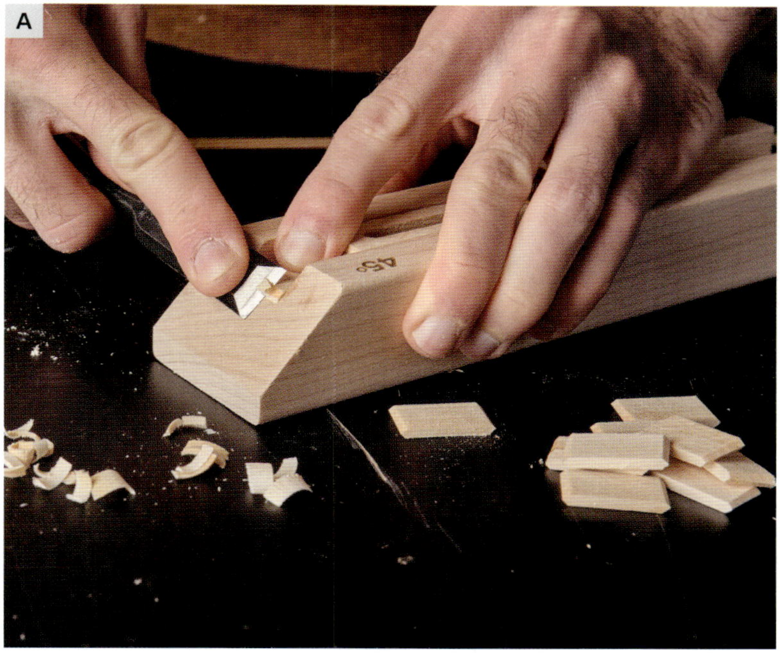

B

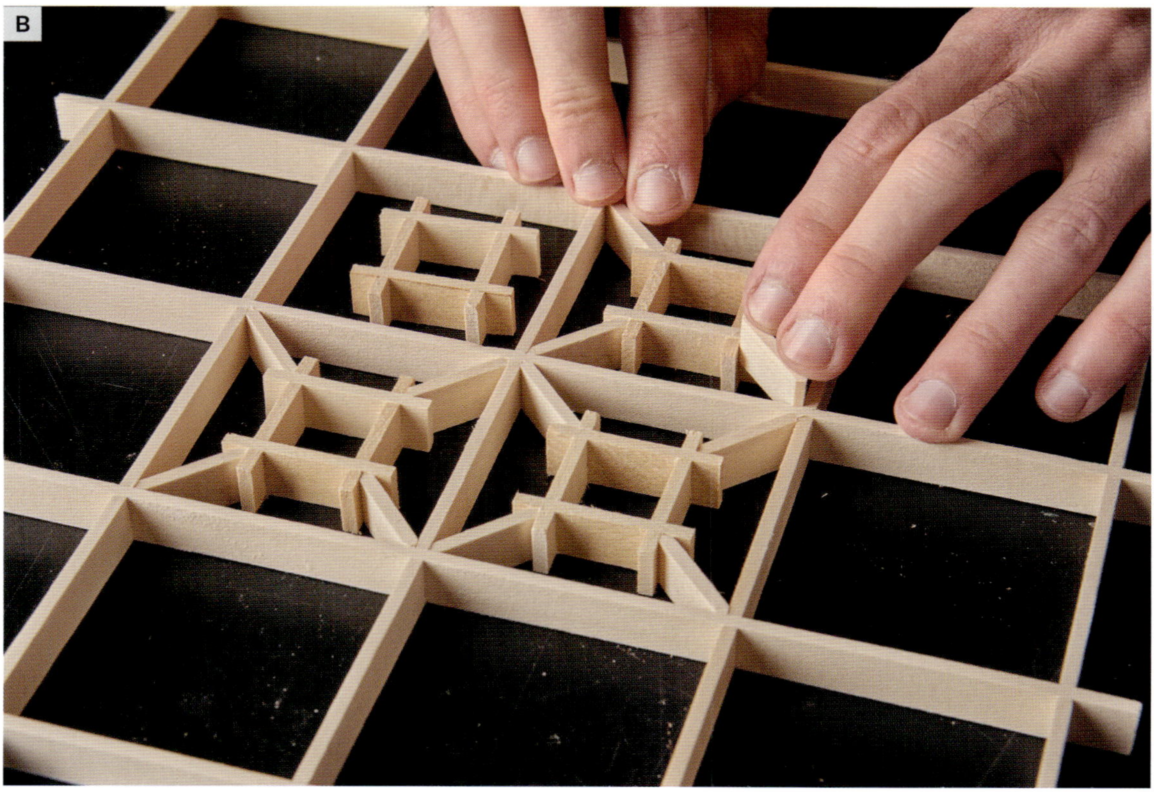

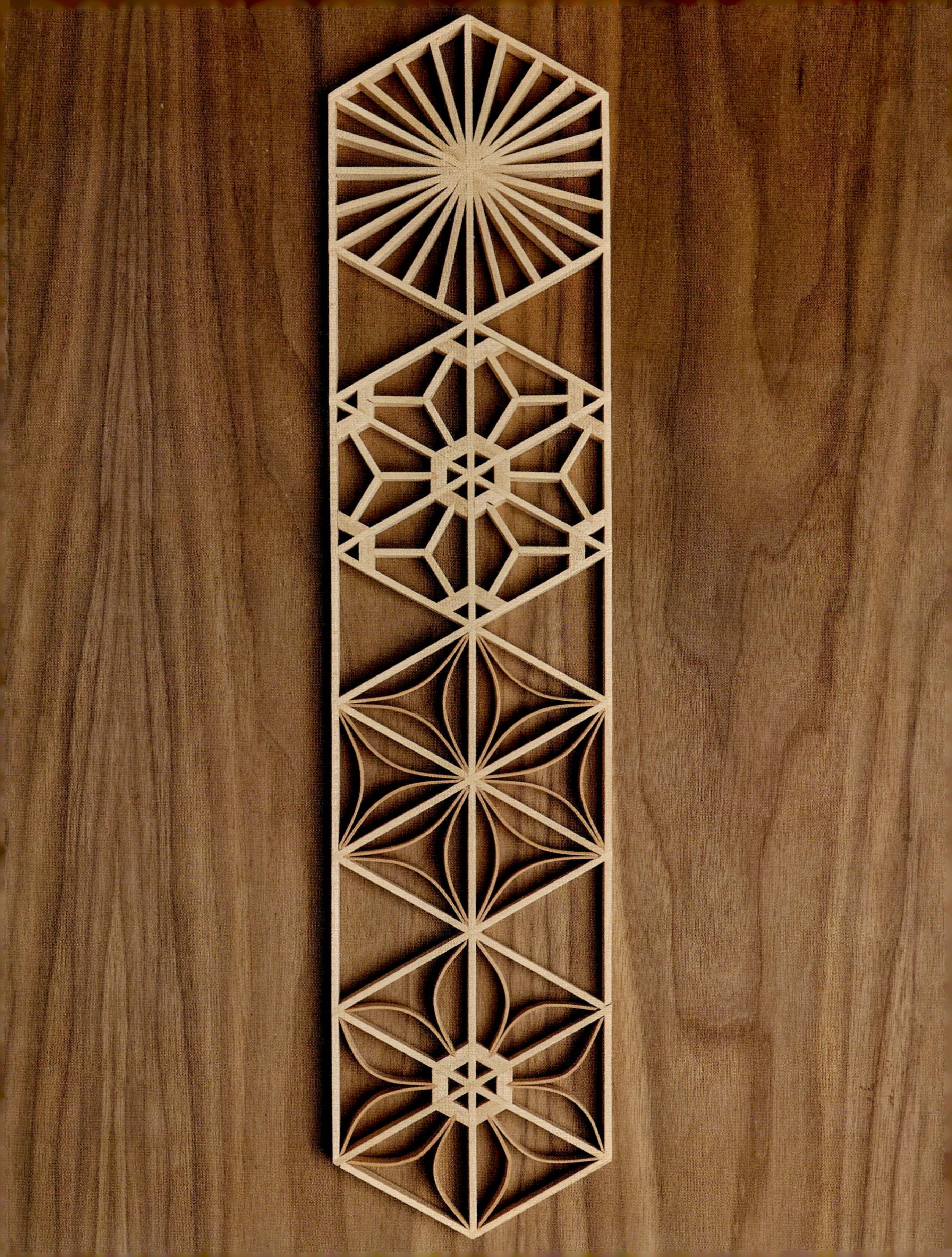

Chapter 5

Making Hexagonal Kumiko Patterns

With the hexagonal grid already established in Chapter 3, we now turn our focus to the decorative patterns that bring it to life. With their six-sided geometry, they create visually captivating designs that feel both organic and structured, reminiscent of natural forms like honeycombs or snowflakes. Hexagonal kumiko patterns are among the most iconic in traditional Japanese woodworking, combining geometric precision with visual elegance. In this chapter, you'll learn how to make two of the most well-known designs that use this grid: asa-no-ha (麻の葉) and shippo (七宝). These patterns showcase the full potential of the hexagonal layout, and their forms can be adapted to create countless other variations such as sakura (cherry blossom — 梅), ume (plum blossom — 梅), and more. Though they may appear complex, each one is built from simple components and repeatable steps, making them approachable with practice and rewarding in both process and result.

◀ From top to bottom: rindo (竜胆), sakura, shippo, and ume.

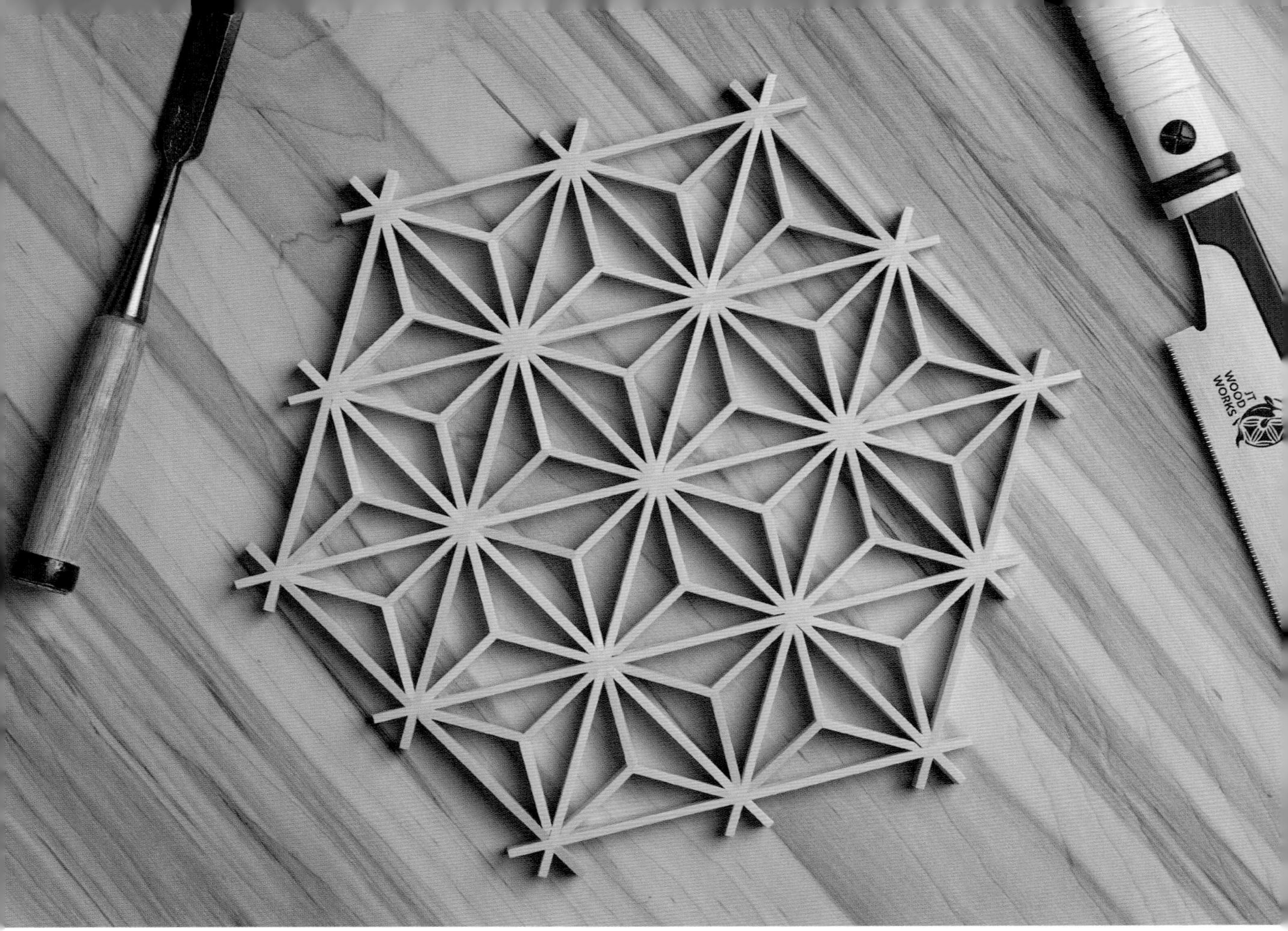

Asa-no-ha (麻の葉)

The first hexagonal pattern covered in this chapter is the hexagonal asa-no-ha pattern. For a brief explanation of the Japanese cultural significance of this pattern, see Chapter 4 (page 53).

Begin by constructing a mitsukude grid, as shown on page 39. Compared to the kaku asa-no-ha pattern, the grid in this hexagonal version is far more complex but the infill pieces are simpler. There are several methods to cut these infill pieces to achieve this pattern. These steps focus on the simplest version, where all three pieces are identical.

HEXAGONAL ASA-NO-HA PATTERN OVERVIEW

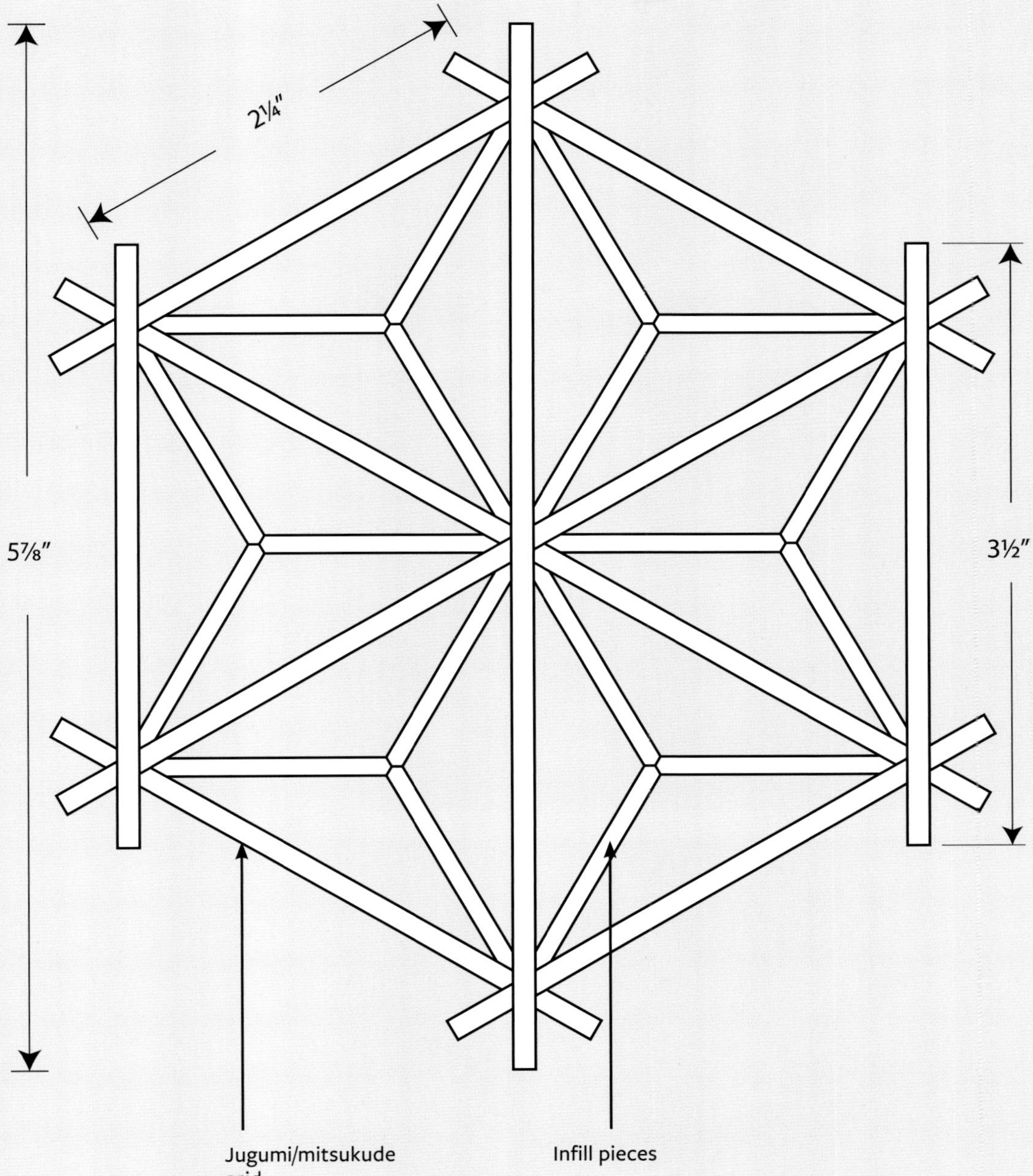

Cutting the infill pieces

The only jigs required for this pattern are 30° and 60°.

1. Roughly measure the length needed for these 18 pieces (from the inside corner to the center of the triangle of the grid) (**A**). Cut several extra pieces to account for possible mistakes.

2. One end of the pieces is trimmed to form a point using the 30° jig (**B**). This end will sit into the 60° angle of the triangle formed by the grid pieces.

3. The opposite ends of these pieces need to be cut using a 60° jig, forming a 120° angle on the end. Insert your pieces in the 60° jig so the previous point cut is against its stop block. Adjust the stop block and cut your pieces as before (**C**). Try to remove as little material as possible to create a centered point on the end.

A

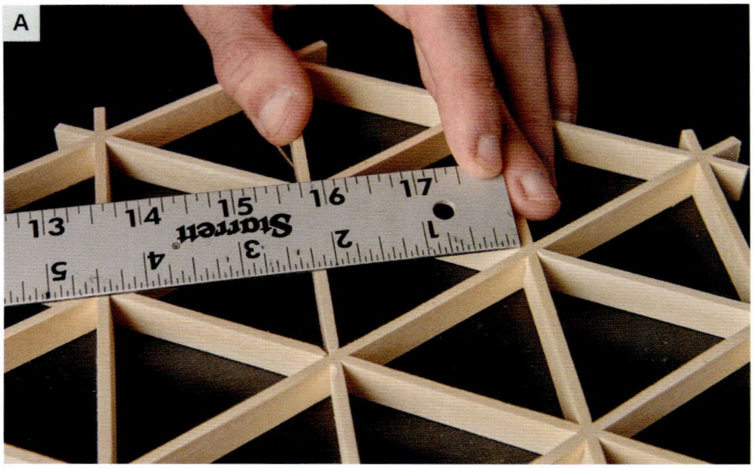

B

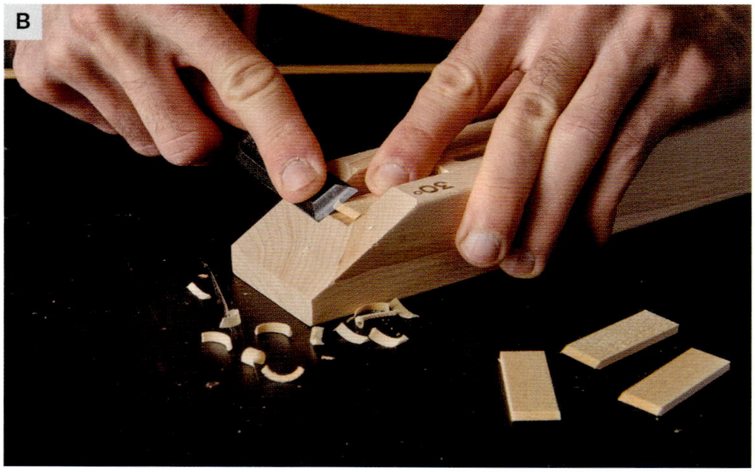

C

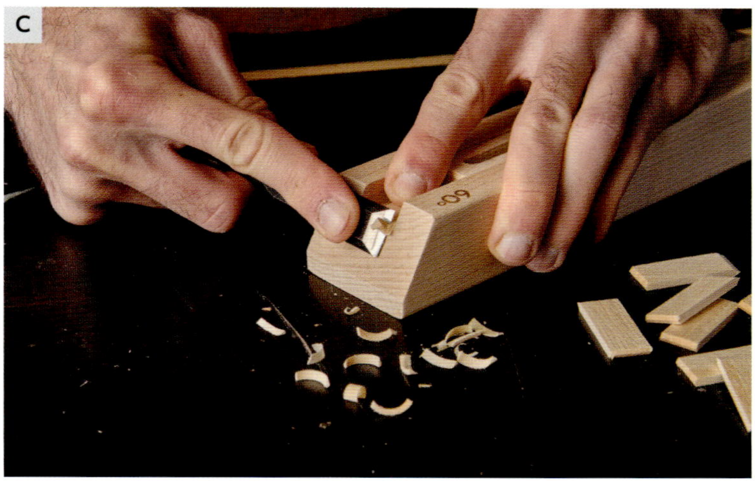

4. Cut the points on the end of three pieces and test their fit (**D**). Work with these three pieces and make small adjustments to the stop block in order to get a snug fit, keeping in mind that any adjustment made is multiplied by three. A small adjustment can make a big difference.

5. Aim for a fit that is snug but not too tight. Tight-fitting pieces can distort the grid, throwing it out of square and making it difficult to fit other pieces. Once the right fit is found, cut the rest of the pieces and fit them in the grid to complete the pattern (**E**).

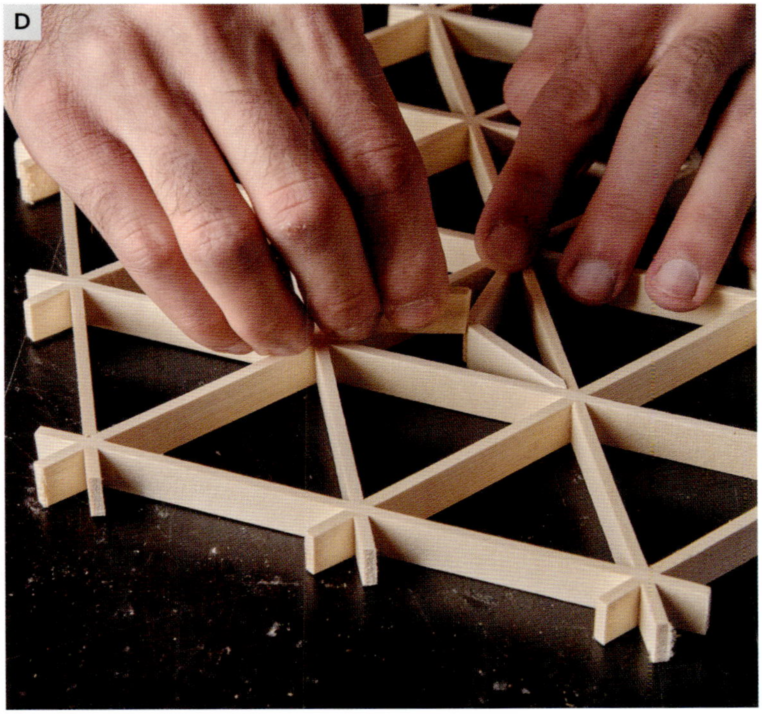

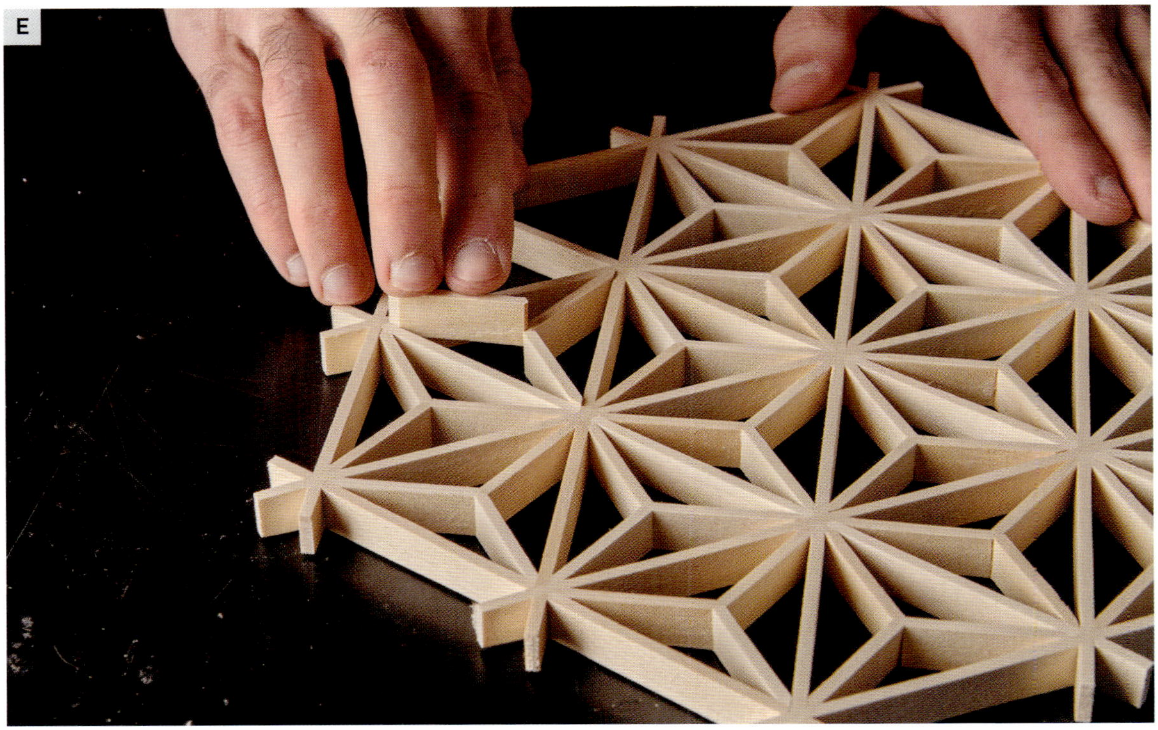

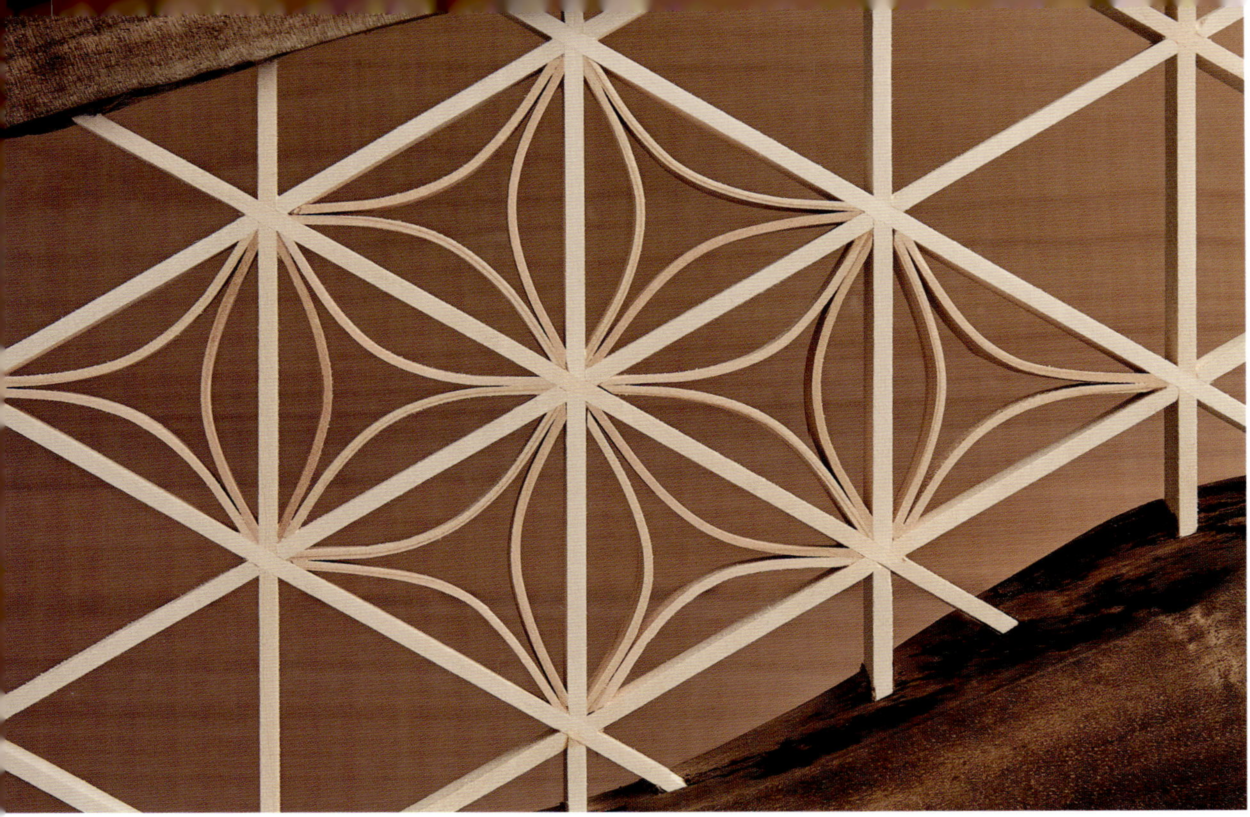

Shippo (七宝)

The shippo pattern is one of the few kumiko patterns that incorporates curves. The curved design goes against but at the same time complements the angular shape of the mitsukude. Shippo, or the "seven treasures" in Buddhist scriptures, refers to gold, silver, lapis lazuli, crystal, agate, red coral, and carnelian. This concept is symbolized by an unbroken pattern of interlocking circles.

This pattern requires thinner pieces so that they can bend more easily. Begin with pieces that are roughly 0.05 in, slightly under $\frac{1}{16}$ in (1.6 mm) in thickness in order to bend without breaking. They can be thicker or thinner if you're working with a larger or smaller pitched grid or prefer a more robust or delicate look. Since these strips are very thin, the best way to prepare them is by using a hand plane. Ensure your plane is sharp and properly tuned to achieve top-quality results. Cedar is a great option to use as it bends fairly easily. Make sure to have straight grain without any knots.

In order to get consistent bends, you'll need a bending form. This is simple to make and can be made from wood you may already have to hand. Start with a short section of 2 x 4 (about 6 in to 8 in /152 mm to 203 mm long), or similar, and curve one of the edges. This can be done in many different ways. I find it easiest to get as close as possible to the final curve with a hand plane and then sand the rest of the way, making sure it's consistent and flows smoothly from one of the side faces to the other. Next, screw on a piece of wood with a small rabbet (groove). The inside corner of the rabbet should line up to the start of the curve on one

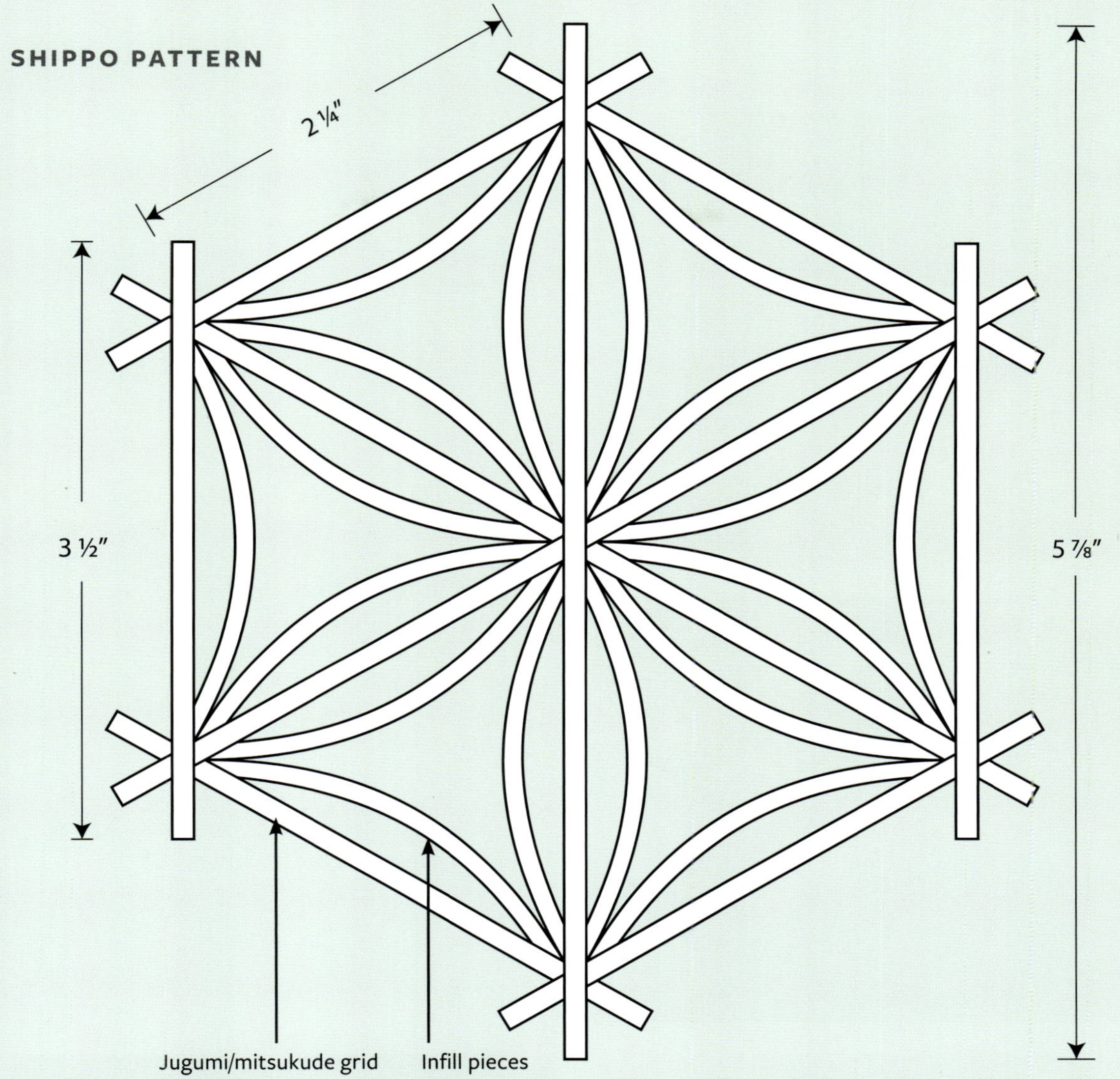

of the faces. Attach some pieces of wood to the edge opposite the curve to act as feet or place this in a vise to help keep it upright while in use.

The length of the infill pieces is based on personal preference and it's a good idea to cut several pieces at slightly different lengths to test them before committing to cutting all the pieces. Adding or removing even $\frac{1}{32}$ in (0.8 mm) in length can drastically change the radius of the curve.

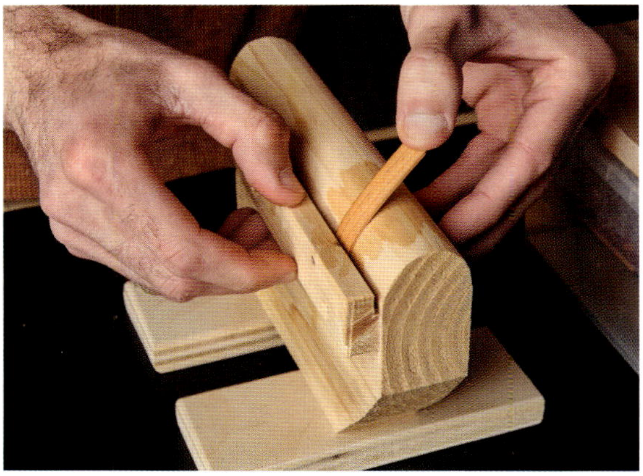

▶ The bending form in use.

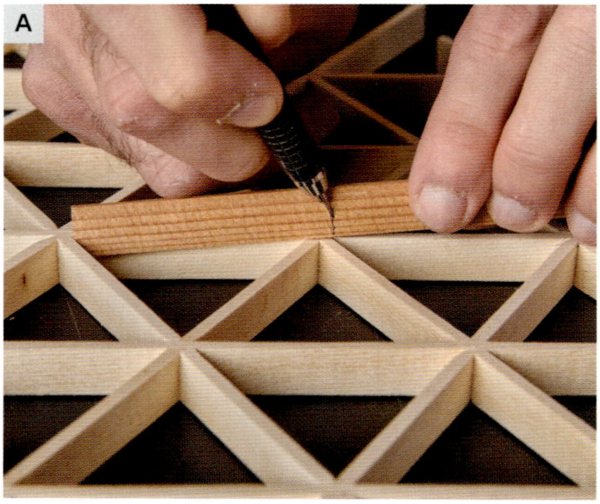

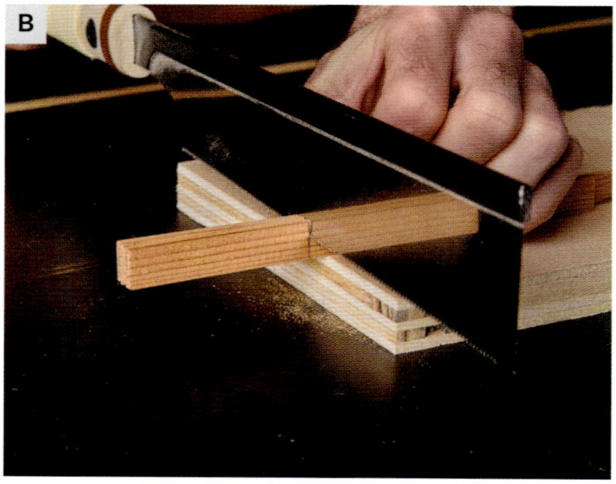

Cutting the infill pieces

The only jig required for this pattern is 30° as well as the bending form.

1. The length of the pieces determines the radius of the curve. A longer piece will produce a more drastic curve, and a shorter piece will produce a more subtle curve. A good starting point is to place the strip into the corner of the grid and mark it at its neighboring triangle's corner (**A**).

2. Cut the pieces needed for your project (**B**). Cutting four or five at a time helps speed up the process. Eighteen pieces are needed for one complete pattern, but cut several extra pieces as some may break during bending.

3. Start by cutting a 30° bevel on one end of each piece. Unlike the pieces prepared for other patterns, don't flip the piece to make a centered point in the strip. This bevel is cut on one face only (**C**).

4. While cutting the opposite end, make sure to cut the bevels on the same face (**D**).

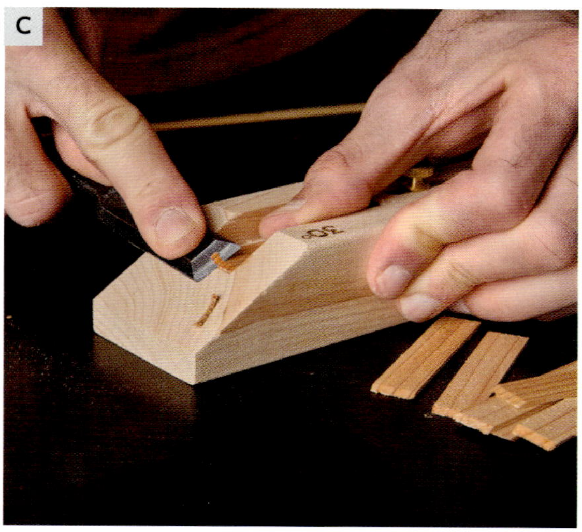

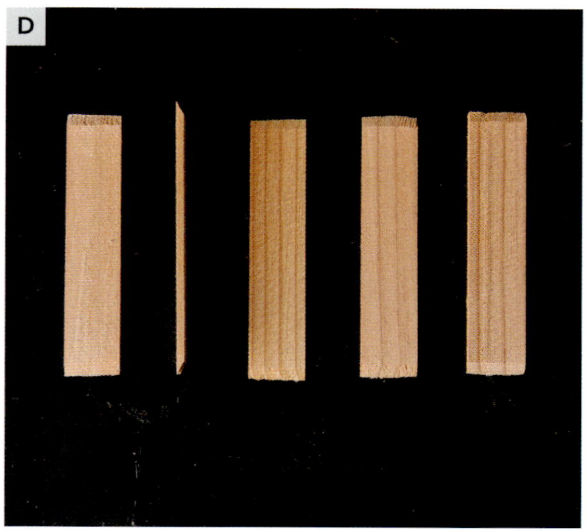

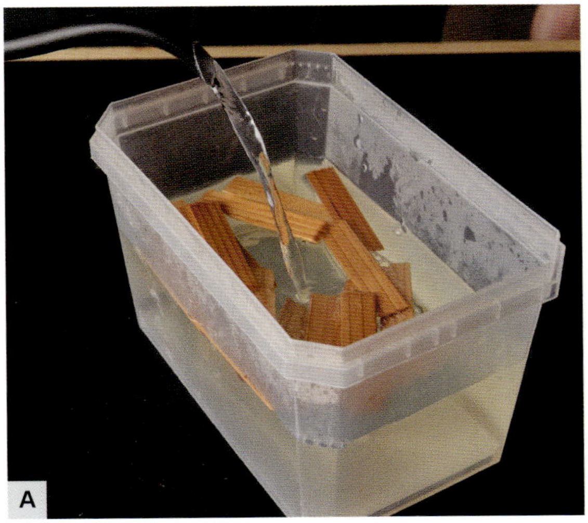
A

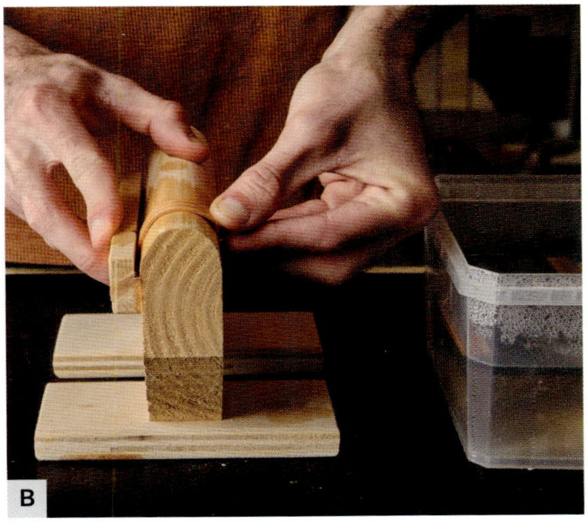
B

Bending the pieces

1. Soak the pieces in **boiling water** for about ten minutes (**A**). This loosens the fibers of the wood to help them bend easier. Temperature matters! Hot tap water won't work.

2. Place one end of a piece into the rabbet of the bending form, facing the bevel toward the curve of the jig. Slowly bend the piece along the radius and hold for a few seconds (**B**). Flip the piece end to end and bend again in the same direction to ensure the bend is as uniform as possible. Repeat for the rest of the soaked pieces.

3. Once you have three bent pieces, place them in the grid while they're still wet. Be careful not to damage the fragile ends.

Assemble the pattern

1. After the wood fully dries (this can take several hours), remove the infill pieces and glue them in place. Use a small brush or toothpick to apply wood glue into the corners of the grid and carefully slide the pieces back in place (**C**).

2. Once the glue is set, sand and trim the pattern as needed.

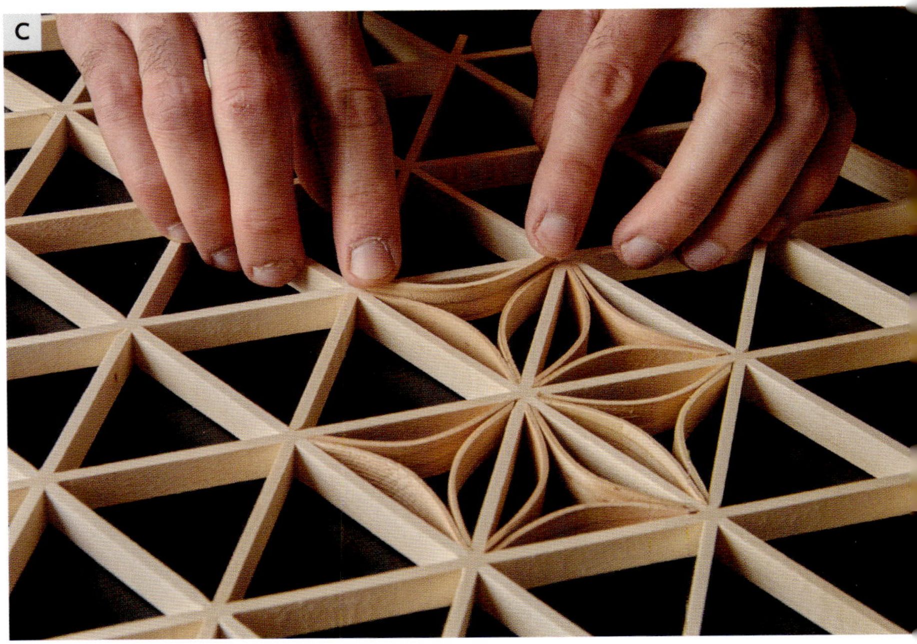
C

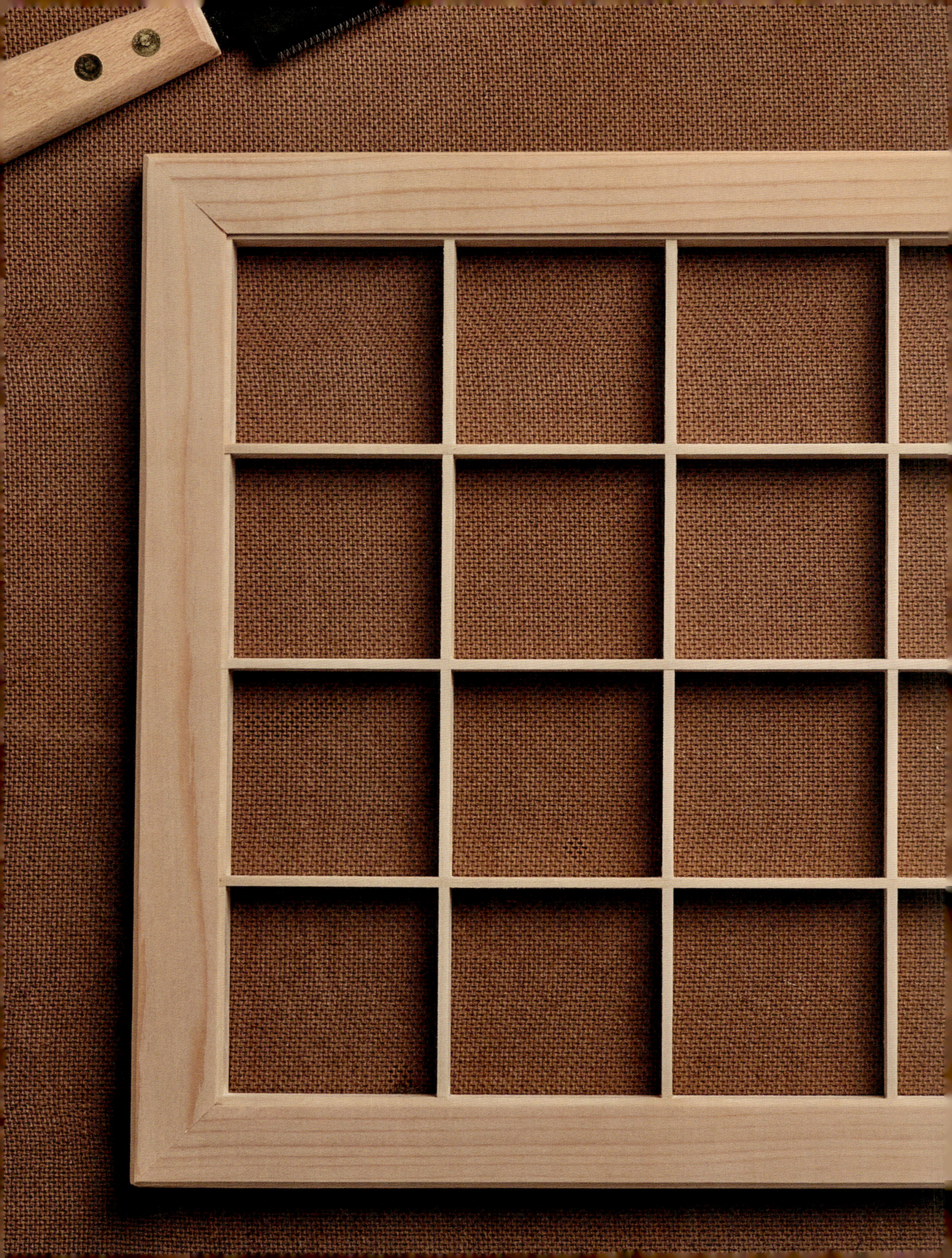

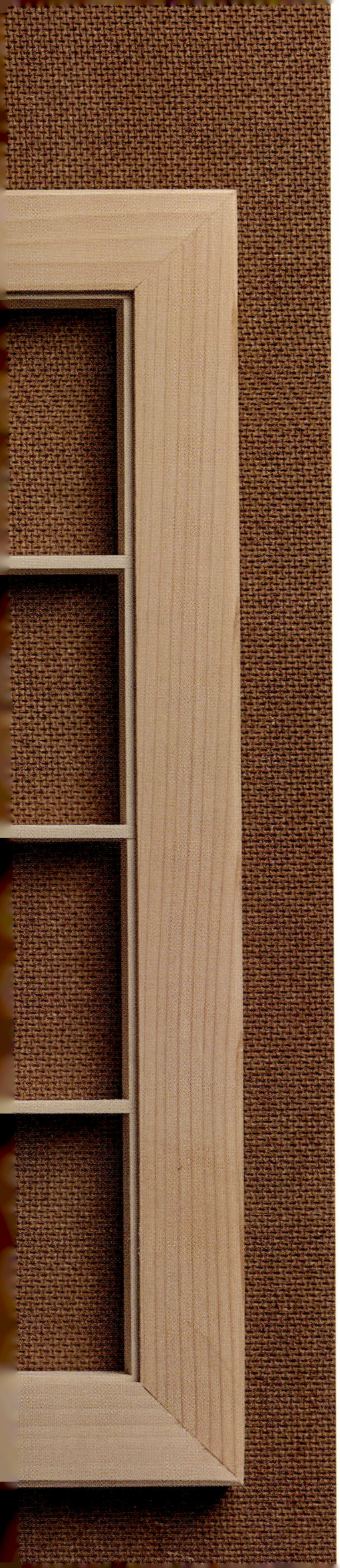

Chapter 6

Framing a Kumiko Panel

Framing a kumiko panel is a straightforward but essential step that both elevates and protects your work. It also serves a functional purpose in many of the projects featured throughout this book, from cabinet doors to wall hangings and beyond. A thoughtfully built frame not only supports the kumiko structurally but also enhances its visual impact by providing contrast and definition. Whether you're showcasing a single pattern as decorative art or incorporating it into a larger piece, the frame plays a key role in presenting your craftsmanship. In this chapter, you'll learn how to build a custom wood frame that complements the intricate geometry of kumiko, while keeping the focus right where it belongs, on the pattern itself.

There are many frame styles that work well with kumiko, each offering its own aesthetic and functional qualities. This chapter introduces the core principles of building a square, rabbeted, mitered frame. Additional frame styles are explored in later chapters.

◀ A square kumiko grid in a simple mitered frame.

Trim and measure the panel

1. Before cutting any frame parts, trim the extra "tabs" or overhanging ends of the kumiko panel (**A**). These should only be removed after the grid has been glued. If the panel isn't secured with glue, pieces may loosen or fall out during trimming.

2. Carefully measure your finished kumiko panel (**B**). It's best to aim for a snug fit — not too tight, not too loose. Keep in mind that even slight discrepancies can affect the final look, so take accurate measurements and double-check your work.

Cut the frame parts

1. Before cutting the joinery, add a rabbet or groove on the inside edge of each piece to house the kumiko panel (**C**). A $\frac{1}{16}$ in to $\frac{1}{8}$ in (1.6 mm to 3.2 mm) wide rabbet is usually enough to create a secure fit without adding too much bulk or covering the kumiko with the frame. The depth of the rabbet should match the depth of the kumiko.

2. Miter the corners at 45° for a clean, seamless look (**D**). Cut one piece at the measurements taken for each side, top, and bottom.

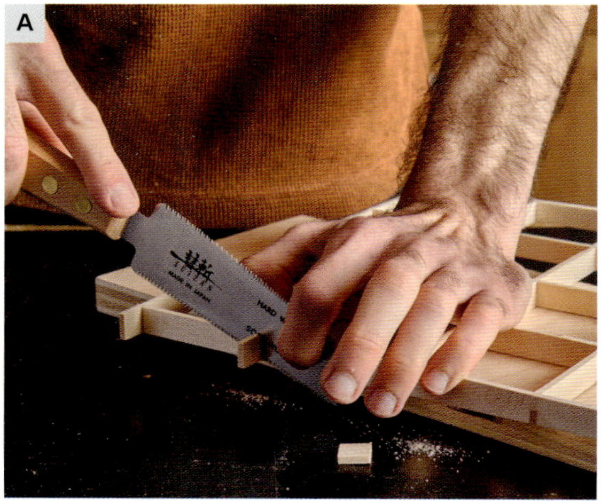
A

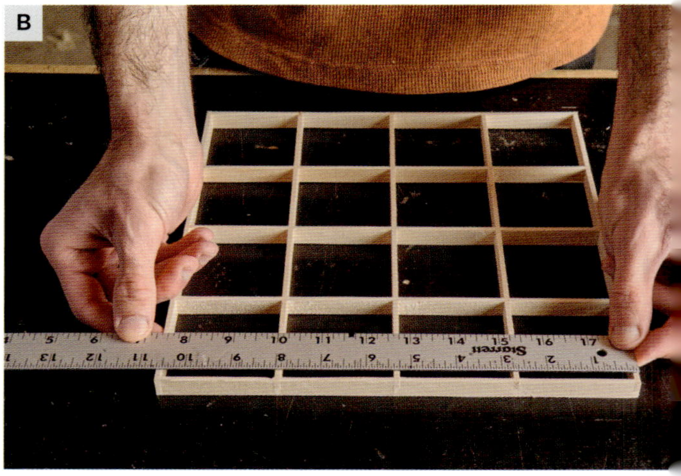
B

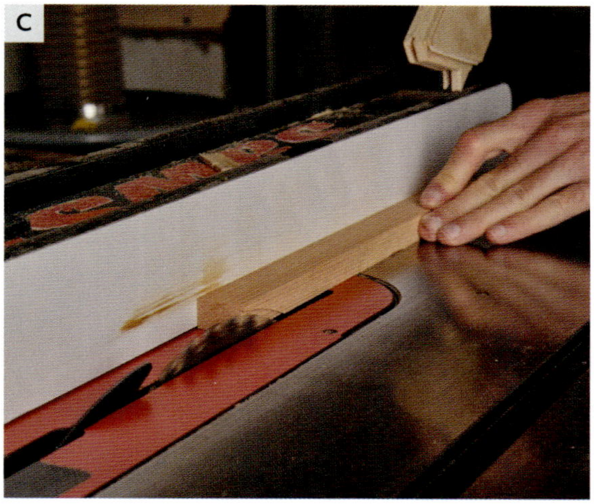
C

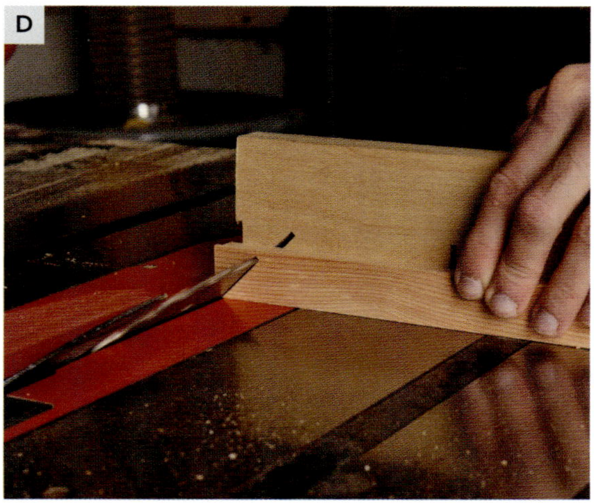
D

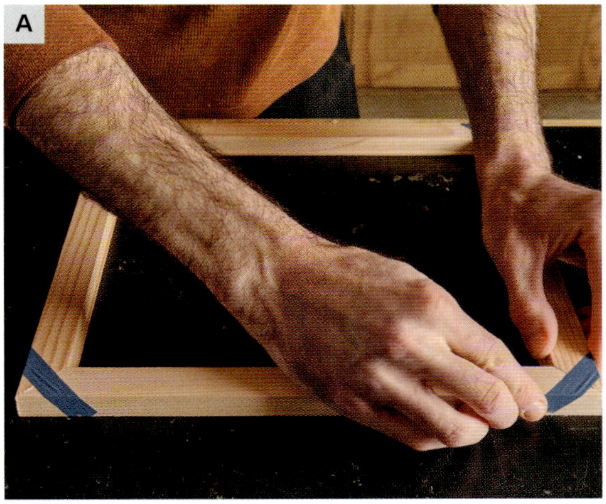
A

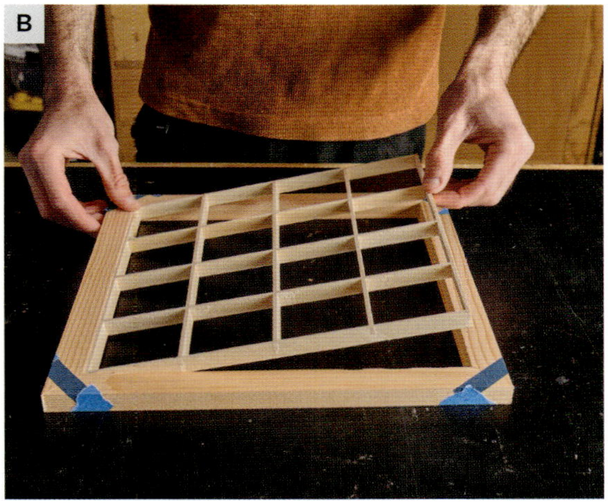
B

Glue and clamp the frame

1. Before gluing, dry fit the frame parts around your kumiko panel. This is your chance to check for gaps, adjust the miters, and make sure the rabbet depth allows the panel to sit flush or slightly recessed, depending on your preference. If needed, fine tune the joints with a shooting board, chisel, or sanding block to get tight, clean corners.

2. Apply glue to the joints and clamp the frame together. Stretching masking tape over the corners works well here (**A**).

3. Insert the kumiko panel to make sure it fits properly (**B**). It may be challenging to fit if the frame is too tight.

4. Check it's square by measuring diagonally from corner to corner (**C**). Both diagonal measurements should be equal. If the measurements are off slightly, add a clamp diagonally to the corners with the longer measurement and slowly tighten it until both diagonal measurements are equal. Let the glue dry fully.

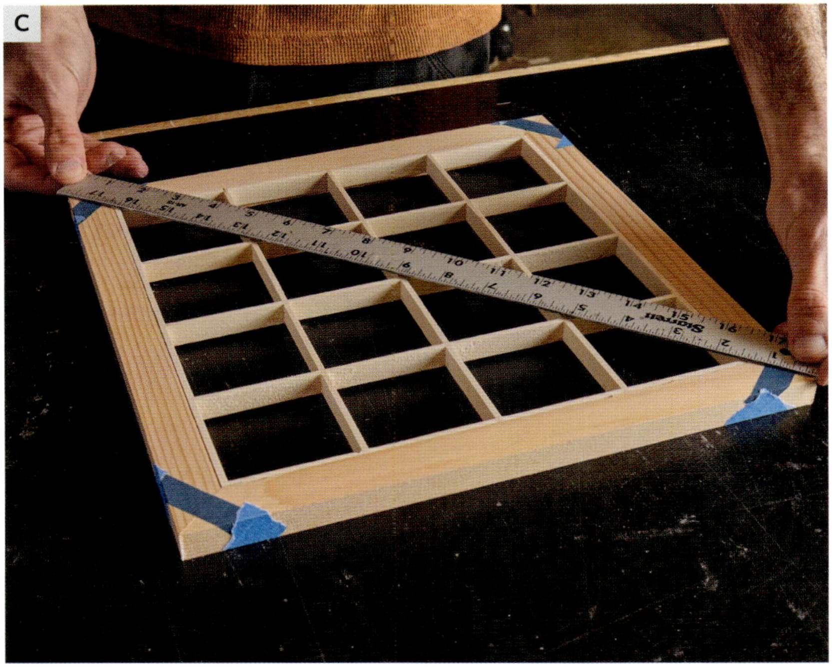
C

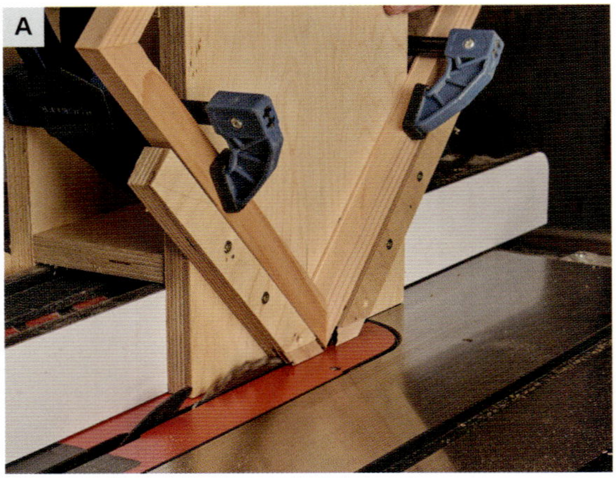

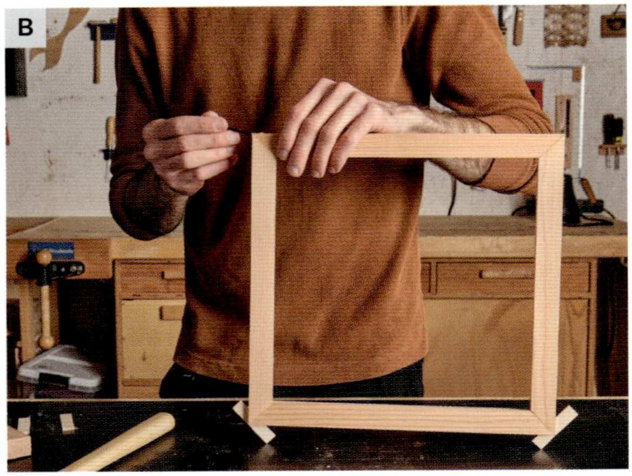

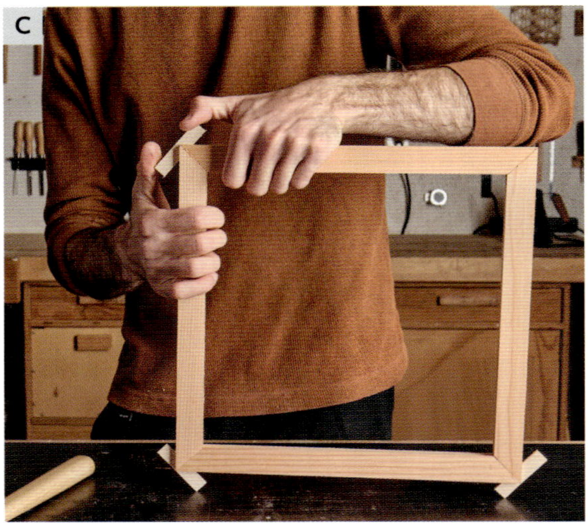

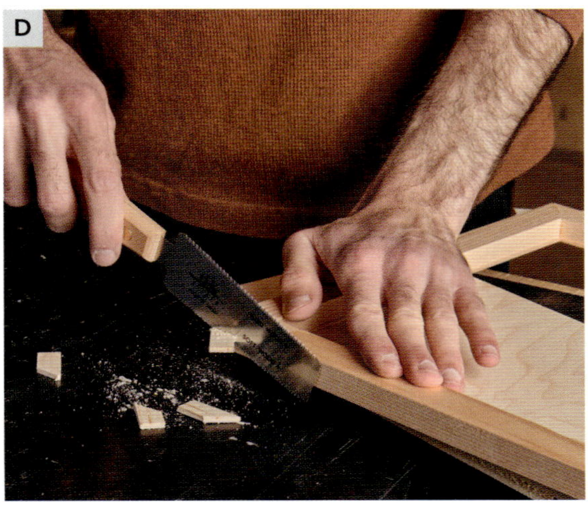

Reinforce and finishing touches

1. After the glue has cured, reinforce the joints using splines (see Glossary on page 172). These strengthen the corners and add a nice visual detail. Splines can be cut in a variety of ways; in this case, a DIY spline jig is used (**A**). The jig straddles the table saw fence and securely holds the frame in the correct orientation for accurate cuts.

2. Apply glue into the cut using a small brush or toothpick (**B**). Cover both walls and the base of the cut.

3. The spline's thickness should match the kerf of the table saw blade. Insert a spline into each corner, ensuring they are fully seated to avoid gaps (**C**).

4. After it has dried, flush trim the splines and sand the entire frame, paying extra attention to the corners and inside edges where glue may have squeezed out (**D**).

5. Ease the edges of the frame with a chamfer or roundover for a softer, more refined feel. Clean off any dust and apply your preferred finish — oil, wax, shellac, or a film finish, depending on how and where the framed kumiko will be displayed.

▶ Traditional shoji screens show how thoughtful framing enhances both structure and beauty.
Photo by John S Lander/LightRocket via Getty Images.

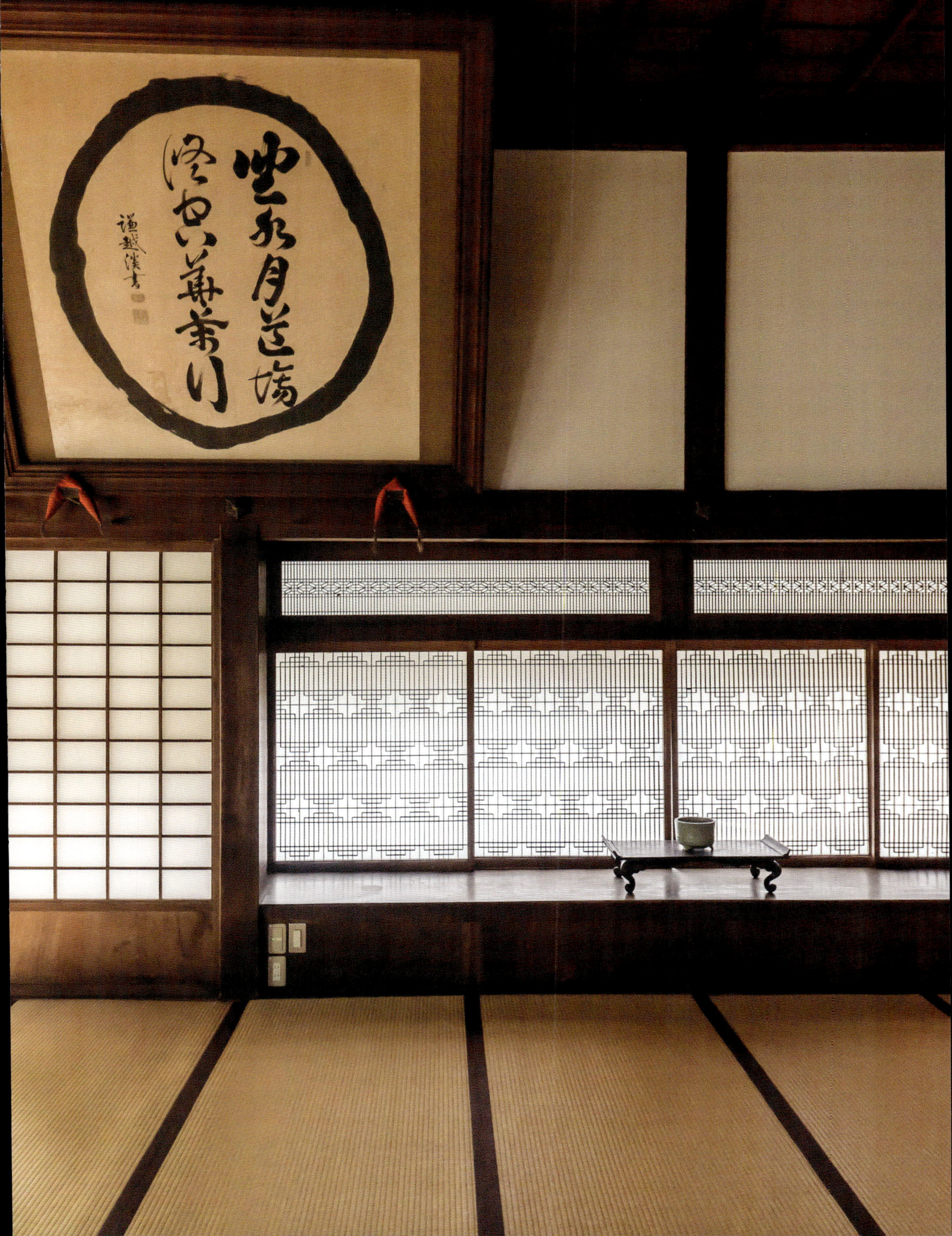

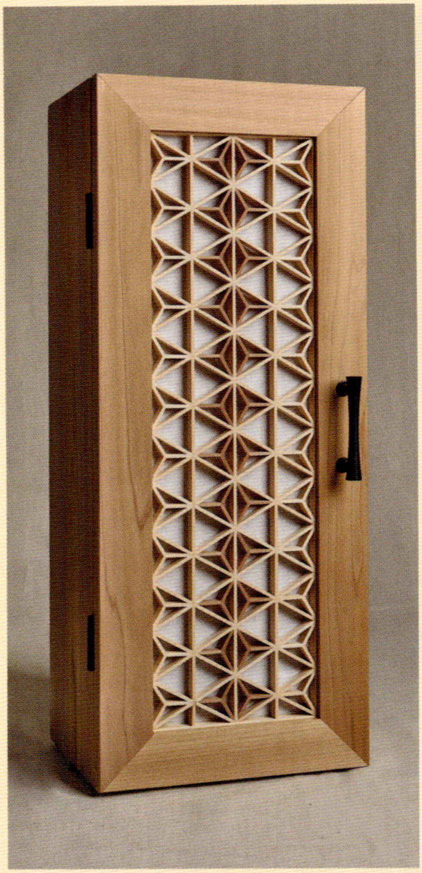
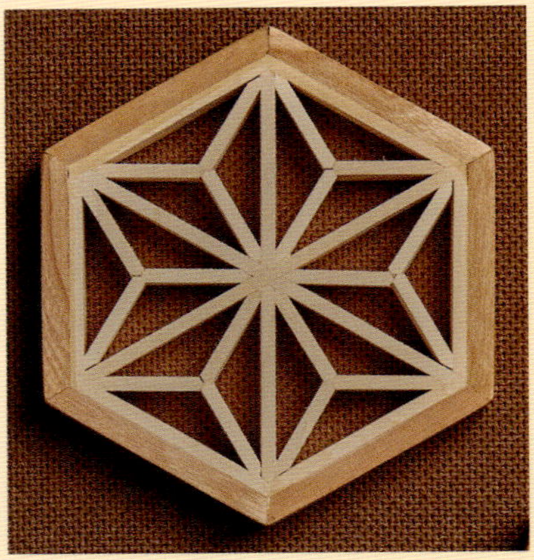
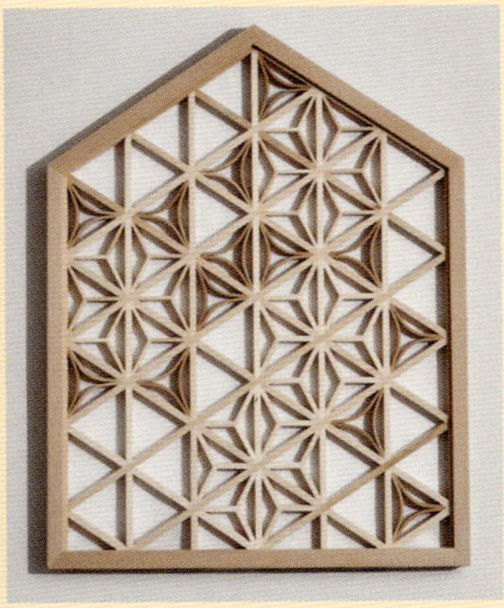
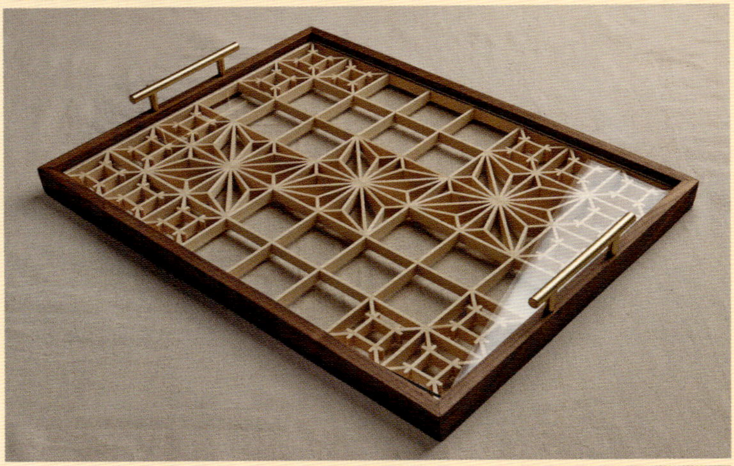
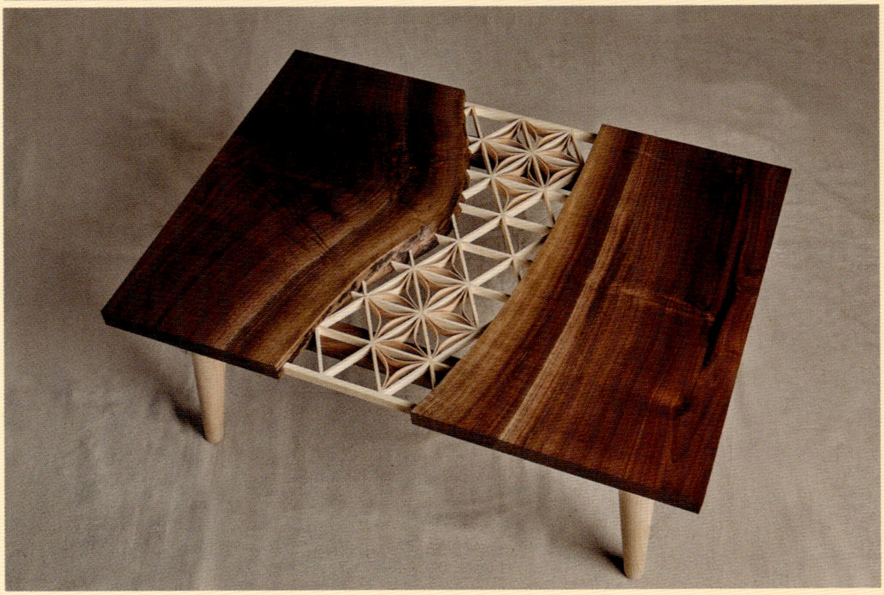
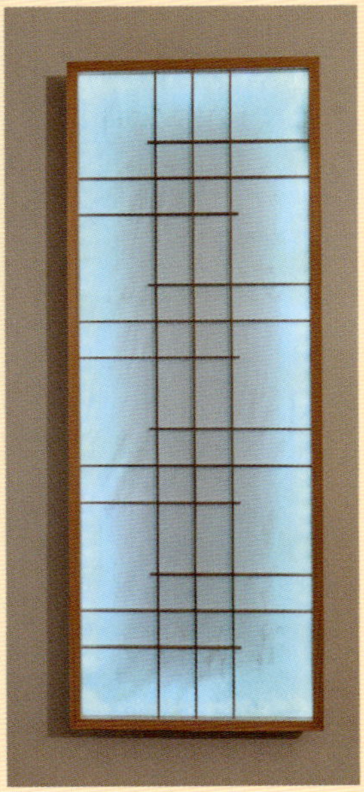

Chapter 7

The Projects

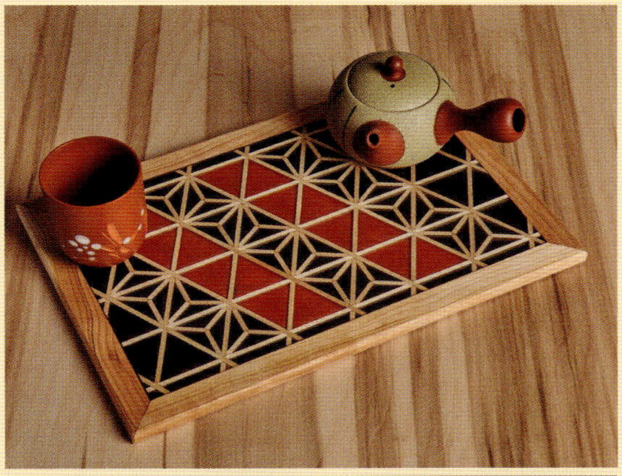

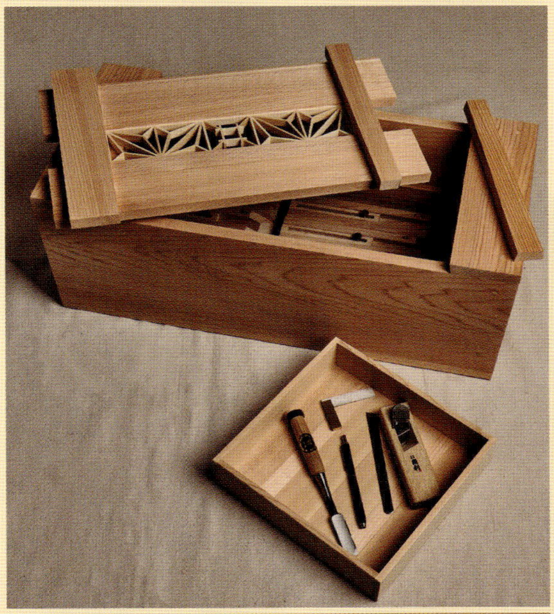

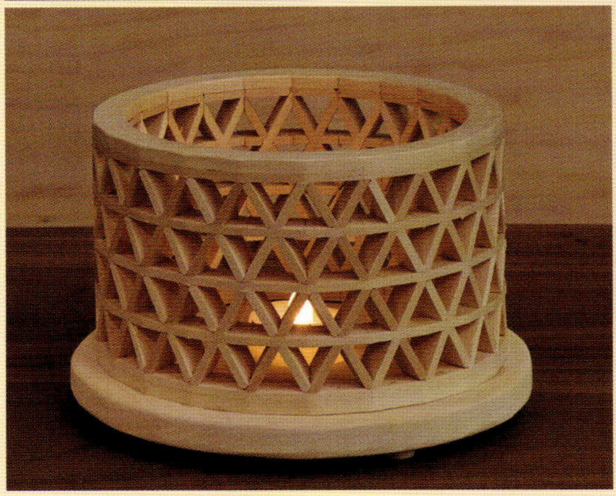

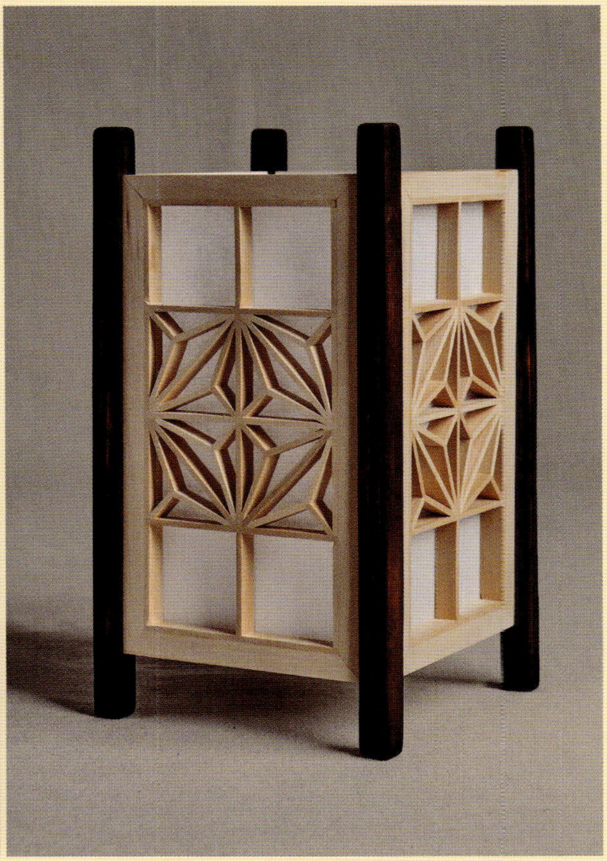

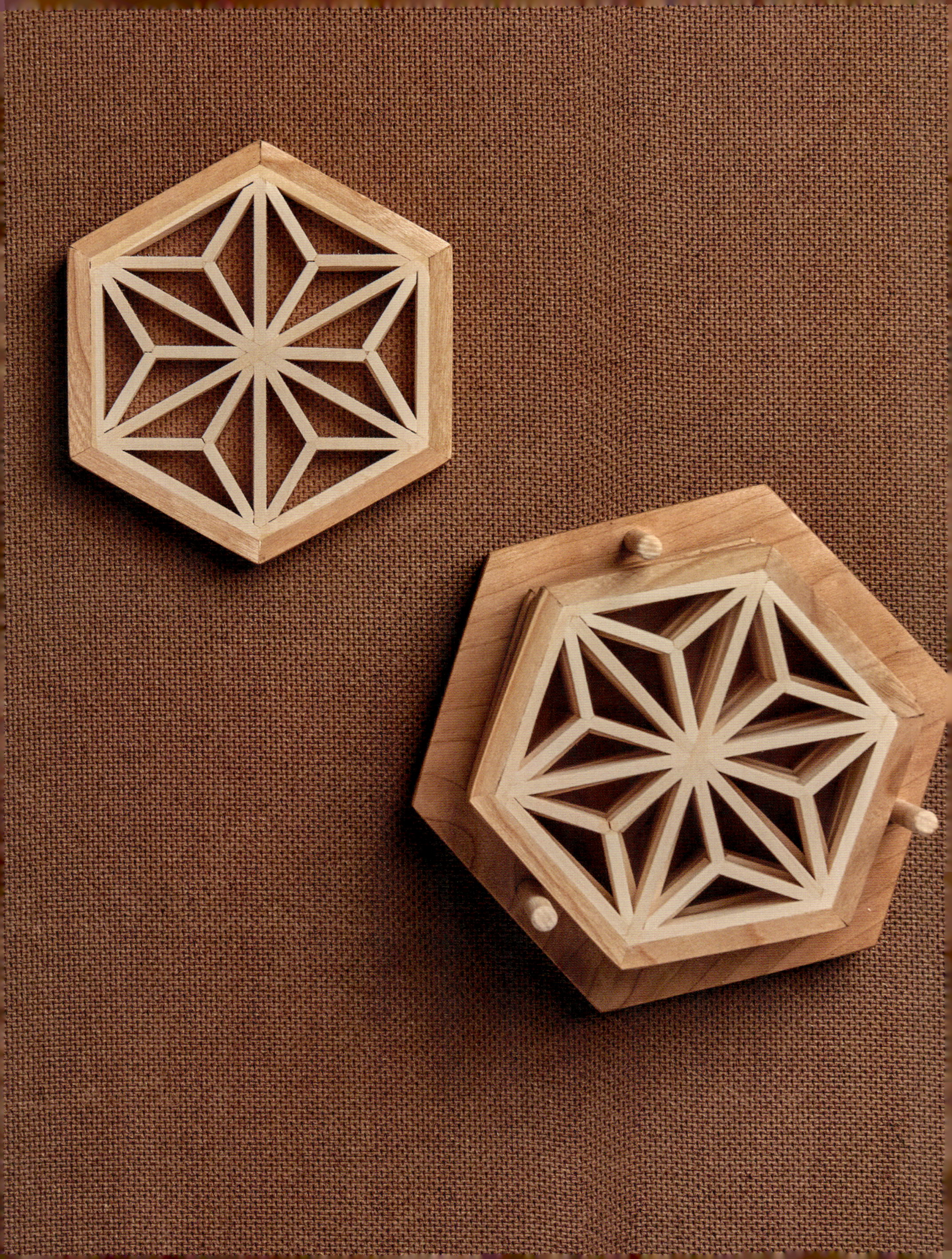

Project 1

Kumiko Coasters

This project takes kumiko off the workbench and into everyday use. In this chapter, you'll craft a set of four coasters featuring the asa-no-ha pattern, each bordered by a hardwood frame, and build a matching holder designed to store and display them neatly.

It's a compact project that invites creativity in combining fine detail with functional design.

The coasters themselves highlight the asa-no-ha pattern while the hardwood border frames the work and protects the edges in daily use. The holder is a minimalist structure with three dowels to cradle the coasters securely, while keeping the pattern visible when not in use.

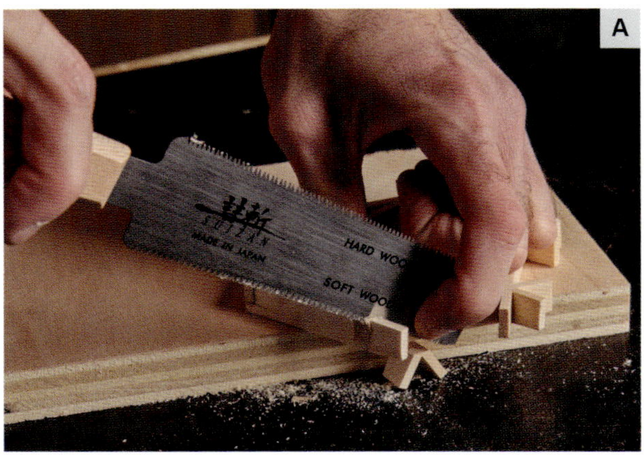

Begin by making four single hexagon mitsukude, the grids introduced on page 39, with a grid spacing of $1\frac{5}{8}$ in (41 mm). Fill each one with the asa-no-ha pattern covered on pages 68 to 71. Be sure to glue all the grid and infill pieces together.

Trim the tabs

After constructing the grids, use a flush trim saw to cut off the small sections that extend past the hexagon (**A**).

ASA-NO-HA COASTERS WITH FRAMED BORDERS

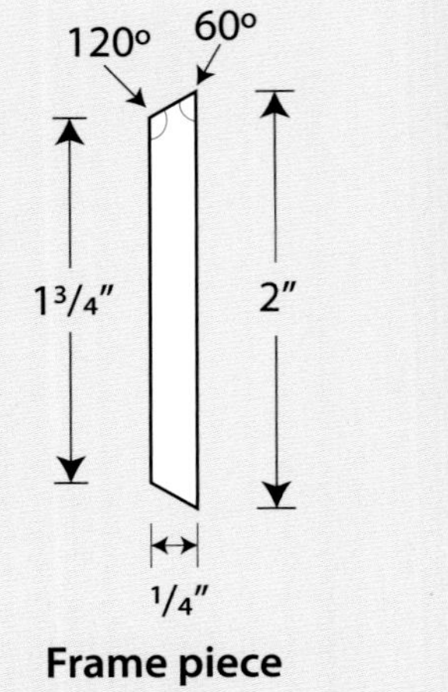

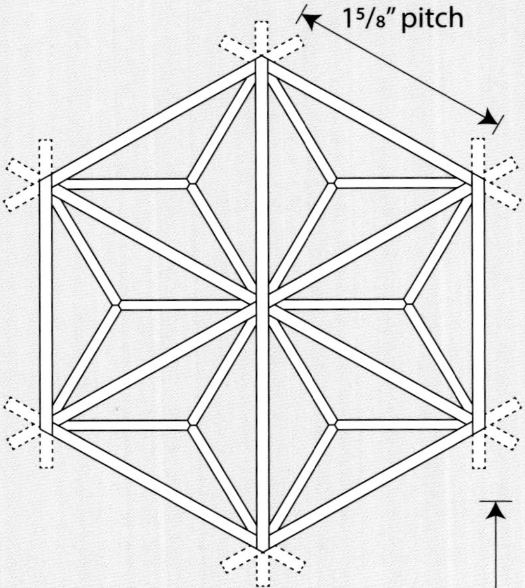

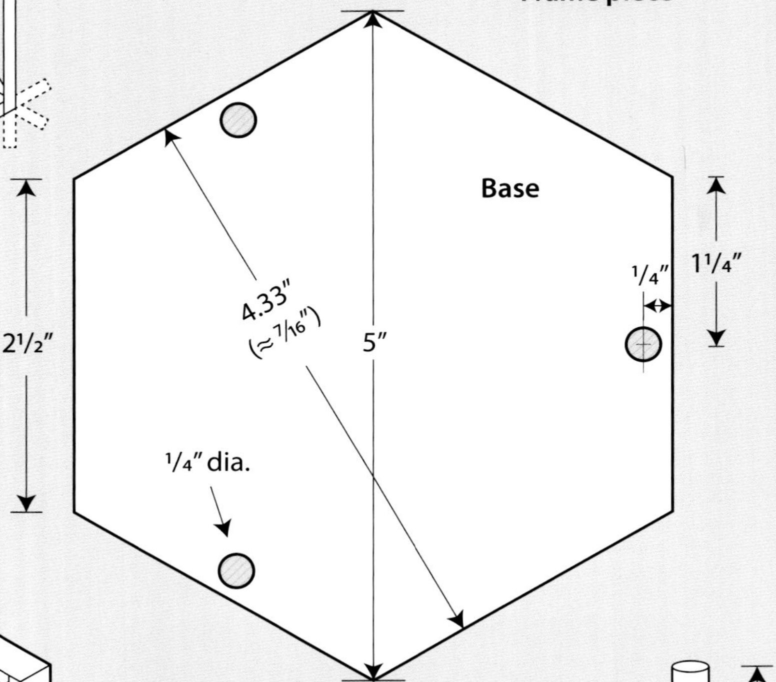

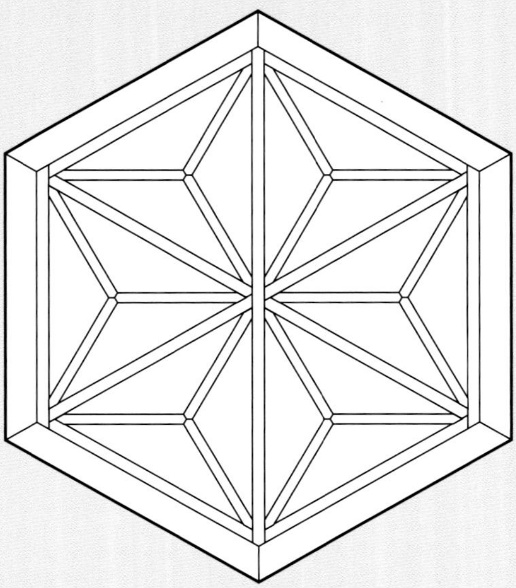

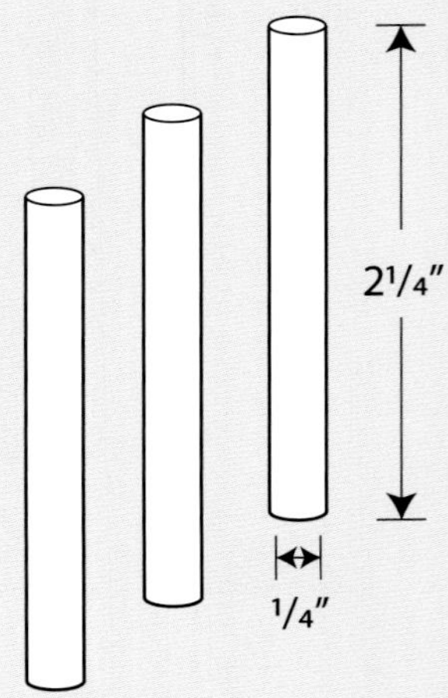

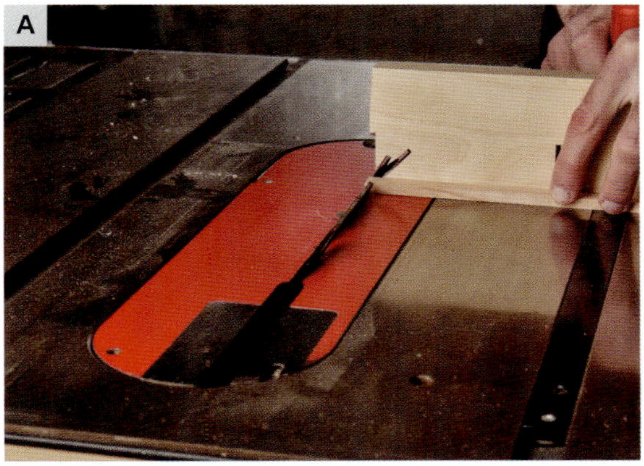

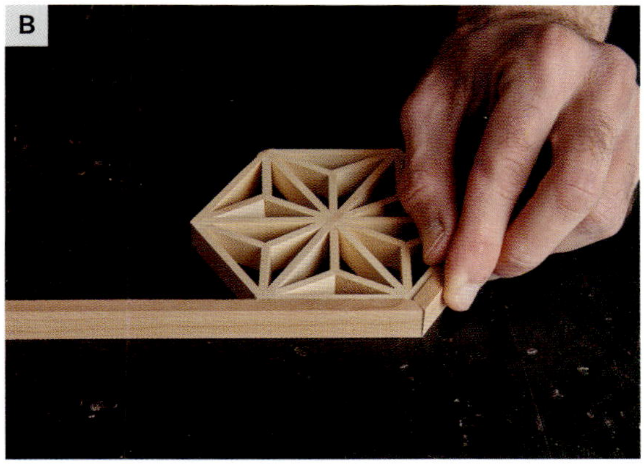

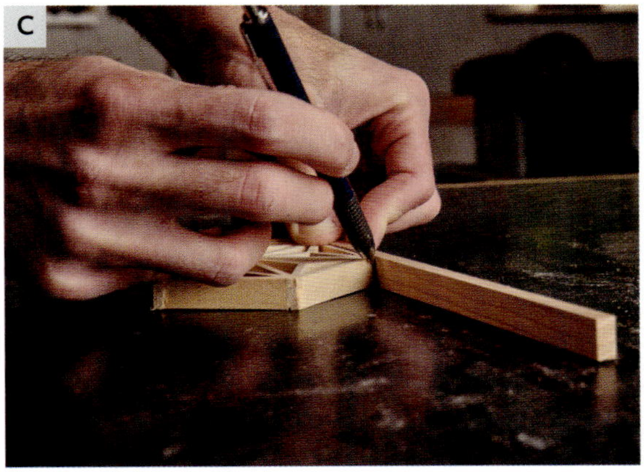

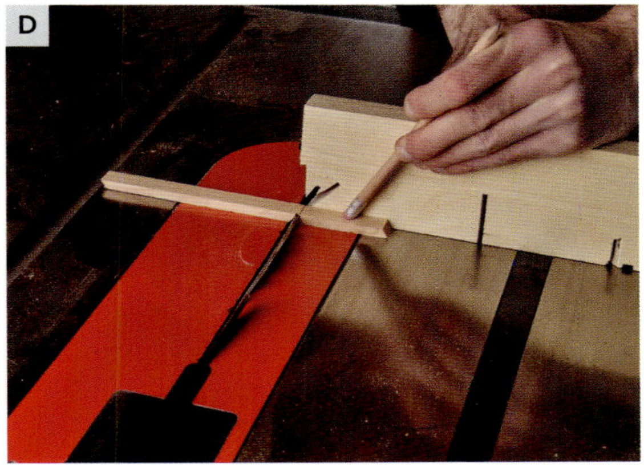

Make the frame

The frame is constructed from ¼ in x ½ in (6.4 mm x 12.7 mm) material. Hardwood options such as maple, walnut or cherry (shown here) work well for this project.

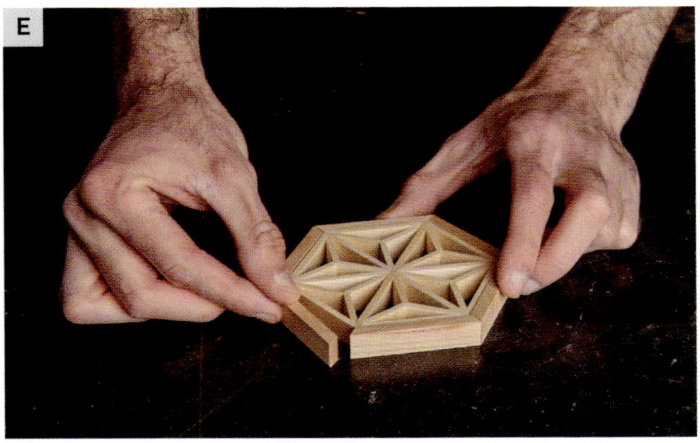

1. Cut one end of two frame pieces at a 60º angle (**A**) and align them with a corner of the kumiko panel (**B**).

2. Mark the opposite corner where the next cut should go (**C**), then trim the piece to fit (**D**). Repeat this process around the hexagon until you've cut all six frame pieces for the four coasters (**E**).

Tip: Minor variations in your kumiko can lead to slight differences in the frame piece dimensions. To make assembly easier, keep track of which frame piece fits best with each kumiko panel and mark their positions accordingly.

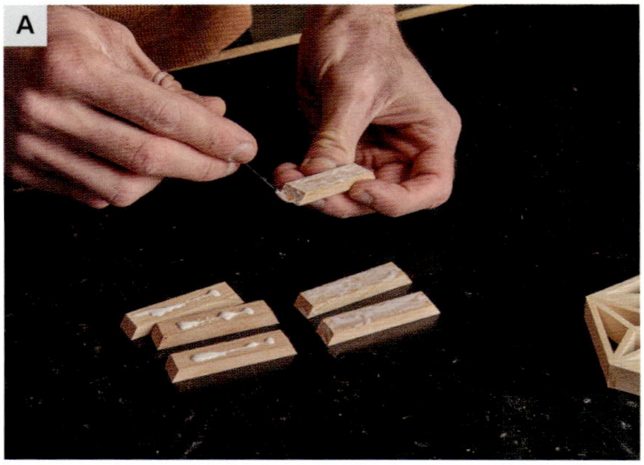

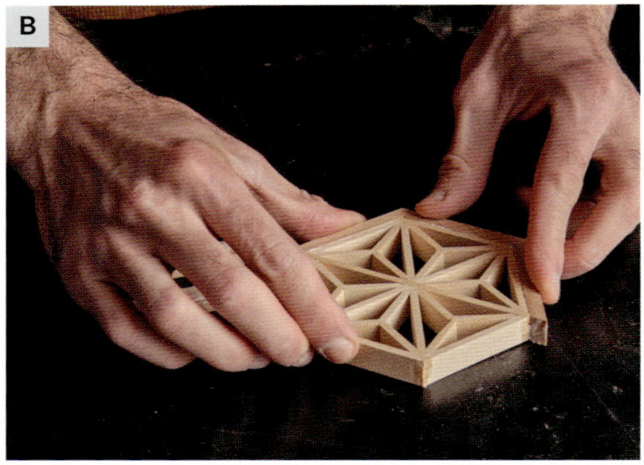

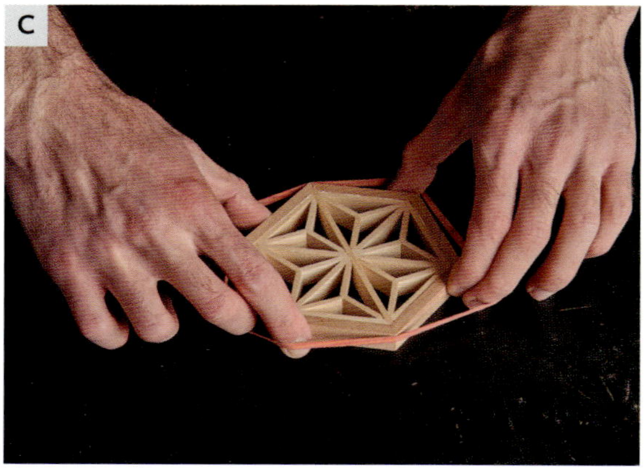

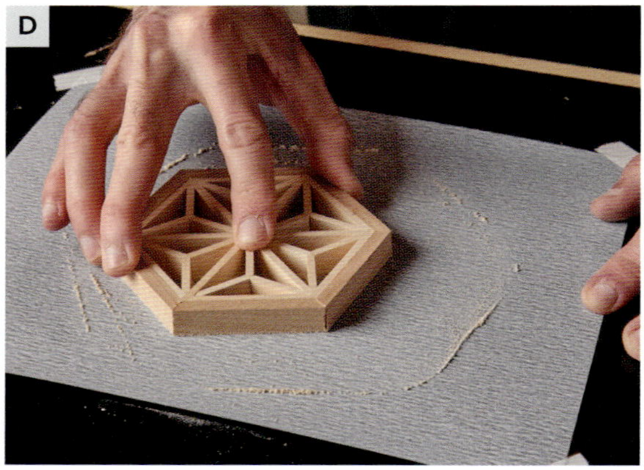

Glue the frame

1. Apply wood glue to the inside edges of the frame pieces as well as the miters (**A**).

2. Press them onto the kumiko panel (**B**). Use masking tape or rubber bands to hold everything in place while the glue dries (**C**).

3. After the glue has fully dried, sand the coasters to ensure they are flat and free of any inconsistencies (**D**).

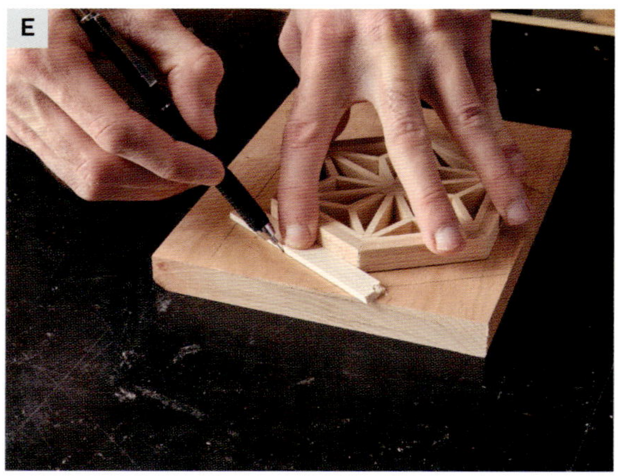

Make the base

1. The base can be made from ½ in (12.7 mm) material to match the coasters, or you can use ¾ in (19.1 mm) material for a sturdier, more substantial look. The base is a hexagon, 1 in (25.4 mm) larger than the coasters. To mark it, place a coaster on your base material and use a ½ in (12.7 mm) spacer to trace around it, creating the larger hexagon (**E**). Then, cut along the marked lines (**F**).

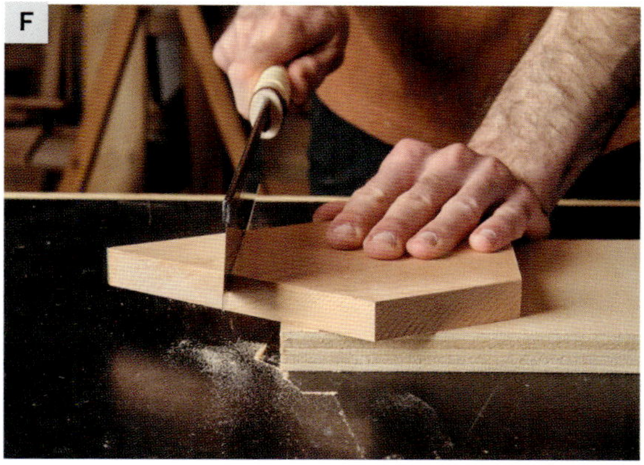

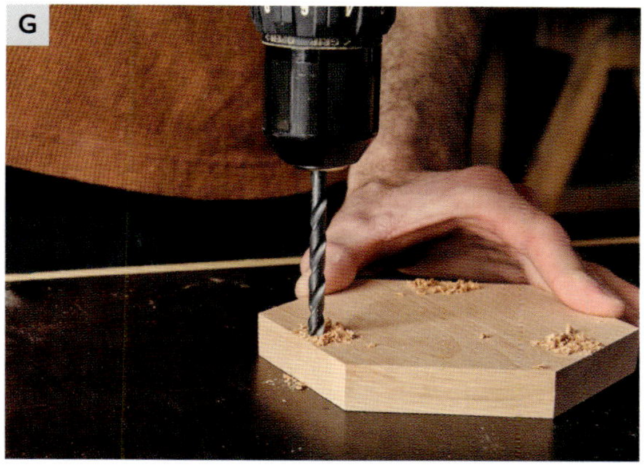

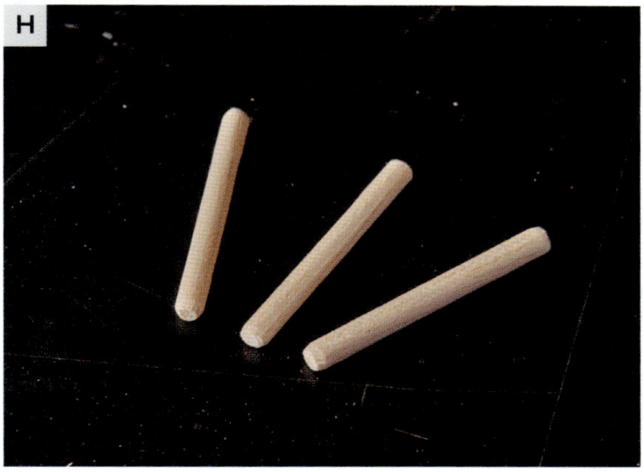

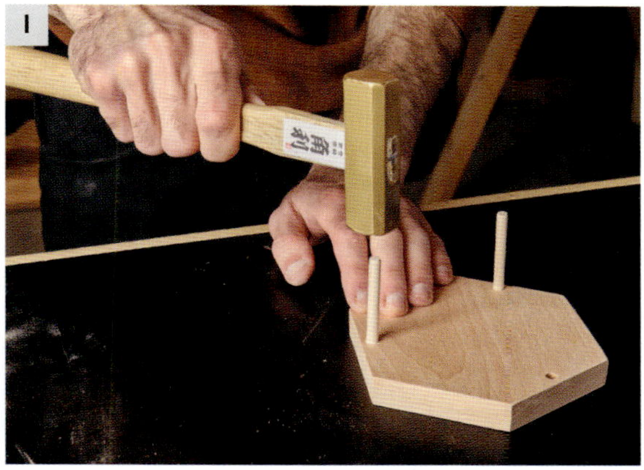

2. Mark the dowel locations as shown in the illustration on page 86, then drill each hole ¼ in (6.4 mm) in diameter and ⅜ in (9.5 mm) deep (**G**).

3. Cut three ¼ in (6.4 mm) dowels to a length of 2¼ in (57 mm) (**H**). Chamfering both ends (using 220 grit sandpaper is a great option) will make it easier to insert the dowels into the holes and give the exposed ends a cleaner, more finished appearance. Apply glue to the holes and tap the dowels into place (**I**).

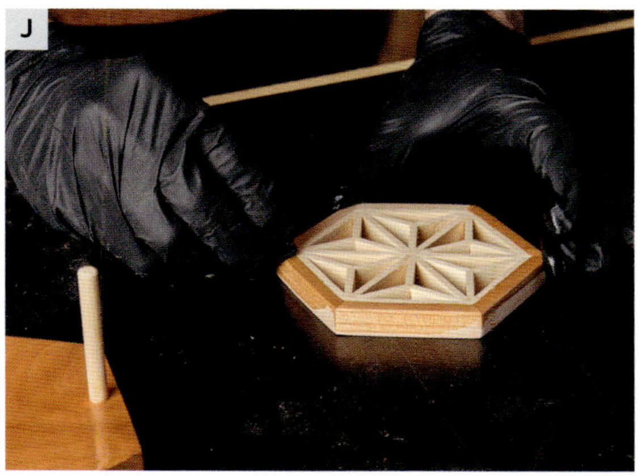

Finish

To protect the coasters from moisture and condensation, apply a durable finish (**J**). A film-forming finish like polyurethane works well, but keep in mind it may add an amber tone to lighter woods. To avoid this, consider applying the finish only to the hardwood frame or use a water-based alternative for a clearer look. Applying the finish by spraying will help get it into the tight corners of the kumiko.

Project 2

Shoji-Inspired Decorative Panel

Many of the projects in this book are designed to push the boundaries of kumiko, but this art panel leans into its traditional roots. While the design is more conventional, I encourage you to make it your own — experiment with different wood species for contrast, adjust the thicknesses of the components to highlight certain shapes, and see how subtle changes can transform the overall feel. Let this panel be a starting point for your own interpretations of kumiko. This art panel is built using ¼ in (6.4 mm) thick mitsukude, with asa-no-ha pieces at ⅛ in (3.2 mm) and 3/16 in (4.8 mm) thick and the shippo pieces slightly thinner than ⅛ in (3.2 mm). All the parts are made from basswood, except for the shippo and frame, which is made from red cedar.

Cut the panel to size

Once you've finished designing, assembling, gluing, and sanding your panel, it's time to cut it to size. You can shape it however you'd like — square, rectangular, diamond, hexagon, or even a pentagon like the one shown here (**A**).

A

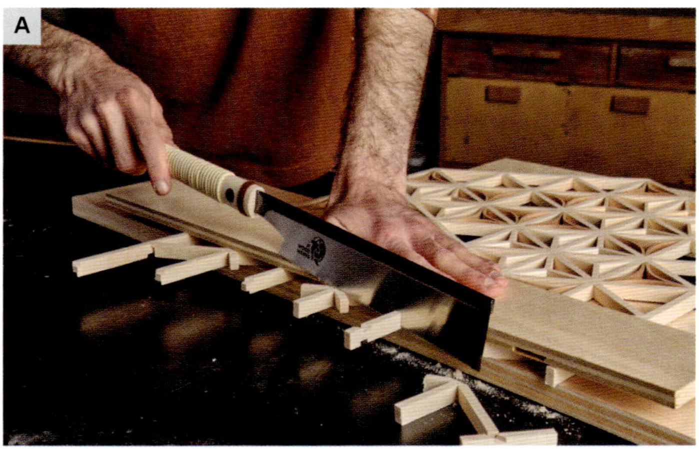

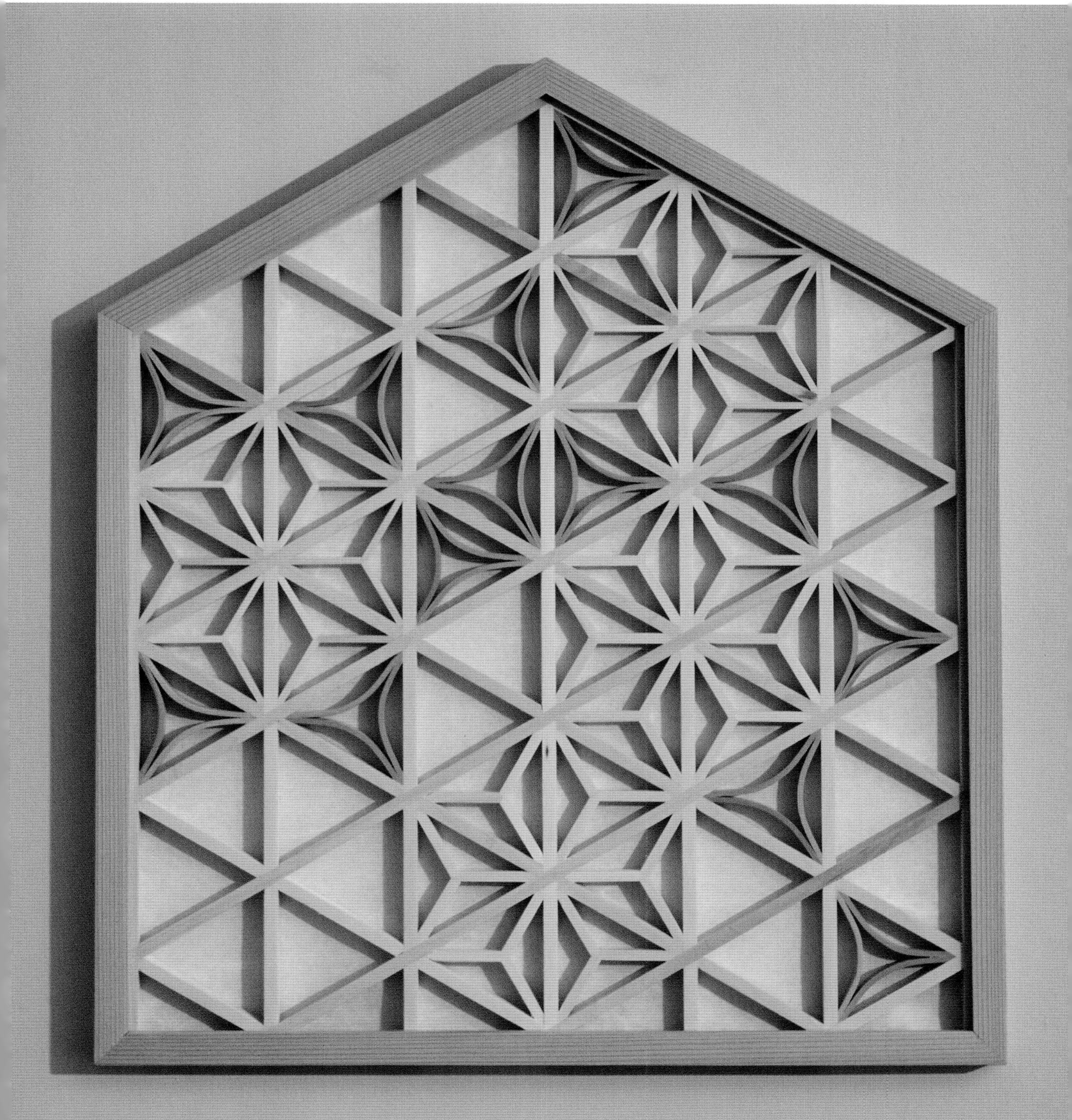

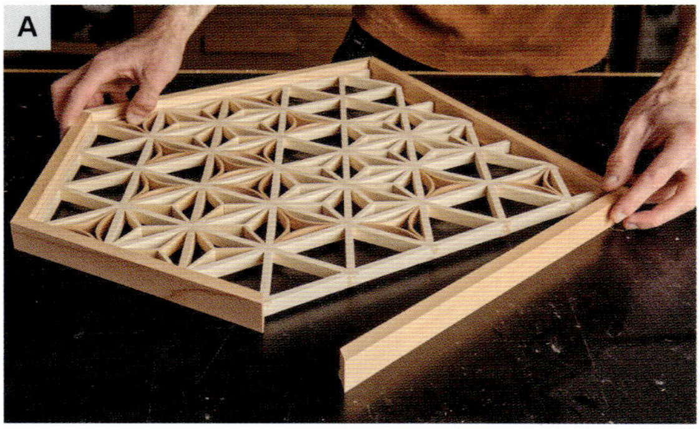
A

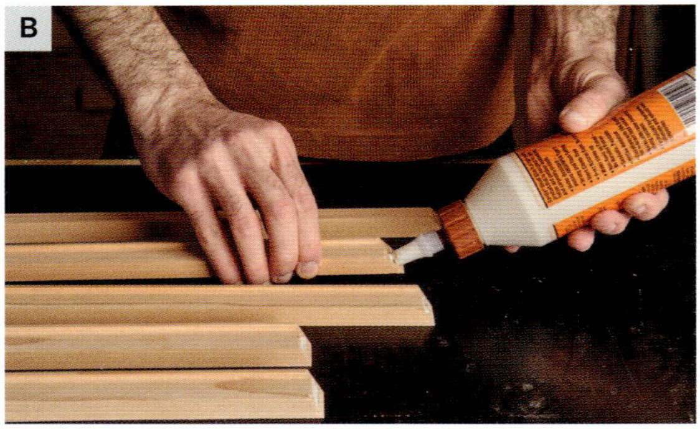
B

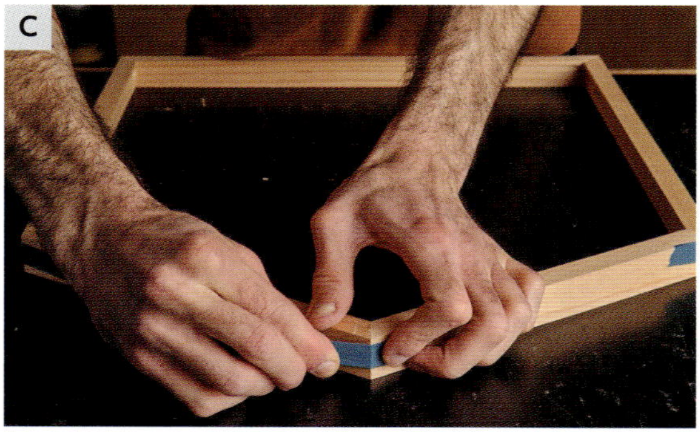
C

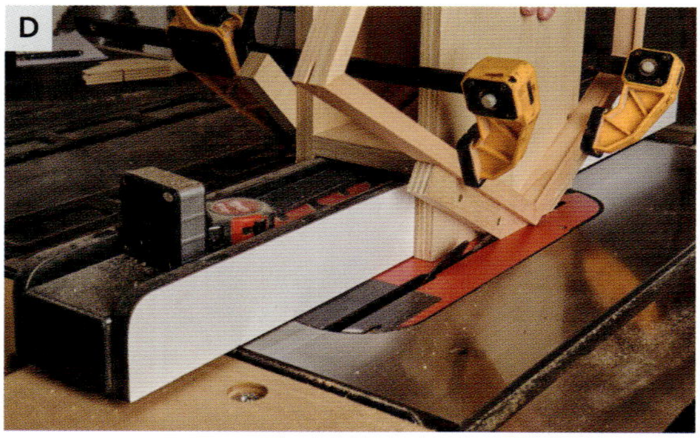
D

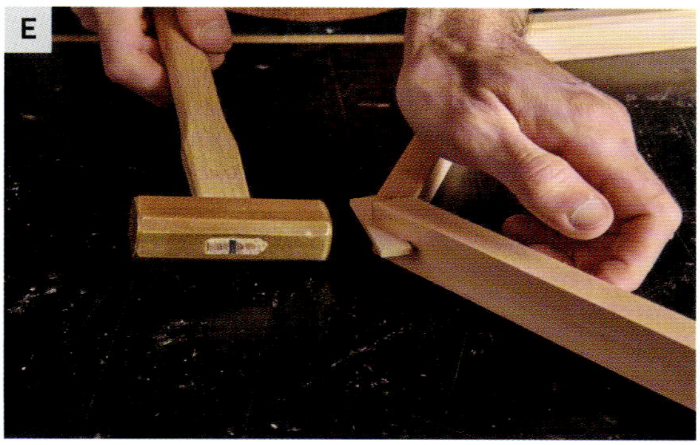
E

Make the frame

The frame pieces measure 1 in (25.4 mm) deep by ⅝ in (16 mm) wide, with a ¾ in x ⅛ in (19.1 mm x 3.2 mm) rabbet cut along the inside face of each piece. They are made in the same way shown on pages 76 to 80.

Cut a rabbet on all the parts and then cut a miter on the ends of two frame pieces. Align them with the corners of the kumiko panel. Mark the opposite corner to locate the next miter, then trim the piece to fit. Repeat this process around the panel, cutting and fitting each frame piece one by one. Make sure the rabbets and miters are all facing the correct direction, so they align properly with the panel. The angles of the miters will correspond to the angles on the kumiko panel (**A**).

Glue and reinforce the frame

1. Apply wood glue to the mitered corners of the frame pieces (**B**), then press them together and use masking tape to hold the joints snug while the glue sets (**C**).

2. After the glue has fully set, cut grooves for the reinforcing splines (**D**).

3. Glue and insert the splines into the cuts (**E**). You can use the same wood as the frame for a more cohesive look or choose a contrasting wood to add visual interest and enhance the design (**F**).

4. Once the glue has dried, flush trim the splines (**G**) and sand the frame.

Apply shoji paper

Adding shoji paper to the back of the kumiko panel will add a more traditional feel and help separate the artwork from the wall it's being displayed on. It can be adhered to the panel with either double-sided tape or nori glue (糊).

1. To apply shoji paper using double-sided tape, start by cutting the paper slightly larger than the kumiko panel. Apply thin strips of double-sided tape along the back edges of the kumiko, and along some of the central kumiko pieces for extra hold (**H**).

F

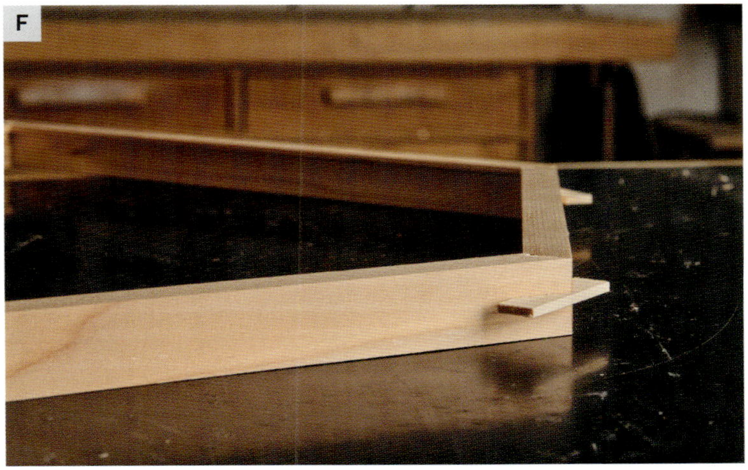

G

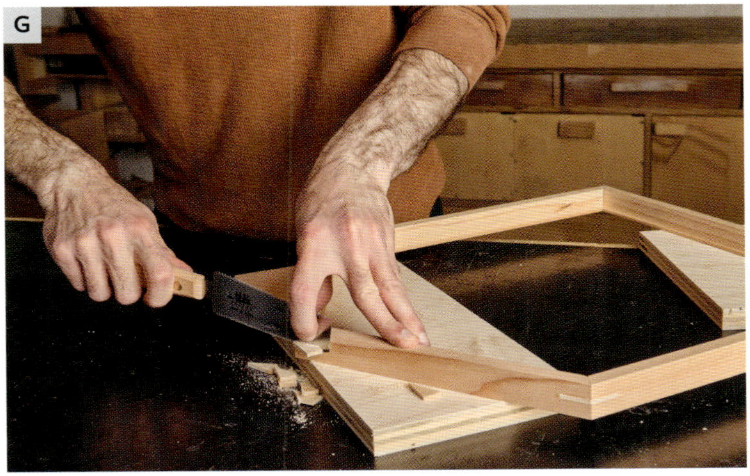

H

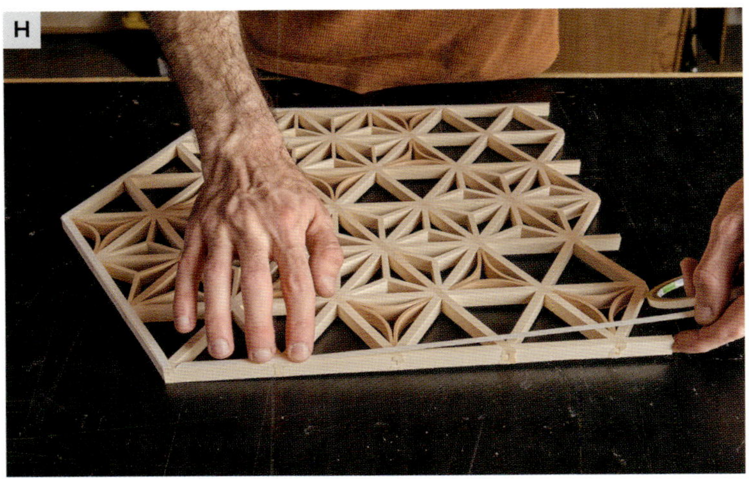

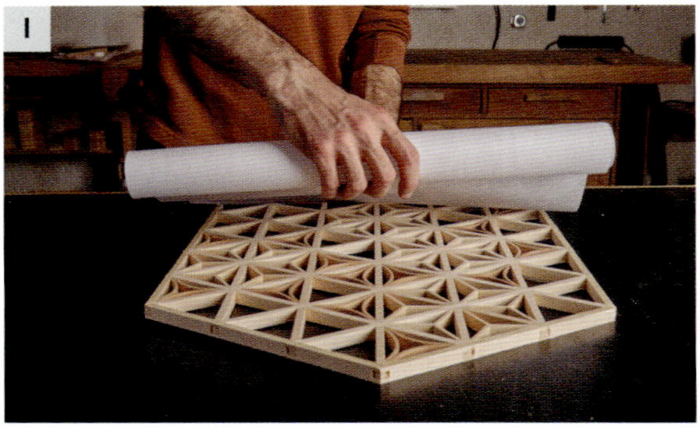

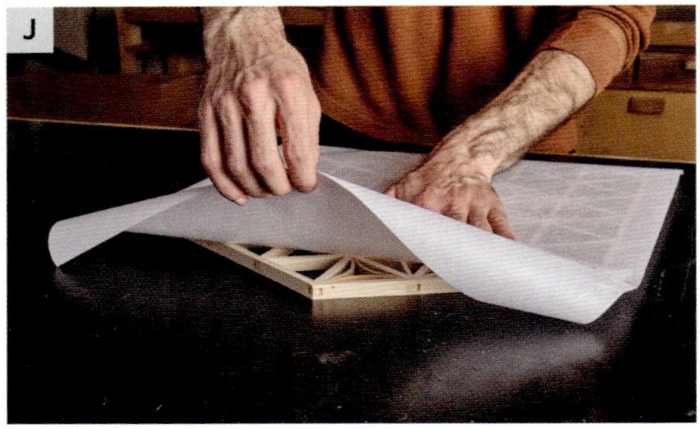

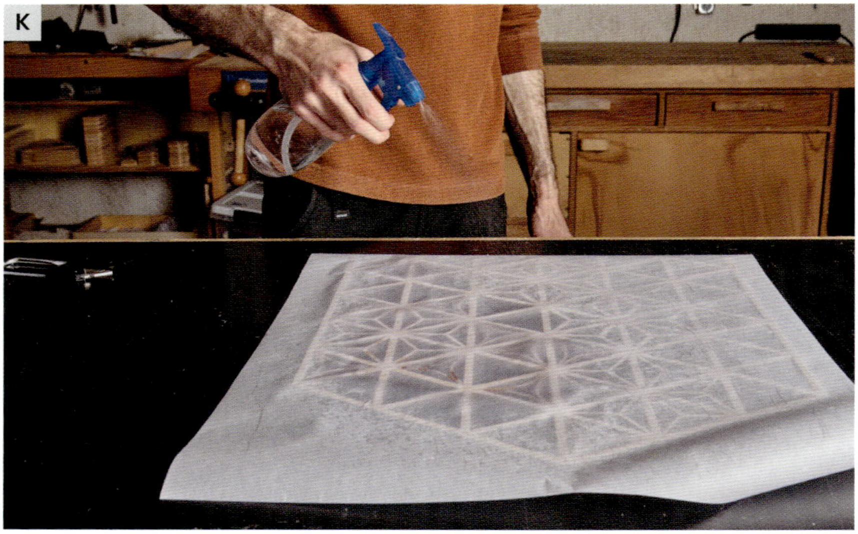

2. Carefully position the paper over the panel, starting at one edge (**I**) and pressing it down gradually to avoid wrinkles or bubbles (**J**).

3. Once it's fully adhered, lightly mist the back of the paper with a spray bottle (**K**). This helps tighten the paper as it dries. After it's dry, trim off the excess for a clean, finished look (**L**).

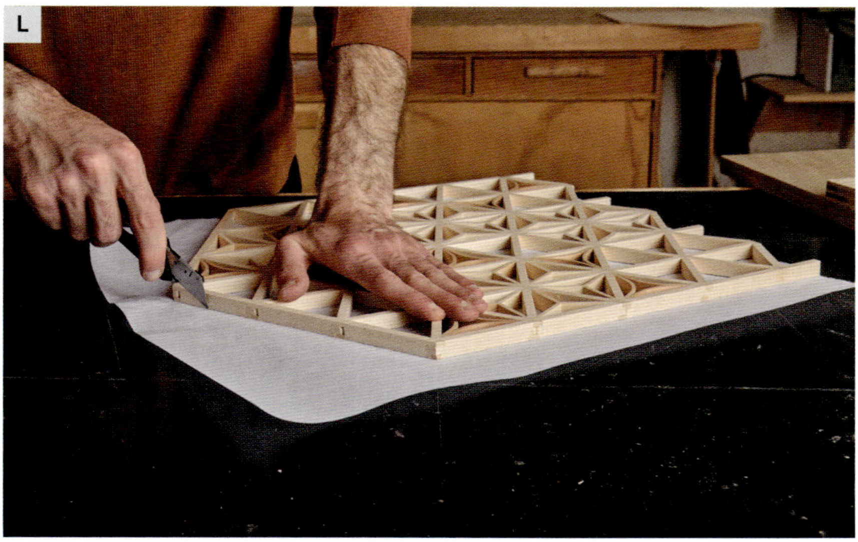

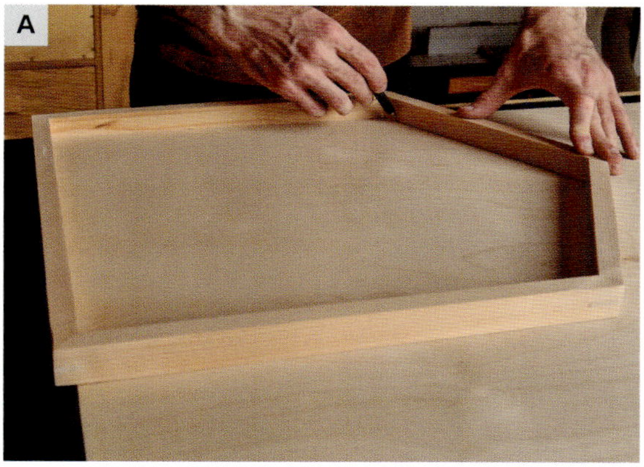
A

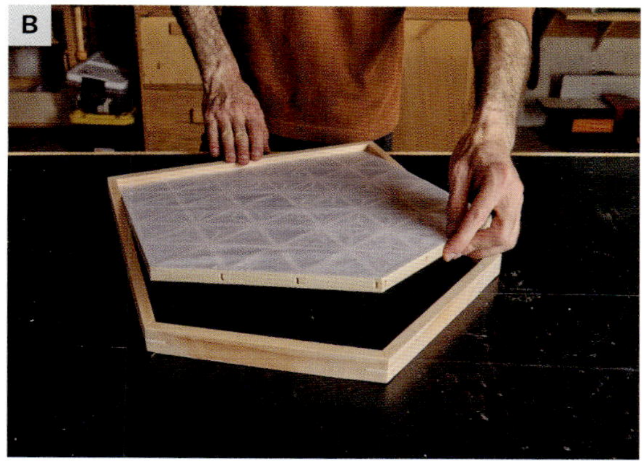
B

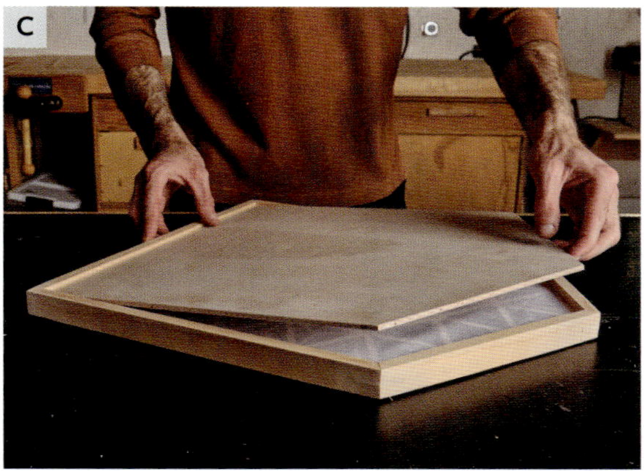
C

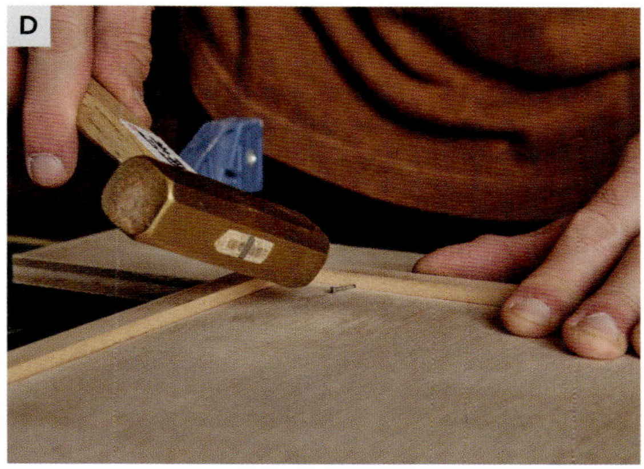
D

Cut the back panel and assemble

If you'd like, now is a great time to apply your choice of finish to the frame or leave the wood raw for a more natural feel.

1. Trace the inside of the frame onto a sheet of ⅛ in (3.2 mm) plywood to use as a back panel (**A**) and cut this shape out.
2. Next, insert the kumiko panel into the frame (**B**) and then the back panel (**C**).
3. Hammer small nails into the inside of the frame, up against the back panel (**D**). These will secure the back panel in place.
4. Add a picture frame hanger to the top (**E**), and it's ready to display.

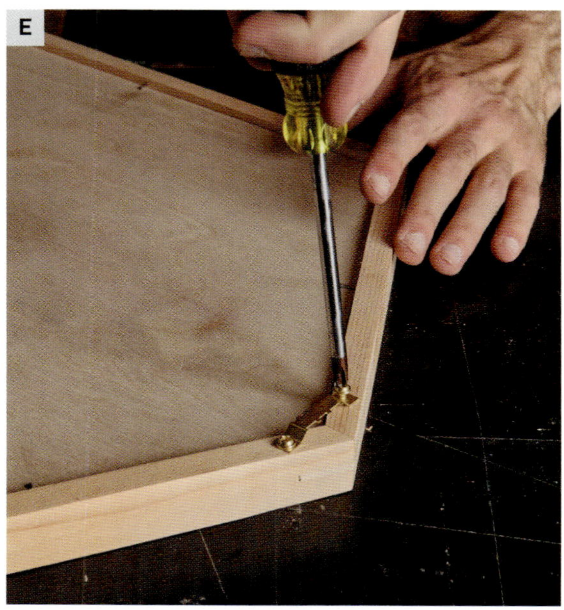
E

Project 3

Kumiko Serving Tray

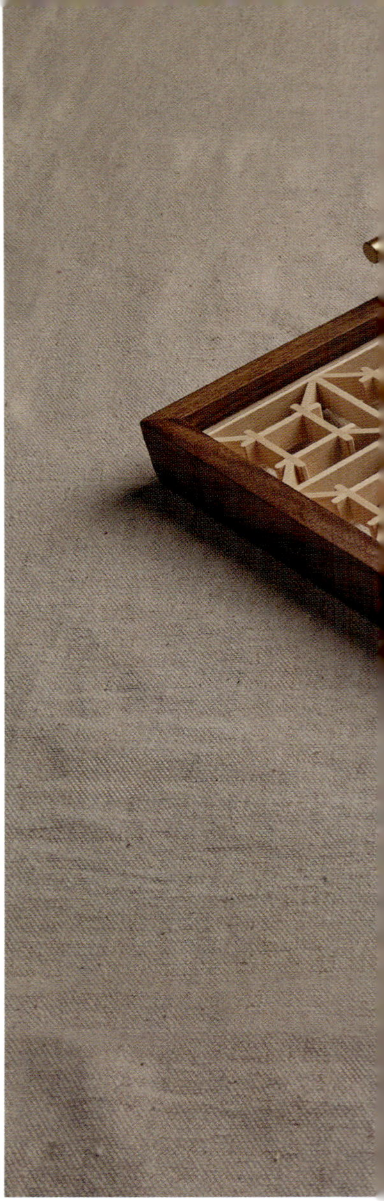

Sometimes, all it takes is a small detail to turn a simple object into something special. What might otherwise be a plain or utilitarian item becomes something unique. Adding kumiko to a serving tray does just that, transforming a basic, functional piece into one that invites curiosity, encourages conversation, and carries the quiet beauty of kumiko. This tray is a perfect example of how tradition can live in the everyday.

When laying out the kumiko for this tray, I chose to balance complexity with openness. Three staggered kaku asa-no-ha patterns form the focal point of the design, their rhythmic geometry drawing the eye to the center. To anchor the composition, izutsu patterns are placed neatly in the corners, creating a quiet frame around the more intricate work. Rather than filling every available space, open areas are left between the patterns. These spaces act like pauses in music; they give the design room to breathe and allow the viewer's attention to rest before returning to the details. The interplay of fullness and emptiness makes the finished piece feel harmonious rather than overwhelming.

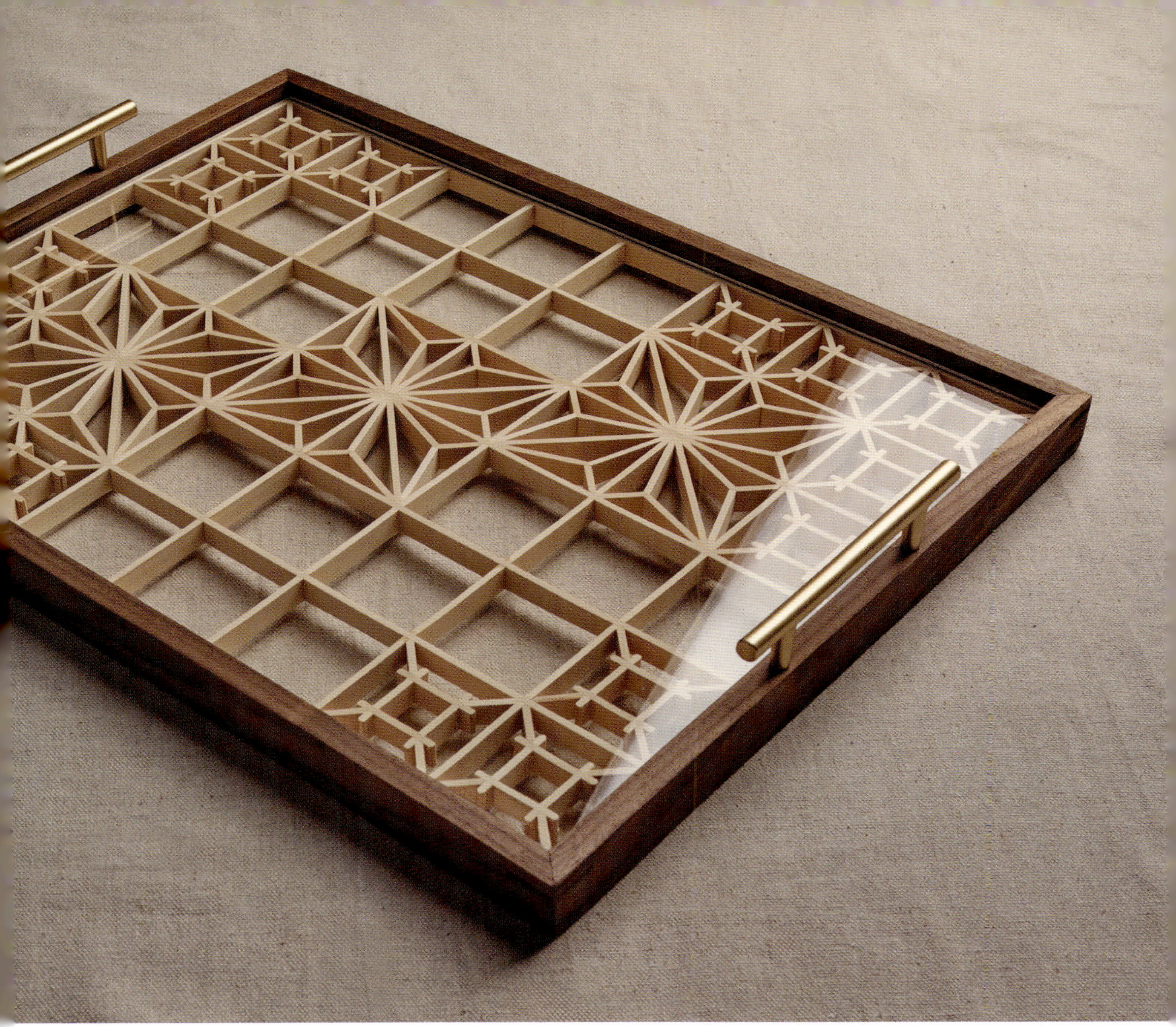

Making the frame

1. Before building the frame, make a kumiko panel of your choice using the techniques covered in previous chapters. Refer to the diagram for the panel dimensions. Once your kumiko panel is complete, begin building the frame, which also forms the sides of the serving tray. This process uses similar techniques covered earlier with slight modifications. Begin with stock measuring ½ in x 1¼ in (12.7 mm x 32 mm) and cut a 45° miter on one end of two pieces. Align each piece with a corner of the kumiko panel, then mark the opposite end to locate the second miter. Trim the piece to fit and repeat this process for the remaining sides (**A**).

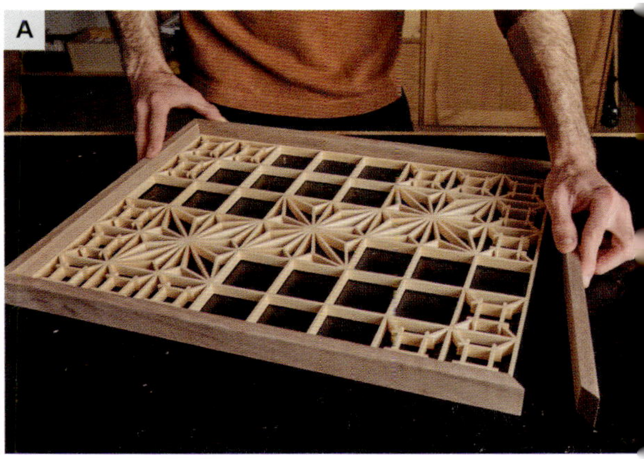
A

PATTERN ARRANGEMENT FOR KUMIKO TRAY

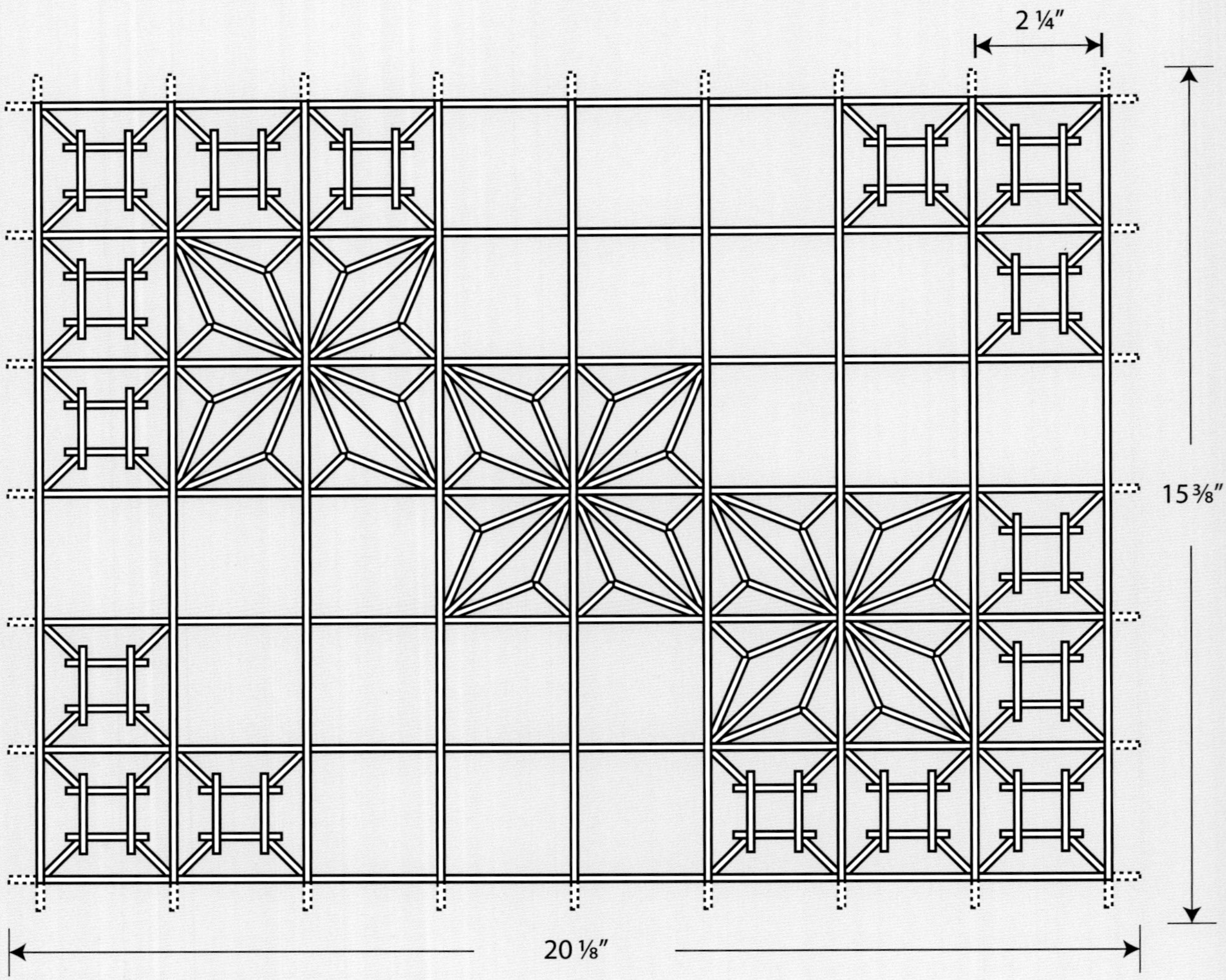

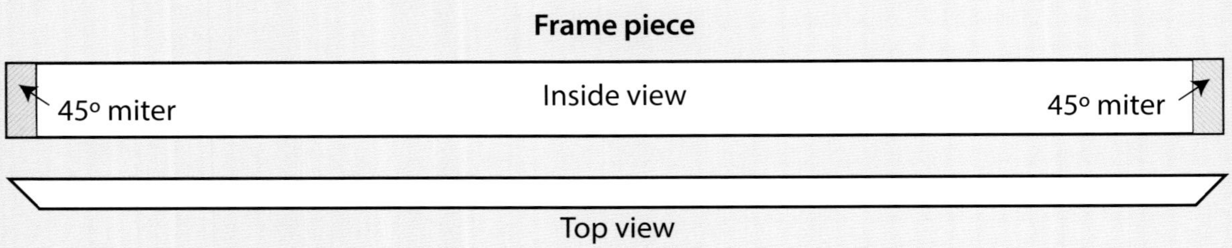

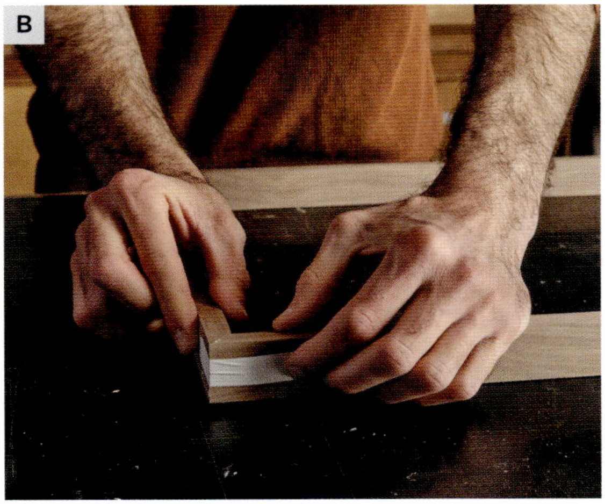

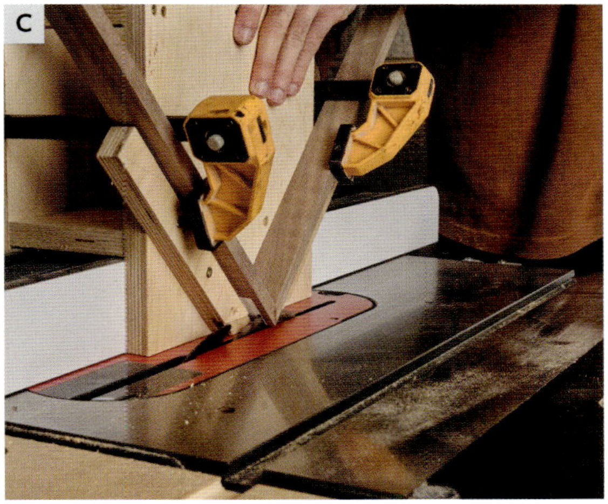

2. Apply wood glue to the mitered corners of the frame pieces, then join them together and secure the joints with masking tape to keep them tight as the glue dries (**B**).

Reinforce the frame

1. After the glue has fully set, make cuts into the corners for the reinforcing splines (**C**). Since this is an item that's intended to carry some weight, it's a good idea to add more than just one spline in each corner.

2. Glue in splines with wood that matches the frame for a seamless look or use a contrasting species to highlight the detail (**D–E**). After the glue has dried, flush trim the splines and sand the frame smooth.

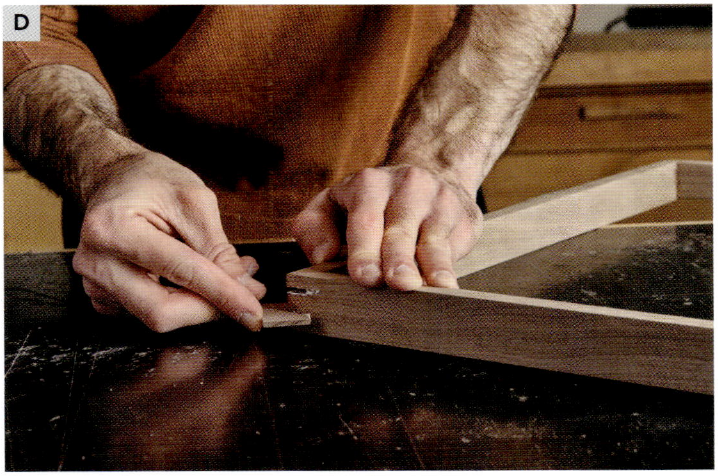

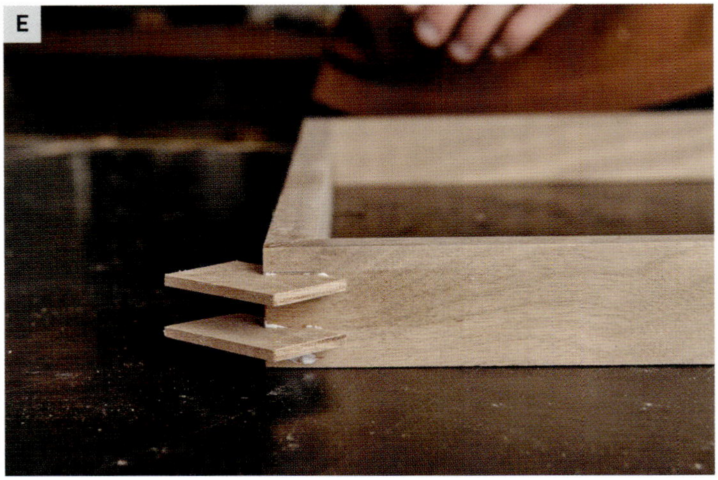

Drill for the handle

The style of handle you choose will have a big impact on the overall look and feel of the serving tray. In this example, a simple brass handle will be paired with this walnut frame, offering a contrast that complements the wood without drawing attention away from the kumiko.

1. The handle is mounted using screws that pass through the side of the frame. After carefully measuring and marking the screw locations for your specific hardware, drill through the tray wall using a bit sized for your screws (**A**).

2. Add a countersink or counterbore on the bottom with a larger drill bit to recess the screw heads (**B**). This is especially helpful if your screws are too short to pass through the entire depth of the side piece.

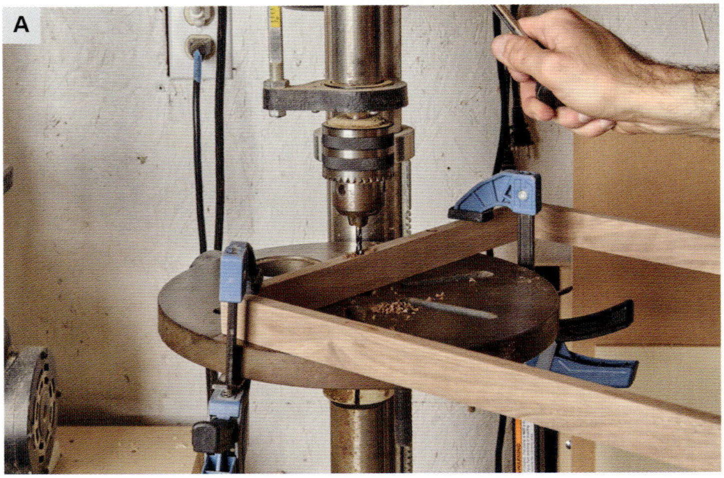

A

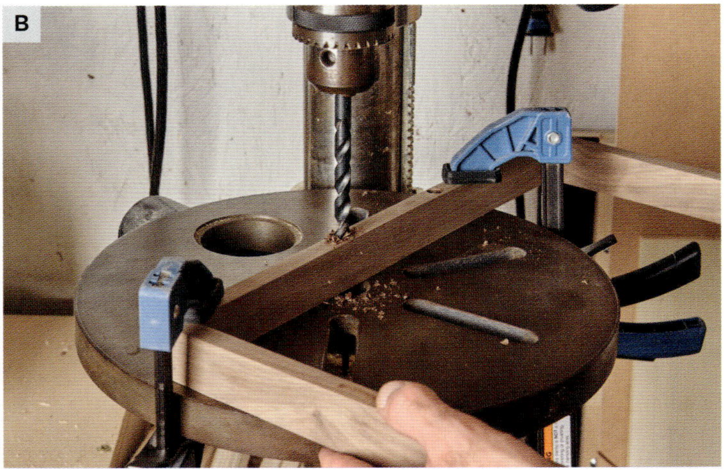

B

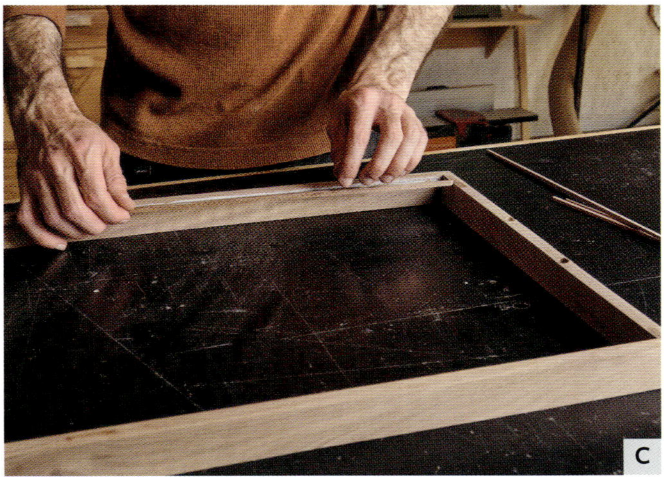

C

Secure the kumiko and finish

1. A slim ⅛ in x ⅛ in (3.2 mm x 3.2 mm) strip of wood is glued along the inside of the frame to support the kumiko panel. These strips run the full length of each interior side, with mitered corners for a clean fit. Once in place, they create a hidden ledge that keeps the panel from falling through the frame. This method mimics a traditional rabbet joint but in reverse. Instead of removing material from thicker stock, the ledge is built up using these small strips (**C–D**).

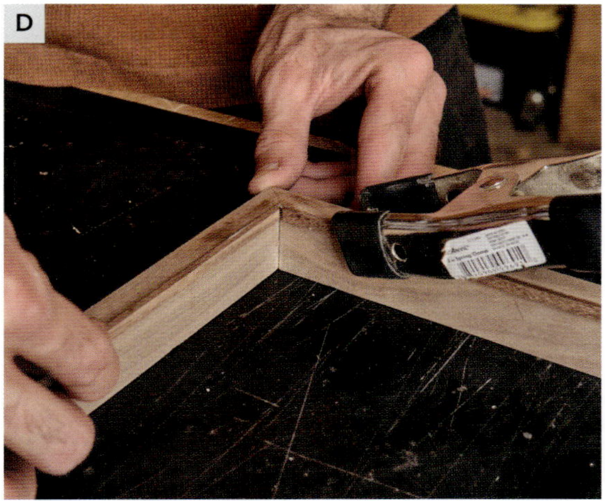

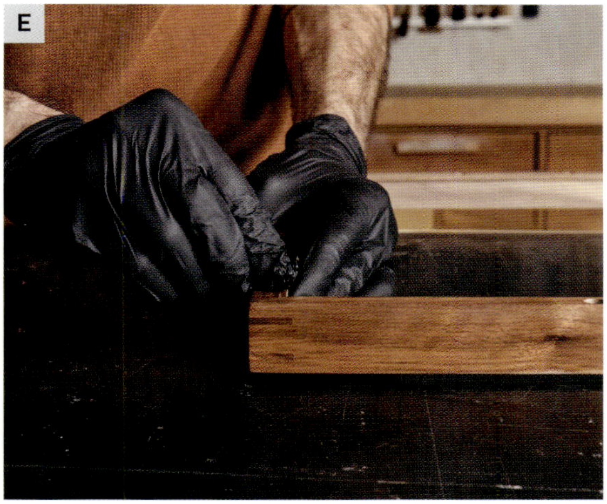

2. Do all the final sanding and apply a finish to the frame to protect it from wear during everyday use (**E**).

3. Once the finish has dried, attach the handle (**F**).

4. The kumiko is intentionally not attached to the frame to allow for removal for maintenance or repair (**G**). For added security, feel free to add double-sided tape to attach it.

5. To increase durability and functionality, you might also consider adding a piece of glass or clear acrylic over the kumiko. This helps protect the delicate work while creating a smooth, usable surface.

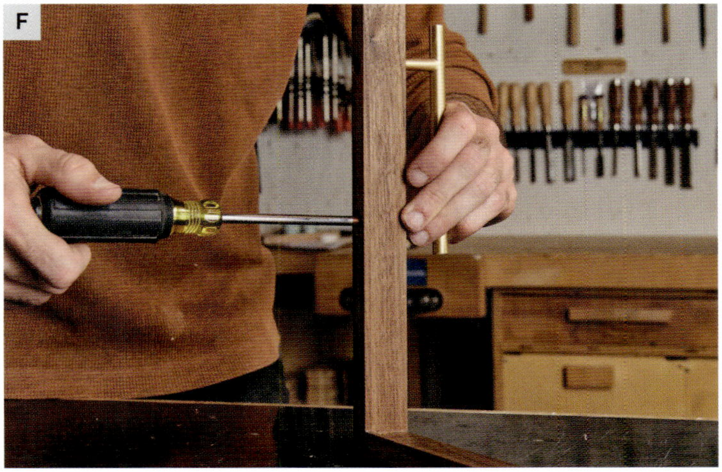

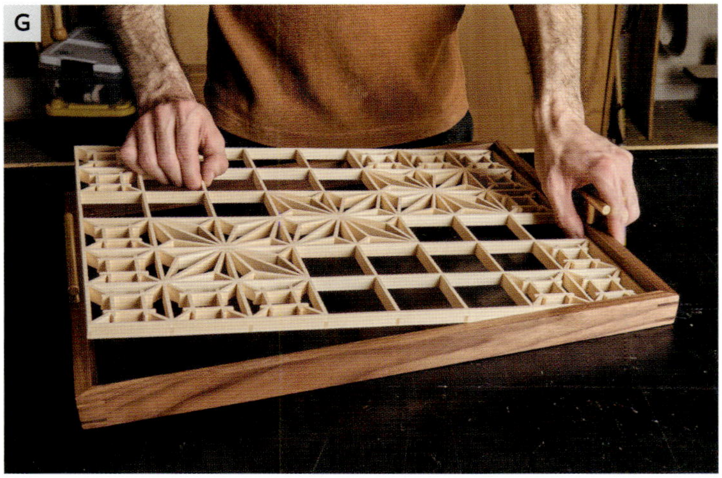

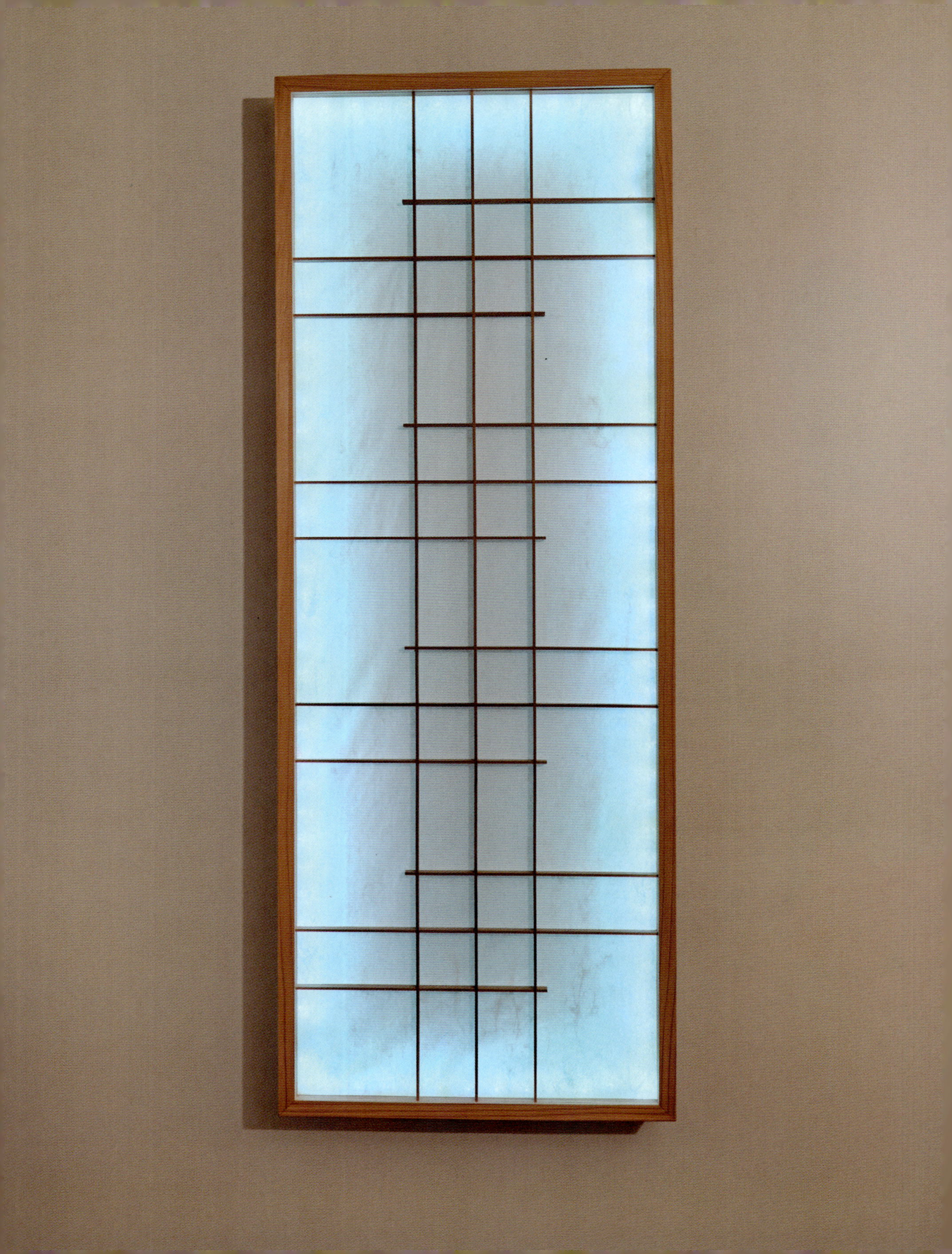

Project 4

Light Panel

Lighting is a great way to showcase the beauty and detail of kumiko, and this project does just that through a clean, minimalist design. While it features an open lattice without a traditional infill pattern, the layout allows you to add one in the central squares if you choose. Made from lightweight cedar and lit from within by an integrated LED strip, the panel creates a soft, ambient glow. Whether hung vertically or horizontally, it's a striking piece, ideal for bringing a quiet elegance to any room.

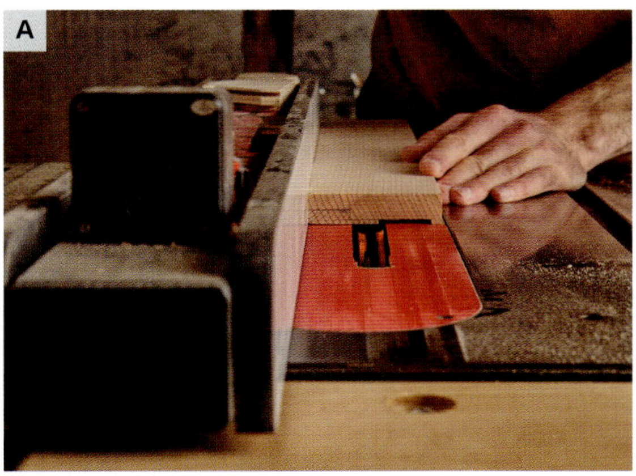

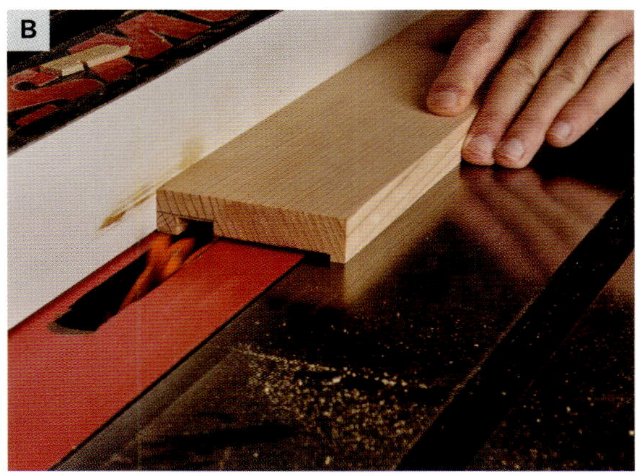

Rabbet the frame

After making the kumiko to the dimensions shown on the next page, begin by cutting the stepped rabbets on one face of each frame piece. You'll need two pieces at 17¾ in (450 mm) and two at 48 in (1219 mm) for the final dimensions, but it's best to start with stock that's a couple of inches longer to allow for fine tuning.

1. Cut the rabbet, starting from the center and moving outward to ensure the workpiece is fully supported during the entire process (**A**).
   A dado stack will help remove material quickly and efficiently (**B**).

LIGHTING PANEL LAYOUT

Note: The exact exterior dimensions will ultimately be guided by the precision of your kumiko panel. Small variations in the panel can subtly influence the finished size.

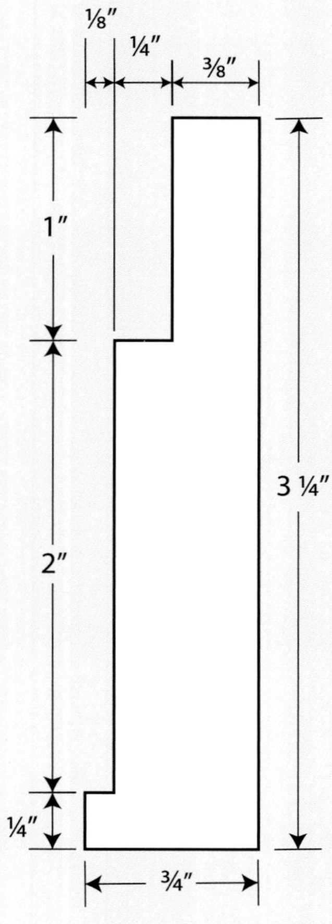

Frame profile

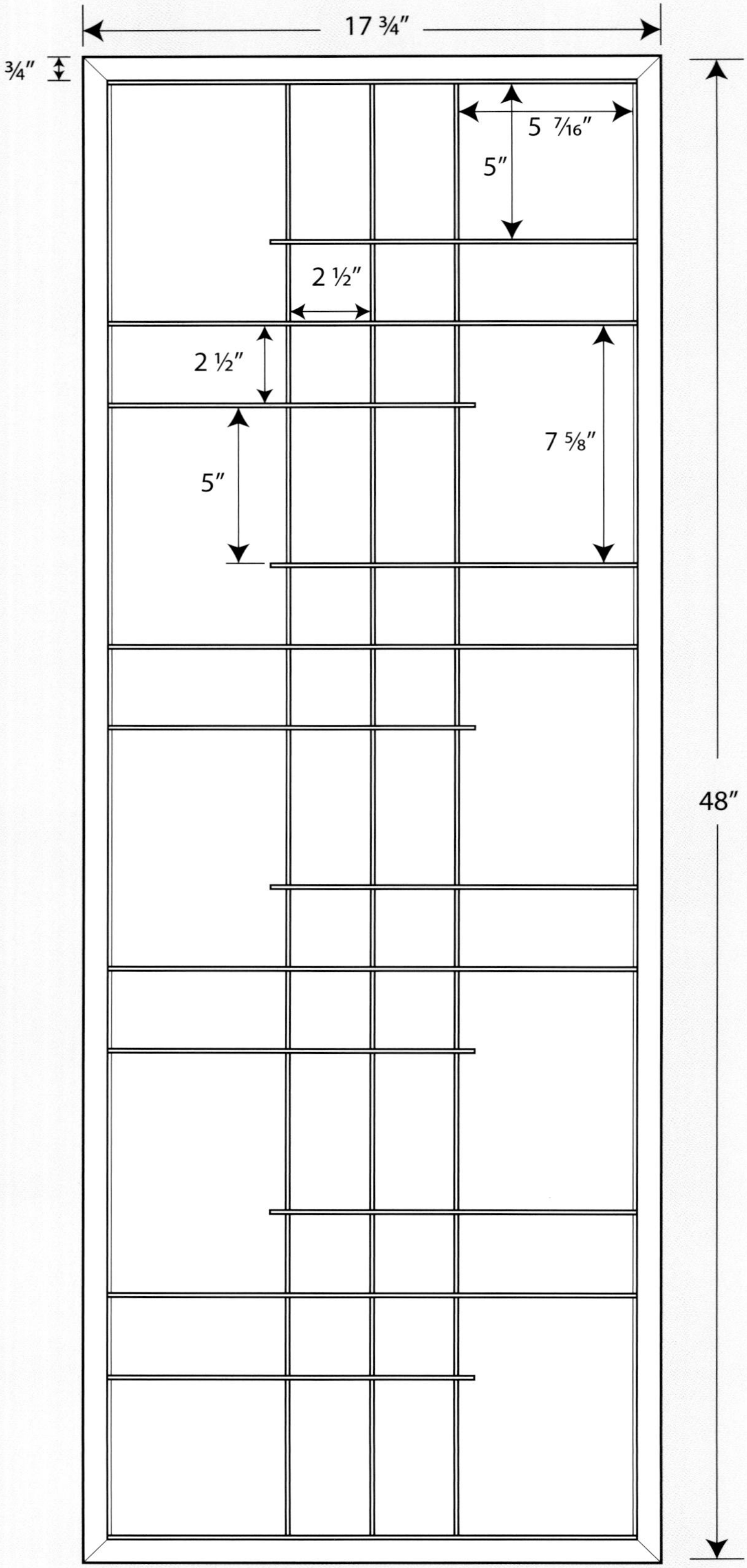

C
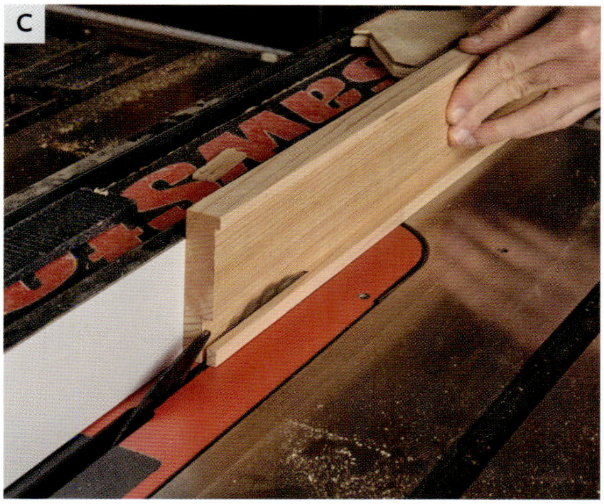

D
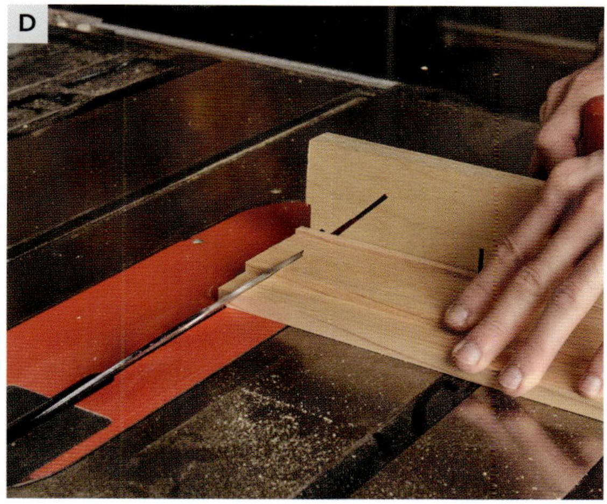

2. Once most of the material is cleared, switch to a standard ripping blade to remove the remaining material with the stock on edge, against the table saw fence (**C**).

Miter and assemble the frame

1. Start by cutting a 45° miter on one end of two pieces (**D**). Align each piece with a corner of the kumiko panel, then mark the opposite end to position the second miter (**E**).

2. Trim each piece to fit, and repeat the process for the remaining sides, paying attention to the orientation of the rabbets and miters.

3. Apply wood glue to the mitered corners, join the pieces together, and secure the joints with masking tape to hold them tight while the glue dries (**F**). Ensure the frame is square and that the kumiko panel has a snug fit within it.

E
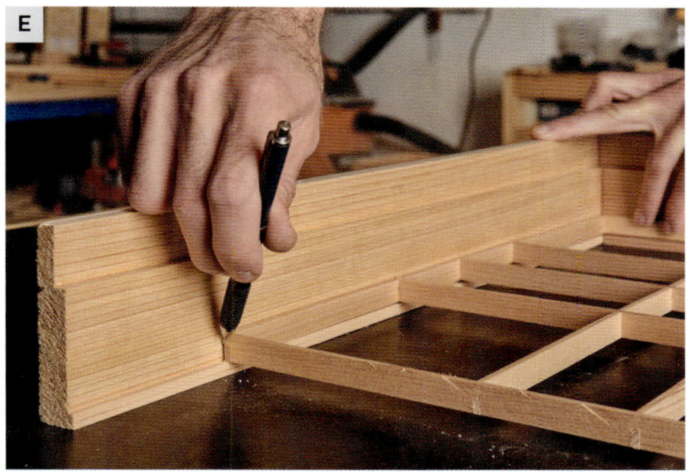

F
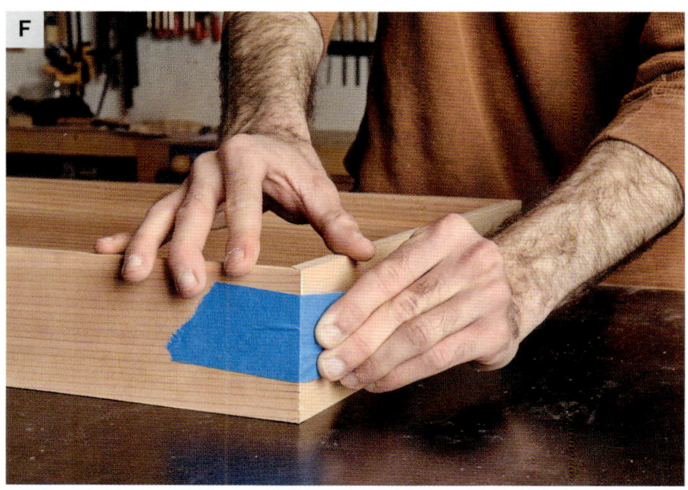

A

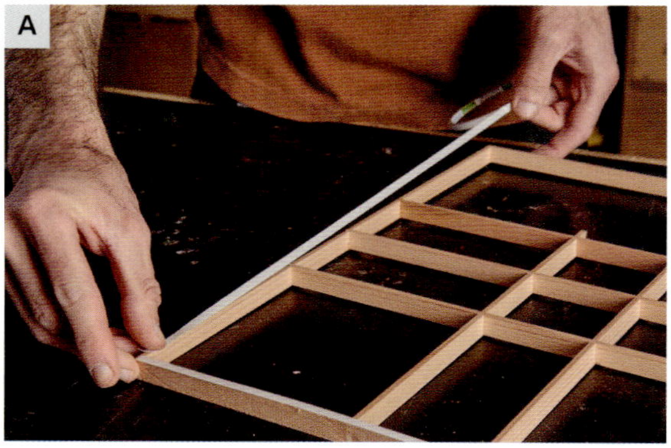

B

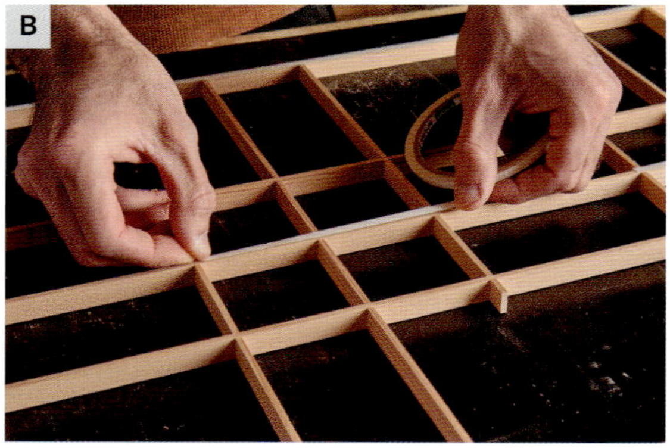

C

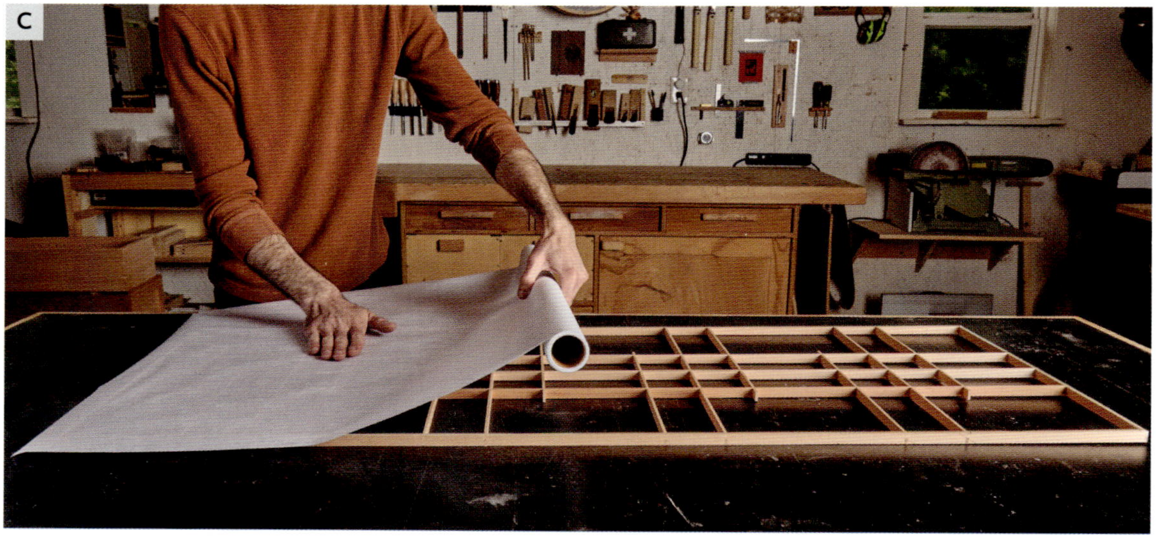

D

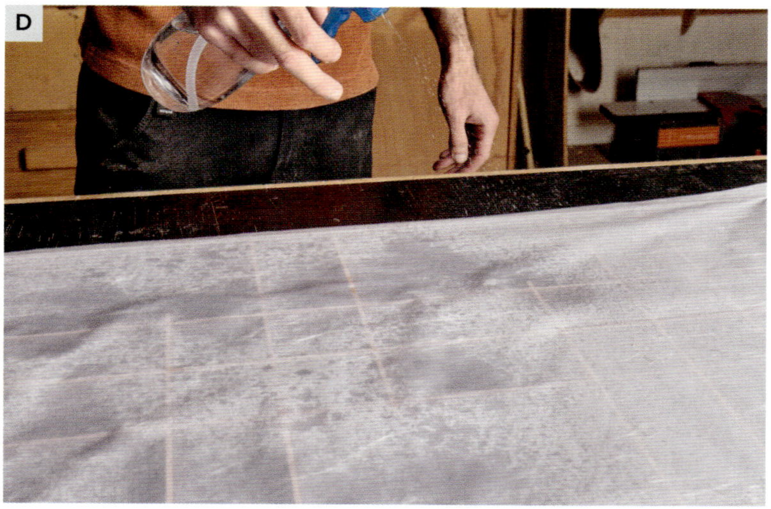

Apply shoji paper

This is the ideal time to apply the shoji paper backing. For step-by-step guidance, refer to pages 93 to 94 (**A–D**). As an alternative, you can use a white or frosted glass or acrylic sheet which offers a similar soft, diffused look while adding extra durability. Keep in mind that those options may add additional weight to the final piece.

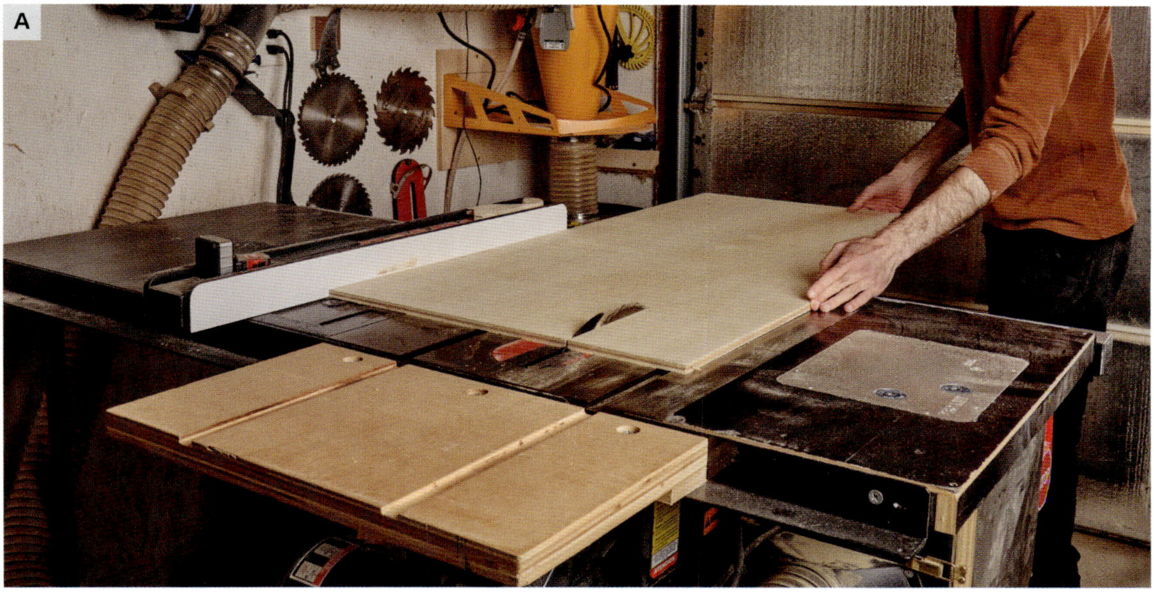
A

Cut the back panel

1. Measure, mark, and cut the back panel from ½ in (12.7 mm) plywood (**A**), ensuring it fits snugly within the rabbet of the frame to prevent light from escaping. However, make sure it's not too tight, allowing for easy removal when needed (**B**).

2. Pre-drill holes to attach the back panel with screws. Place the first screw about 3 in (76 mm) in from each corner along the edges. Add a screw centered on each short side and three evenly spaced along the long sides. Position the holes as close to the edge of the plywood as possible and drill at a slight angle outward to ensure the screws bite into the rabbet of the frame. Be careful not to angle too much and drill through the sides (**C**). After drilling all the holes, remove the back panel for the next step.

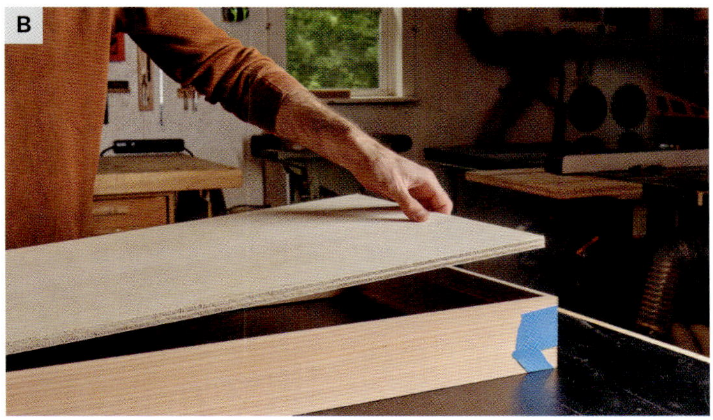
B

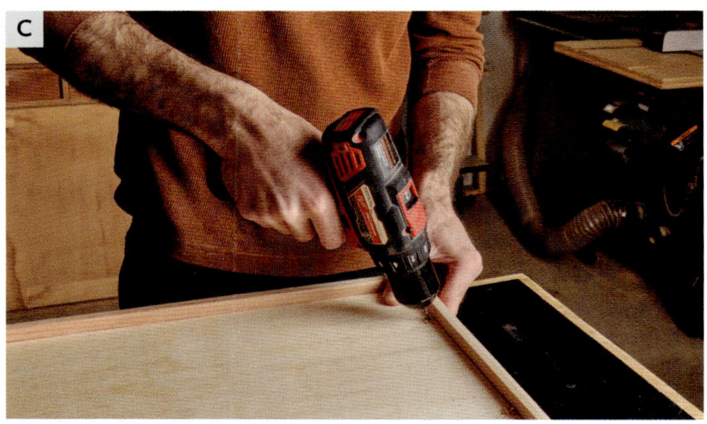
C

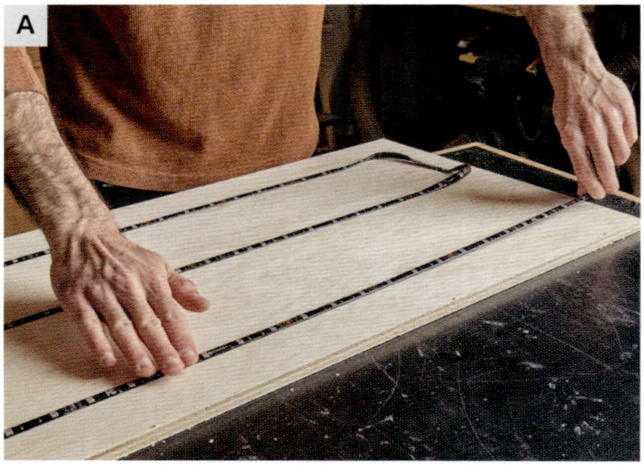

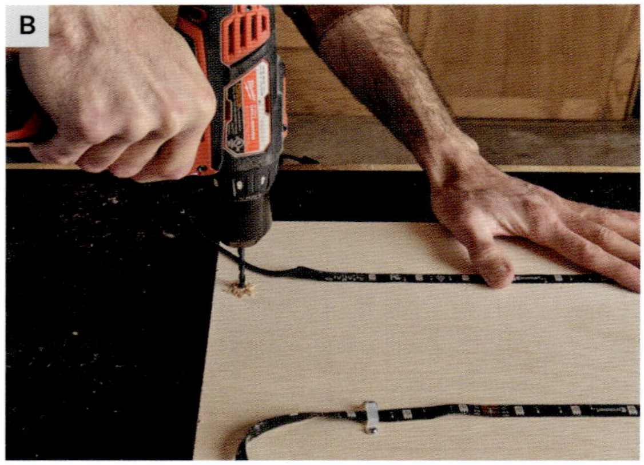

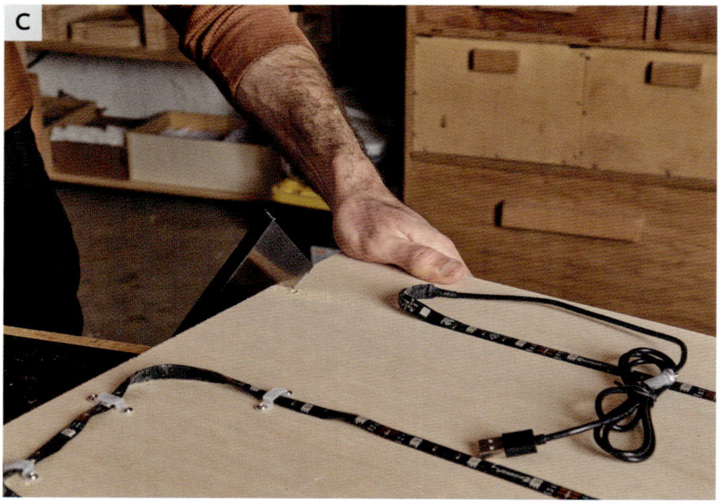

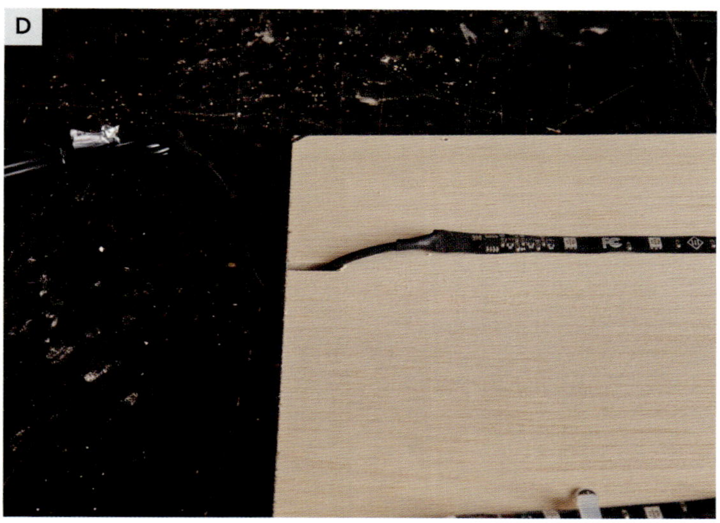

Finish and assembly

Before assembling the parts, apply a finish of your choice to the frame to protect the wood and bring out its natural beauty. A dimmable LED light strip with adhesive backing makes lighting installation quick and simple.

1. Adhere the strip to the inside of the back panel, keeping the spacing consistent (**A**). A 16 ft (5 m) strip works well for this design.

2. Whether you're using a plug-in or battery-powered strip, drill a small hole through the back panel (**B**) and create a notch for the cable to pass through (**C–D**). Mounting the battery pack on the outside makes for easy access when it's time to recharge or replace the batteries.

Safety tip: Be sure to use LED lighting that's rated for enclosed spaces, as some strips can generate heat and pose a potential fire hazard.

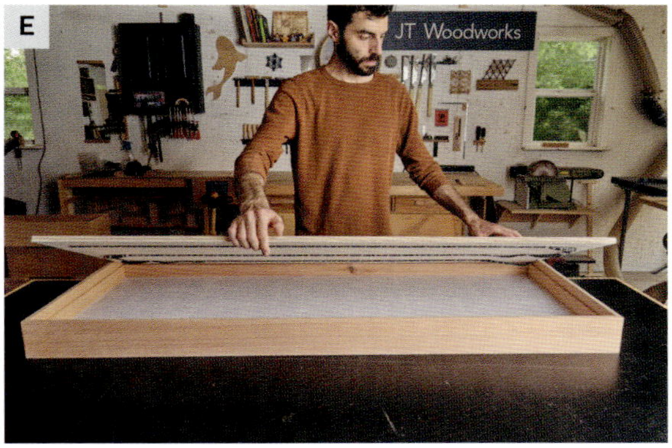

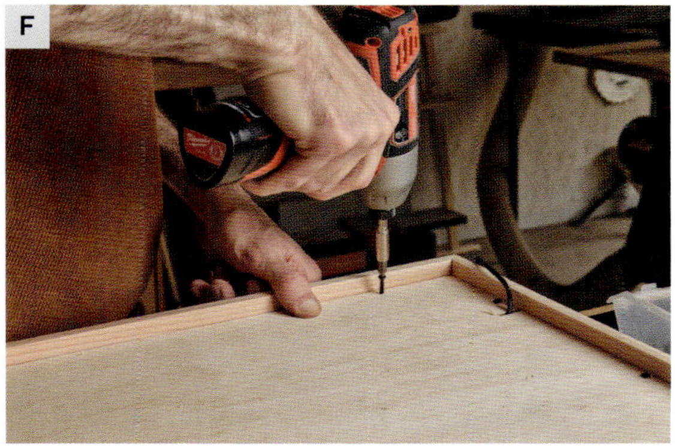

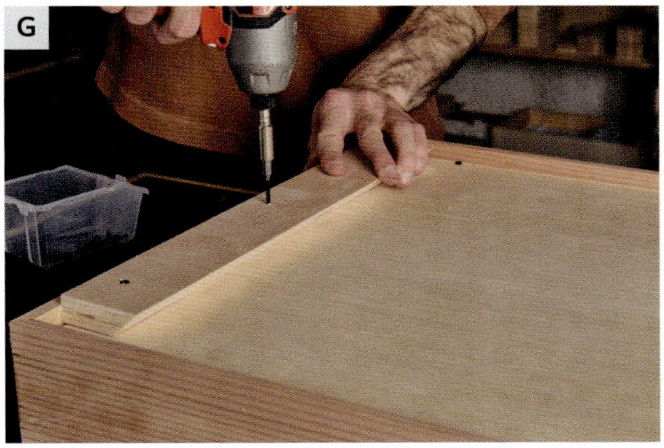

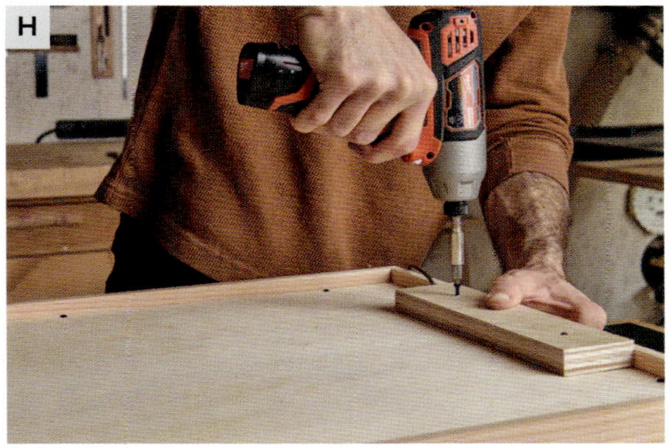

3. Start assembly by inserting the kumiko panel into the frame. If the fit is loose, consider adding small retaining strips behind the kumiko and secured to the inside of the frame. Make sure these supports are removable, in case the panel needs to be taken out for maintenance.

4. Insert the back panel (**E**) and screw it to the frame (**F**).

5. For easy mounting, use a French cleat and make sure to add a spacer on the opposite end to ensure it hangs evenly (**G–H**). This panel can be hung vertically or horizontally to fit your space.

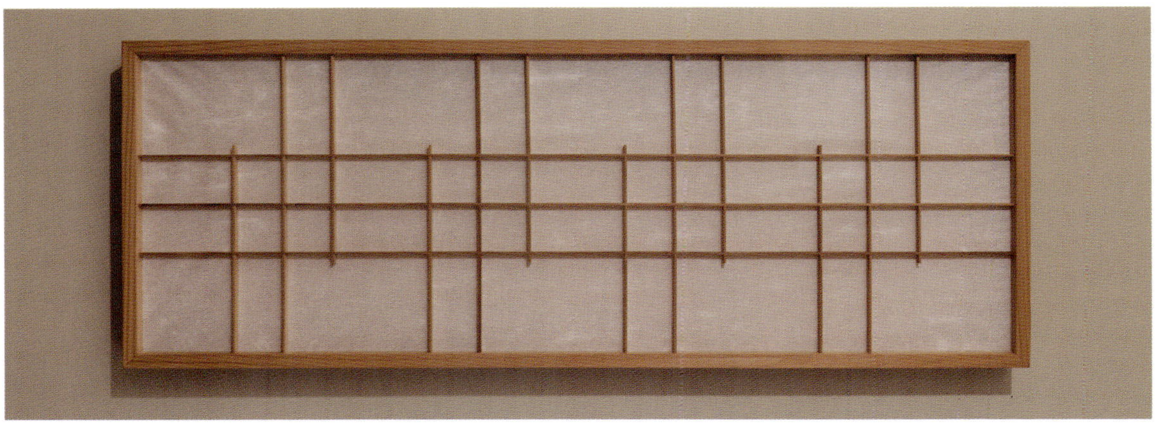

Project 5

Kumiko Andon

In Japanese, "andon" (行灯) refers to a traditional paper-covered lantern. Historically, andon were used in homes and along streets during the Edo period and typically consisted of a wooden or bamboo frame, a paper shade, and an oil lamp or candle inside. Today, andon can also describe modern light fixtures inspired by that style, like this one. This lantern features an "inverted" kaku asa-no-ha pattern. When making this pattern, instead of placing the first diagonal pieces from the center of the grid and extending out to the corners, position them so they span from the center of one side to the center of the adjacent side. From there, complete the rest of the pattern as normal.

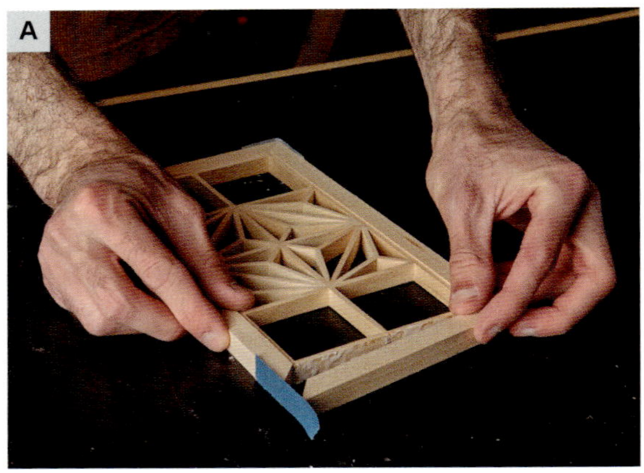

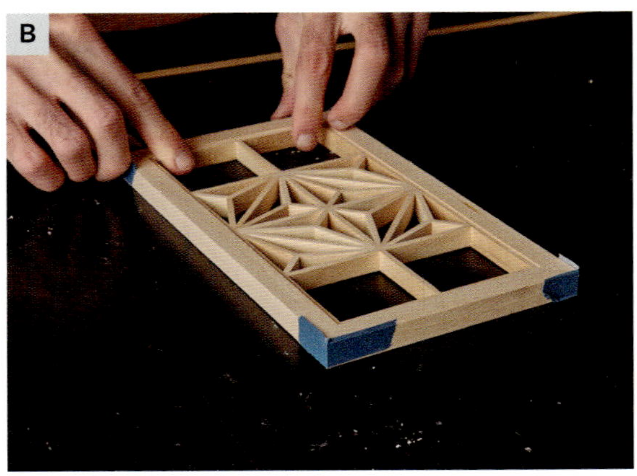

Frame the kumiko

1. Make four kumiko panels to the dimensions shown. Once complete, it's time to build the frame. Start with stock measuring ½ in x ½ in (12.7 mm x 12.7 mm) and for a more unified and simpler look, use the same wood species as the kumiko. Cut 45° miters and fit the pieces around the kumiko panels.

2. Apply glue to the panel edges, press the mitered frame pieces into place, and secure them with tape or clamps until dry (**A–B**).

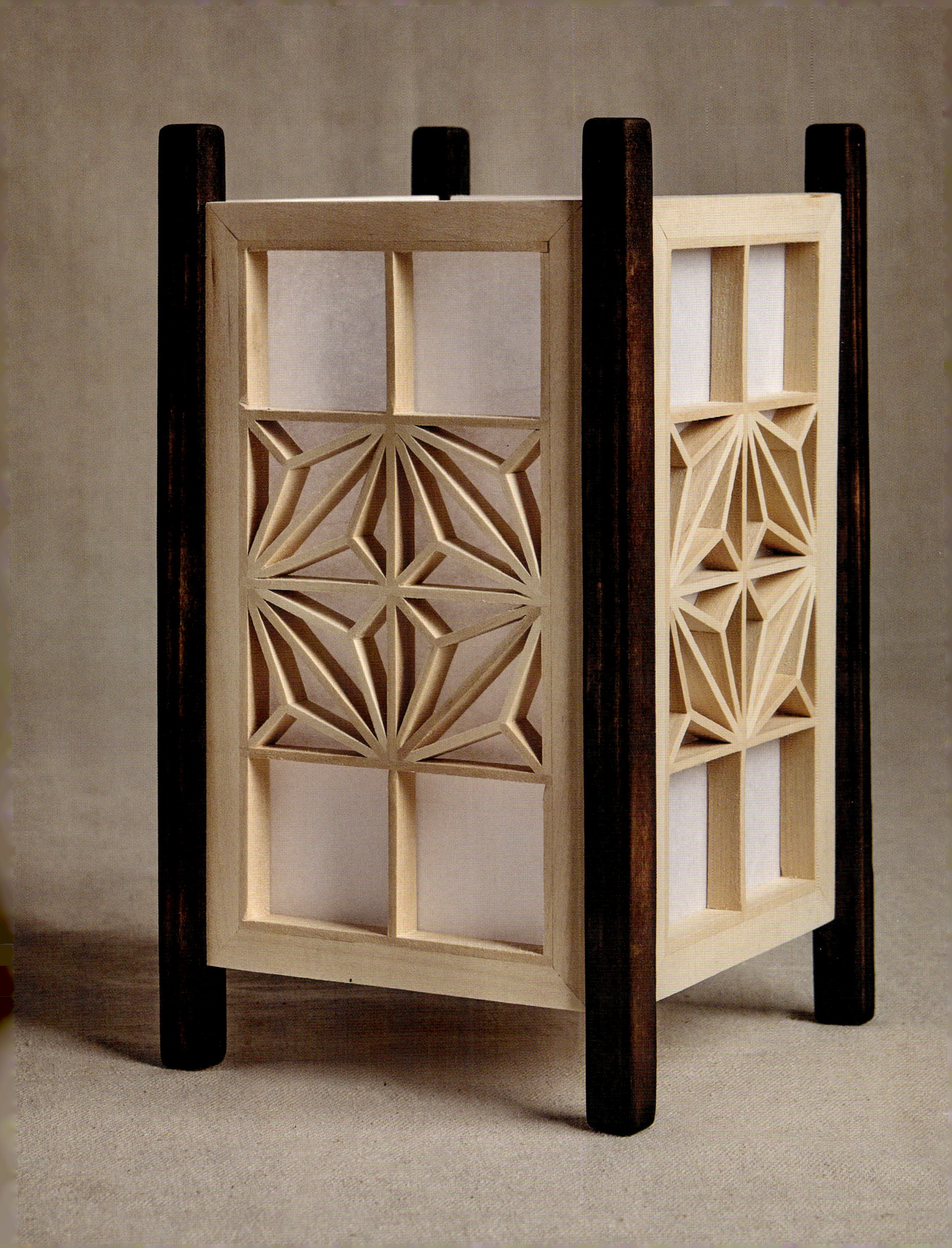

INVERTED ASA-NO-HA PATTERN FOR AN ANDON

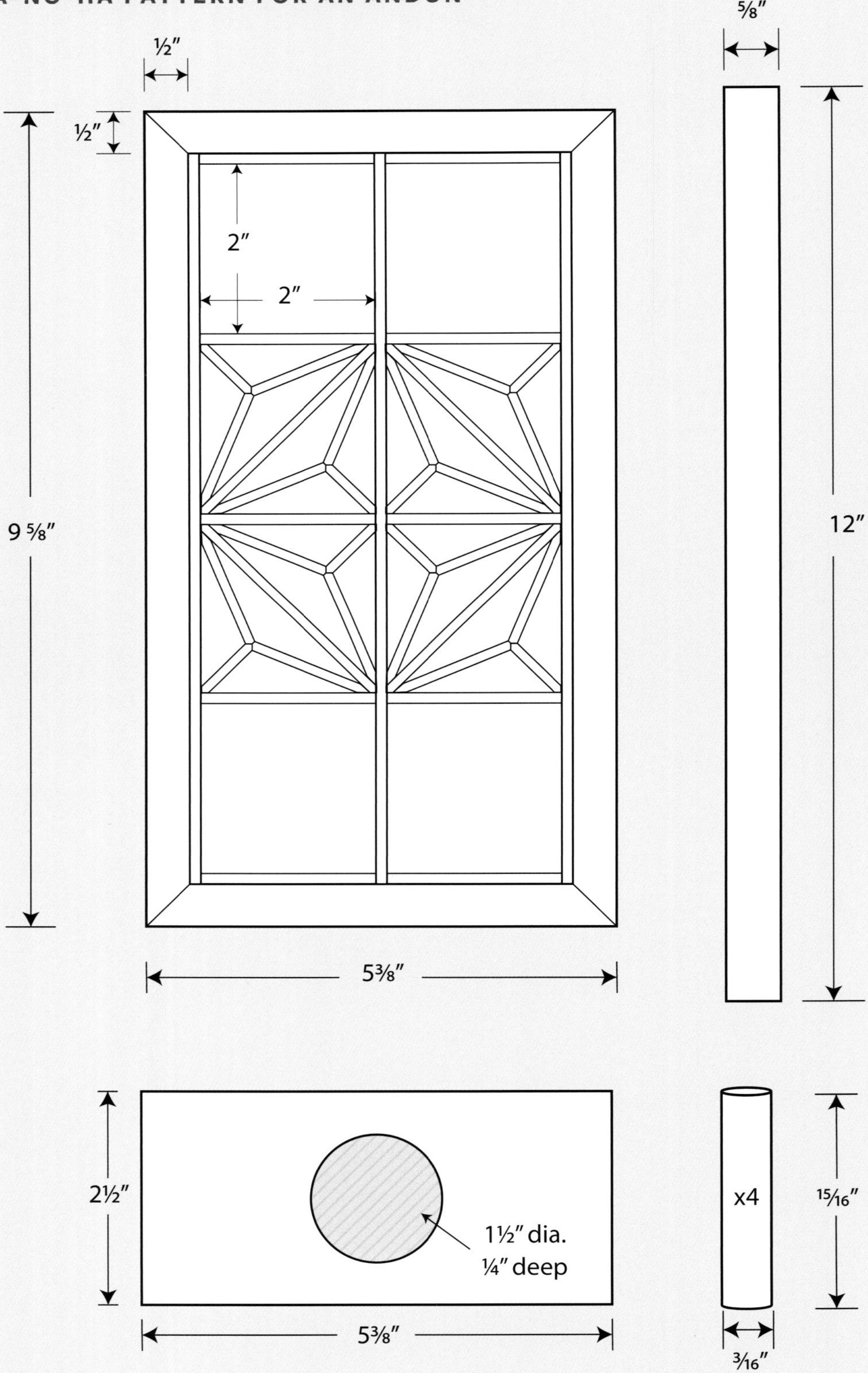

Making the legs

1. For the legs, use stock measuring ⅝ in x ⅝ in x 12 in (16 mm x 16 mm x 305 mm). A wood with minimal or no heavy grain patterns will give the best results when burning. In this example, poplar is used.

2. Add a subtle chamfer to both ends of each leg piece. Using a small block plane works well here (**A**). This will soften the edges and create a more polished, professional look. Ensure the chamfer is consistent on all pieces.

3. Now it's time to burn the legs. Use a torch to carefully scorch the pieces, aiming to change the color without causing them to catch fire (**B**–**C**). Use even, consistent strokes for the best results, ensuring you burn all four sides and the ends of each leg.

   Safety tip: Always wear protective clothing and work on a non-flammable surface when using a torch. You should also keep a fire extinguisher or water source nearby for safety.

After burning, the pieces may still be hot, so handle them carefully or allow them to cool before proceeding. The soot created during the burning process can stain the kumiko panels, so be sure to wipe it off with a rag.

If you prefer not to burn the wood, you can use a darker species like walnut or mahogany instead. This will create a similar visual effect, though burned wood offers a more traditional touch, referencing yakisugi (焼杉), a Japanese technique historically used to preserve wood through controlled charring.

A

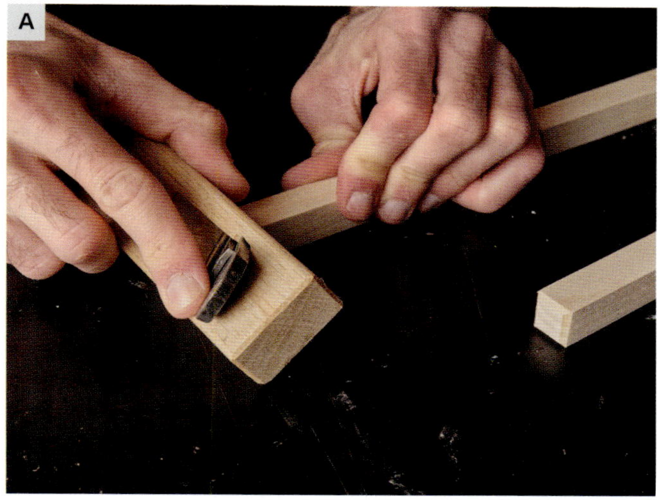

B

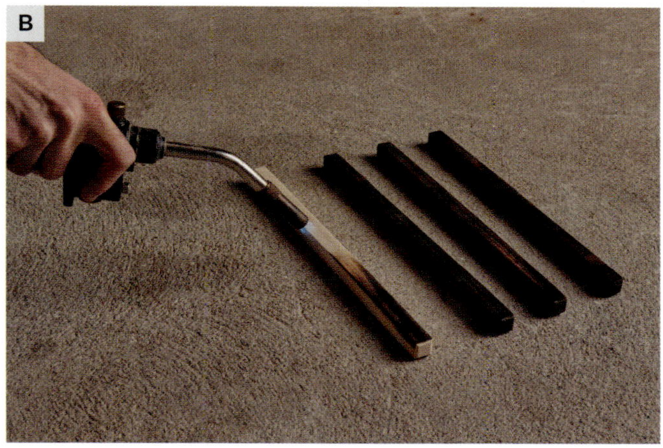

C

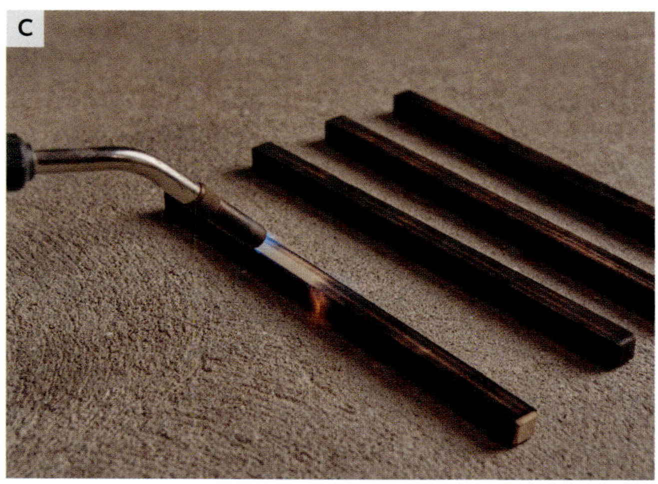

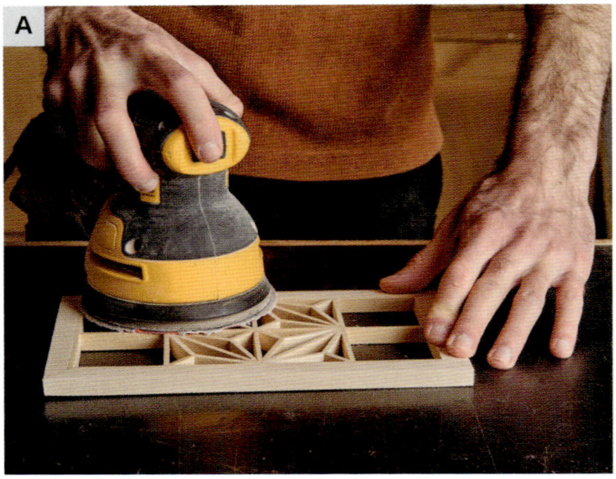

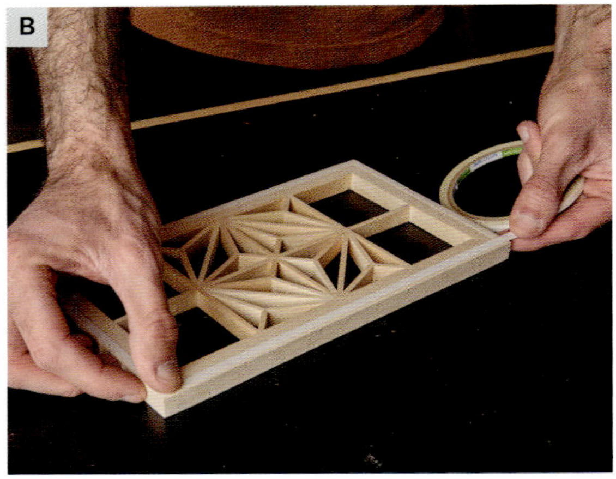

Sand and apply shoji paper

1. Once the glue on the kumiko panels has fully dried, sand them smooth with fine-grit sandpaper, such as 220 grit (**A**). Ensure the panels and frames are flush with each other.

2. Apply shoji paper to the back of each panel. For detailed instructions, refer to pages 93 to 94. Traditionally, shoji paper is applied only to the kumiko and not the surrounding frame. However, since the inside of these panels will be visible, extend the paper to the outer edges of the frame to maintain a clean, finished appearance (**B–D**).

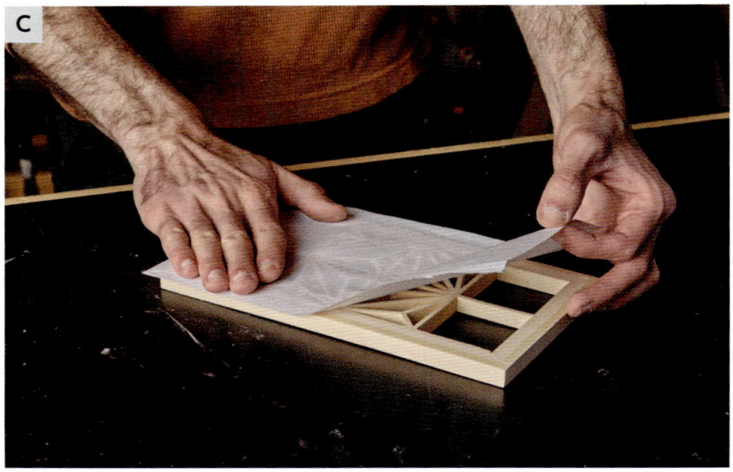

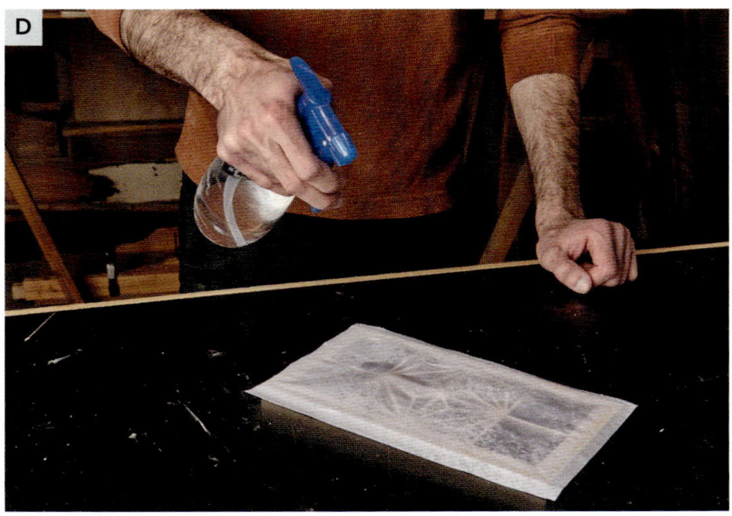

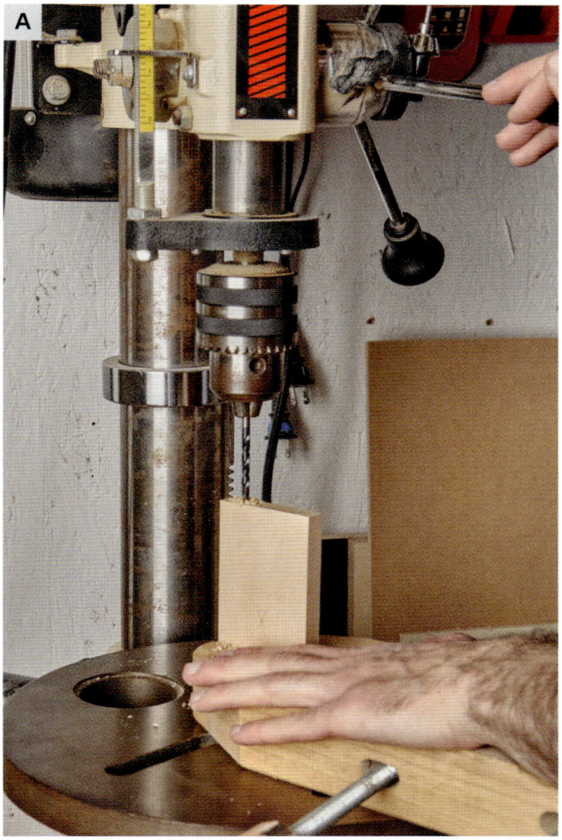

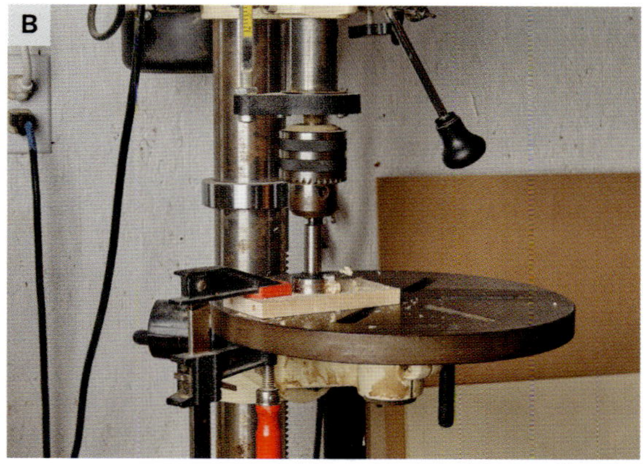

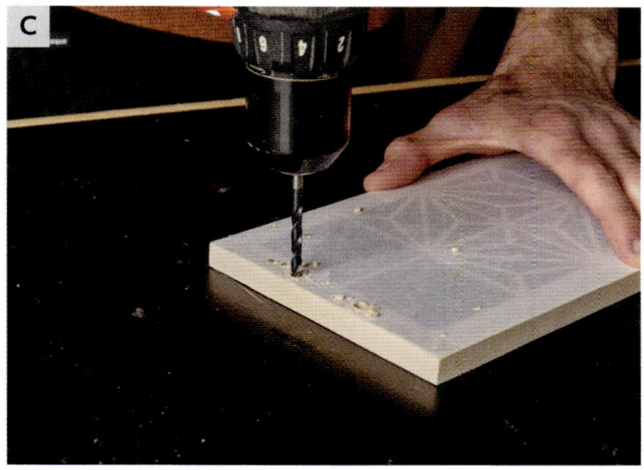

The tealight bracket

1. Cut a piece of wood for the tealight holder, measuring $2\frac{1}{2}$ in x $5\frac{3}{8}$ in x $\frac{1}{2}$ in (64 mm x 137 mm x 12.7 mm).

2. This piece will be attached to the kumiko panels using four $\frac{3}{16}$ in (4.8 mm) dowels. Measure and mark the dowel locations on both ends, placing them $\frac{1}{2}$ in (12.7 mm) in from each edge and centered with the width of the piece. Use a $\frac{3}{16}$ in (4.8 mm) drill bit to drill these holes perpendicular to the end grain to a depth of $\frac{3}{4}$ in (19.1 mm) (**A**).

3. Next, drill a $1\frac{1}{2}$ in (38 mm) hole, $\frac{1}{4}$ in (6.4 mm) deep, in the center of the piece for the LED tealight (**B**).

4. Transfer the dowel hole locations to two of the kumiko panels, positioning them so the tealight piece sits flush with the bottom of the frames and is centered across their width. Drill the holes to a depth of $\frac{1}{4}$ in (6.4 mm) (**C**).

5. Cut four sections of $\frac{3}{16}$ in (4.8 mm) dowels, each $\frac{15}{16}$ in (23.8 mm) long. This length is slightly shorter than the combined depth of the holes, allowing the pieces to sit flush and leaving space for air to compress within the joint.

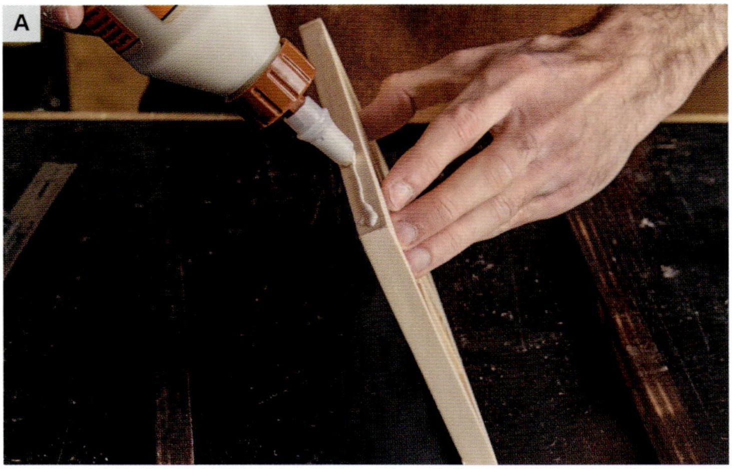

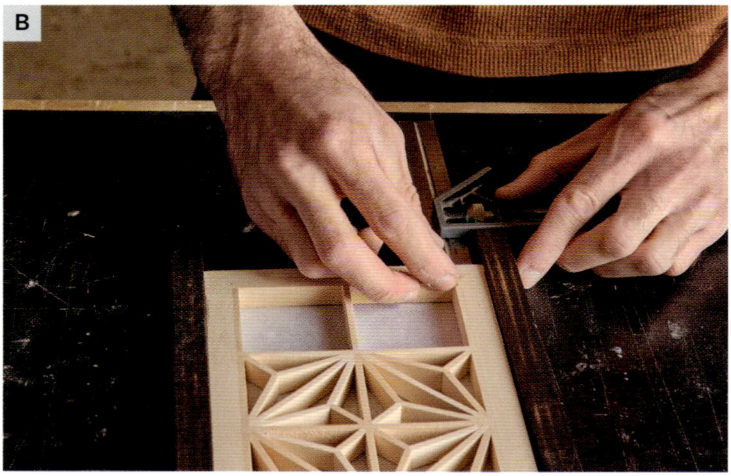

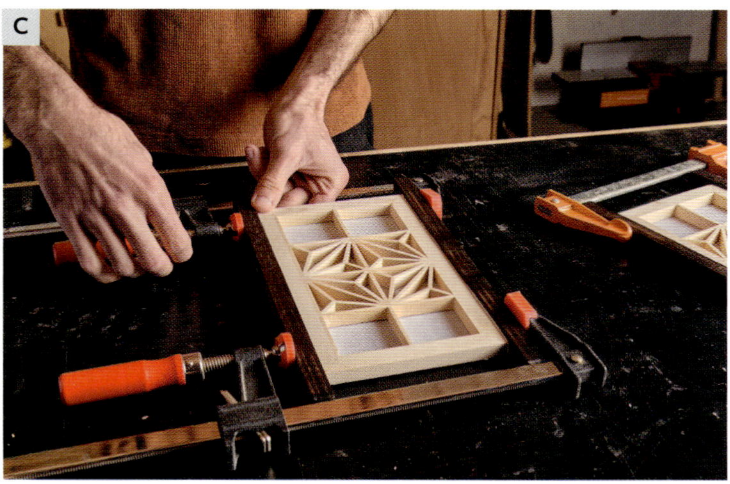

Assemble the lamp

1. Glue one leg to each side of the two kumiko panels that have the holes drilled from the previous step (**A**). Make sure the panels are centered vertically on the legs and flush with the back, so the legs extend ⅛ in (3.2 mm) proud from the front of the kumiko panels (**B–C**).

2. Once the initial glue-up is dry, attach the remaining sides and the tealight holder. Since aligning all the parts at once can be tricky, start by gluing the tealight holder in place using the dowels (**D–H**). Then glue and clamp one side panel, followed by the opposite side (**I**). Make sure each panel is centered vertically on the legs and sits flush with its back edge, meeting the initial panels at the inside corners.

3. After the glue has dried, the lamp construction is complete. Adding a finish to the legs is a great way to deepen their color. Mask off the kumiko panels to protect them from any unwanted finish, then apply the finish of your choice to the legs. Insert an LED tealight into the recessed hole and enjoy.

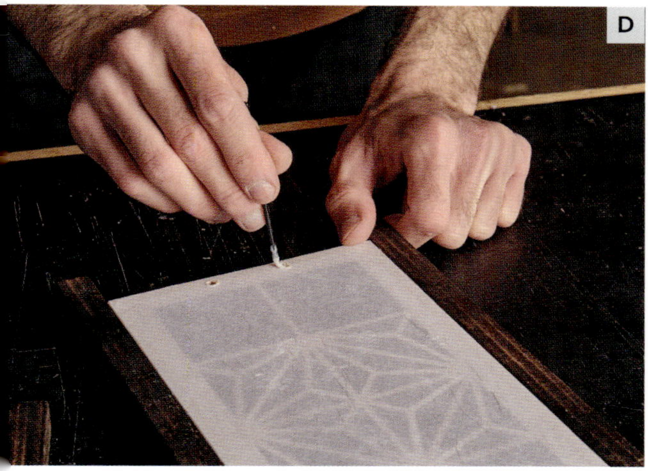
D

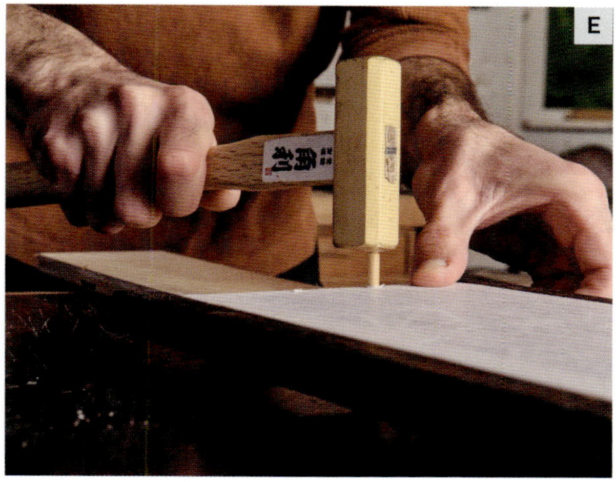
E

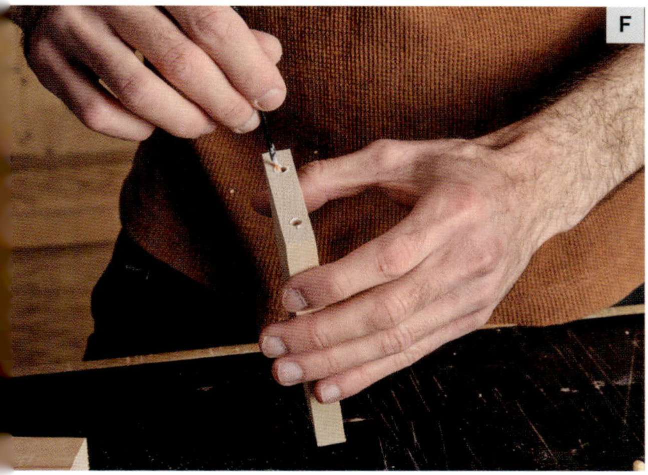
F

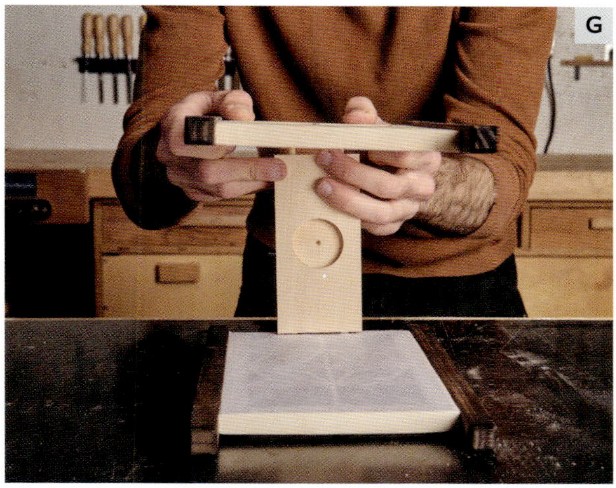
G

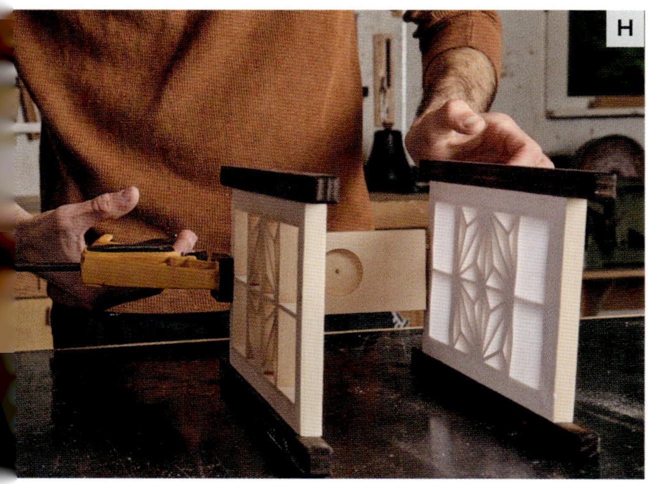
H

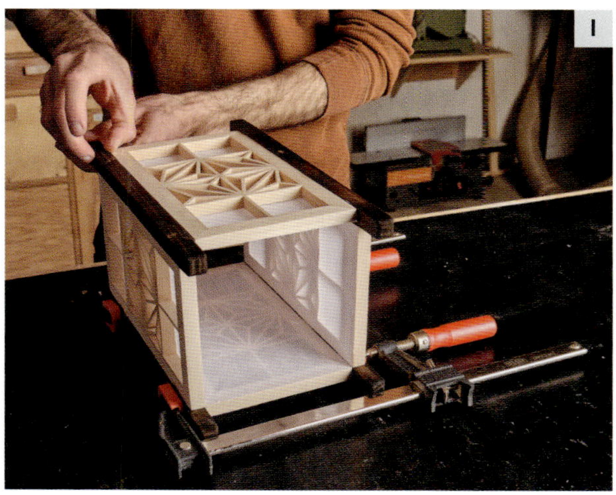
I

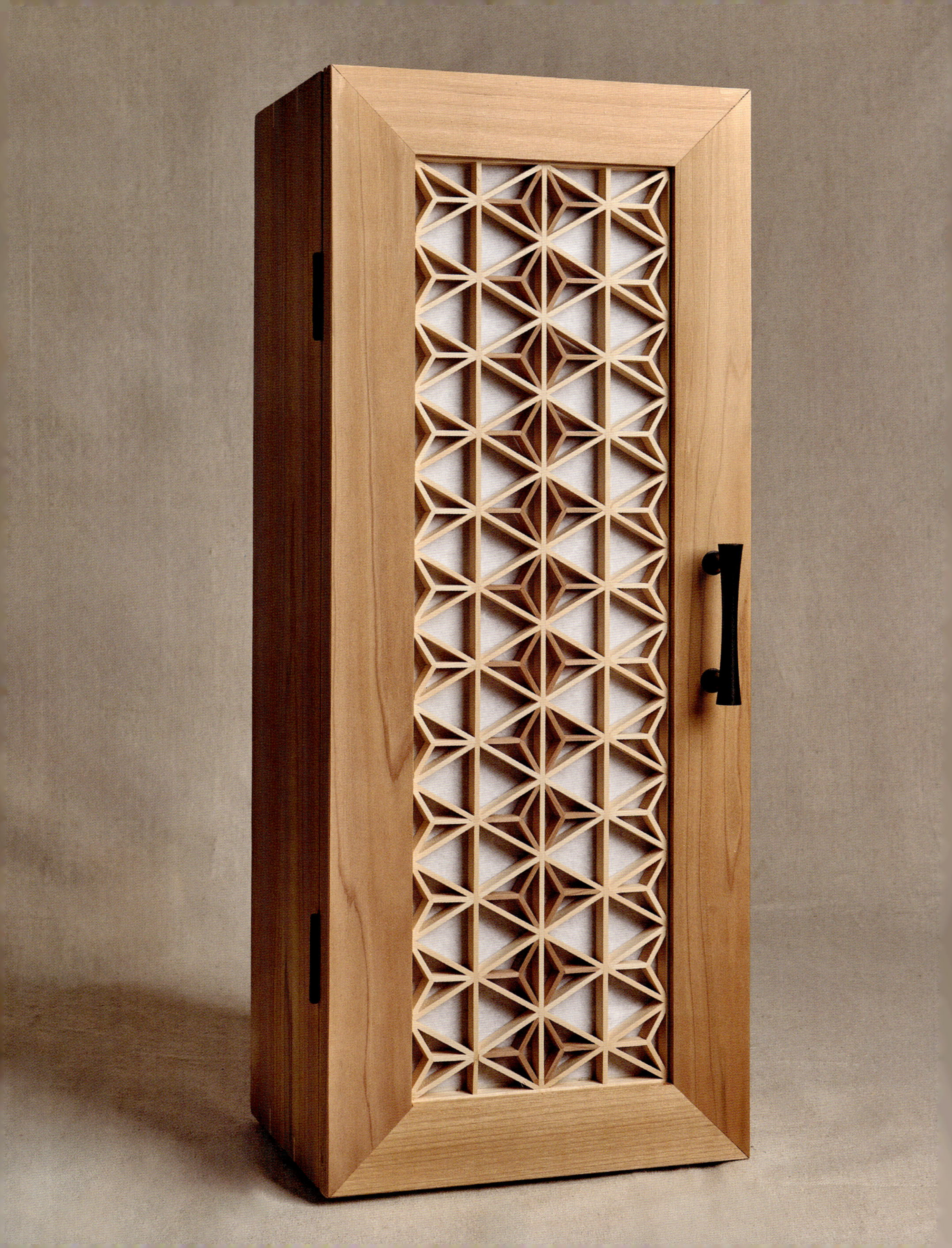

Project 6

Cabinet with Kumiko Door

This kumiko cabinet is designed to be both approachable and practical. Its clean lines and modest size make it an ideal project for a range of skill levels, while the kumiko panel in the door offers a moment of artistry that elevates the entire piece. Inside, adjustable shelves provide flexibility for storage or display, making it useful in almost any room.

The cabinet can be wall-mounted or placed on a counter with added feet for a more grounded presence. Construction is kept intentionally simple, including a plywood back panel and mitered joinery, so your focus remains on integrating kumiko into the structure, rather than getting caught up in complex joinery.

This panel is set on a 1¾ in (44 mm) grid, with bands of asa-no-ha running vertically along the edges and through the center. Varying the wood species in these sections can draw the eye to different areas and introduce subtle layers of contrast. When these choices echo the woods used in the cabinet carcass, the panel feels intentional and unified, tying the kumiko work seamlessly into the whole piece.

CABINET WITH ASA-NO-HA DOOR PANEL

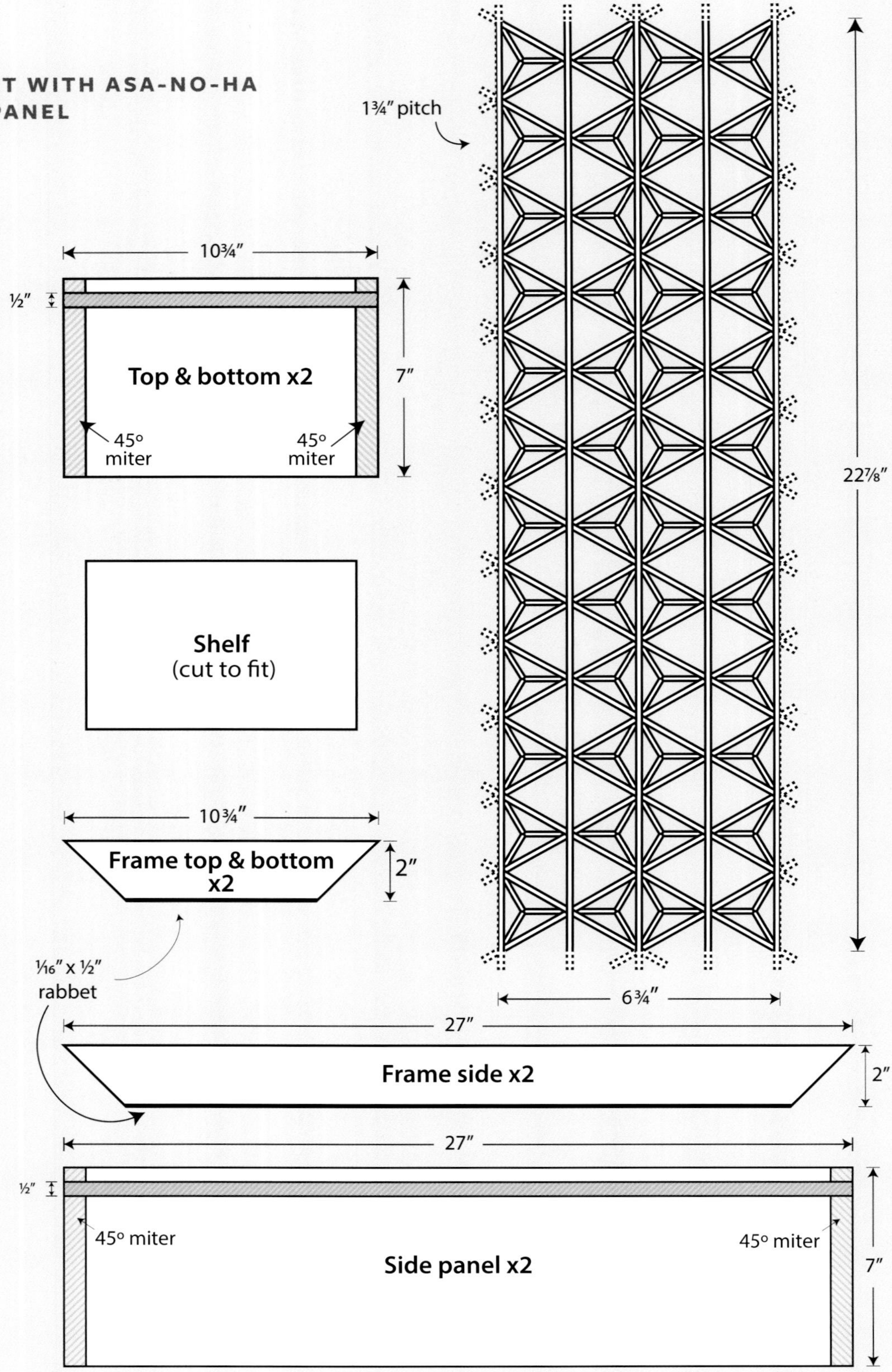

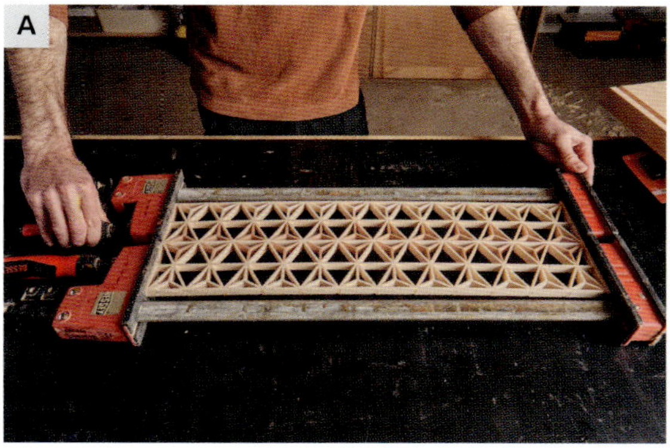
A

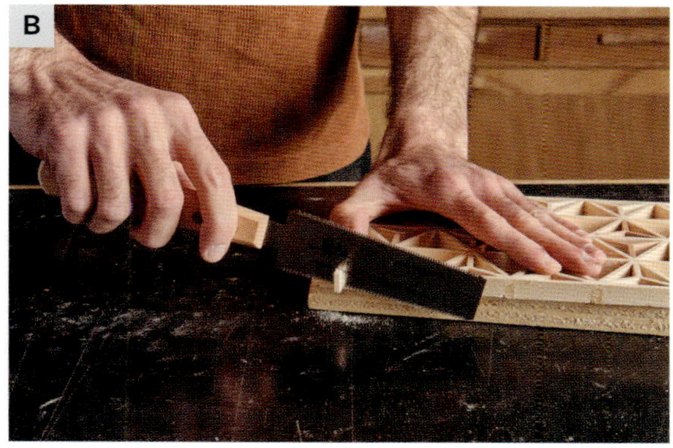
B

Prepare the kumiko

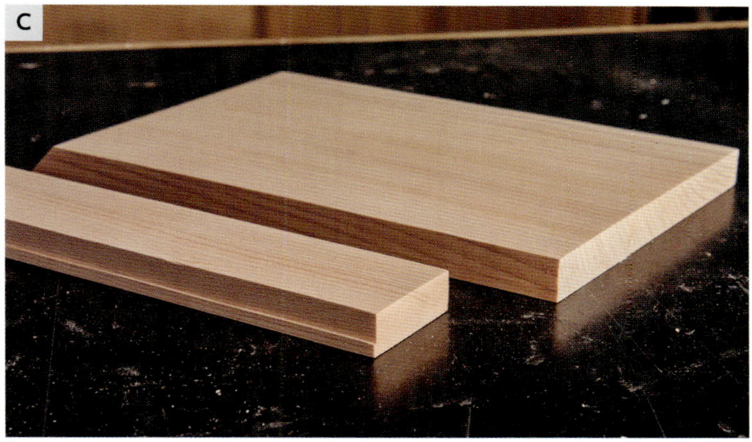
C

1. After completing the kumiko panel, cut it to its final size and glue a $\frac{1}{8}$ in (3.2 mm) strip along the ends to cap the panel and give it a more polished, finished appearance (**A**).

2. Trim off excess material (**B**).

Cutting the parts and joinery

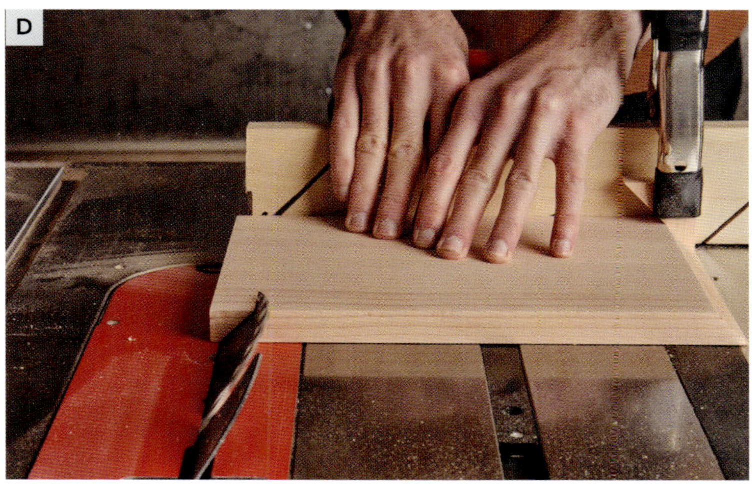
D

1. Begin by cutting a $\frac{1}{16}$ in x $\frac{1}{2}$ in (1.6 mm x 12.7 mm) rabbet into the frame parts. This will provide a ledge for the kumiko panel to sit in. Next, cut the carcass panels to width, leaving them and the frame pieces slightly oversized in length (**C**).

2. This cabinet is designed with an overlay door, meaning the final exterior dimensions of the cabinet and the door will match. To ensure consistent sizing, use a stop block when cutting the frame and carcass pieces to length (**D**). This guarantees that all components are equal in length.

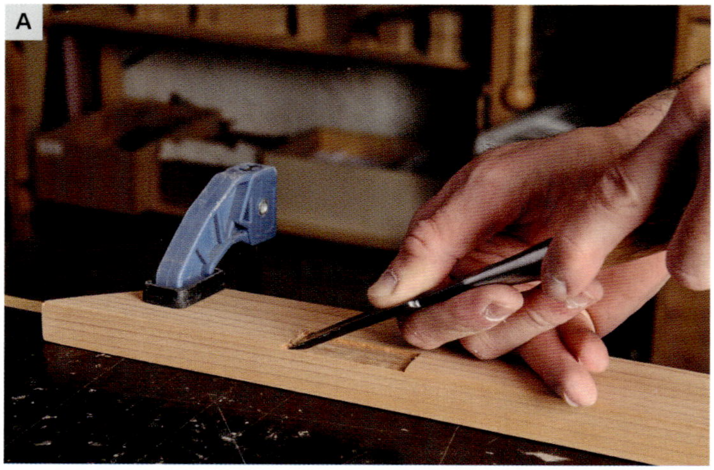

Mortise for hinges

Depending on the type of hinge you choose, it may be easier to cut the mortises before assembling the door frame and cabinet carcass.

1. This design also accommodates concealed (European-style) hinges, which often come with soft-close options that add a refined touch. For a more traditional or minimalist aesthetic, standard mortise hinges can be used (**A**).

2. When cutting the mortises, be sure to orient the joinery correctly on both the frame and the corresponding side panel so the door opens in the desired direction (**B**).

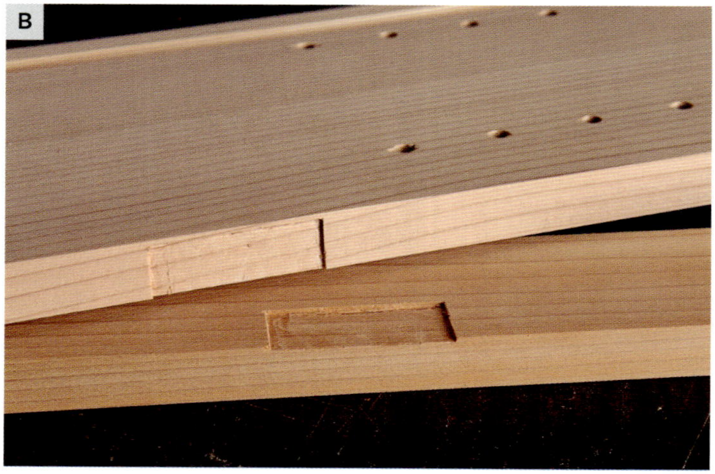

Glue the frame

Glue the frame together (**C**). Once the glue has dried, reinforce the miter joints with splines for added strength and a decorative detail (**D**).

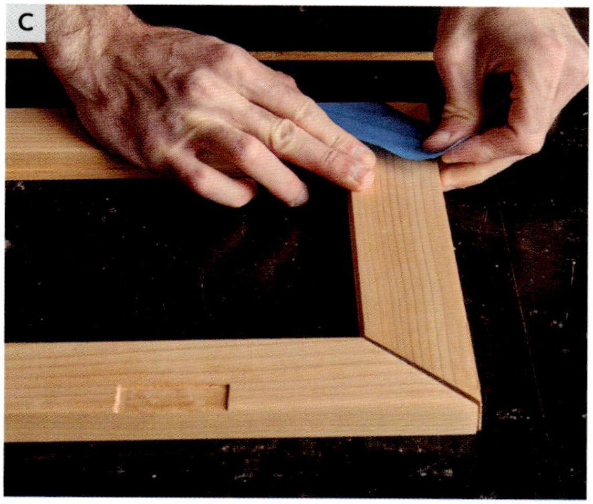

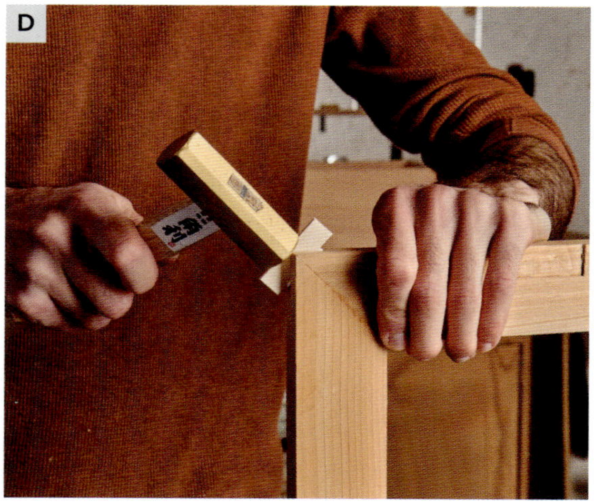

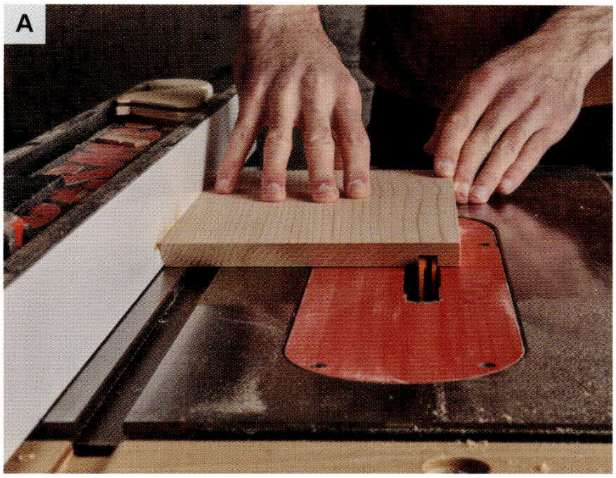

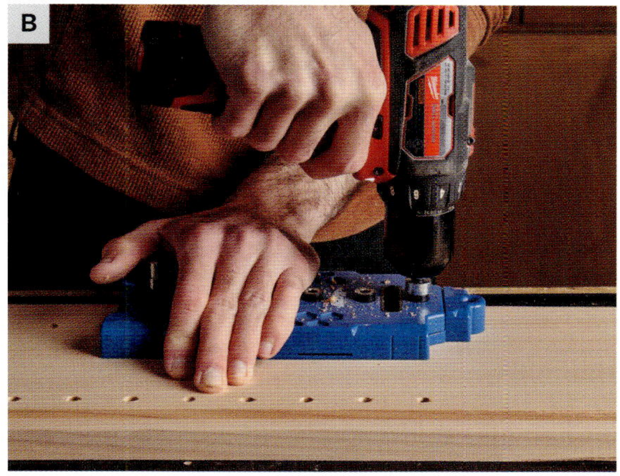

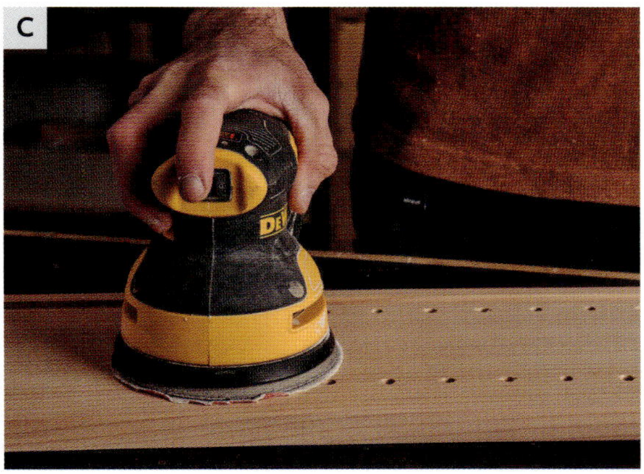

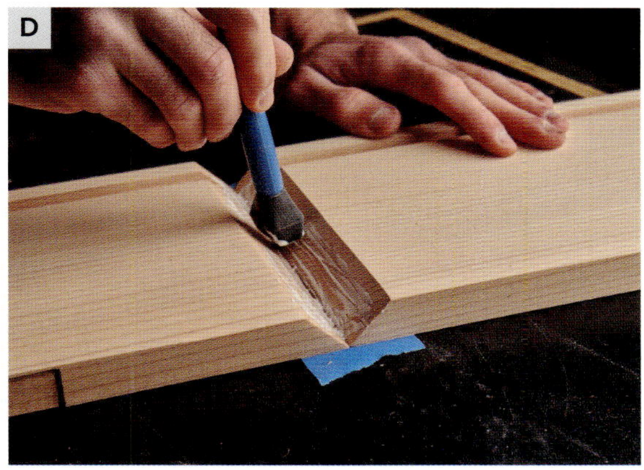

The cabinet carcass

1. Cut a groove into the inside face of each carcass panel to accommodate the back panel (**A**); ½ in (12.7 mm) plywood works well here — it's stable, lightweight, and won't expand or contract with seasonal changes.

2. Drill shelf pin holes on the inside of the cabinet. You can measure and mark these individually or use a shelf pin jig for greater speed and accuracy (**B**).

Glue the carcass

1. Before gluing the carcass together, now is the ideal time to sand the interior surfaces of the panels (**C**).

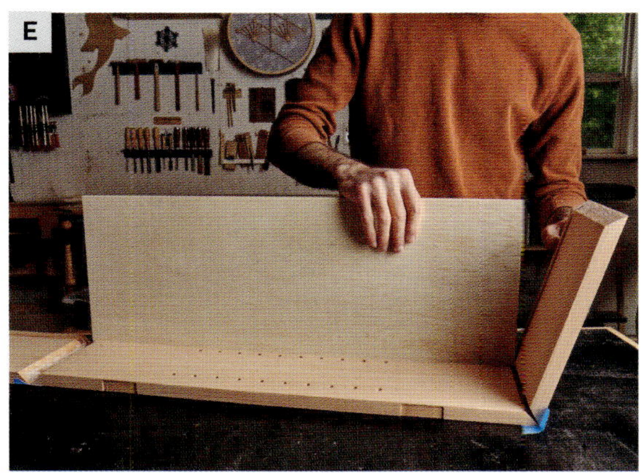

2. Apply glue to the miter joints (**D**), insert the back panel (**E–F**), clamp, and let the carcass dry.

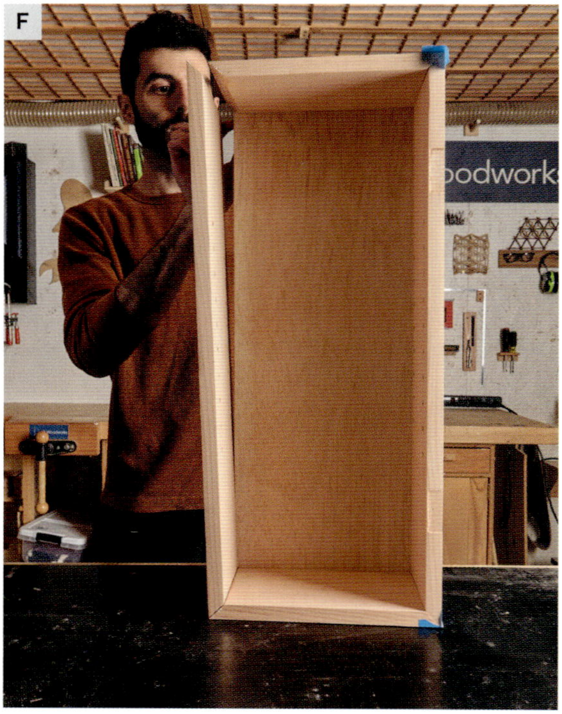

F

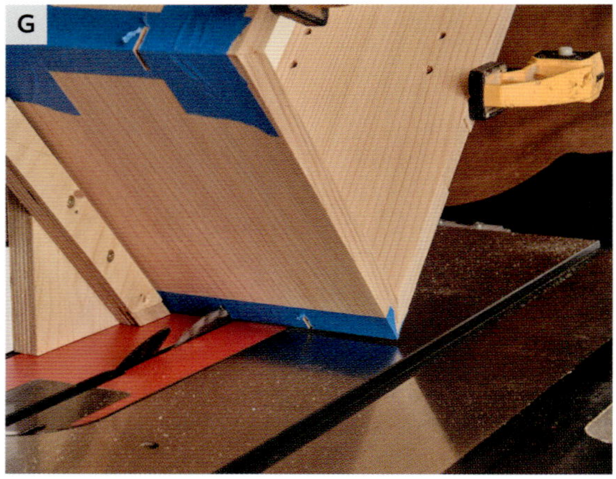

G

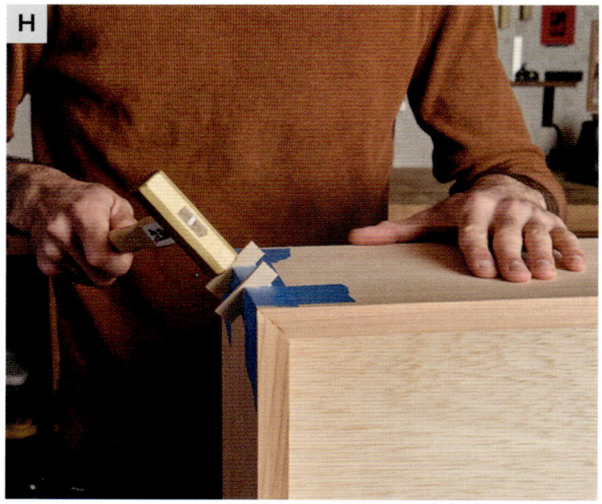

H

3. Once dry, mark and cut slots for splines at each corner (**G**). Two splines per corner, made from a contrasting wood, add strength and visual interest. Position them 2¼ in (57 mm) in from the front and back edge and at a depth of ½ in (12.7 mm).

4. Glue the splines in place, allow them to dry, and then flush cut them (**H**).

Make the shelf

Take accurate measurements for the interior shelf. Measure the inside width and depth of the cabinet, then cut a shelf panel slightly undersized in both dimensions — just enough to allow easy insertion and ensure the shelf doesn't interfere with the door's ability to close properly. Use ½ in (12.7 mm) thick material for the shelf (**I**). This is a good balance between maximizing interior space and maintaining structural strength.

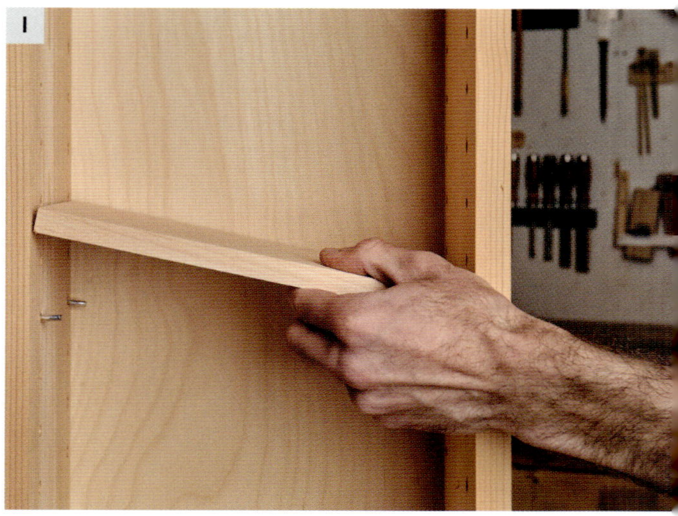

I

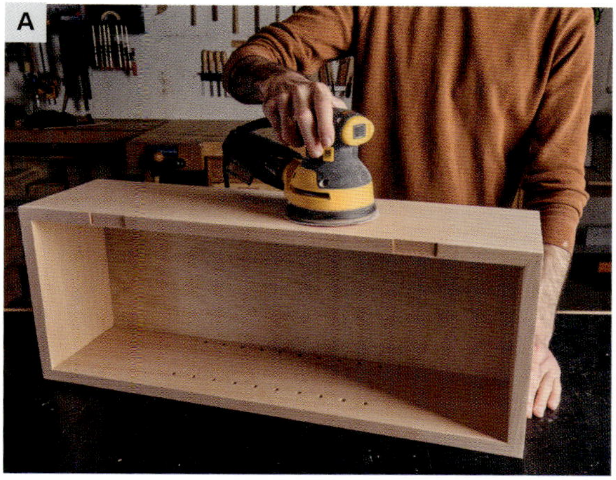

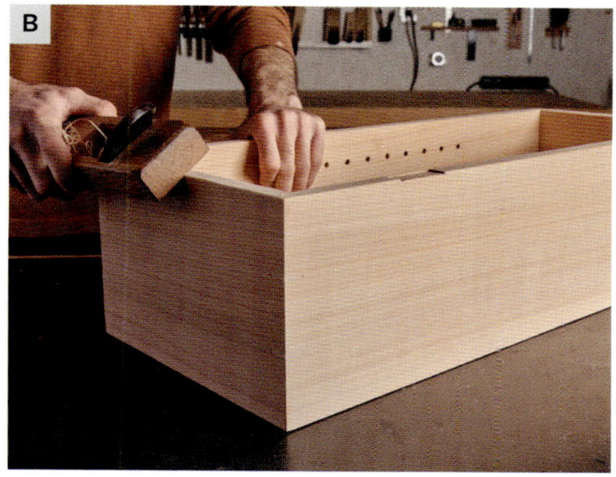

Finishing touches

1. Sand all surfaces smooth (**A**) and consider adding a small chamfer to the outer edges of both the carcass and the door frame (**B**). This subtle detail creates a clean shadow line and can help mask minor imperfections where the door and carcass meet.

2. Now is the time to apply finish to both the cabinet and the door frame. Whether you opt for oil, lacquer, or another wood finish, apply it evenly and allow it to fully dry before final assembly. You can also opt to leave it unfinished to allow the cabinet to patina over time.

3. Choose a handle or knob that complements the overall aesthetic of the cabinet. You can install it centered on the frame or closer to a corner (**C–D**). Corner placement is often more ergonomic if the cabinet will be wall-mounted.

4. If you would like to include a shoji paper backing, now is the time to apply it to the back of the kumiko panel (see pages 93 to 94). Shoji paper not only adds a soft look to the kumiko but also protects items inside the cabinet from dust and gives the piece a more traditional feel.

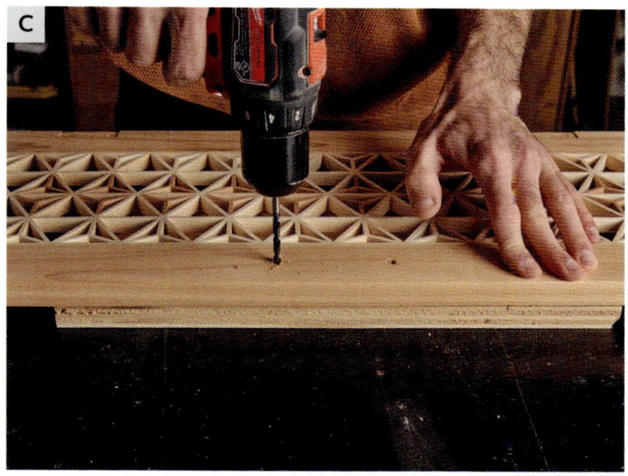

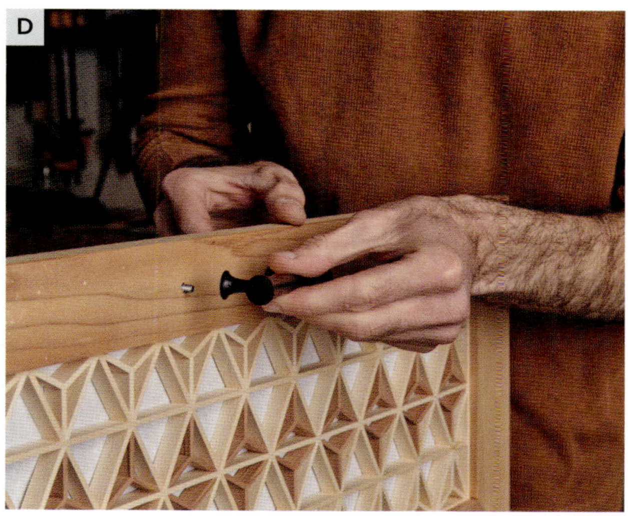

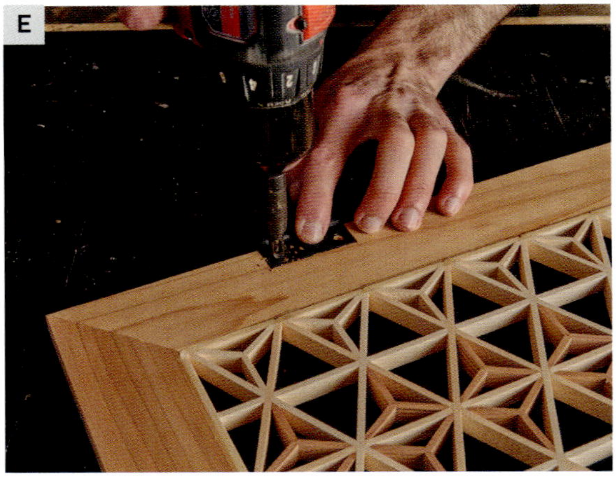

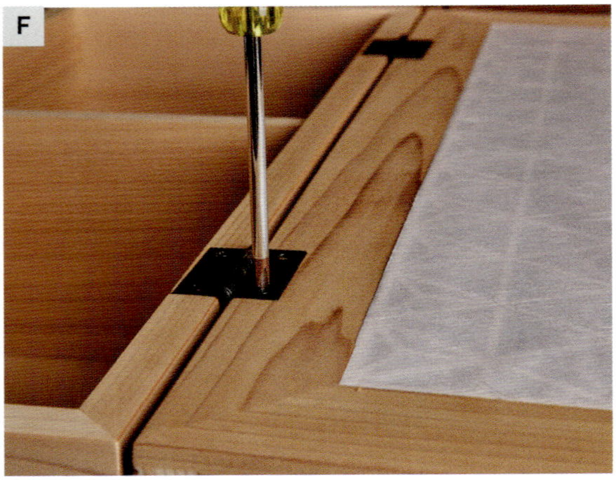

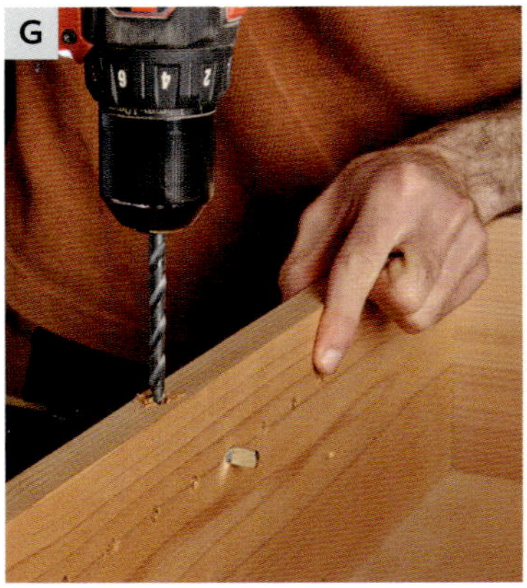

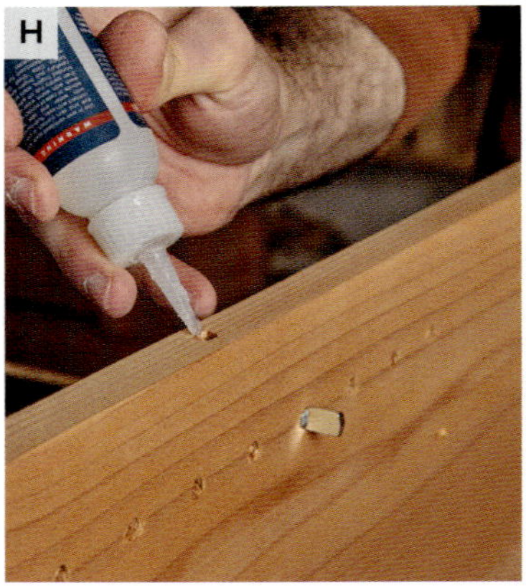

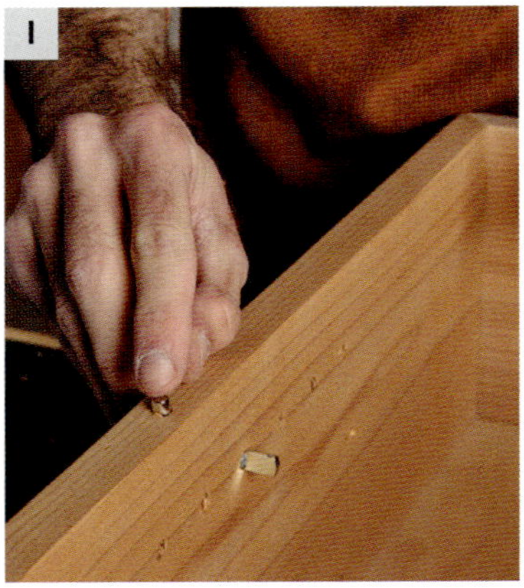

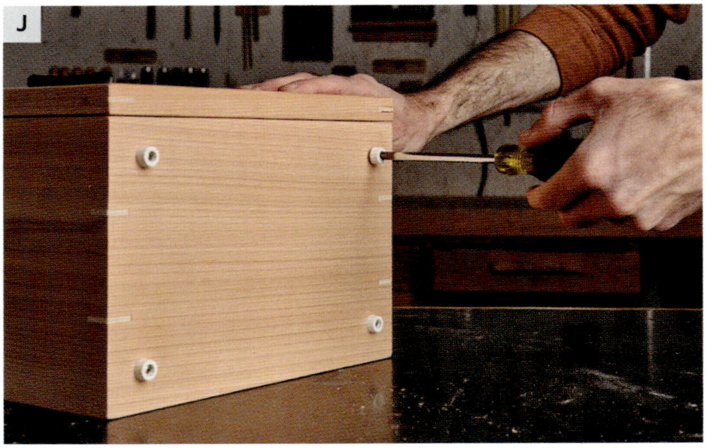

5. Install the hinges and secure the door to the cabinet (**E–F**). Using a self-centering drill bit ensures the screw holes are in the correct locations.

6. If using mortise hinges, consider adding a magnet catch to help keep the door closed (**G–I**).

7. If you plan to hang the cabinet, install a French cleat to the back panel near the top. Add a small block near the bottom edge to act as a spacer, helping the cabinet sit flat against the wall. If the cabinet will rest on a countertop, consider adding small wooden or rubber feet to the bottom (**J**). This raises the cabinet slightly, preventing the door from rubbing against the counter surface when opening or closing.

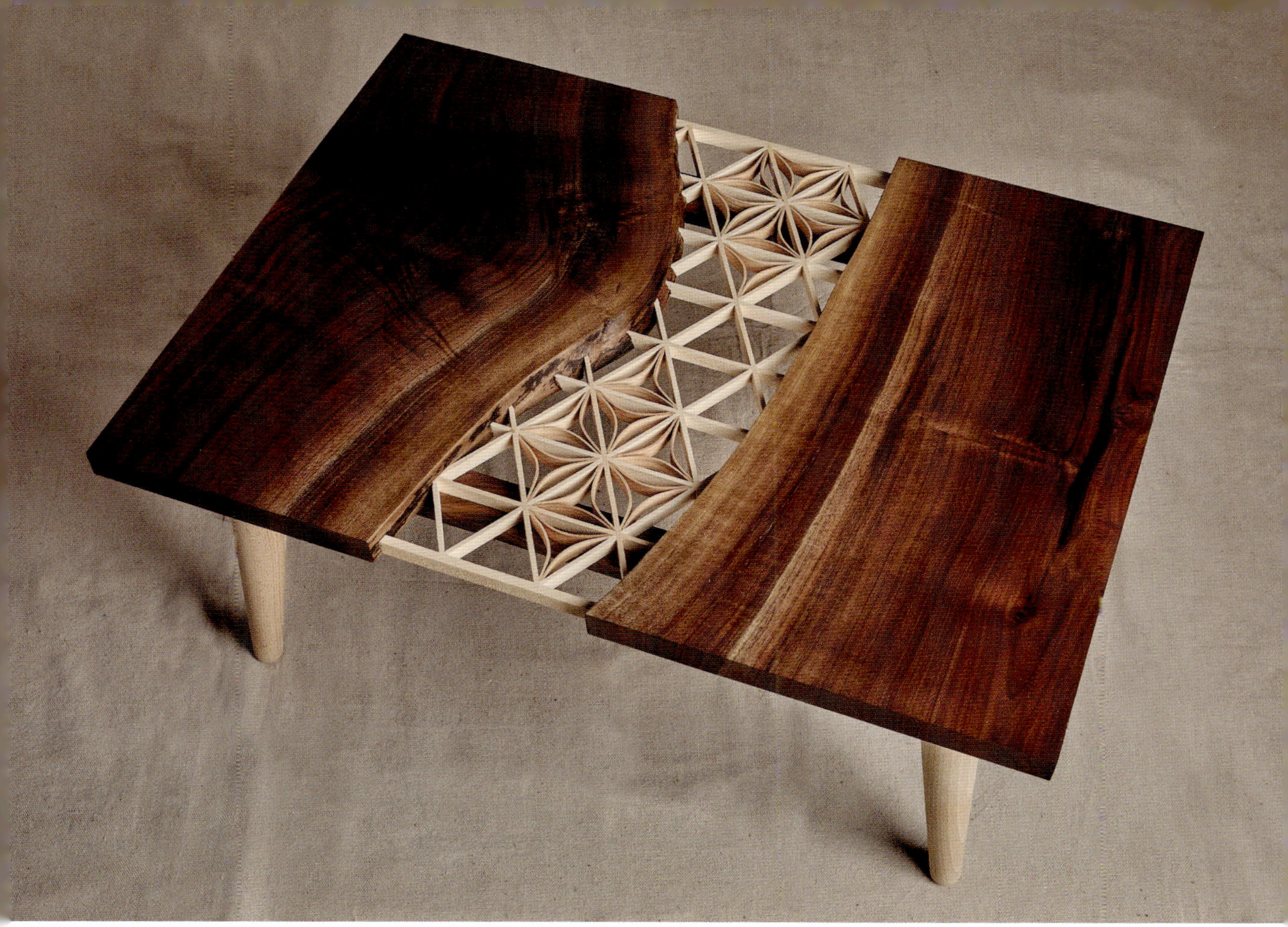

Project 7

Kawa Table

In Japanese, kawa (川) means river. This table draws from that imagery. The kumiko flows through the center like a winding stream, framed by the live edges of a hardwood slab. It's a reimagining of the popular epoxy or glass-style river table, but instead of using synthetic materials, this design celebrates the warmth and intricacy of wood.

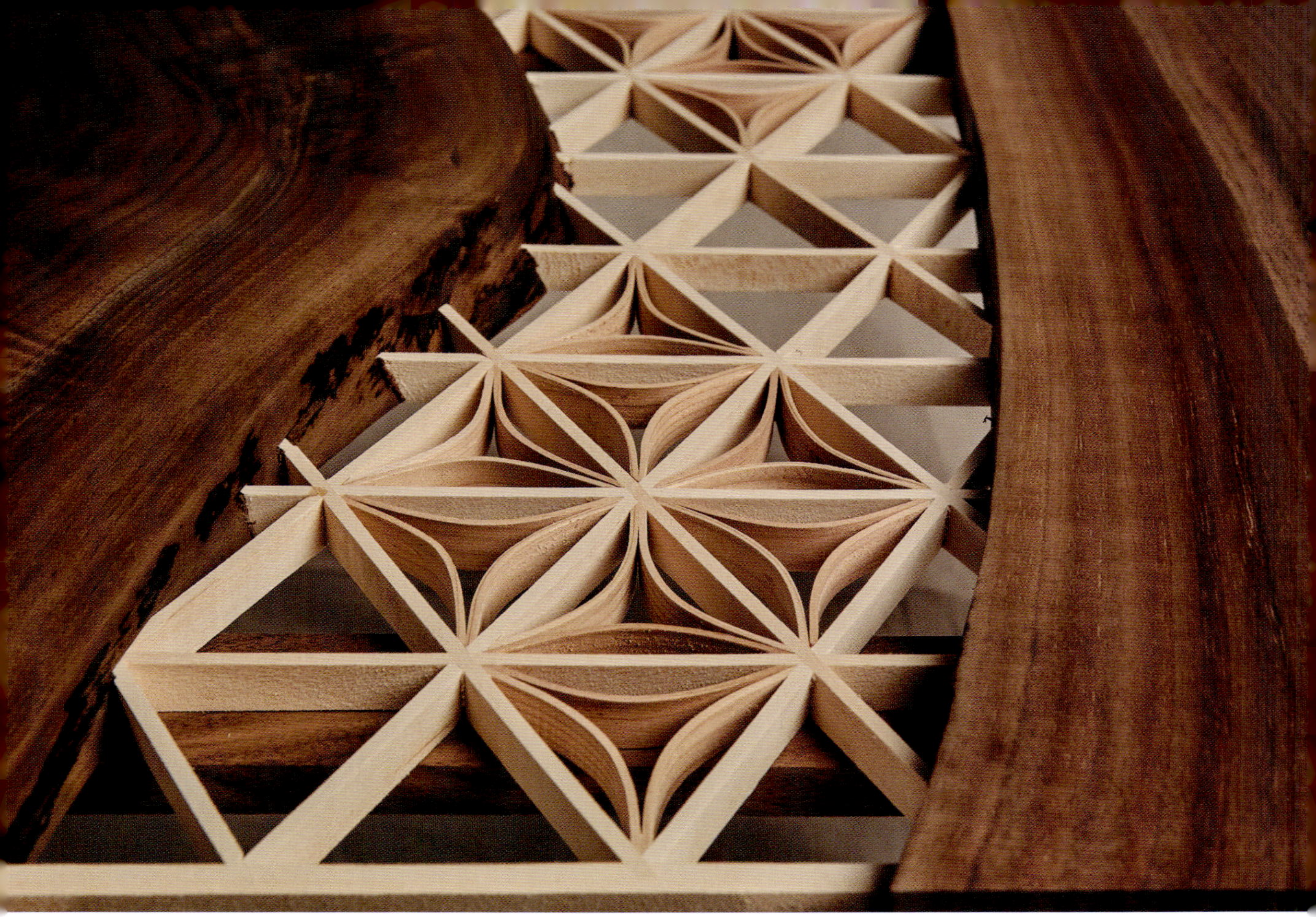

The geometric precision of the kumiko contrasts beautifully with the organic movement of the slab. The irregular edges, natural voids, and unique grain patterns in a live edge slab embody the spirit of wabi-sabi (侘び寂び), the Japanese philosophy that embraces imperfection, impermanence, and the quiet beauty of natural materials. Each table is inherently one of a kind. If you prefer a more minimalist look, square, milled boards can be used instead of live edges. The construction remains the same, but the result feels more refined and modern. Either way, this project invites you to explore the balance between structure and nature, precision and irregularity.

To build this table, start with a slab that's at least ¼ in (6.4 mm) thicker than the kumiko panel. This allows the kumiko to sit properly within the slabs and ensures a visually satisfying reveal on top. Because every slab is different, varying in shape, thickness, and character, precise measurements are intentionally left out of this chapter. This project is meant to adapt to the unique materials you select, encouraging a more intuitive approach to the build.

Cutting the slab

1. Start by finding the center of your slab and drawing a line down its length (**A**). This can be tricky with irregular shapes but do your best to find a balanced center. It may not be square to the ends.

2. Using a track saw or a circular saw with a straight edge, cut along this centerline to split the slab in two (**B**).

3. Next, decide on the orientation of the two halves. Flip them, rotate them, and adjust the center spacing between them to find a layout you like (**C**).

4. Once you're happy with the arrangement, secure the slabs together using double-sided tape and strips of plywood across the top to hold them in place (**D**). With the slabs fixed, trim the ends square to the outer edges.

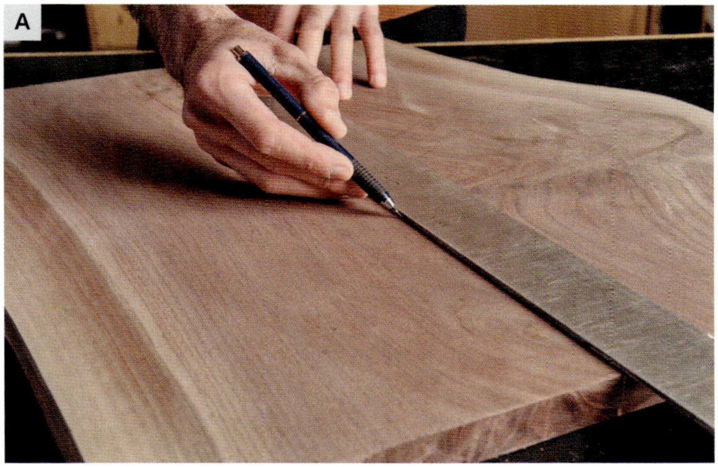

A

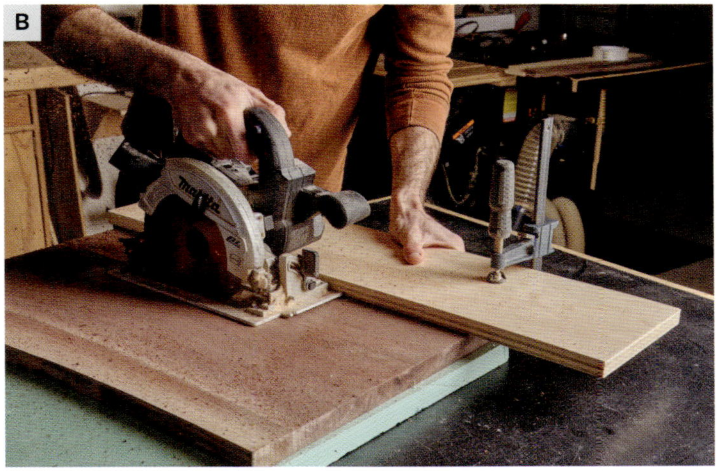

B

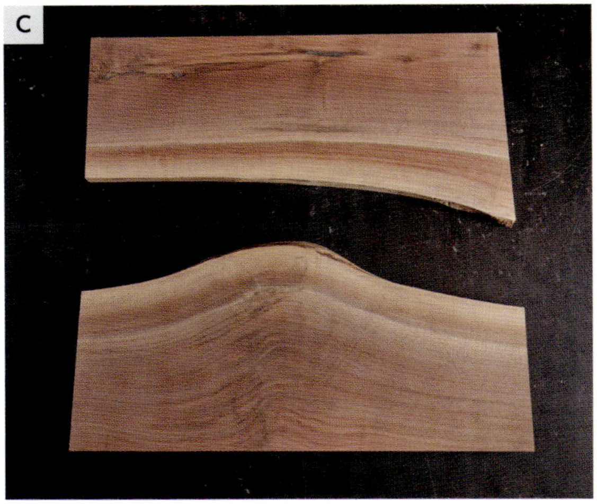

C

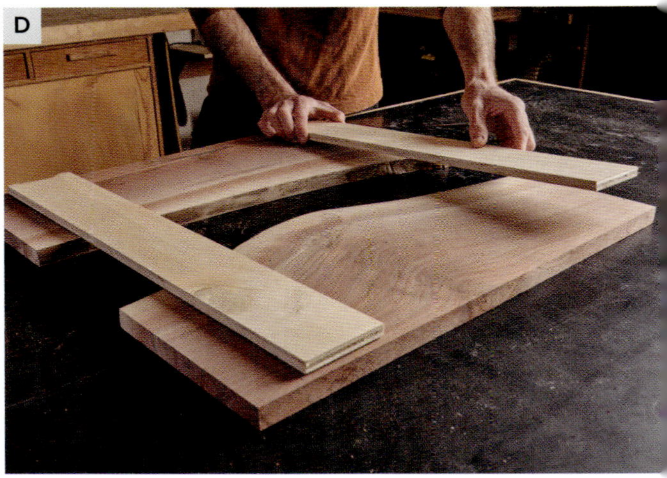

D

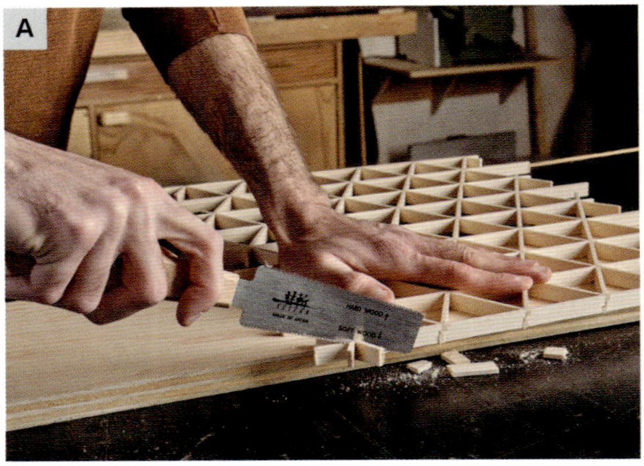

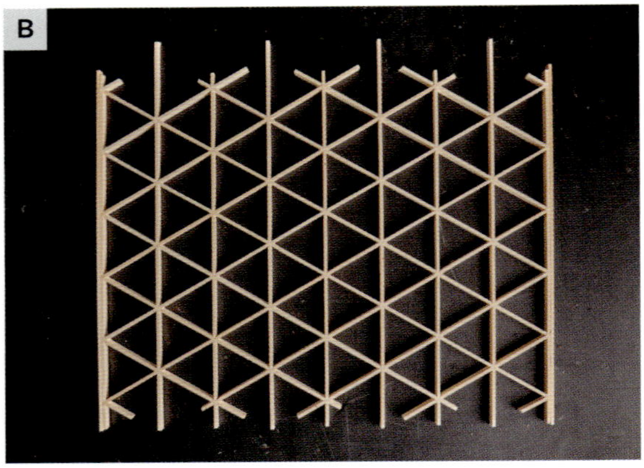

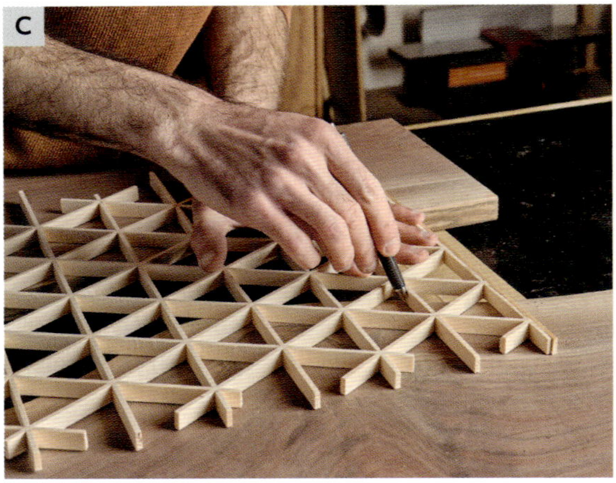

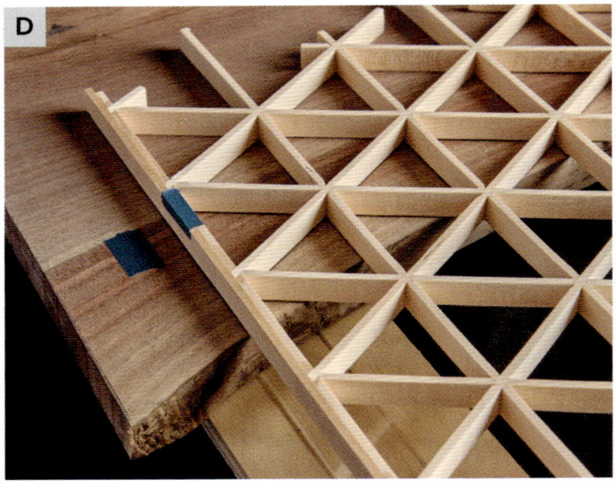

Make and inlay the kumiko grid

1. With the width of the "river" established, make a kumiko grid that's roughly 5 in (127 mm) wider than the opening and 2 in (51 mm) shorter than the total slab length. This gives you flexibility when positioning it later. Use a pitch of your choosing — 2¼ in to 3 in (57 mm to 76 mm) is a great option. Glue the kumiko grid together, but don't add the infill pattern just yet. Trim off the tabs on the ends of the kumiko panel (**A**).

2. Glue on ⅛ in (3.2 mm) strips to cap the ends (**B**). These strips hide the exposed joinery and give the panel a more substantial appearance. Thicker strips can be used on larger tables to achieve a balanced appearance.

3. Place the finished kumiko panel face-down on the underside of the slabs and adjust it until you find the ideal placement. Secure it temporarily with tape or a weight, then trace the kumiko onto the slab (**C**). It doesn't all need to be marked, about 2 in to 3 in (51 mm to 76 mm) in from the live edge of each slab is enough.

4. Before removing the panel, mark its orientation. Place tape on one corner of the kumiko grid and slab to make reassembly easier later (**D**).

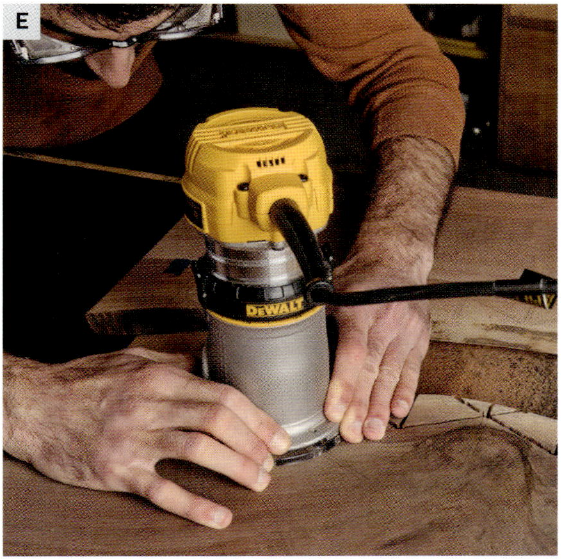
E

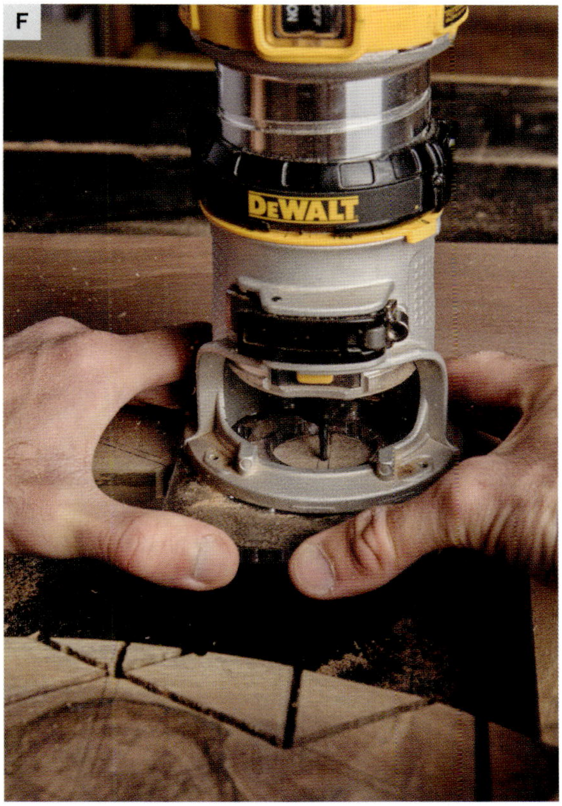

F

5. Use a router and a bit that matches the thickness of the kumiko strips. Set the bit depth to match the depth of the kumiko so it sits cleanly after being installed (**E**). Cut between the traced lines (**F**). Take your time, use a sharp bit, and make slow, controlled passes.

6. Trim the kumiko panel to its final size (**G**).

7. Test-fit it into the grooves (**H**). The fit might be snug, so insert it halfway to check alignment. Make any adjustments, if needed. Don't press the kumiko in fully yet as it may be difficult to remove.

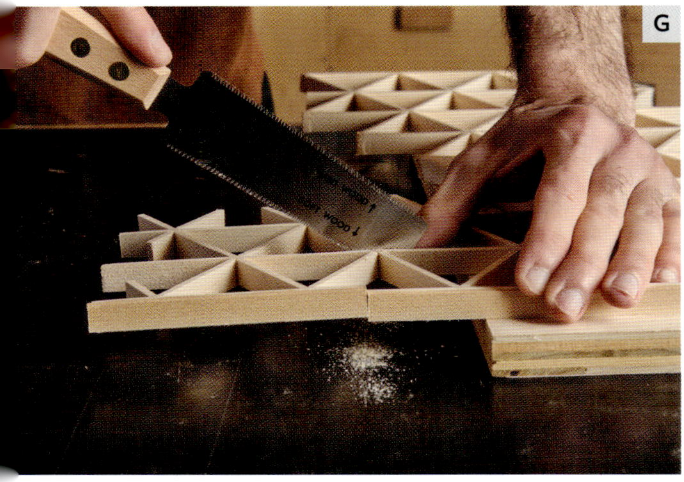
G

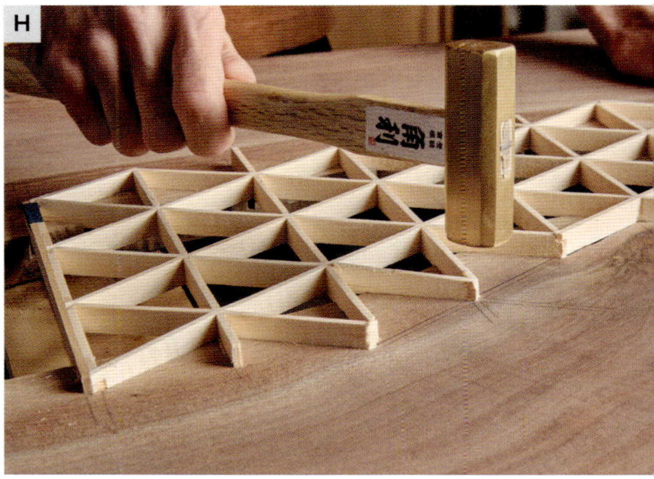
H

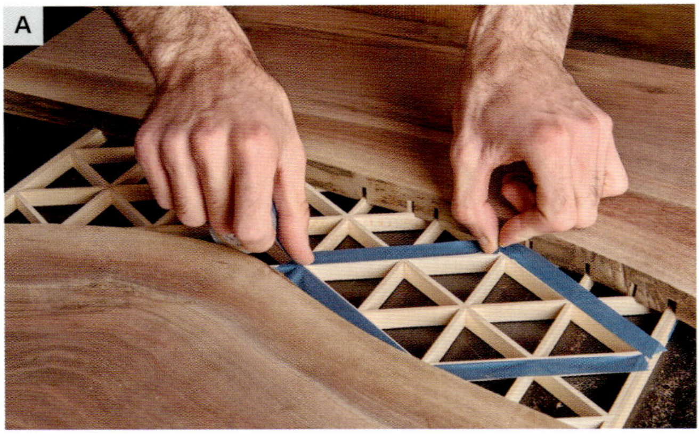

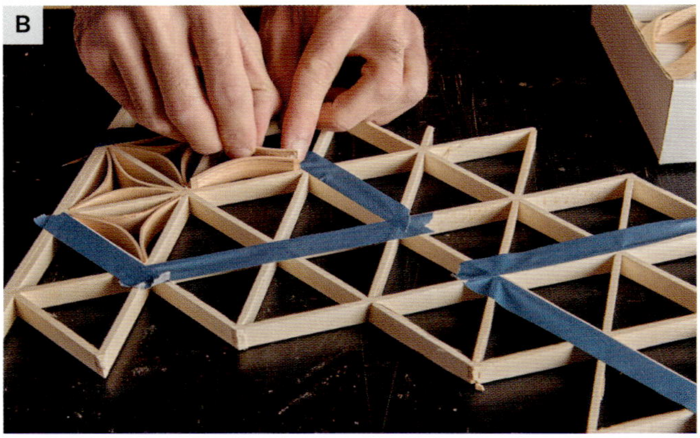

Mark and make the infill pattern

1. While the kumiko is still in place, flip the tabletop right side up and use masking tape to mark where you'd like to add infill patterns (**A**). You can echo the natural curves of the live edges or go with a more symmetrical design. There's no wrong answer.

2. If the plywood support pieces are in your way, carefully remove them now. Just be cautious not to damage the kumiko or slabs during handling.

3. Take the kumiko out of the slabs and create your chosen infill pattern (**B–C**). Once complete, glue the pieces in place and sand the entire panel flat.

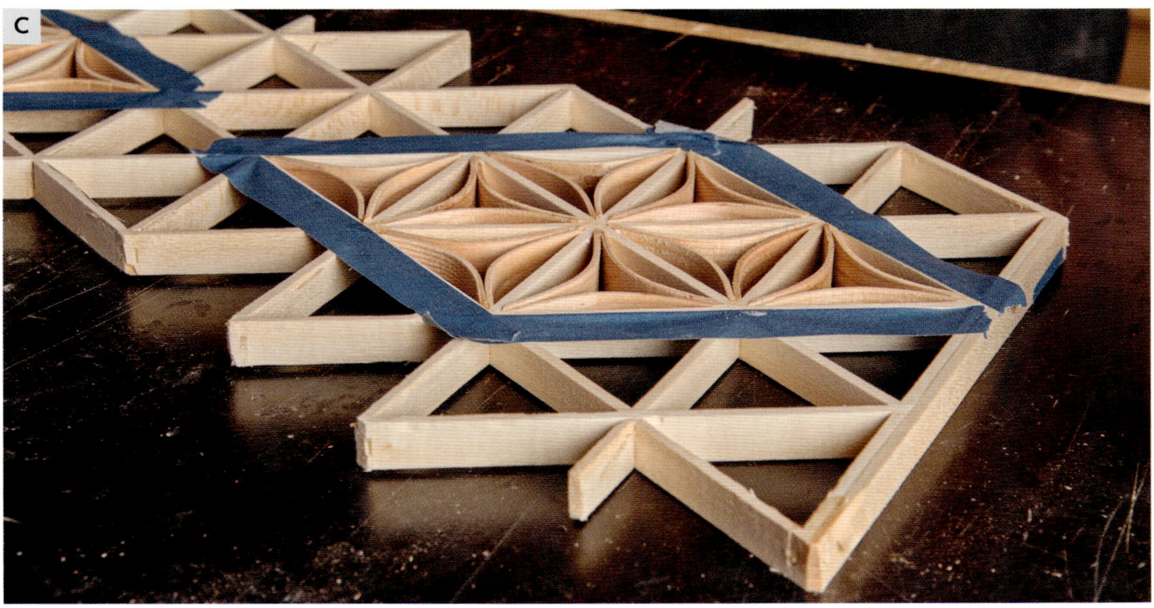

Finish the slabs and glue the kumiko

1. Now is the time to sand and finish the slab surfaces. Choose a durable wood finish that will stand up to the wear of everyday use. You might opt for a finish with multiple coats for added protection (**A**).

2. Be careful not to get any finish into the routed kumiko grooves, as it could affect the fit later.

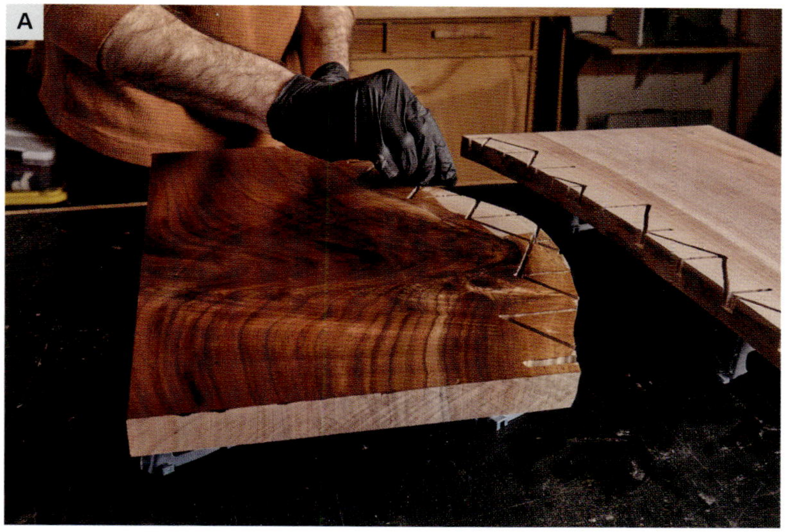

A

3. Once the finish is fully dry, glue the kumiko panel into place. Protect the finished slab during this step by placing foam or a soft cloth beneath it on the workbench. Use a scrap block and a hammer to aid with installation if your panel is tight (**B**).

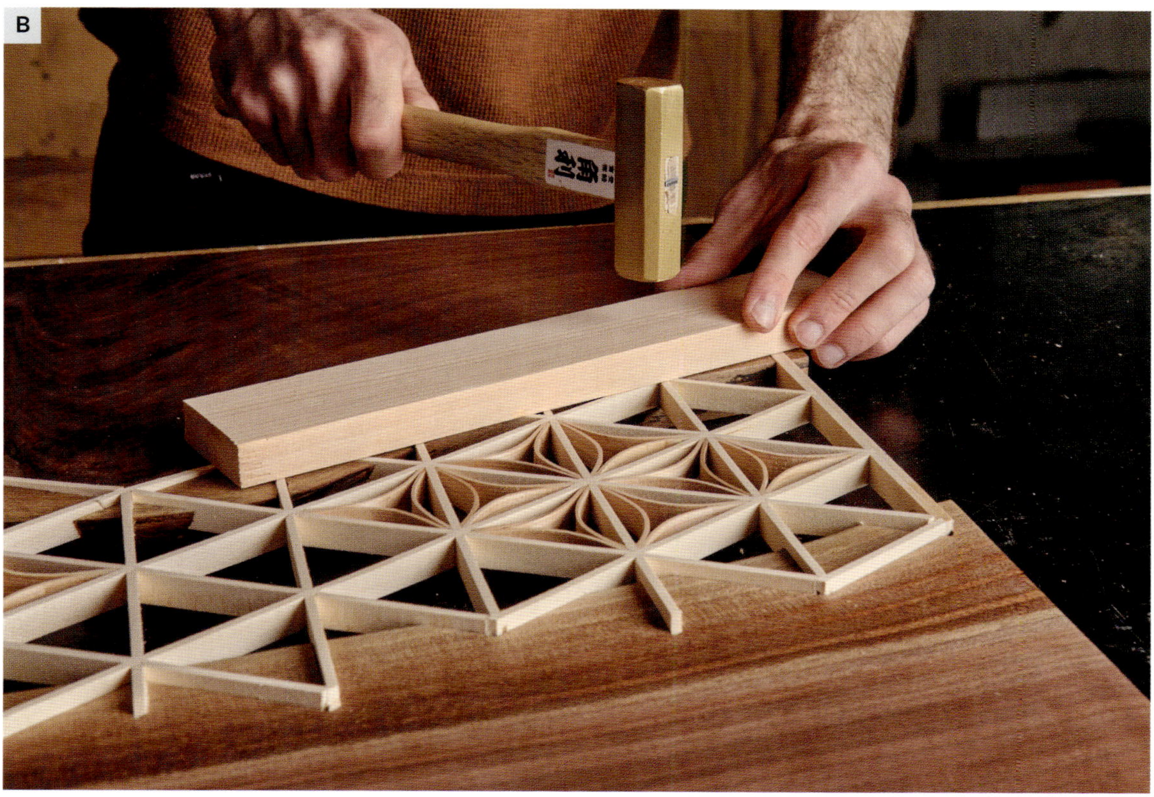

B

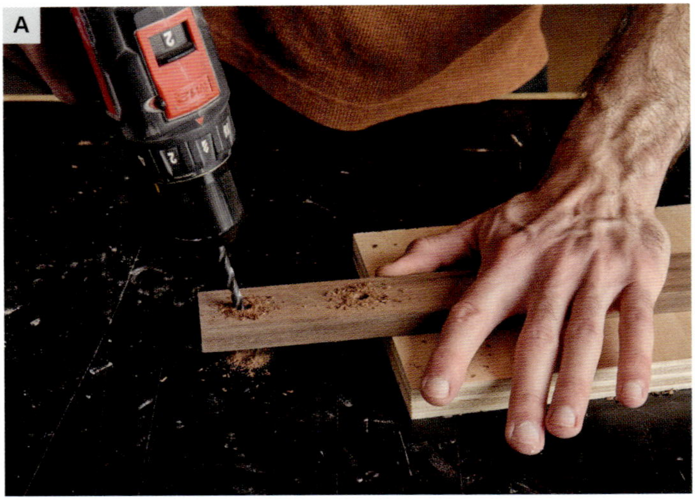

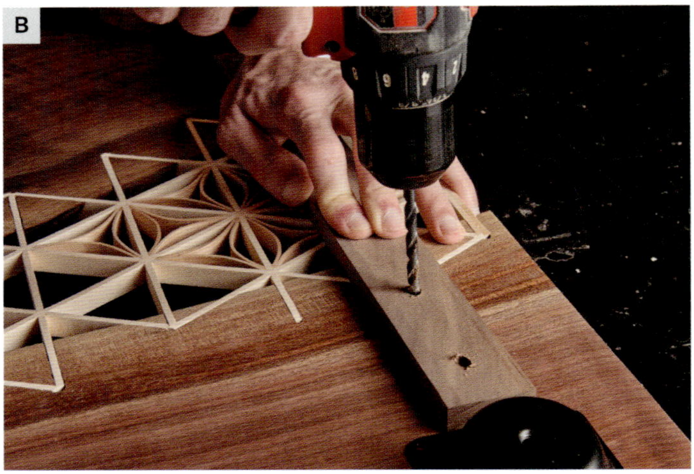

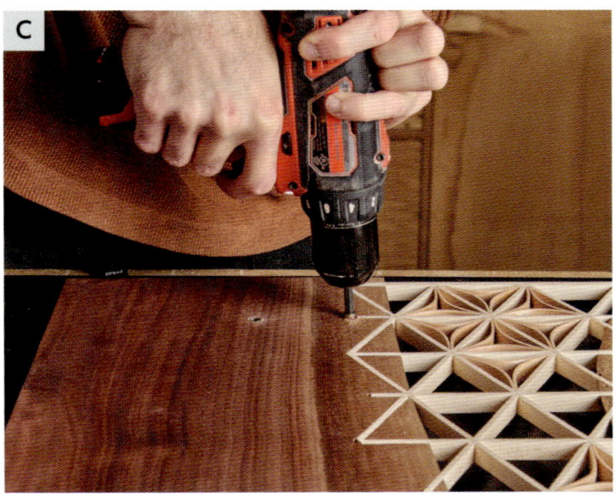

Attach the stretchers

At this point, the only thing holding the tabletop together is the kumiko, so reinforcement is essential. Two wooden stretchers on the underside will strengthen the structure and prevent flexing. The size of the stretchers depends on the size of your table. For smaller tables like end or coffee tables, use ½ in to ¾ in (12.7 mm to 19.1 mm) thick hardwood cut to about 3 in (76 mm) wide and 3 in (76 mm) shorter than the table's overall width. Thicker and wider material should be used for larger tables. The stretchers should be placed near the ends of the tabletop, making sure they won't interfere with the placement of the legs later. Aligning them with the kumiko pattern or centering them over a grid strip adds visual cohesion.

1. Drill elongated holes in the stretchers to accommodate wood movement. Drill straight holes first and then pivot the drill from side to side to elongate them (**A**).

2. Mark the hole locations on the slabs. Drill and install threaded inserts into the slabs (**B–C**).

3. Attach the stretchers using screws sized for the threaded inserts (**D**).

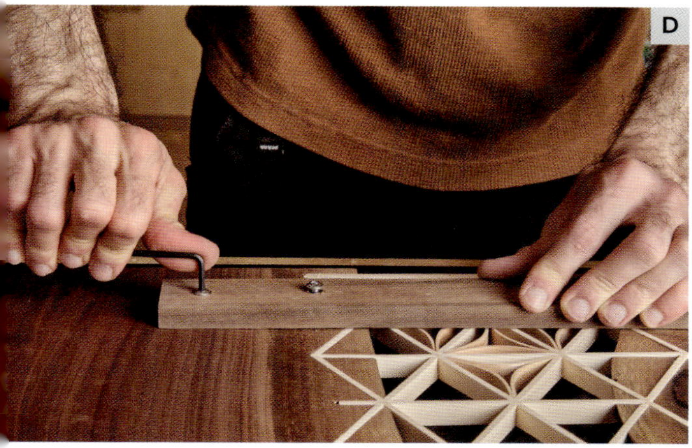

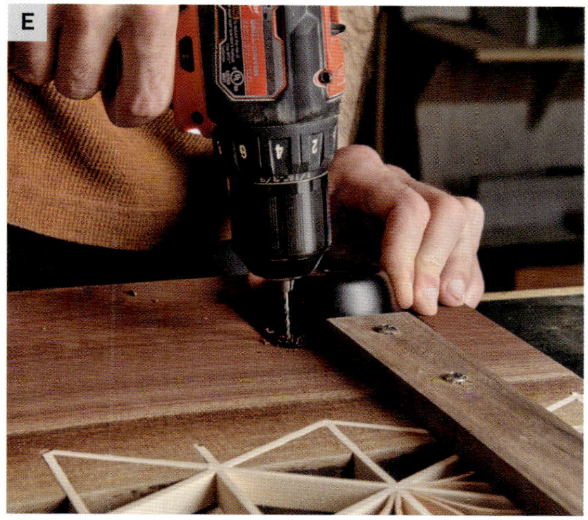

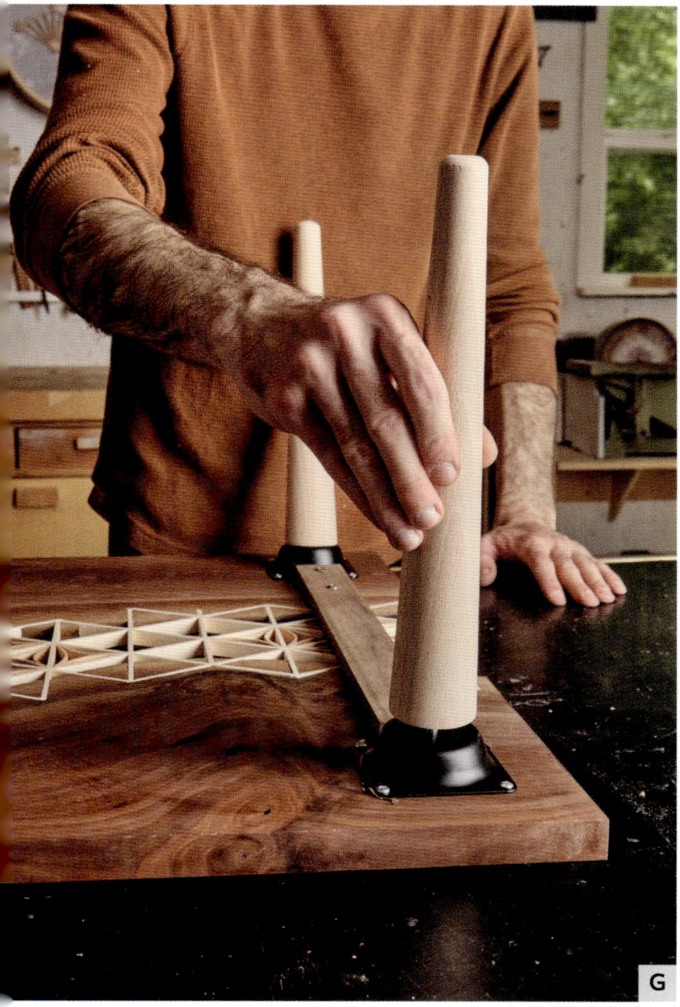

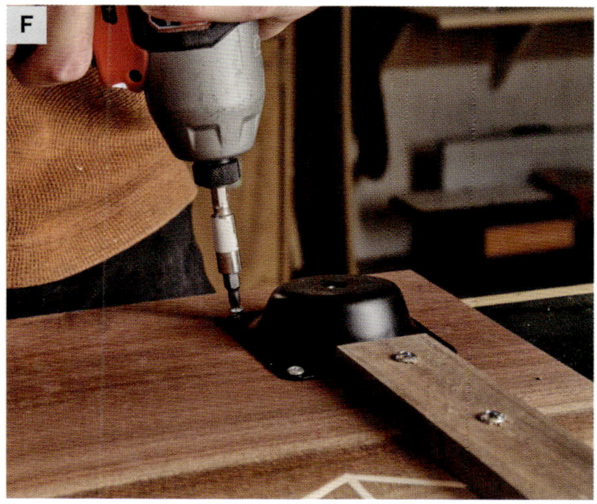

Attach the legs

There are many options for table legs, but since the kumiko is the centerpiece, simple is better. Angled metal brackets with tapered wooden legs are a great choice.

1. Mark the bracket locations, pre-drill the holes (**E**), and screw the brackets into place (**F**). Then attach the legs (**G**).

2. With the legs on, your kawa table is complete. If you'd like to protect the kumiko and create a fully usable surface, consider adding a glass top that spans the entire table.

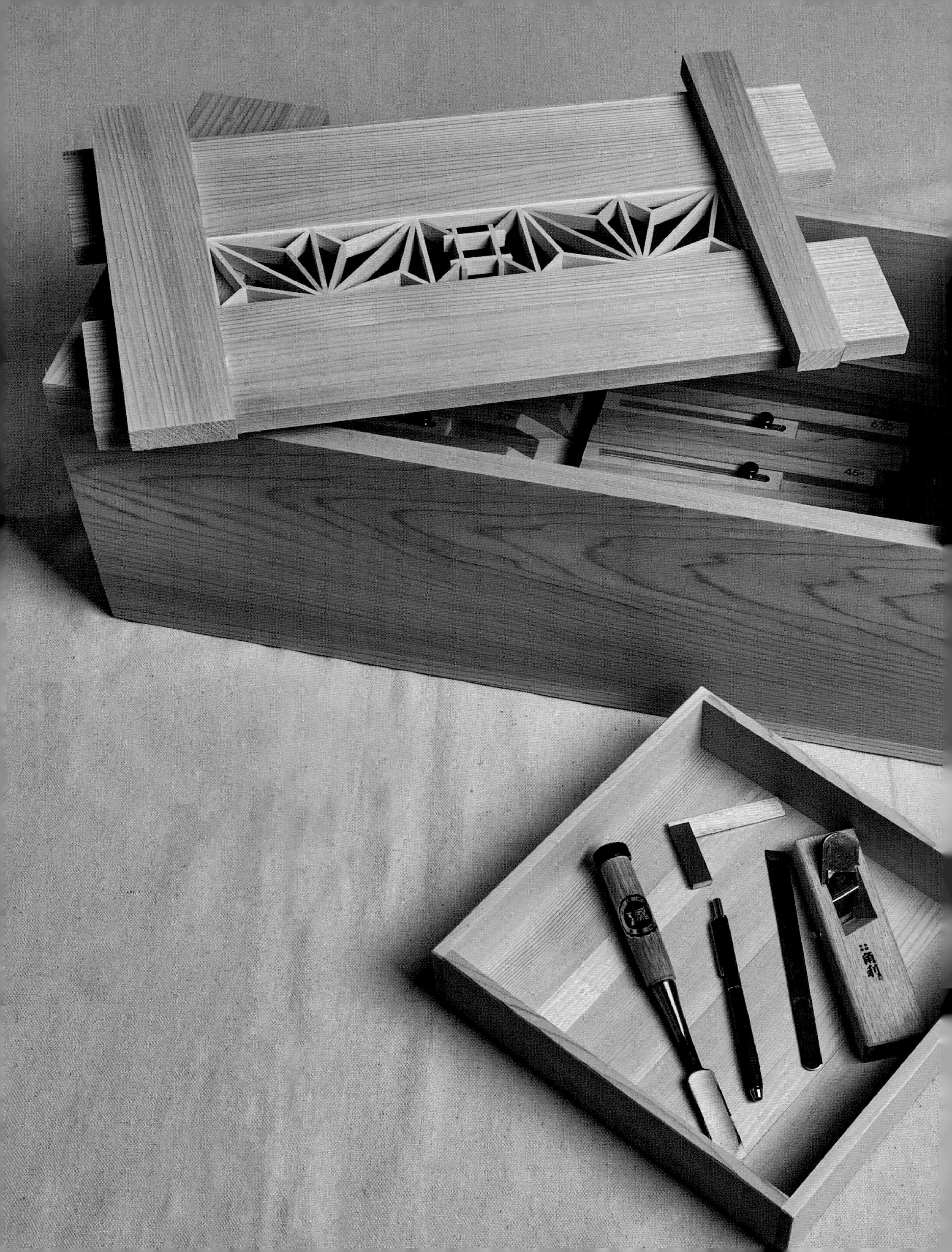
67.5°
45°

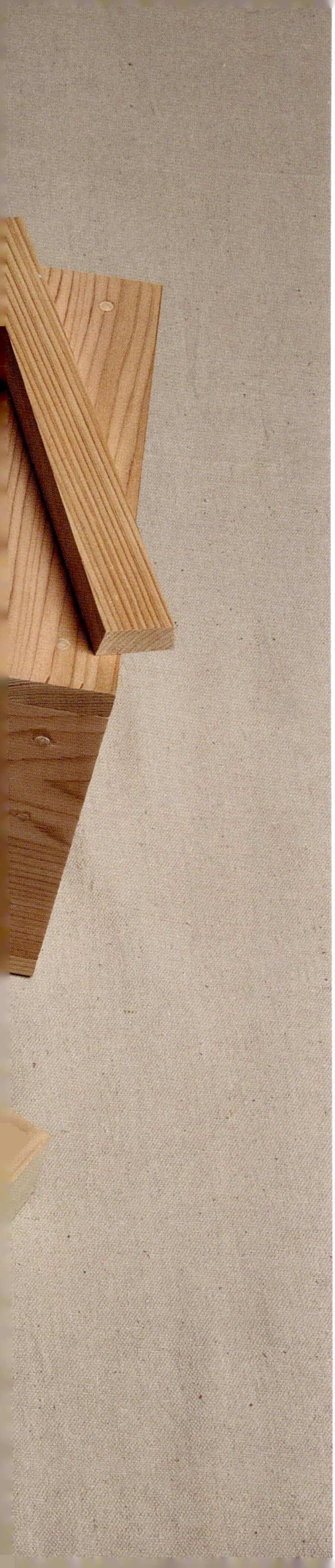

Project 8

Japanese Toolbox

Traditional Japanese toolboxes, known as kōgu bako (工具箱), are simple, strong, and thoughtfully designed. Made primarily from lightweight wood, they often feature sliding lids, clean joinery, and organized compartments. Many are constructed without nails or screws, showcasing the precision and care of the maker. These boxes were used by craftsmen such as carpenters and joiners to carry and protect their most trusted tools. Built for both function and longevity, the kōgu bako reflects the same respect for craftsmanship that defines the tools it holds.

In this chapter, you'll build your own version of this classic form. This toolbox is designed to store the jigs and hand tools introduced throughout this book, keeping them safe, accessible, and ready for use. Its flexible interior can be customized over time to match your growing skills and expanding toolkit. Whether kept in your workshop or brought to a job site, this project will serve as both a practical storage solution and a lasting symbol of your journey into kumiko.

BUILDING A TRADITIONAL TOOLBOX

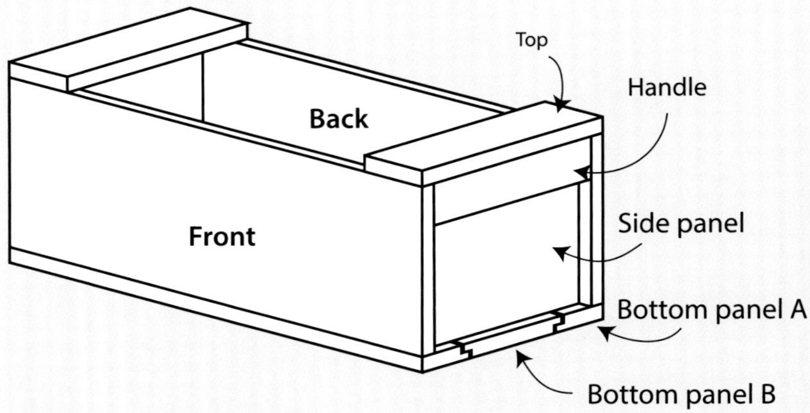

All parts are ¾″

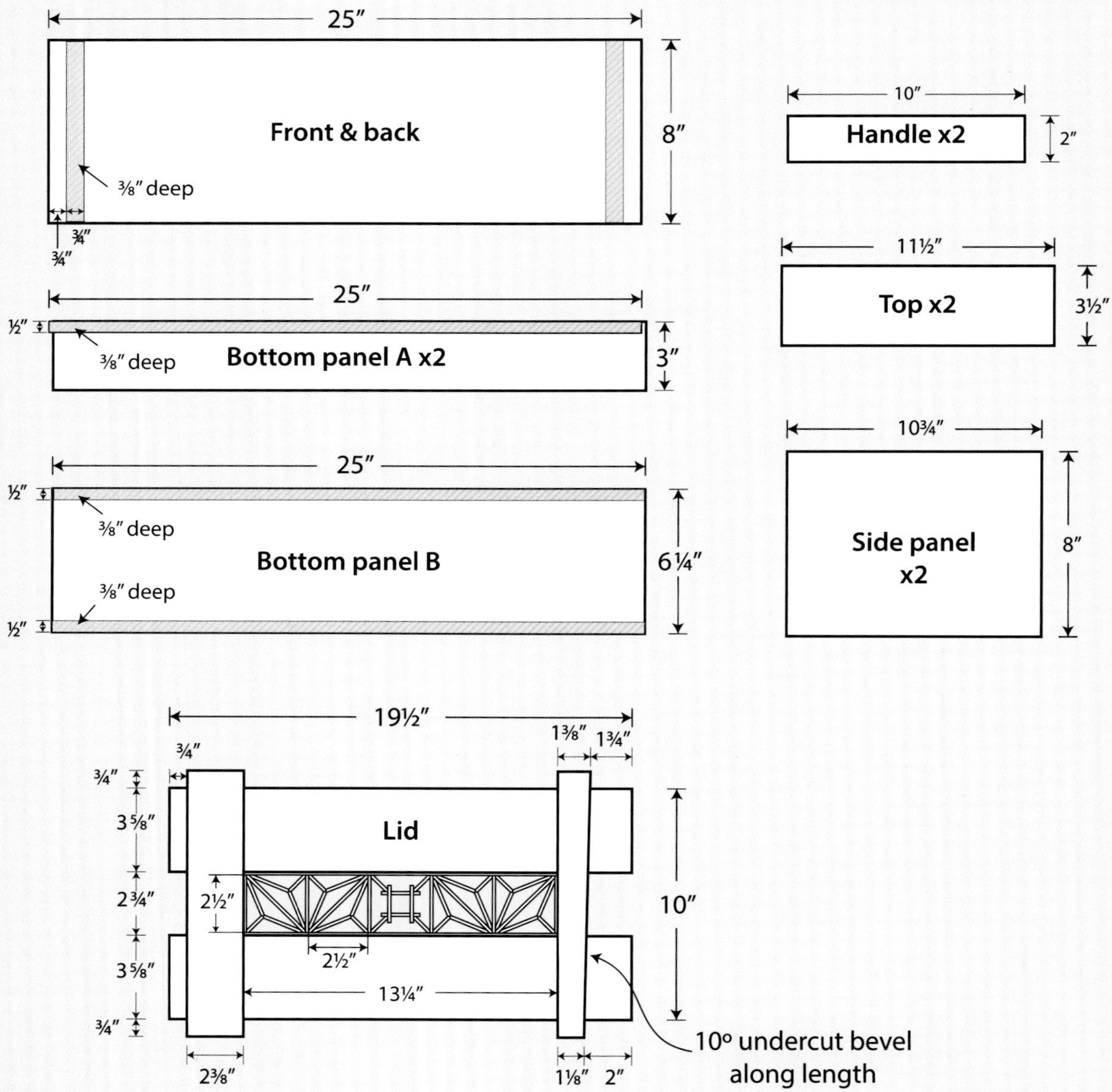

Cutting the parts and joinery

Begin by cutting all the parts for the main body of the toolbox shown here. The lid components and interior parts can be cut later. A lightweight wood such as cedar is ideal as it keeps the toolbox easier to carry, even when filled with heavy tools. All parts should be ¾ in (19.1 mm) thick, except the interior tray and rails. Two of each part is needed, except for bottom panel B, of which only one is needed.

1. Cut the joinery in the front and back panels. A dado blade on the table saw makes this process quick (**A**). For a snug fit, cut the dadoes slightly undersized in width. This will ensure the side panels fit tightly.

2. Before assembly, use a hammer to gently compress the fibers at the ends of the side panels (**B**). This technique, called kigoroshi (木殺し), helps the ends slip into the dadoes more easily. Once glue is applied, the compressed wood will expand slightly, locking the joint tightly in place. Try to compress the fibers and not crush them.

3. With glue applied in the dadoes (**C**), assemble the front, back, and side panels (**D**). Mark, pre-drill (**E**), and secure the pieces using screws (**F**). These screws act as temporary clamps, holding everything tightly together while the glue is drying during the next few steps. They will be removed later and replaced with dowels. Use finish screws with smaller heads to minimize surface damage, ensuring cleaner joinery when the dowels are installed later.

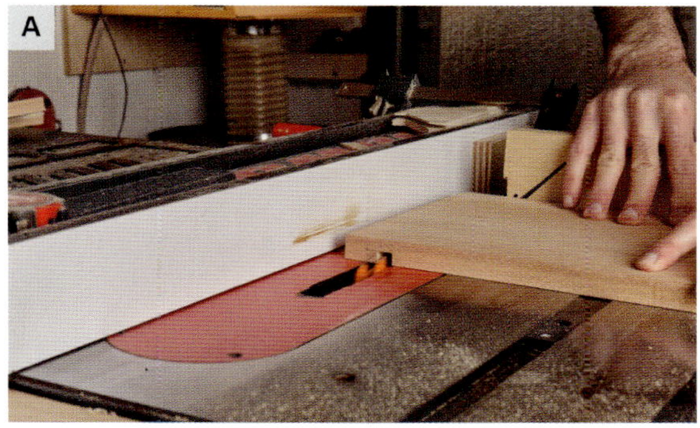
A

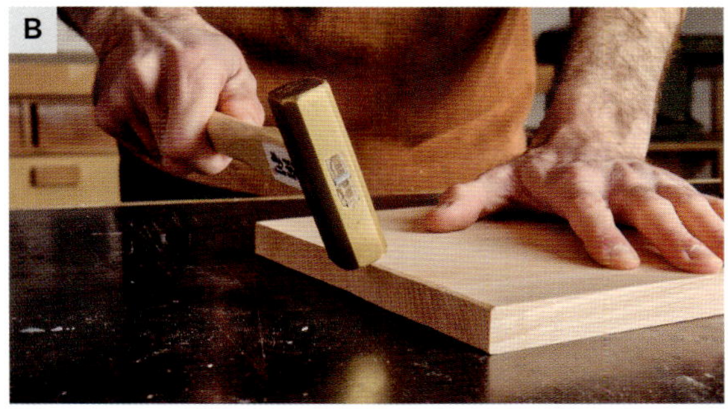
B

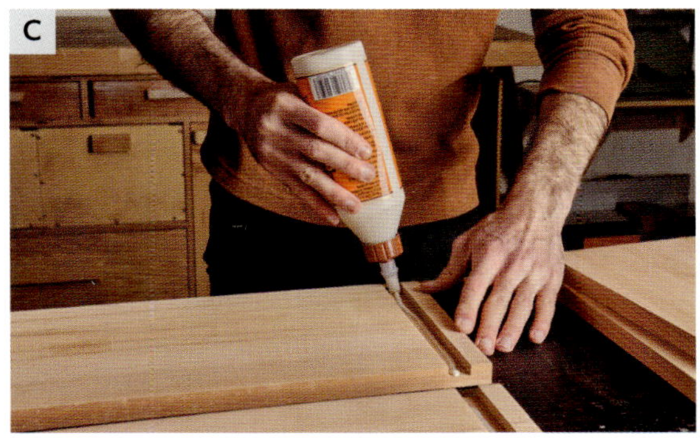
C

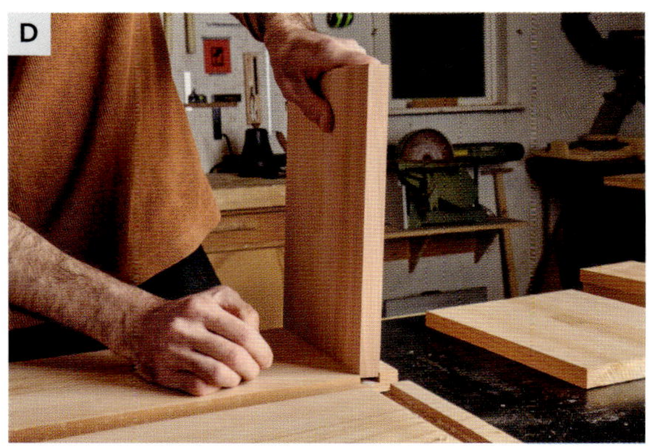
D

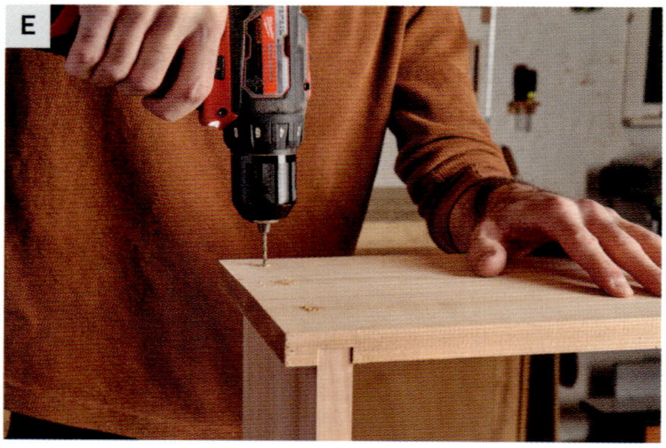

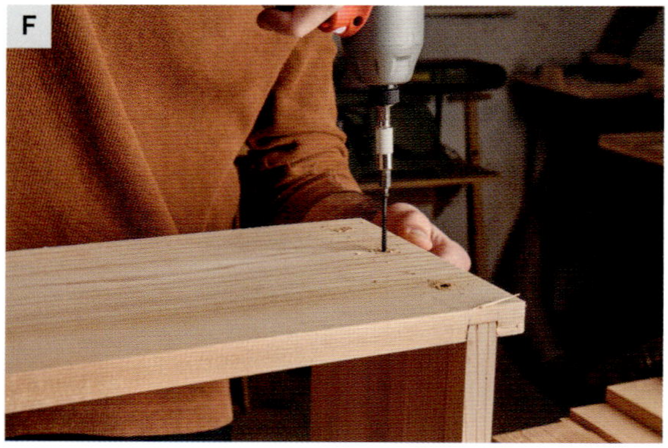

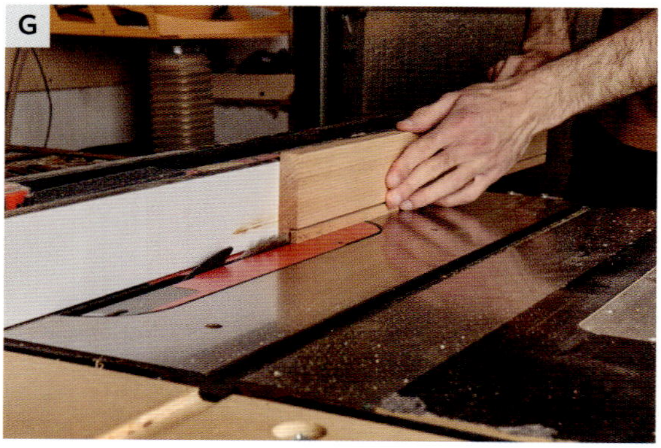

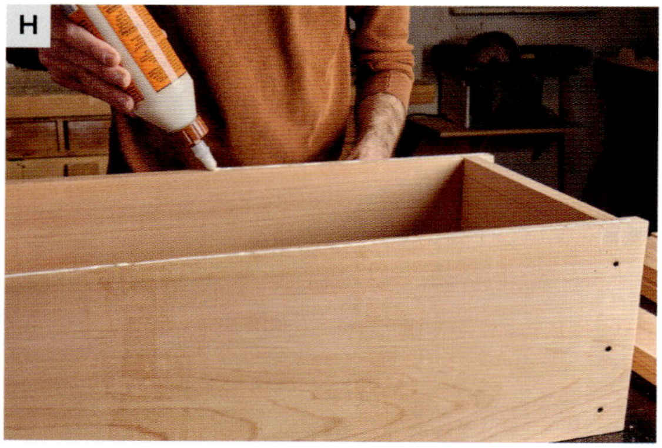

Attaching the bottom

1. Cut the rabbets on all bottom pieces as shown in the illustration on page 138 (**G**).

2. Apply glue to the edges of the front and back panels only and the center of the side panels (**H**).

3. Pay close attention to the orientation of these parts: the rabbets on the A panels should face inward, as this helps support the B panel. Mark, pre-drill, and screw the A panels in place (**I-J**). Ensure the ends and sides are flush.

4. The B panel is intentionally spaced ⅛ in (3.2 mm) away from the A panels to allow for seasonal wood movement. Use spacers for aid with proper alignment and add one screw on either end through the center of the B panel to secure it to the side panels.

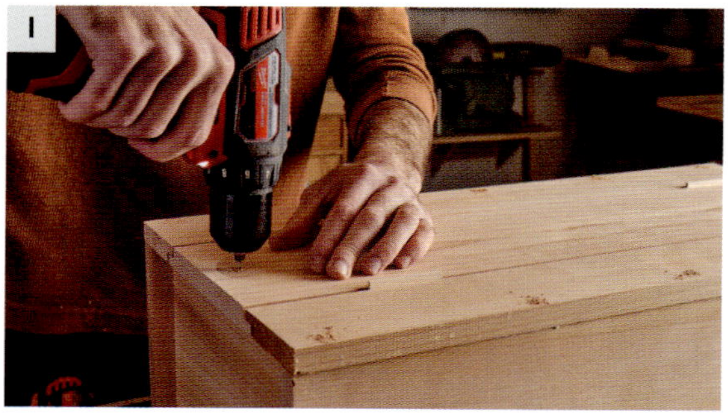

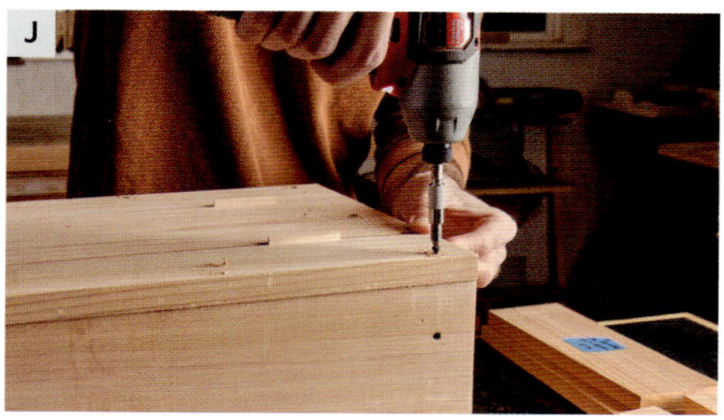

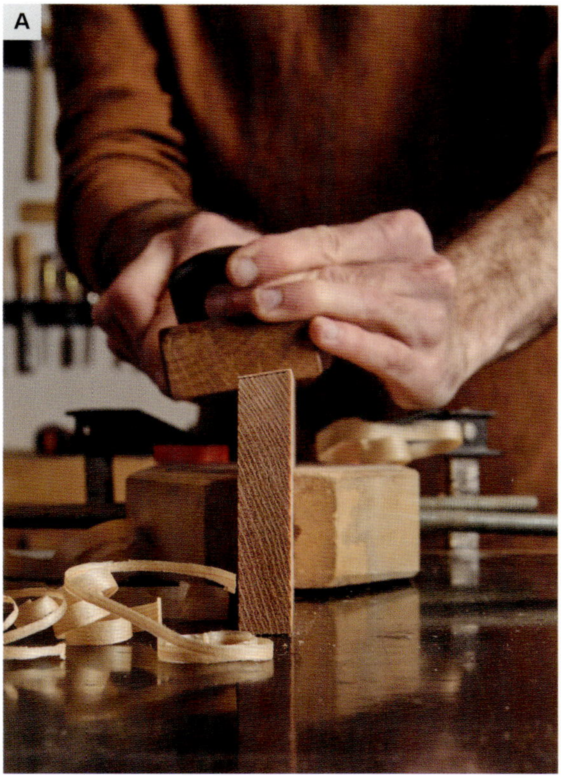

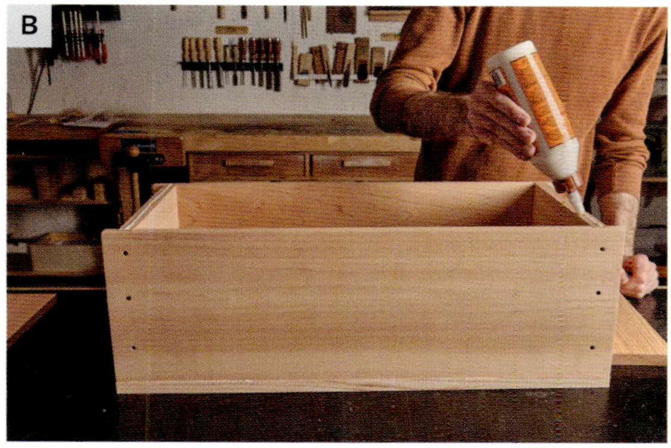

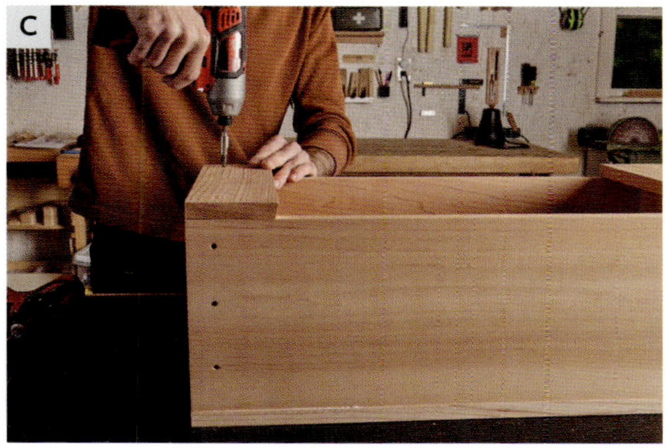

Tops and handles

1. Cut a 10° bevel along the edge of one top piece. This is a crucial step that will allow the lid to lock in place. When securing this piece, make sure the bevel is facing inward (**A**).

2. Apply wood glue to the top edge of the side panels (**B**) and secure the top pieces in place using screws, just as with the bottom (**C**). Make sure the top pieces are flush with the ends of the front and back panels.

3. Next, attach the handles. Apply glue to the inside faces of the handle parts, then secure them to the toolbox using screws driven into the side panels (**D**). The main body of the toolbox is now complete.

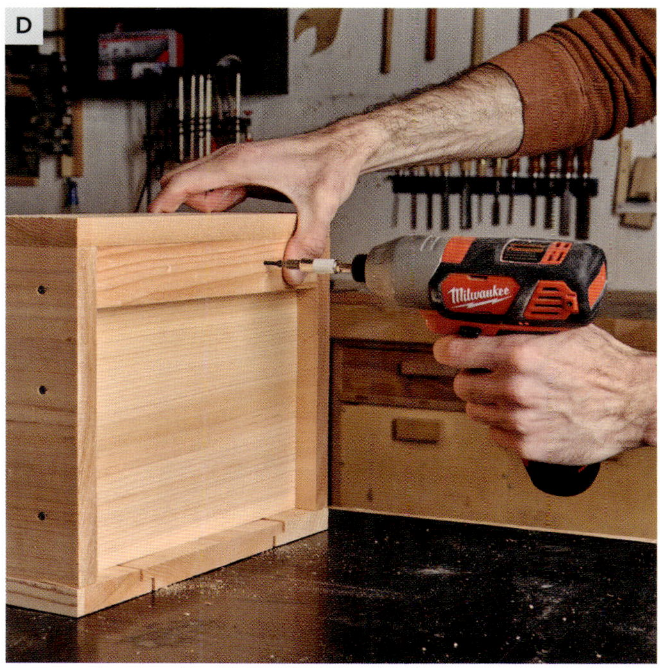

A

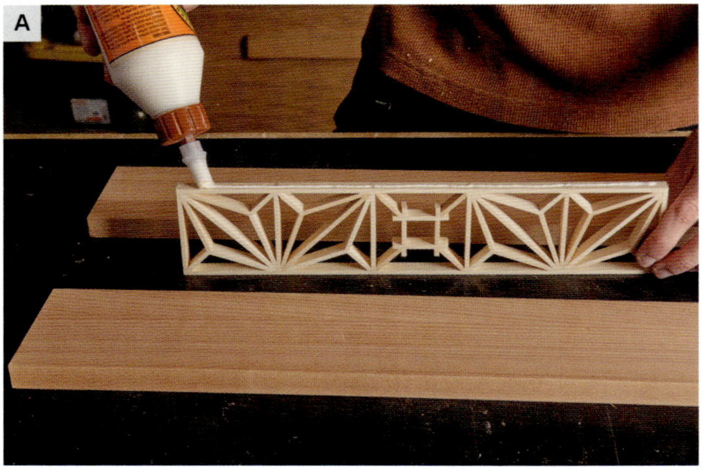

B

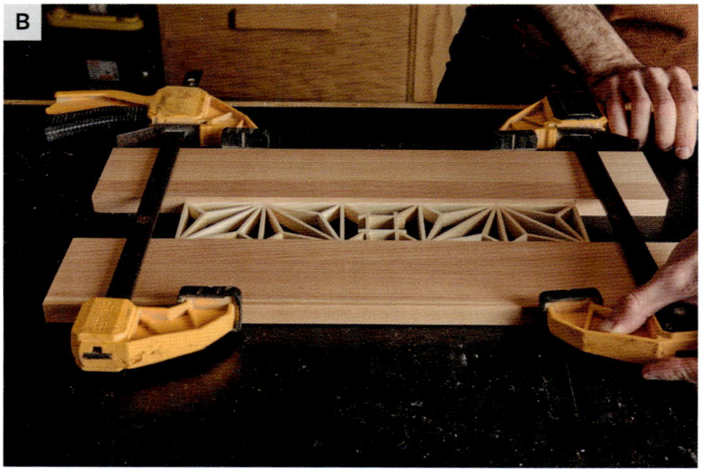

C

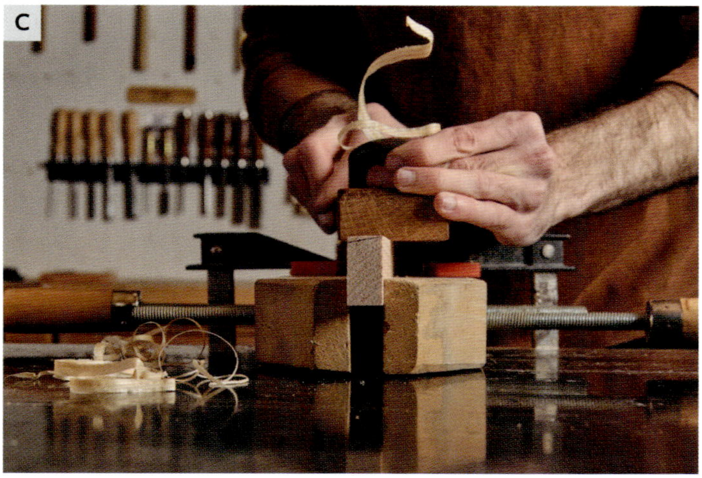

The lid

1. Start by making the kumiko panel. This panel uses a 2½ in (64 mm) pitch with ⅛ in x ½ in (3.2 mm x 12.7 mm) material. Glue both the grid and infill pieces in place, and once the glue has dried, sand the surface smooth.

2. Next, glue the two long lid pieces to either side of the kumiko panel (**A**). The kumiko should be centered between them at 3⅛ in (79 mm) in from each end. Make sure the back face of the kumiko is flush with the back of the lid pieces (**B**). This sets the kumiko panel ¼ in (6.4 mm) below the surface of the lid, allowing objects to rest on top of the toolbox while minimizing the risk of damaging the panel.

3. Now cut the thinner tapered lid guide and add a 10° undercut bevel on the tapered side (**C**). When attaching it to the lid, the bevel should face outward (toward the end of the lid) and downward (toward the top surface of the lid).

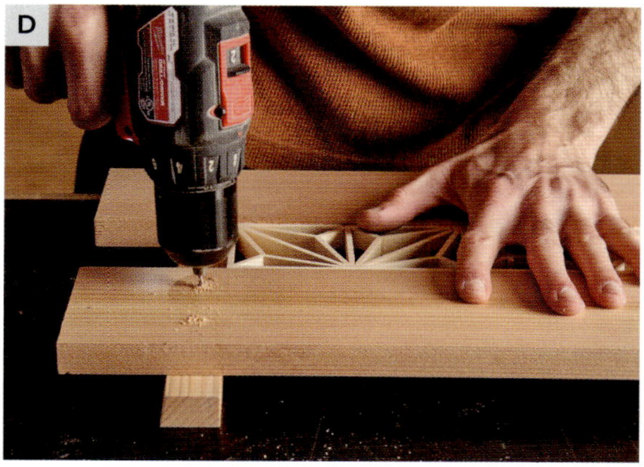

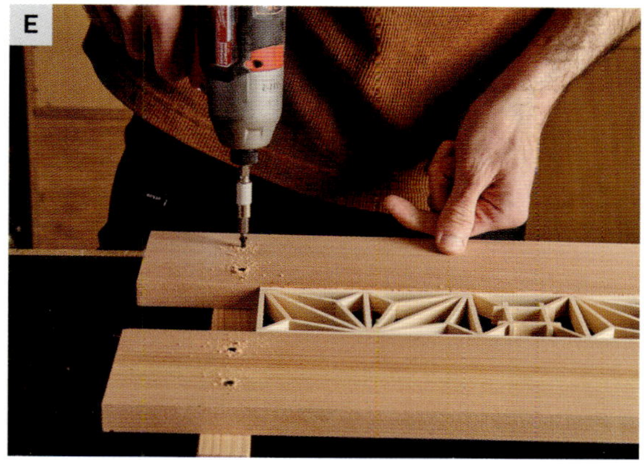

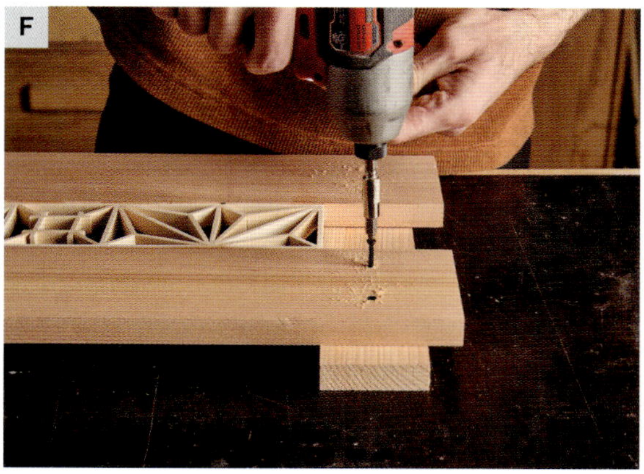

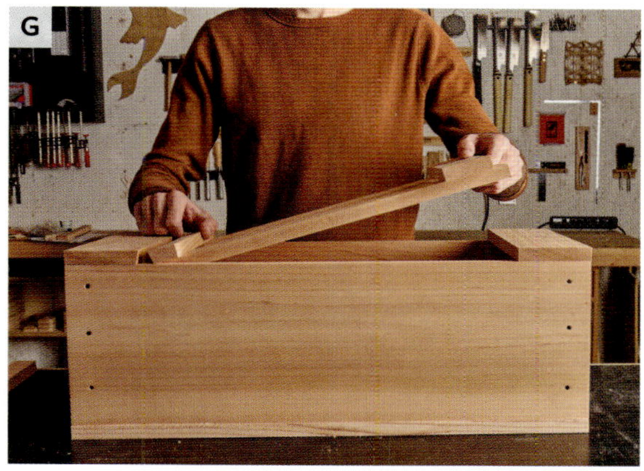

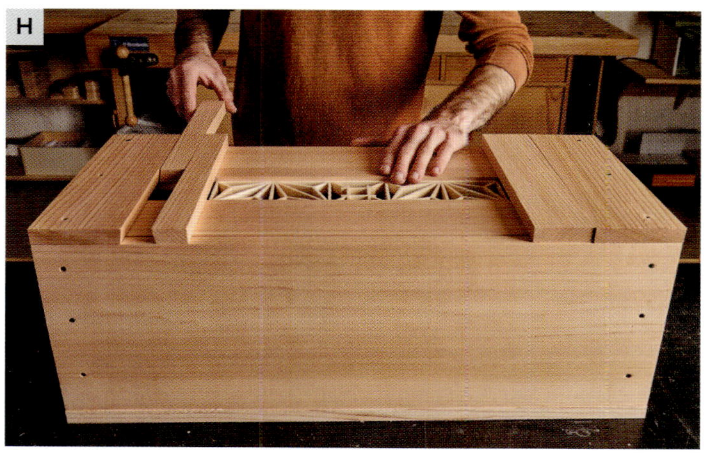

4. Position both guide pieces accurately to the measurements shown and square to the lid. Secure them using screws from underneath (**D–F**). This keeps the top face clean and free of visible fasteners.

5. With the lid assembled, you can now fit it into the toolbox. Insert the end with the beveled guide piece into the side of the toolbox that has the beveled top piece. Then lower the lid into place and slide it closed (**G**). Make any adjustments necessary to ensure smooth operation.

6. To hold the lid closed, use a wedge with a 10° bevel cut along both edges (**H**). Cut it to size for your specific spacing. This locks the lid in place securely.

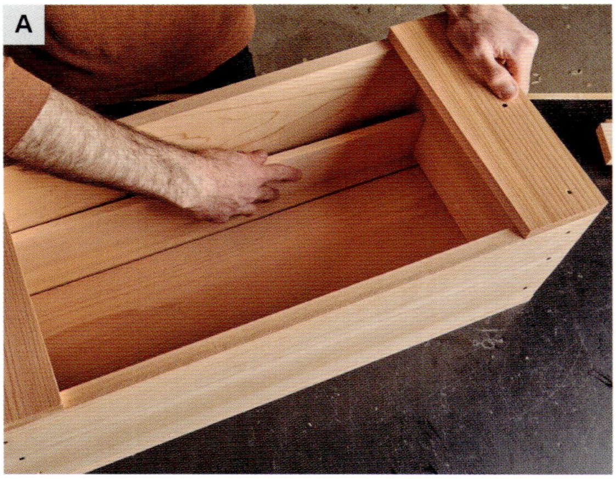

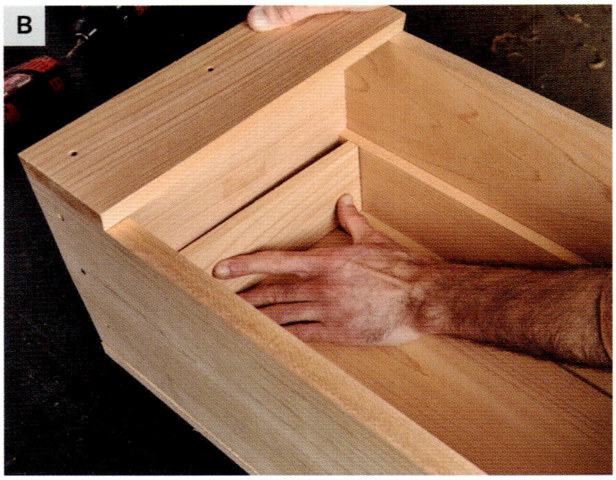

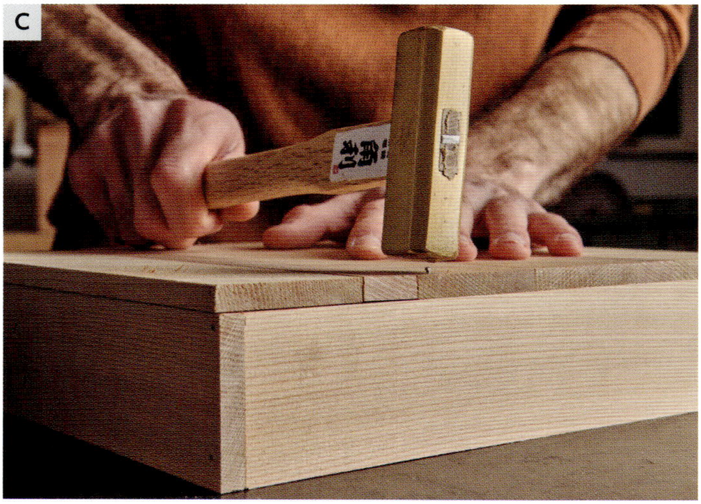

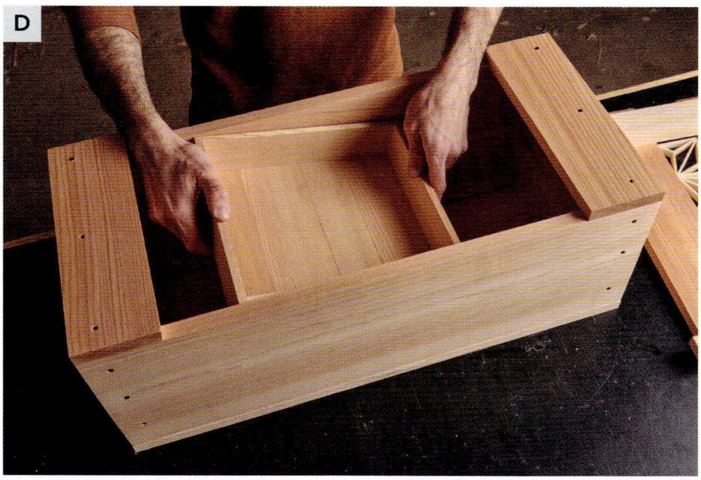

Inner compartments

1. To add functionality to the toolbox, consider installing a sliding tray. Start by cutting ¼ in (6.4 mm) thick material to run along the inside walls of the toolbox (**A**). These will act as supports for the tray. The width of these parts will determine the height of the lower storage compartment.

2. Next, cut two shorter pieces to fit snugly between the longer parts and press them against the side panels to lock everything in place (**B**). While you can glue these supports in, keeping them friction-fit or adhering them with double-sided tape allows you to remake or replace them later if your storage needs change.

3. The sliding tool tray is built using simple construction with small nails and can be made to any size that fits within the lid opening (**C–D**). It's a great spot for organizing smaller items like marking gauges, pencils, or layout tools.

Finishing

1. Now you can remove the screws and drill out the holes for dowels (**A**). Miller dowels are a great choice for strength but standard ¼ in (6.4 mm) round dowels work just as well. Remove the screws with care, as any non-glued panel may shift out of alignment. Remove one screw at a time and glue in a dowel before removing another screw (**B–C**).

2. Applying a finish is optional. Leaving the wood unfinished allows it to naturally age, developing a rich patina and character over time.

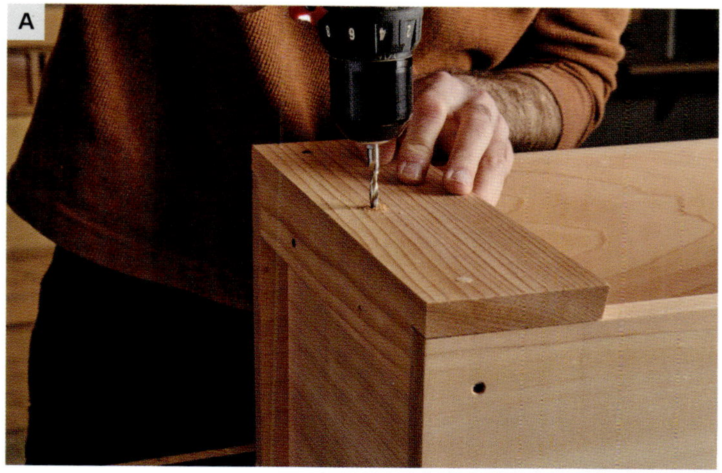

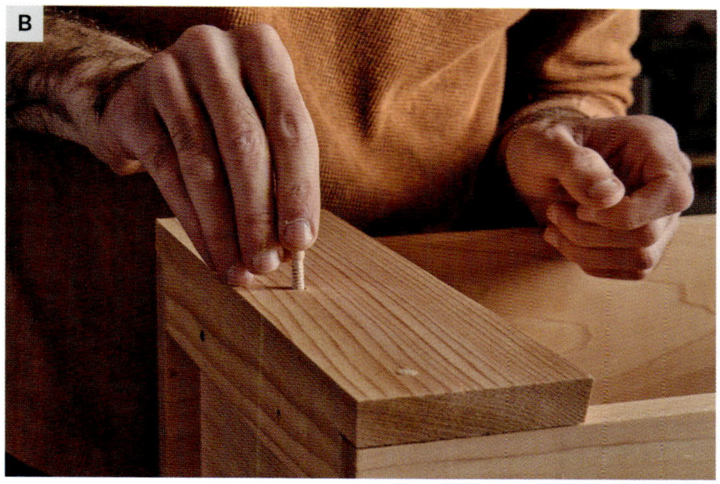

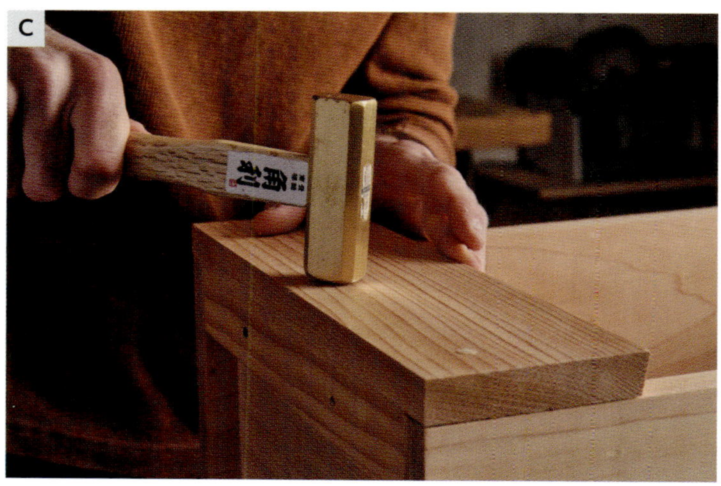

Project 9

Kumiko and Epoxy

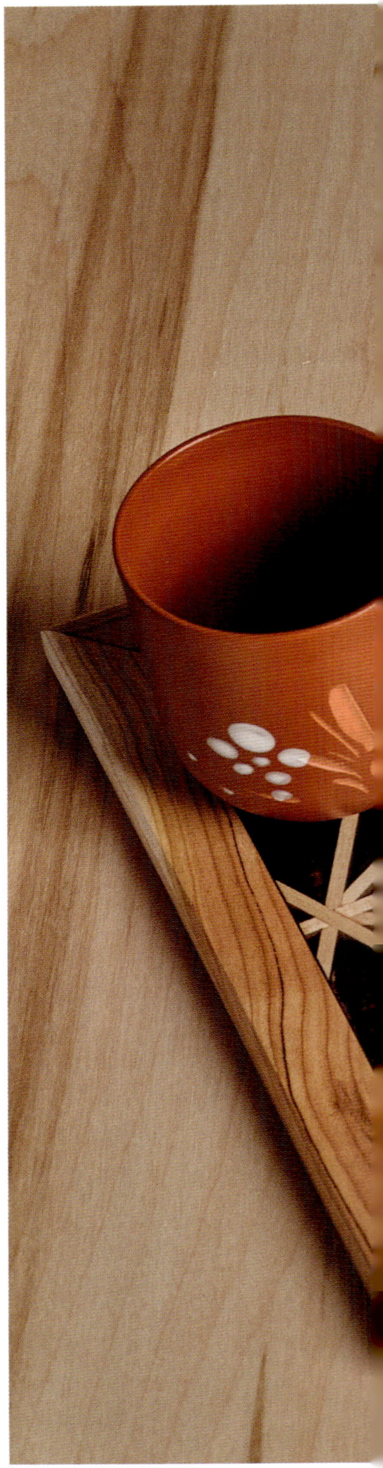

This project brings together two very different worlds: traditional Japanese woodworking and contemporary resin techniques. By filling the open areas in a kumiko pattern with epoxy, we're putting a modern twist on a centuries-old craft.

Epoxy has become a popular material in the woodworking scene for its versatility and visual impact, but when used thoughtfully, it can complement kumiko rather than overpowering it. The goal here is to create something eye-catching while still honoring the precision, intention, and restraint that define traditional kumiko.

This chapter will walk you through the process of preparing your kumiko panel for resin, working with epoxy safely and effectively, and turning the completed piece into a functional and artistic charcuterie board.

Safety tip: Working with epoxy can be hazardous if proper precautions aren't taken. Uncured epoxy contains chemicals that can cause skin irritation, allergic reactions, or respiratory issues with prolonged exposure. Always wear nitrile gloves, a long-sleeve shirt, and safety glasses when handling epoxy. Work in a well-ventilated area and use a respirator rated for organic vapors if ventilation is limited. Be sure to follow the manufacturer's instructions for mixing ratios and cure times and dispose of any waste material responsibly.

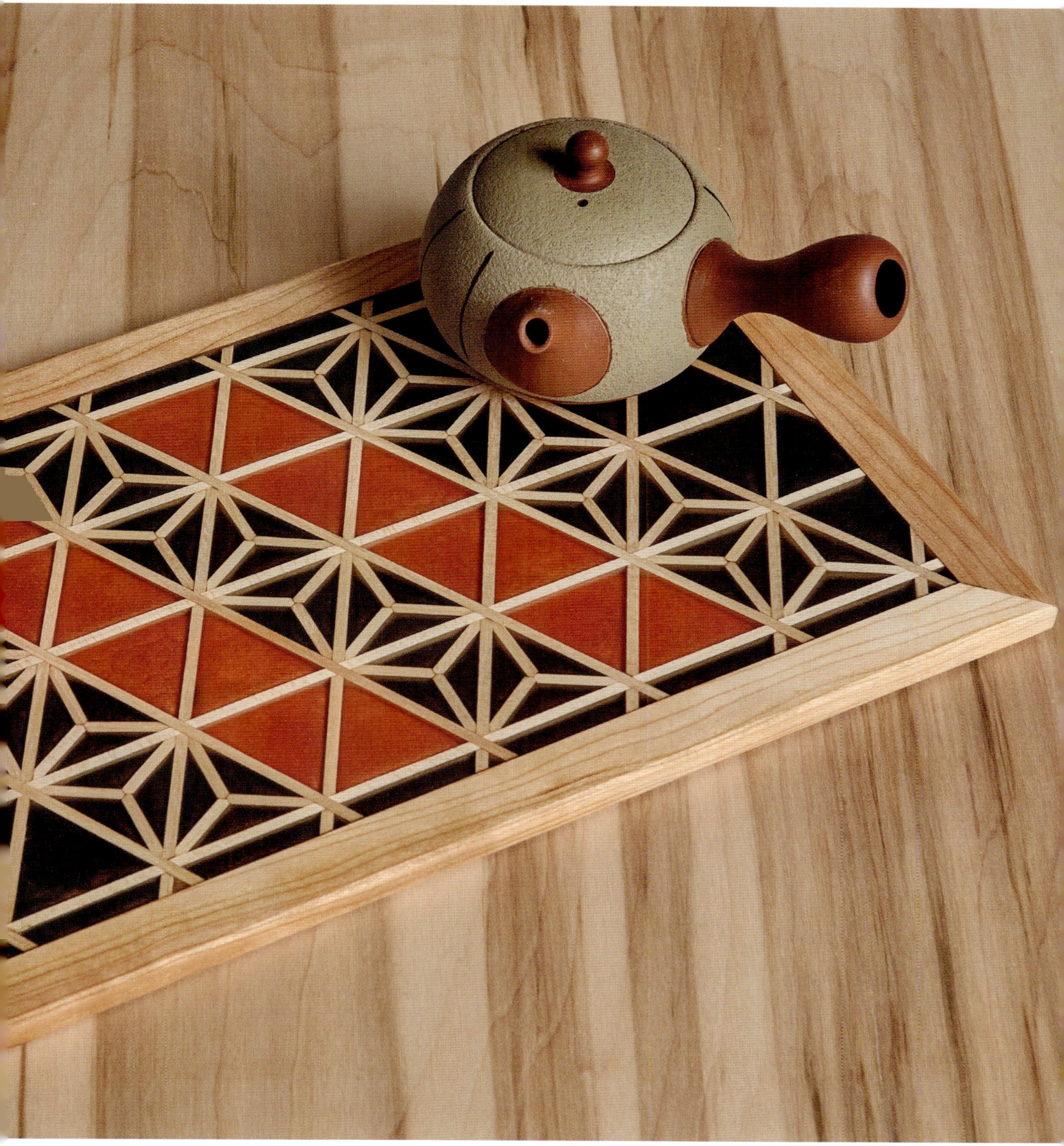

Prep the kumiko for epoxy

In this project, gluing the kumiko pieces is unnecessary. The epoxy will hold everything in place once cured. Make your kumiko to any size you'd like and with any infill pattern and layout. After assembling it and fitting it inside its frame, it's time to prep for the epoxy pour.

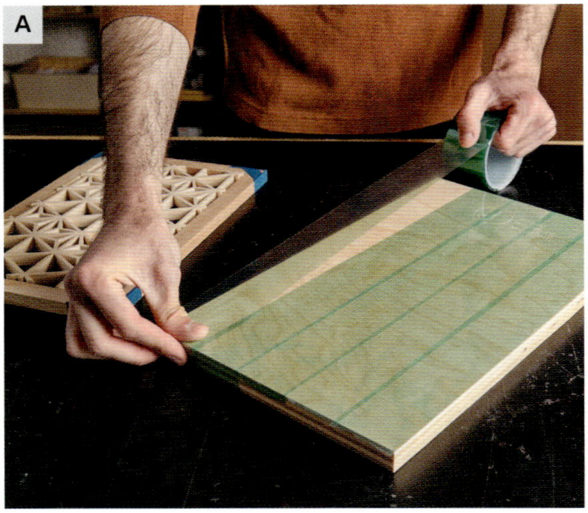

1. Start by covering a flat piece of plywood with resin tape, a non-stick, heat-resistant tape that prevents epoxy from bonding to surfaces (**A**). Applying a demolding agent on top of the tape can help remove the panel later, but it's not essential.

2. Instead of using a traditional mold, you'll use the kumiko frame itself as the mold. Place the framed kumiko panel onto the taped plywood and weigh it down to prevent shifting. Then, run a continuous bead of hot glue around the outer edge of the frame (**B**). This creates a seal to prevent epoxy from leaking underneath. You can also use caulk for this step, but hot glue is quicker to apply and remove.

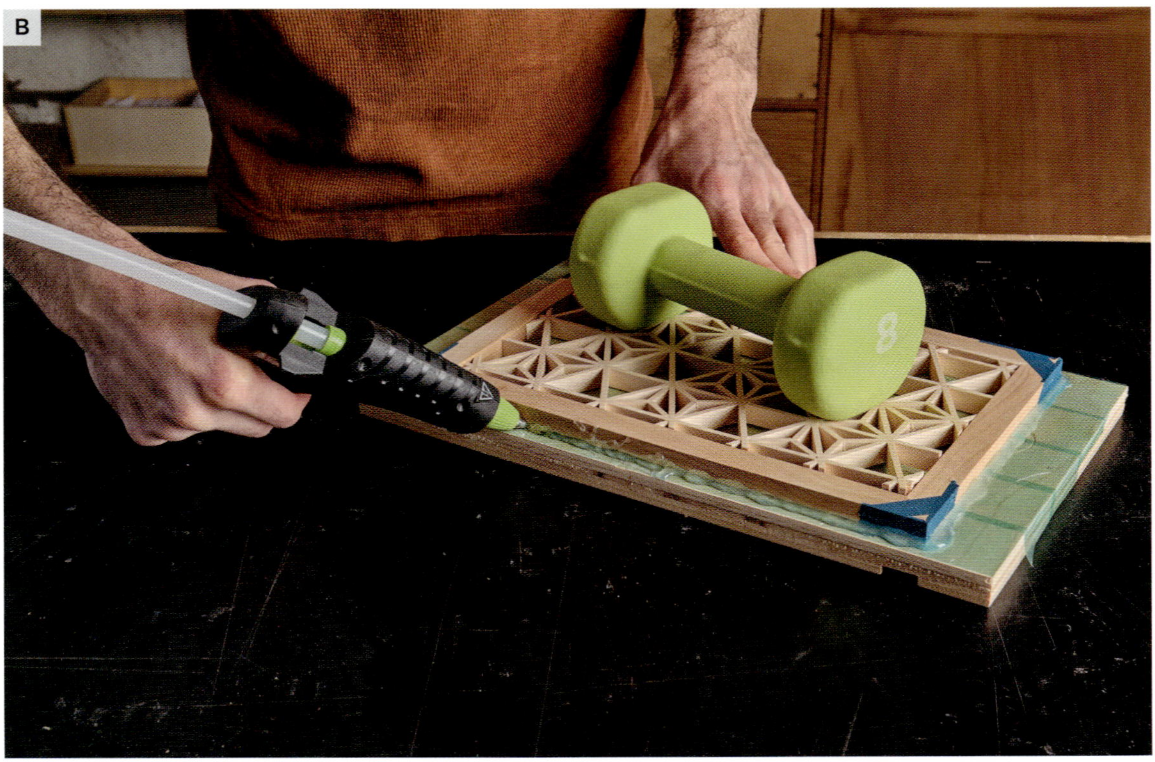

Pouring the epoxy

For this project, use a food-safe, low-viscosity casting epoxy with a long working time. This type flows easily into the tight corners of the kumiko and cures slowly to minimize bubbles.

Epoxy can be expensive, so it's important to calculate how much you need accurately. Use this formula: Volume = Length × Width × Depth × % Fill Area

For example:

If your kumiko panel is 10 in × 8 in, with a ½ in pour depth and 80% open space:
Volume = 10 × 8 × 0.5 × 0.8
Volume = 32 cubic inches

Since 1 fluid ounce is approximately 1.805 cubic inches:
32 ÷ 1.805 = 17.73 fluid ounces

You'll need about **18 fluid ounces** of epoxy.

The exact percentage of open area can be difficult to calculate, but use your best judgment based on how dense or open your panel is. It's a good idea to start with a thin sealing pour about ⅛ in (3.2 mm) deep. This first pour will confirm that your mold is leakproof and slightly seal the wood surface to prevent pigment bleed in the colored layer.

1. Mix the epoxy to the manufacturer's specifications (**A**). Epoxy that is not properly mixed can cause issues while curing, so take your time here. Remove the kumiko grid and pour the epoxy into the frame (**B**).

2. Use a heat gun or torch to remove bubbles by gently sweeping heat across the surface (**C**). The heat temporarily lowers the viscosity of the epoxy, allowing trapped air bubbles to rise and pop more easily. Be cautious not to overheat — holding the tool too close or lingering in one spot can scorch the epoxy or even introduce more bubbles.

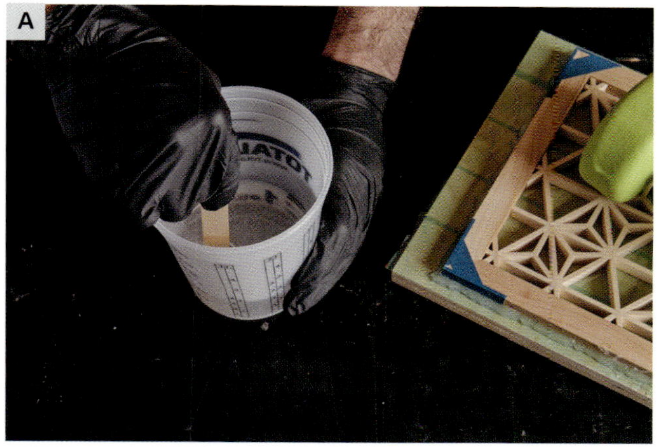

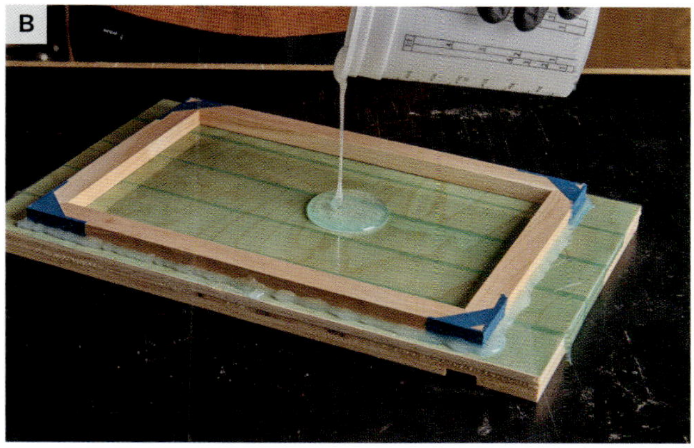

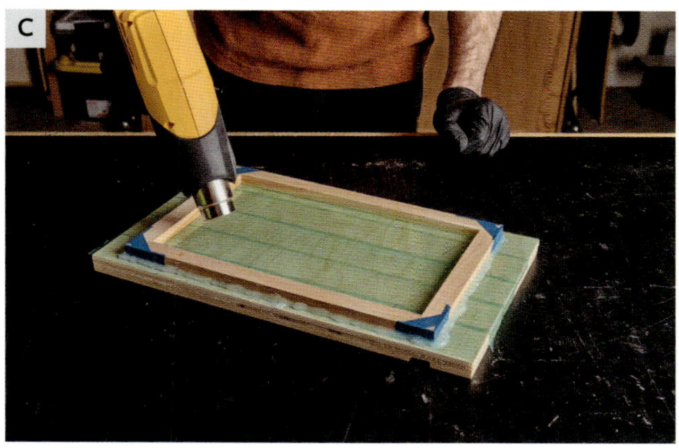

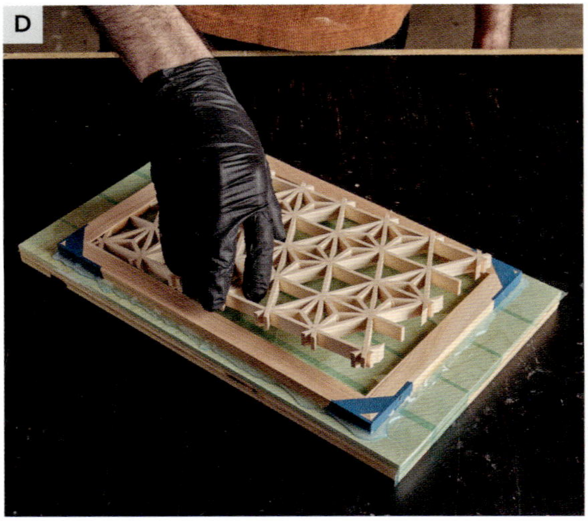
D

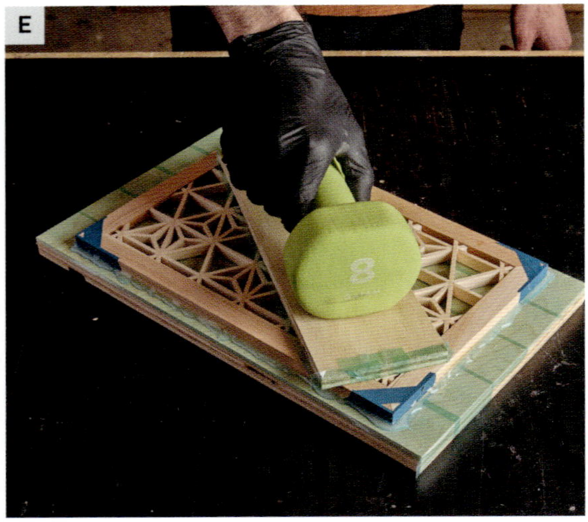
E

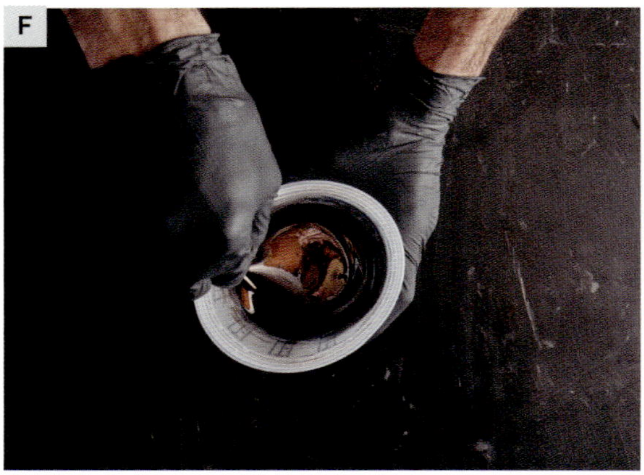
F

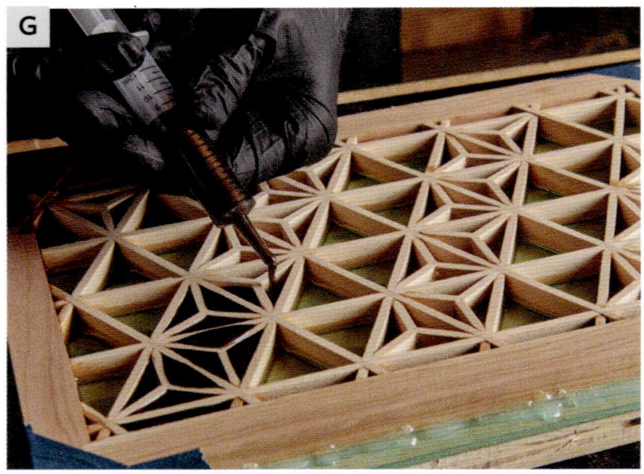
G

3. Carefully lower the kumiko panel into place (**D**) and set a weight on top to keep it from floating to the surface of the resin (**E**).

4. Once the first layer has cured, mix the remaining epoxy. You can add color using liquid dyes, powdered pigments, alcohol inks, or mica powders, depending on the look you want (**F**). The more pigment added, the more opaque the result. If you're using multiple colors, mix separate batches for each. You can also continue with clear epoxy if you choose.

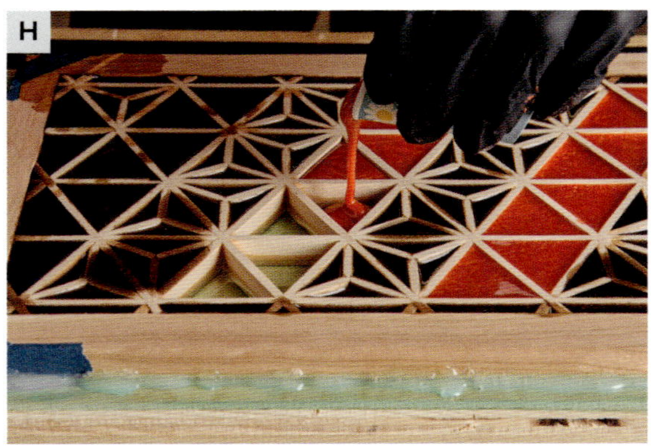
H

5. Carefully pour the colored epoxy into the kumiko panel, filling it just below flush with the top of the kumiko pattern to reduce sanding time later.

For smaller areas, use a dental syringe (**G**). Fill all spaces evenly and let it cure completely (**H**).

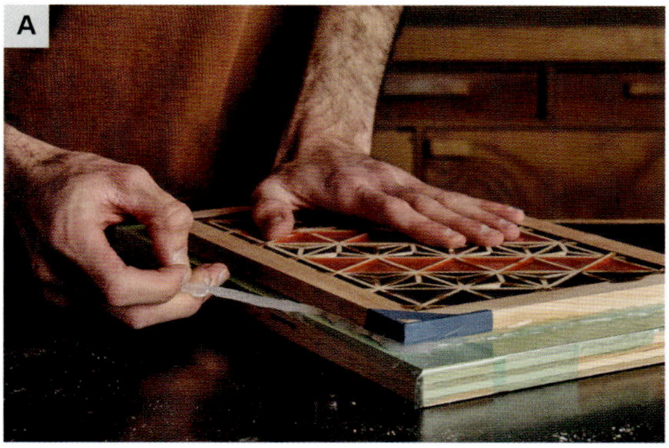

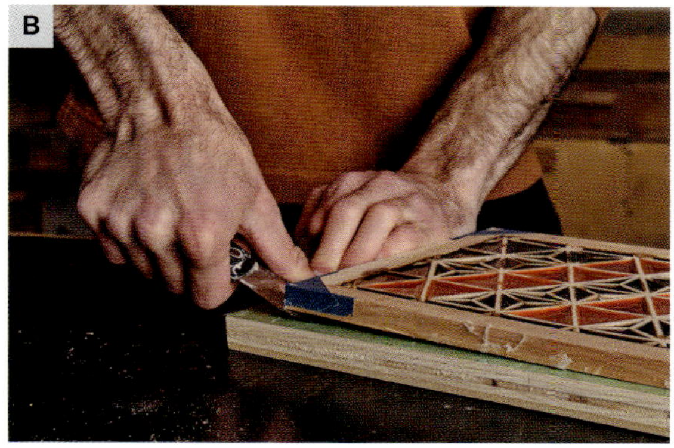

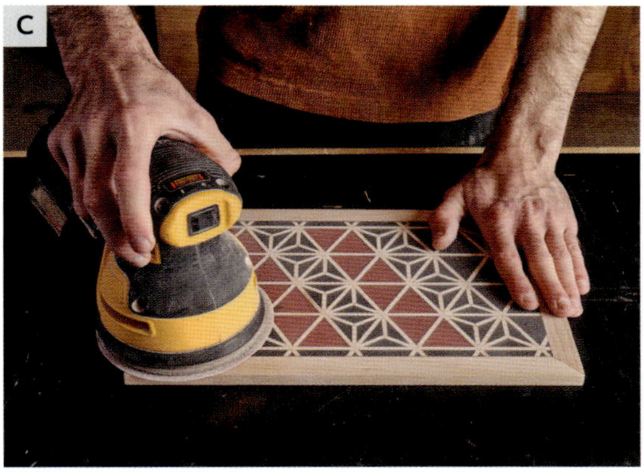

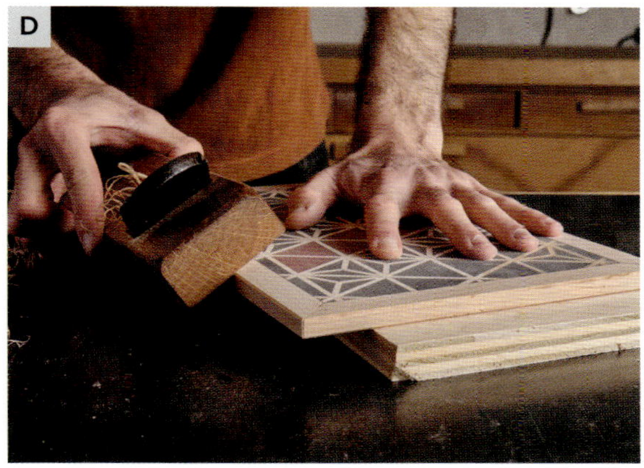

Finishing

1. Once the epoxy has cured, begin by cutting away the hot glue seal with a sharp knife and peeling it off (**A**).

2. Gently pry the panel off the resin-taped board using a putty knife (**B**). If they are difficult to separate, use wooden shims to gradually lift the entire panel.

3. Next, sand all surfaces smooth and flat (**C**). Take care not to concentrate in one area for too long. Excessive heat from friction can soften or smear the epoxy.

4. For finishing touches, you can soften the board's edges with a chamfer or roundover (**D**), add non-slip feet, or drill a hole for hanging. These small details enhance both function and presentation.

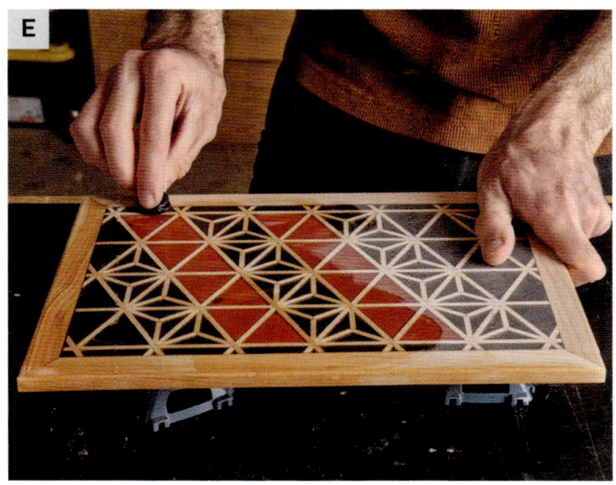

5. Finish the board with a food-safe oil and wax, such as a cutting board oil and wax combo, to bring out the wood's natural beauty and protect it for regular use (**E**).

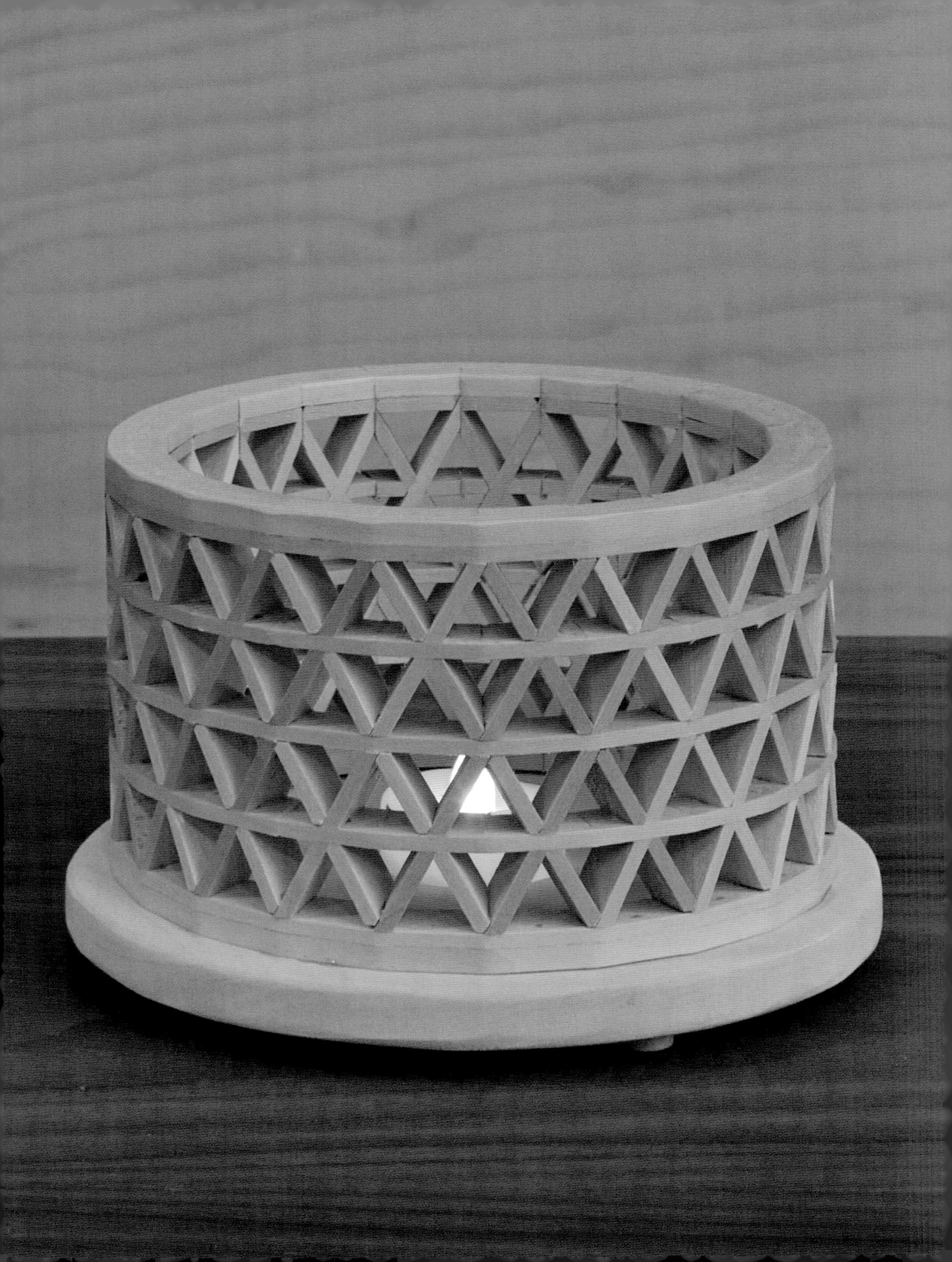

Project 10

Bent Kumiko Evening Lamp

Kumiko is traditionally confined to flat panels. However, I began to question the limitations of this flat form and experimented with bending kumiko into curved shapes, an unconventional approach that has since led to a series of ambitious projects.

The lamp featured in this chapter serves as a more approachable introduction to this innovative technique. While the overall design may appear simple, the process of bending kumiko is anything but. The fragility of the strips, coupled with the stress introduced during bending, makes this technique particularly challenging. Even minor errors in preparation or pressure can lead to breakage or structural failure.

Despite the difficulty, I encourage you to explore this method. Bending kumiko opens up an exciting new dimension of creative possibilities, blending tradition with sculptural expression. For those willing to take on the challenge, it offers a rewarding opportunity to push the boundaries of a centuries-old craft.

PANEL LAYOUT AND PREPARATION FOR BENDING

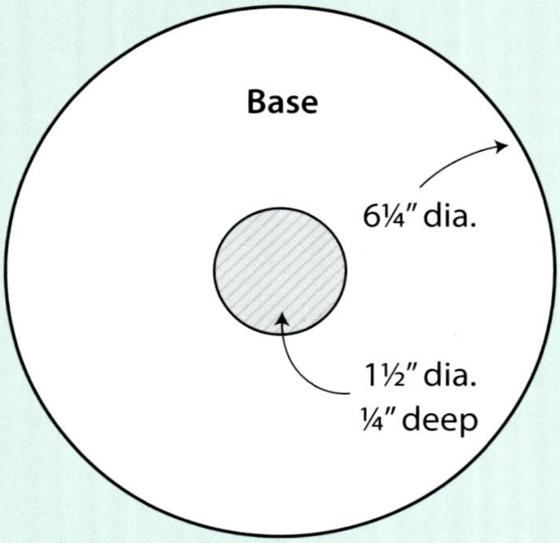

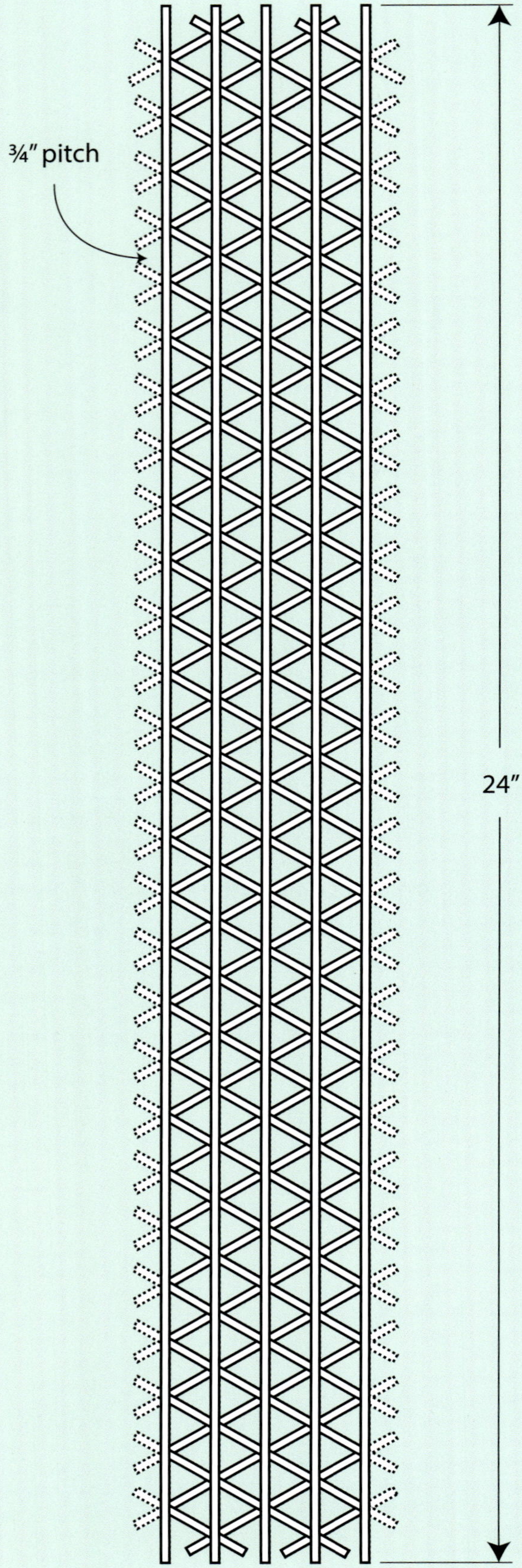

Make the kumiko panel

Begin by constructing the kumiko panel. One critical detail: an A-piece must run the full length of the panel in the direction it will bend. This piece provides essential structural support during and after bending.

This mitsukude is very tight and doesn't offer much space for an infill pattern. The grid can be made larger to accommodate patterns but there are a few things to keep in mind if this route is taken. Not every open space can be filled with pattern infill pieces. Avoid placing infill pieces where bending cuts will be made. Pieces in these areas are prone to breakage or complete removal during cutting. Focus on filling only the central diamond-shaped areas with pattern pieces for asa-no-ha or shippo. These sections remain uncut and will retain their detail. There is an example of this shown in the next chapter.

Important: Use waterproof wood glue during assembly. Hot water will be applied during the bending process, and only high-quality waterproof glue will hold up under those conditions. Water-resistant glue is not sufficient.

1. Once dry, trim the tabs on the panel (**A**).
2. Glue a 3⁄16 in (5.8 mm) thick strip to both long edges of the panel (**B–D**). These will later help define the finished profile. Lastly, sand the panel flat.

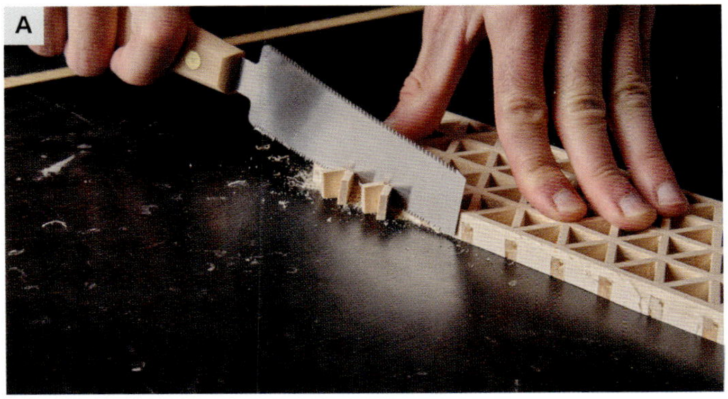
A

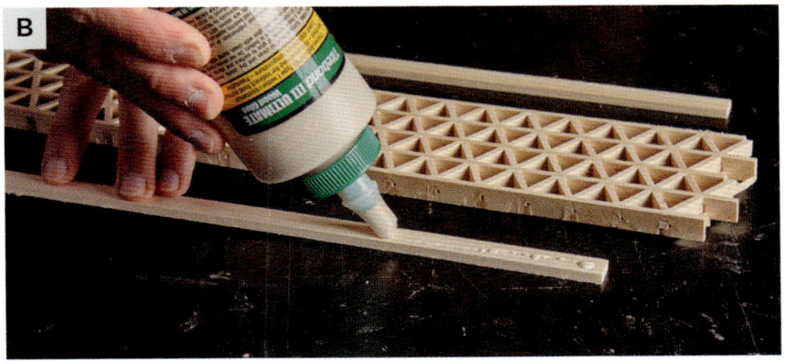
B

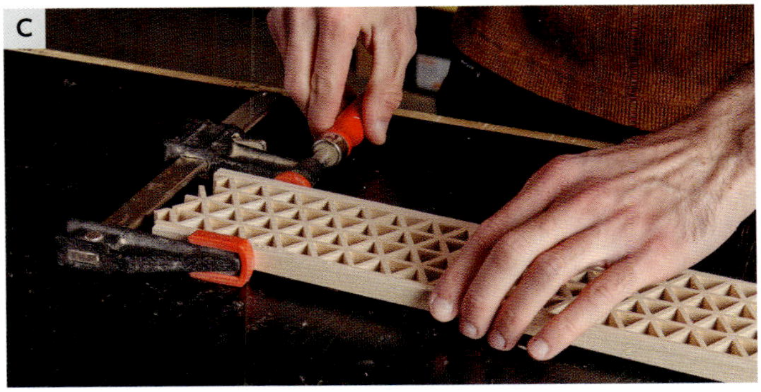
C

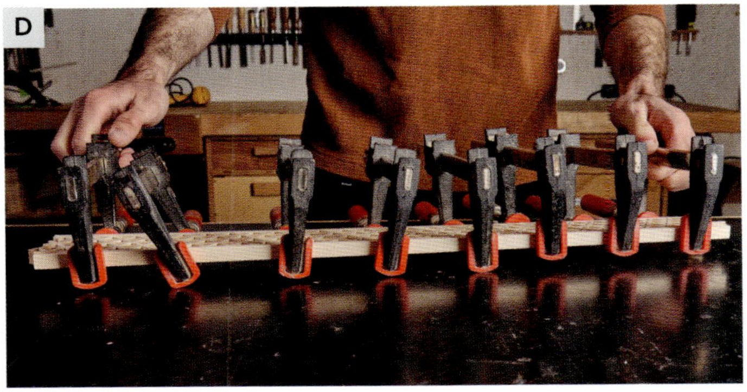
D

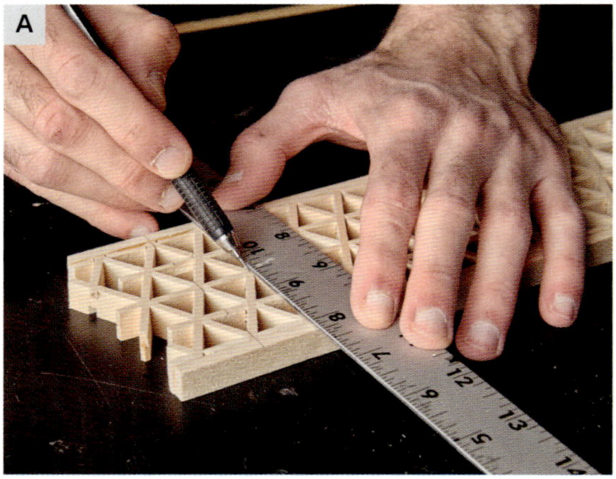

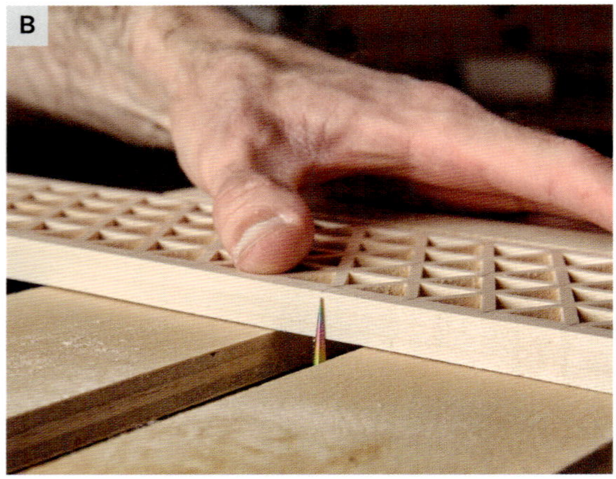

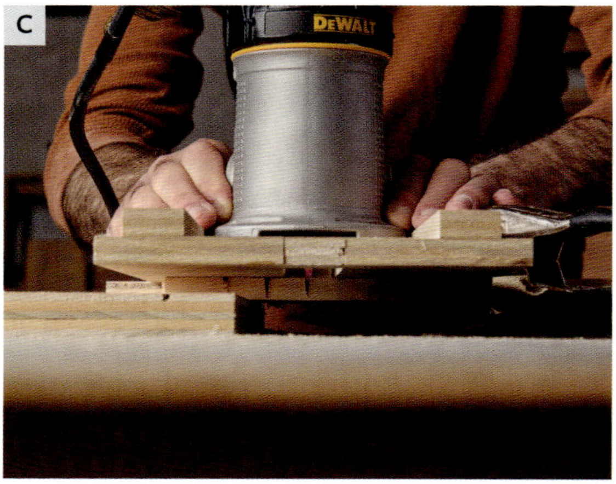

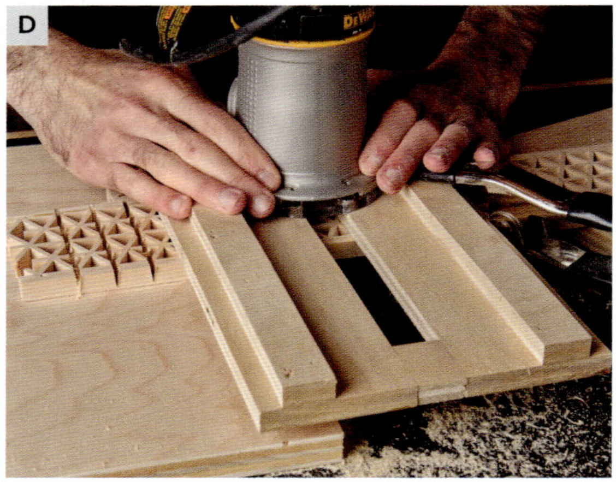

Kerf cutting

1. With the panel face-down (the back side facing up), mark where the kerf cuts will be. These lines should be perpendicular to the panel's long edges and intersect the triangle points in the center of the panel. It's essential that you mark the correct side. This is the back, opposite the side where the full-length A-pieces are visible (**A**).

2. The cuts will be made with a router fitted with a 15º V-bit and with the aid of a shop-made router sled. Alternatively, a straight edge guide can be used.

3. Place the router in the sled and set the cutting depth so that the bit will cut just a hair shy of the panel's full thickness (**B**). Check the depth in multiple spots along the kumiko panel to ensure consistency, accounting for any slight thickness variations.

4. Align the sled so the V-bit tracks precisely along the marked lines (**C**). For ease and safety, elevate the panel and clamp the sled or straight edge guide firmly in place. Make one cut along each line (**D**).

5. After cutting, the panel will be extremely fragile. Handle it with care and clean all kerfs thoroughly to remove sawdust and tear out.

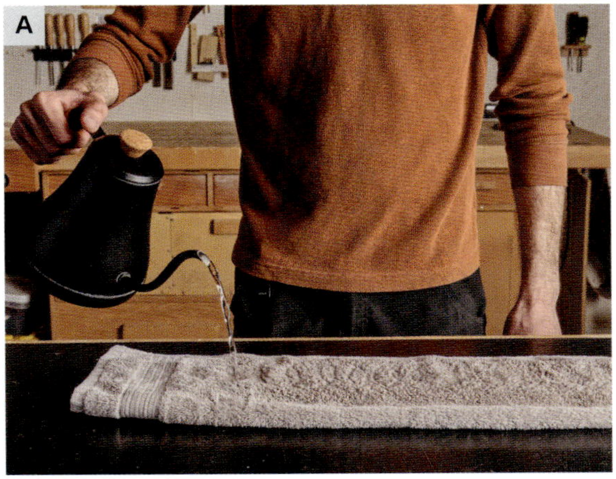

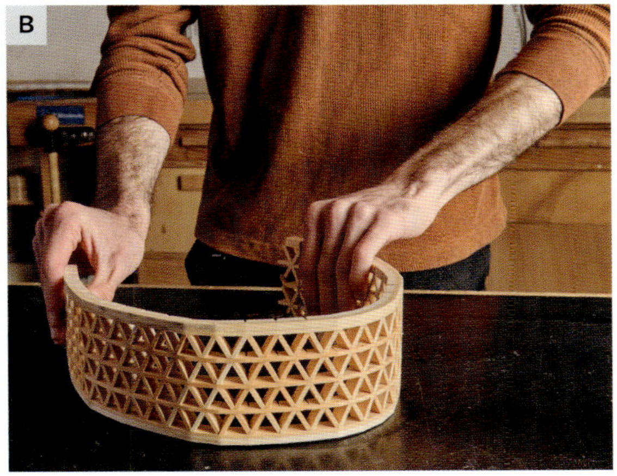

Bending the panel

1. Lay the panel cut-side down on a flat surface. Place a folded towel on top and soak it thoroughly with boiling water (**A**). Temperature matters! Hot tap water won't work. Because the wood is relatively thin, a minute or two of soaking is usually enough.

2. Gently begin bending the panel by hand until all the kerfs close (**B**). If the wood resists, re-soak the towel with boiling water and allow more time. Patience is key here.

3. Once fully bent (**C**), secure the panel in position with masking tape (**D**). This should hold the curve without applying excess pressure — just enough to maintain the shape.

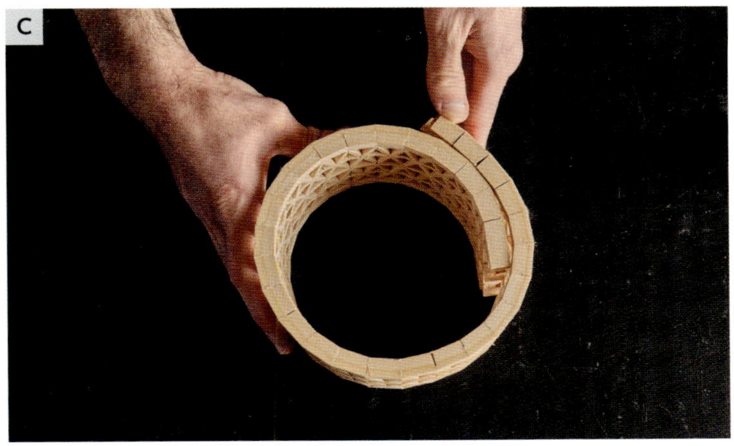

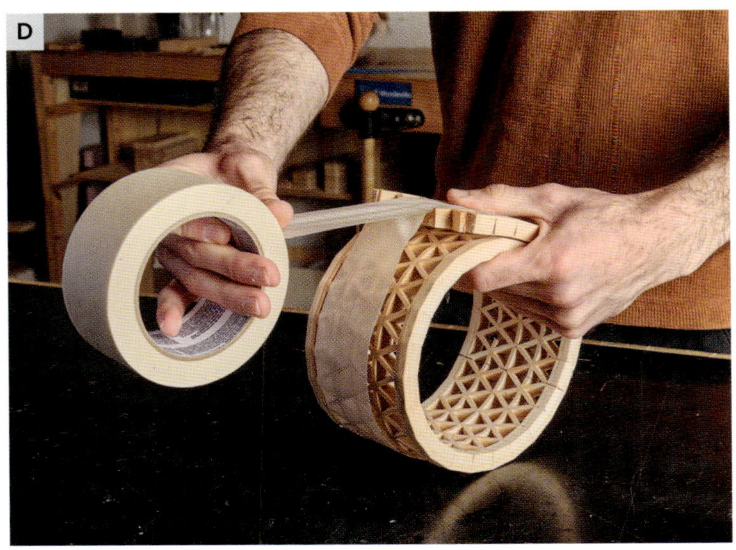

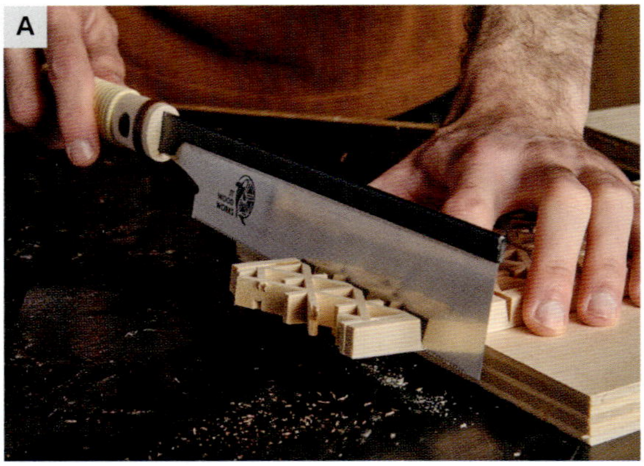

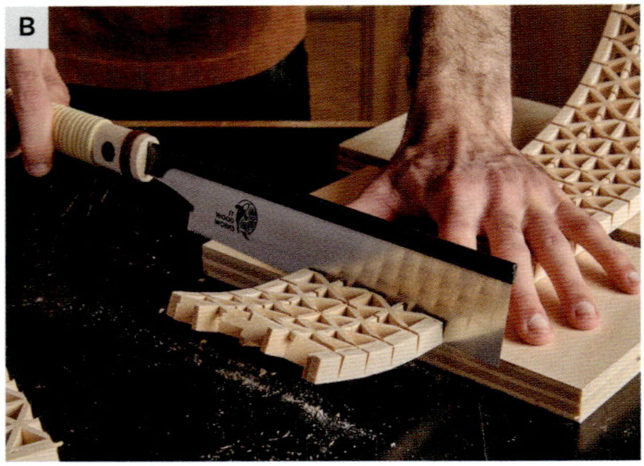

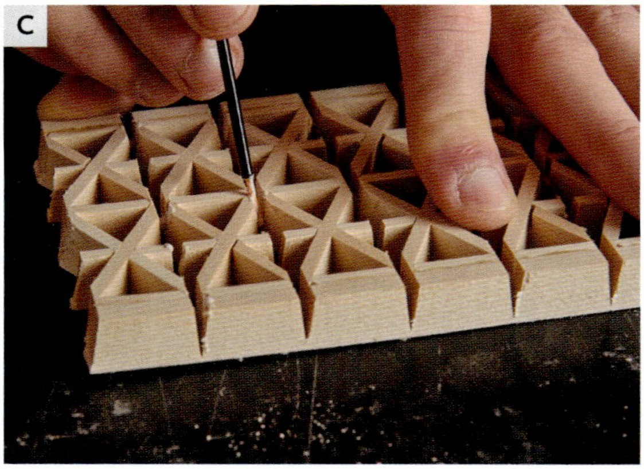

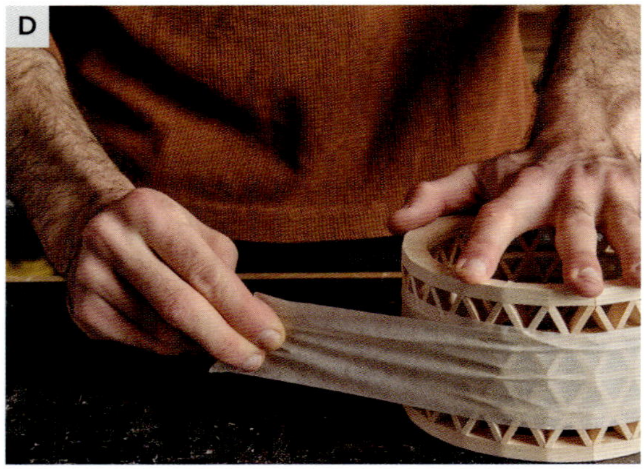

Cut and glue the panel

1. After the panel dries completely, it needs to be cut to size. Carefully unroll the panel and use a dozuki saw to cut the first V-groove on one end of the panel. Follow the angled cut with the saw (**A**).

2. Locate the V-groove that needs to interact with the one just cut so the panel can bend into a complete cylinder. Cut along that V-groove in the same way as the first (**B**).

3. Carefully open each kerf slightly and apply glue inside (**C**). Avoid excess glue to minimize squeeze-out.

4. Resecure the bend using masking tape (**D**) and let the glue dry fully. Make sure all grooves fully close and pay extra attention to the seam. It should be invisible if done properly. Once the glue dries, the panel will be significantly more rigid.

Make the base plate

1. Using ½ in (12.7 mm) thick material, cut the base plate ½ in (12.7 mm) larger in diameter than the kumiko panel (**E**).

2. Drill a ¼ in (6.4 mm) deep hole at 1½ in (38 mm) in diameter directly in the center to hold an LED tealight (**F**).

3. Sand and shape the base plate as desired. Add a chamfer or roundover to the edges to give a more refined look.

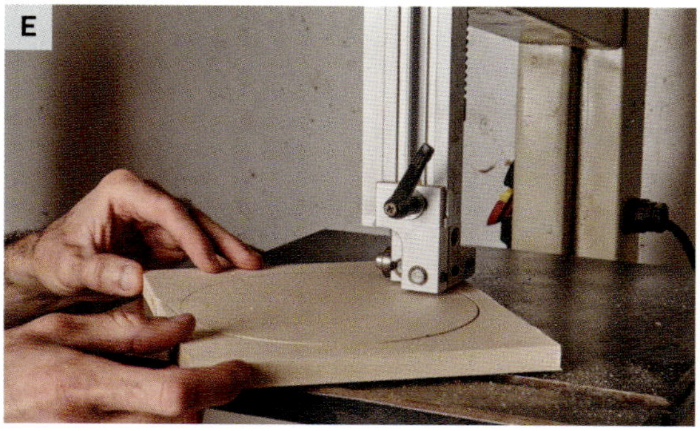

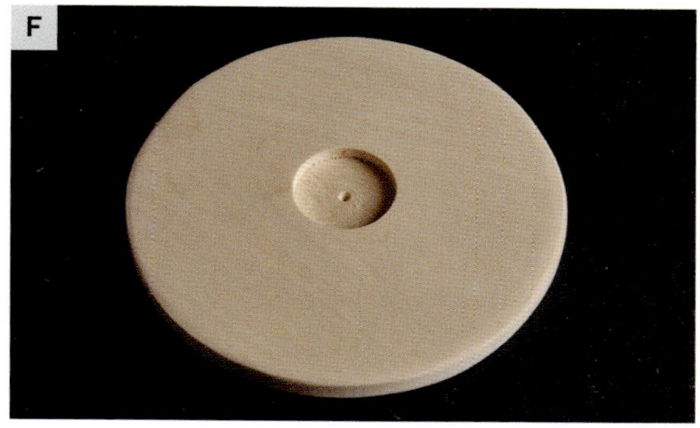

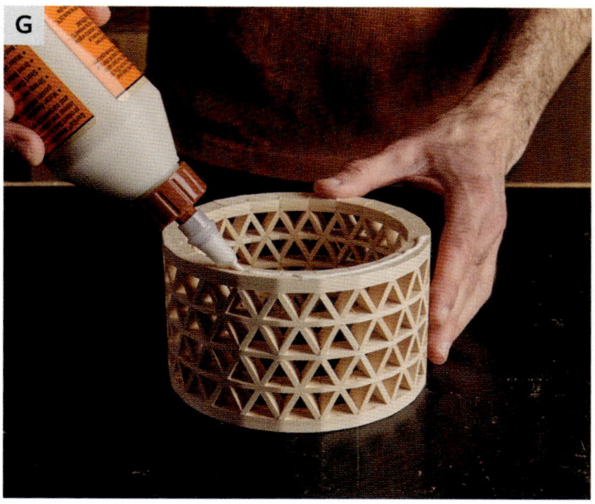

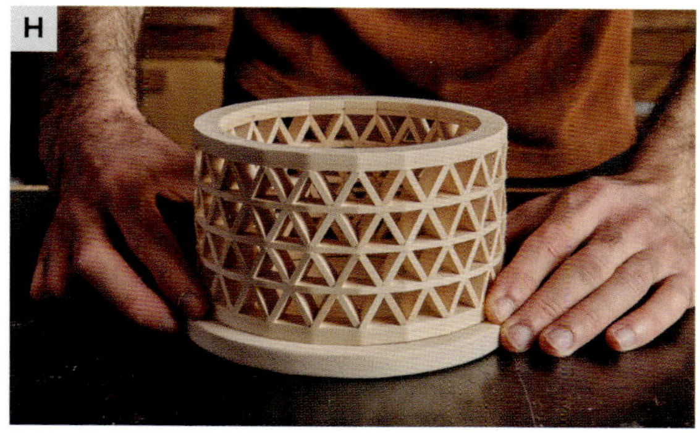

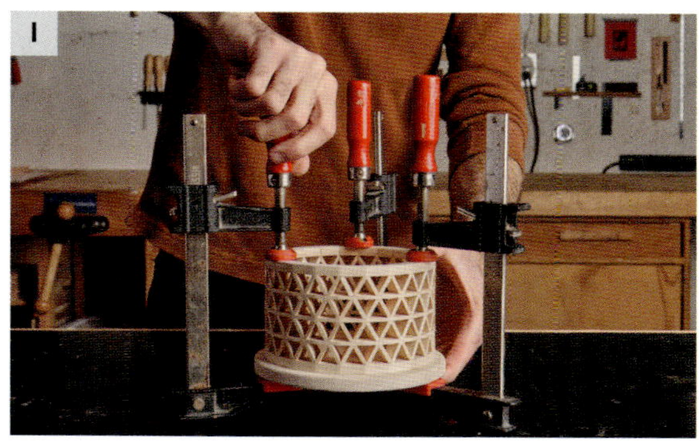

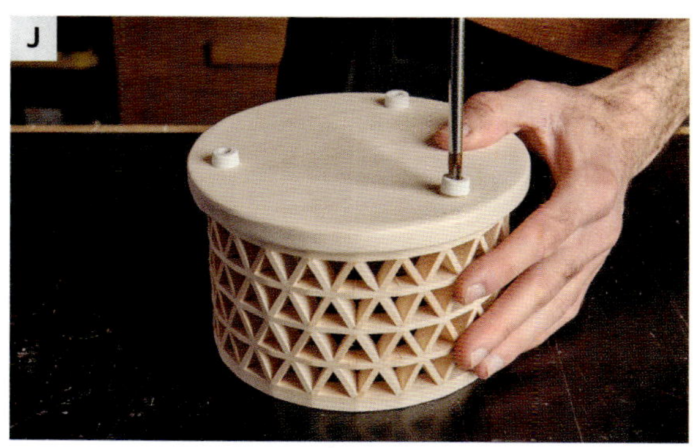

Assembly

1. Apply shoji paper to the inside of the bent kumiko panel, if you'd like (see pages 93 to 94). This can be a bit difficult to do on the inside of a curve and is completely optional.

2. Apply glue to the bottom edge of the kumiko (**G**) and glue it to the base. Position it in the center so the base has an even reveal around the kumiko panel (**H**).

3. Clamp lightly to ensure a solid connection (**I**), and allow everything to dry completely.

4. Once the glue has cured, add small feet to the bottom to give a more finished and polished appearance (**J**), and your bent kumiko lamp is ready to enjoy.

OVERLEAF **Light filtering through a lattice window.**
Photo by Noriko Hayashi for The Washington Post via Getty Images.

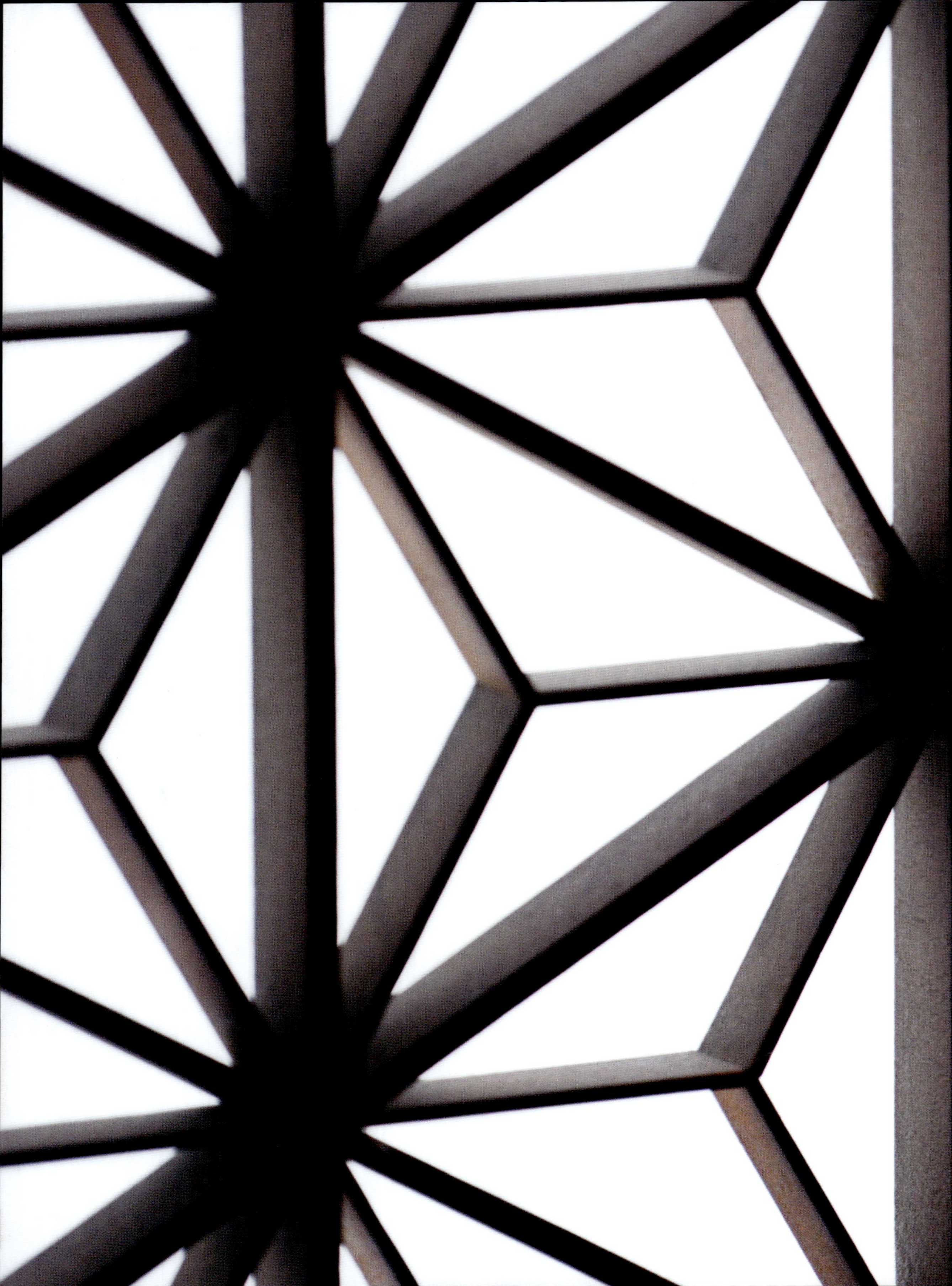

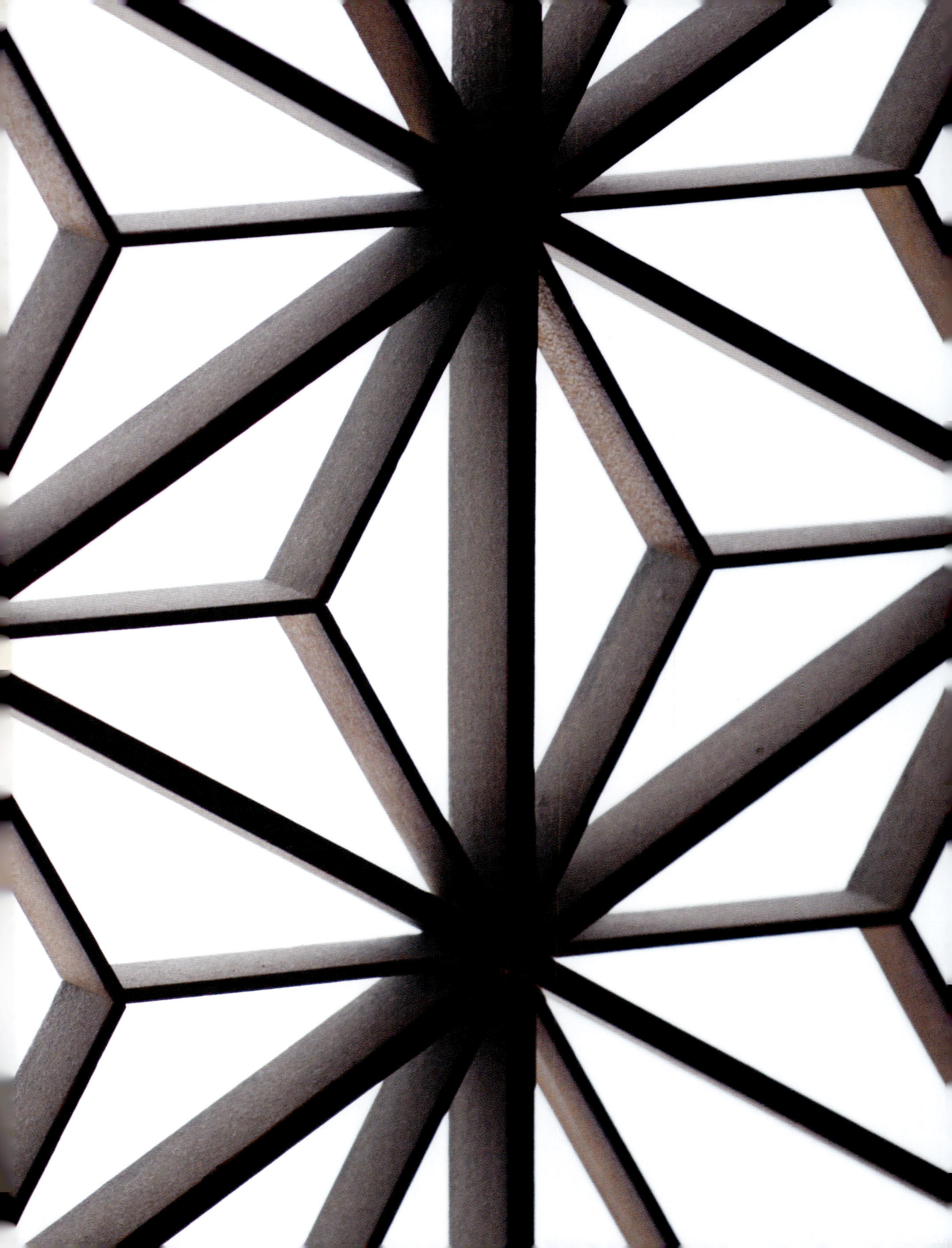

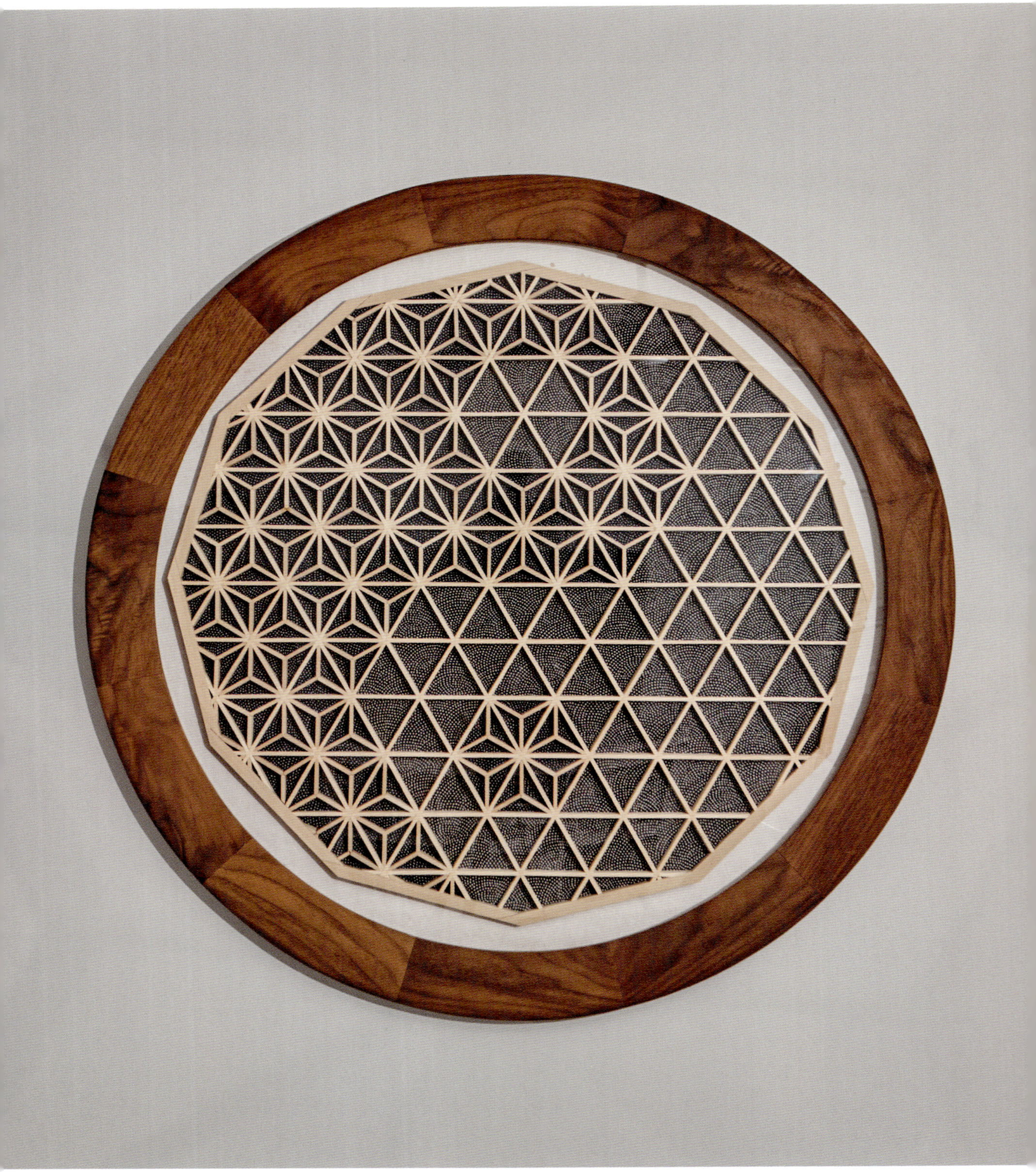

Chapter 8

Kumiko Design Principles

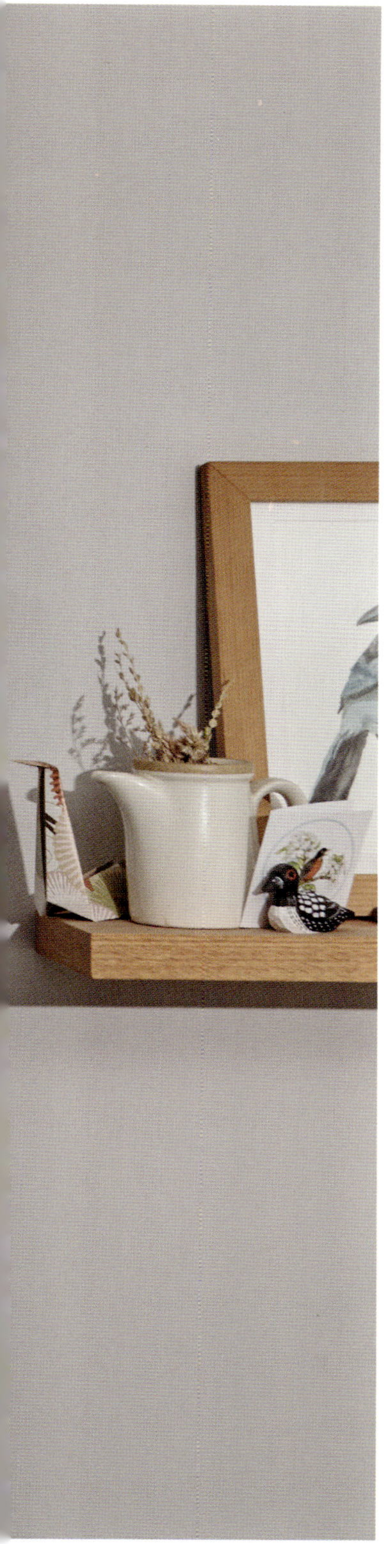

Kumiko is more than a technique; it's a design language. Once you've developed the skills to make patterns like the kaku asa-no-ha, yotsuba izutsu-tsugi, asa-no-ha, and shippo, you gain access to a visual vocabulary capable of expressing mood, balance, and artistry through your work.

This chapter marks a shift from execution to intention. It invites you to begin designing original pieces that feature kumiko, whether as a bold centerpiece or a quiet accent, by exploring considerations of style, proportion, wood selection, and overall cohesion. In doing so, you take a step onto what the Japanese call the Shokunin no Tabi (職人の旅), or "Craftsman's Journey."

Shokunin no Tabi is more than the development of technical skill; it's a lifelong path of refinement, curiosity, and quiet respect for the material, the craft, and your own evolving sensibilities. As you begin to make design decisions, balancing boldness with subtlety, structure with spontaneity, you're not just assembling parts — you're learning to speak through wood.

◀ A framed kumiko panel with an artistic representation on the yin-yang symbol.

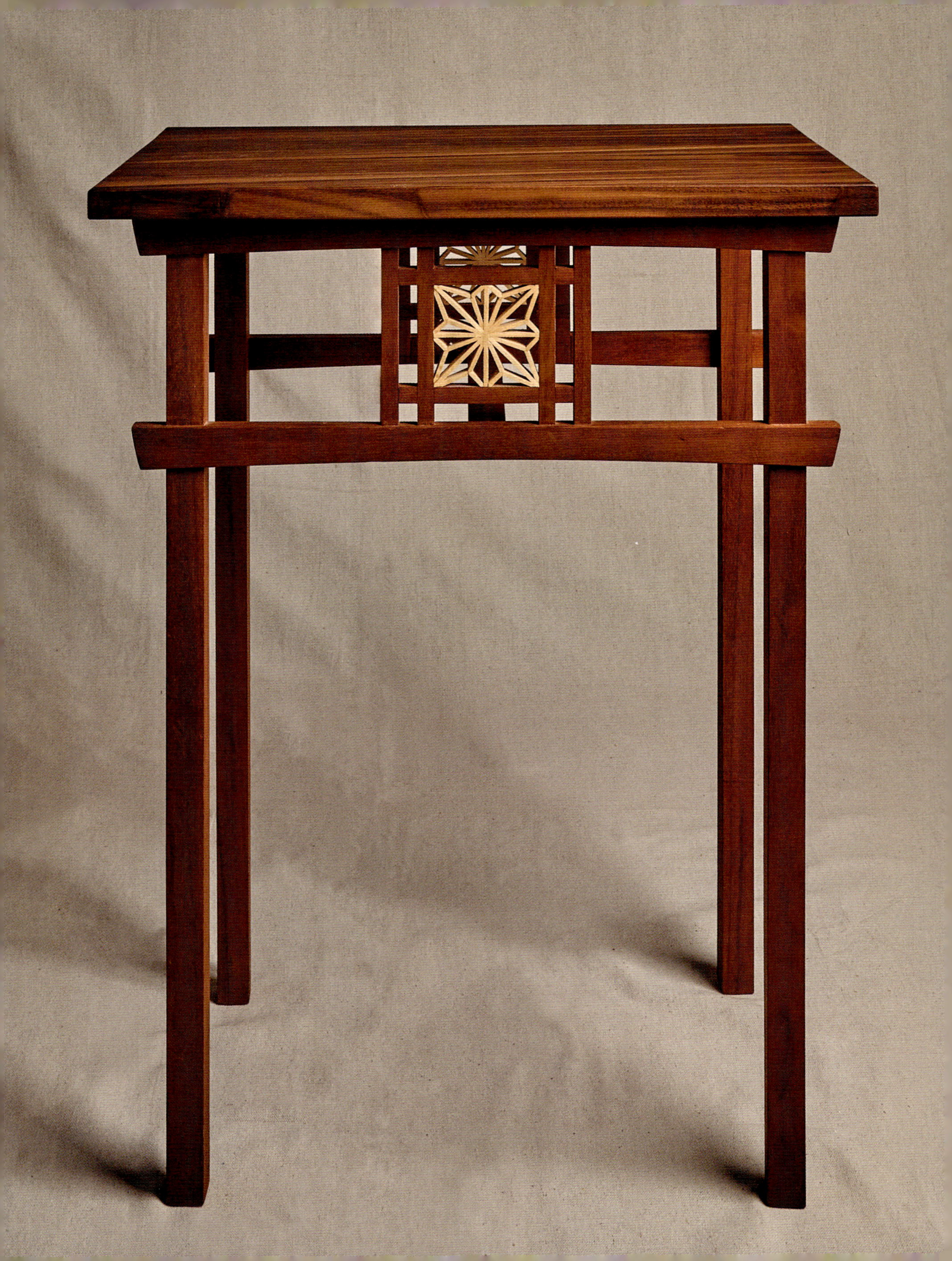

◀ Torii Table. An end table modeled after the torii gates commonly seen at Shinto shrines.

▶ Kumiko and epoxy pendant light.

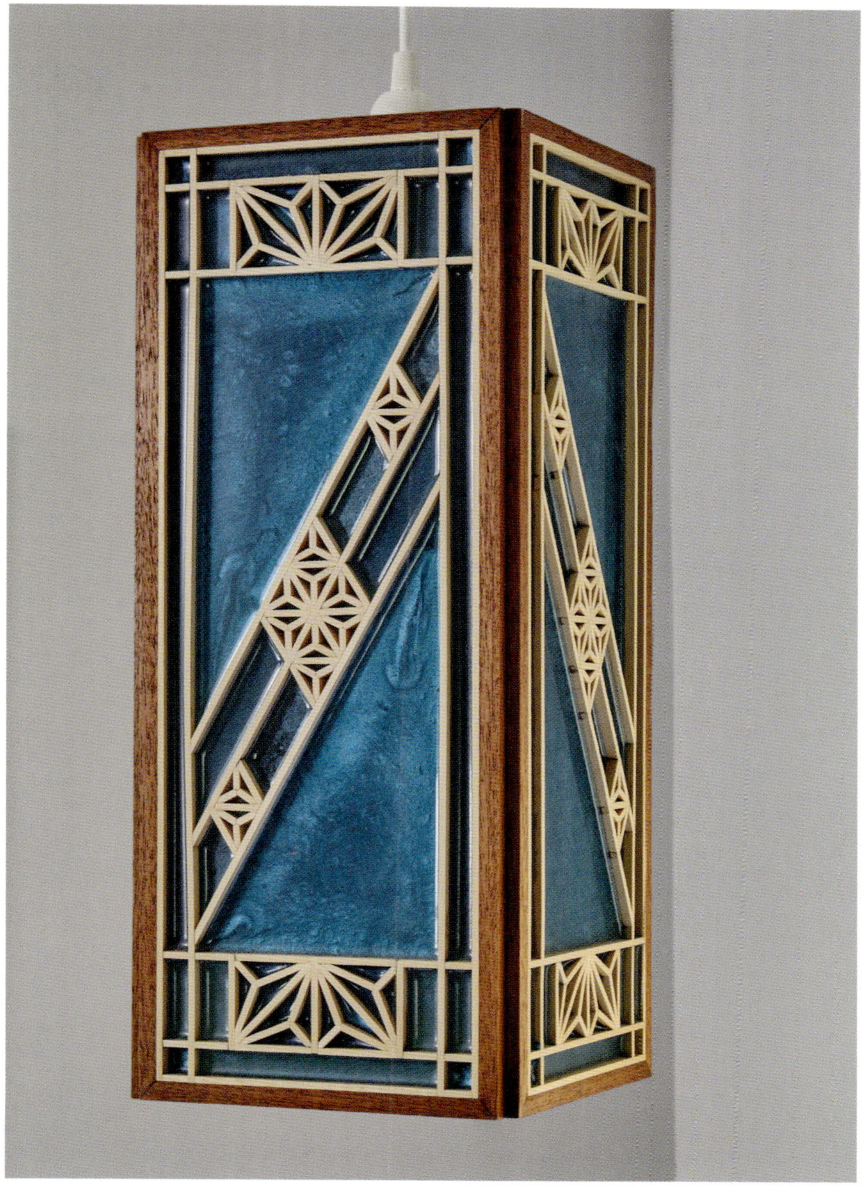

Sketching, testing, and reworking your ideas is part of this path. You may not get it right the first time, or even the tenth, but each iteration deepens your understanding. Each choice, from grain direction to pattern placement, reflects not just what you know but how you see. And this, more than any template or jig, is what defines the work of a true shokunin.

Highlight or Subtly Integrate

One of the first choices to make in designing a kumiko project is how prominent you want the pattern to be.

- Highlighting kumiko: When kumiko is meant to stand out, such as in a panel in a cabinet door, a shoji-inspired room divider, or the focal point of a wall hanging, think of it as the "voice" of the piece. Keep the surrounding materials and lines clean and minimal to allow the pattern to shine. Let kumiko play the role of sculpture within structure.
- Subtle integration: Kumiko can also play a supporting role, used sparingly in drawer faces, lampshades, or mirror frames. Here, it functions more as a texture or detail, offering interest without dominating the design.

Knowing which role you want kumiko to play will shape every other design decision.

▶ Kumi-koi. An art piece where epoxy takes center stage, with kumiko used sparingly to weave in a dialogue with the past.

Thinking in Proportion

Good proportion is what makes a piece feel balanced and comfortable. Kumiko is inherently rhythmic and geometric, which can either enhance or fight with the overall form if not scaled thoughtfully.

- Frame-to-pattern balance: When framing a kumiko panel, avoid overly thick rails and stiles that overpower the pattern. Conversely, if the kumiko grid is too dense or fine for the scale of the piece, it may appear visually noisy. A good rule of thumb is to design the kumiko cell size to be roughly in harmony with the surrounding frame, neither dwarfing nor dwarfed.
- Pattern density: A kaku asa-no-ha may be best showcased in fewer, larger cells to emphasize its starburst structure. The shippo pattern, with its interlocking curves, tends to lose clarity in smaller grids and is best used in medium to larger-scale cells where its overlapping circles can be fully appreciated. And remember it's perfectly okay to leave some areas of the kumiko grid unfilled. Negative space can create balance and emphasize the surrounding patterns. Consider what the eye needs — space to rest or detail to study?

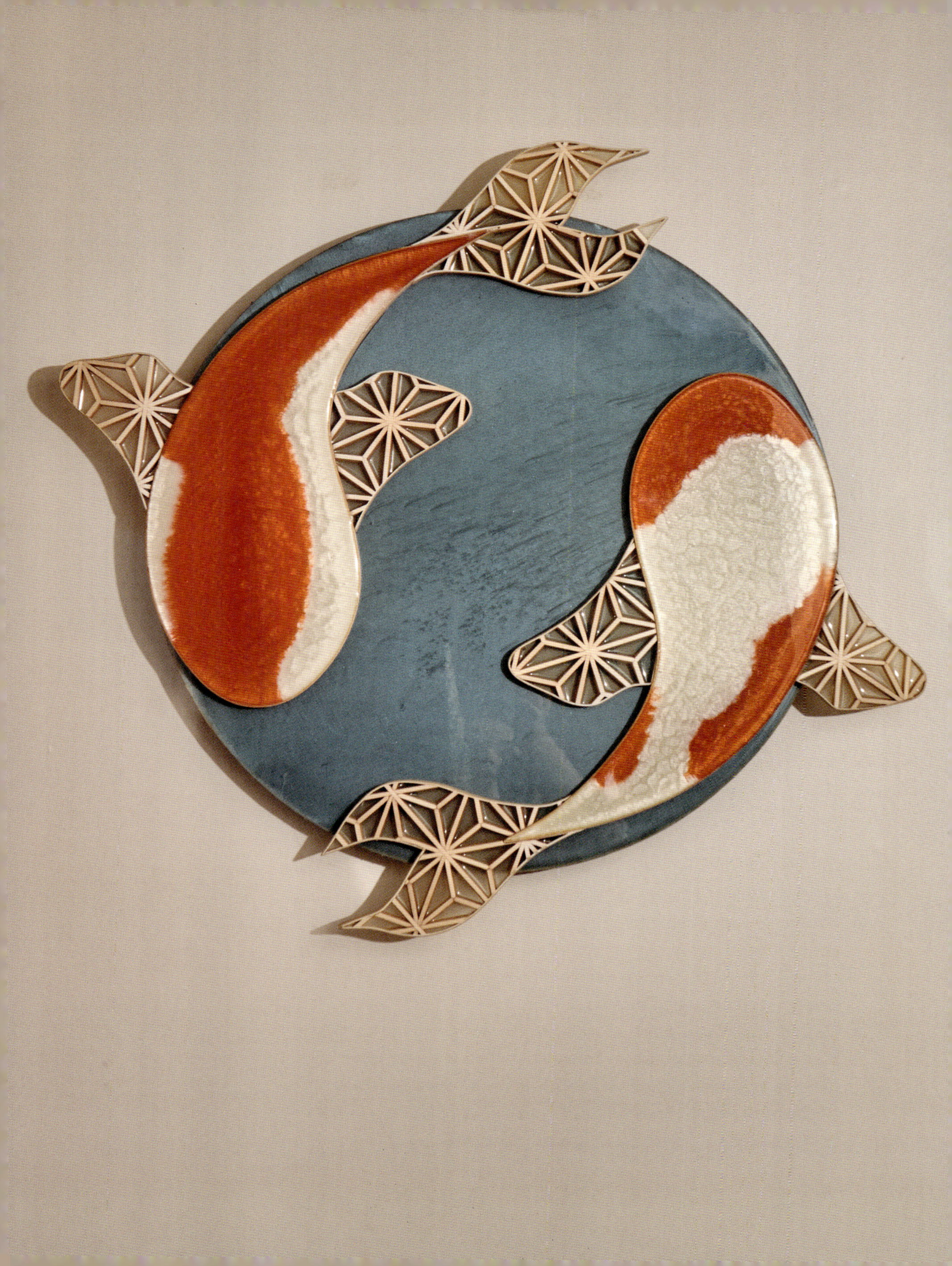

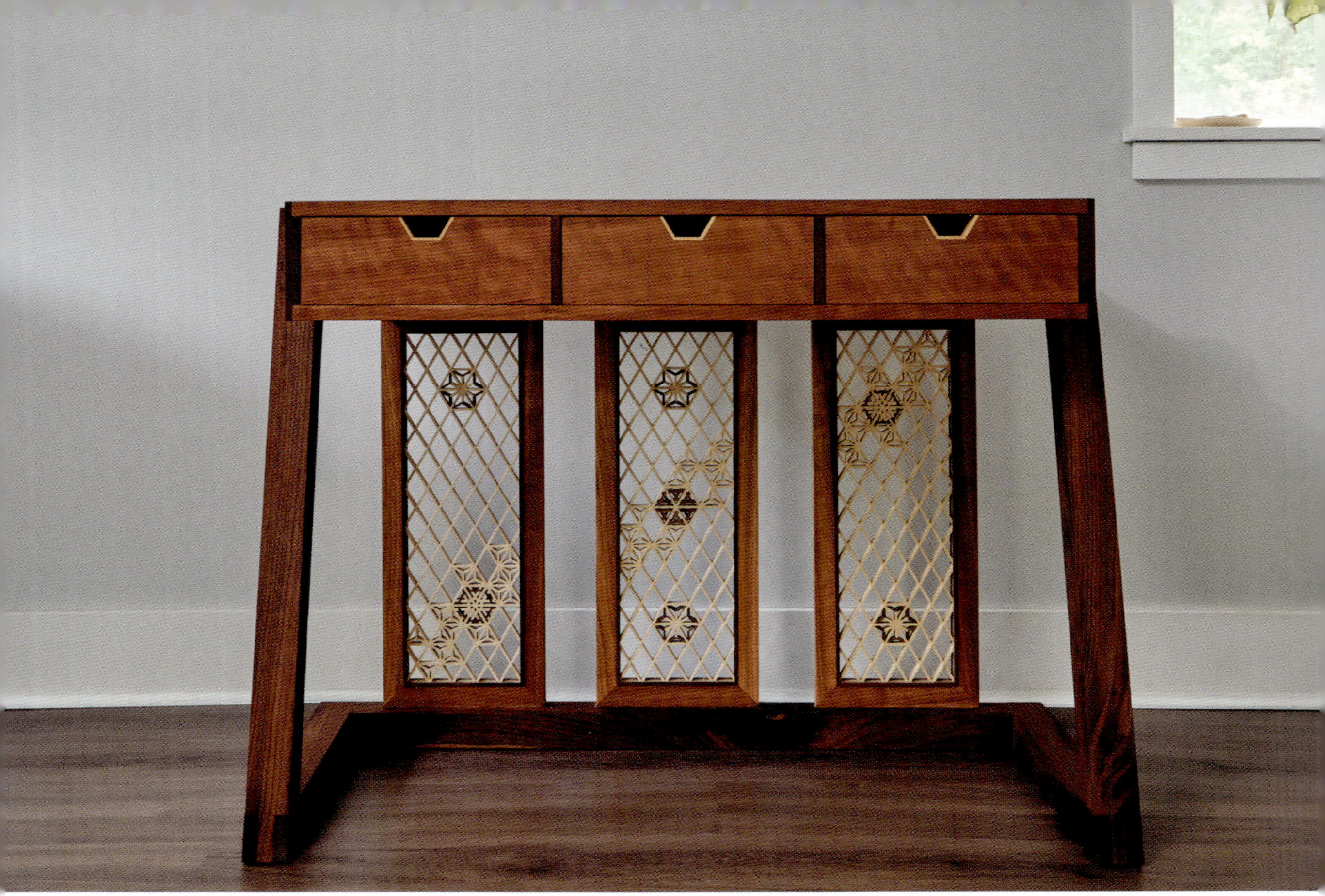

- Overall form: A tall cabinet, low bench, or wide mirror all offer different kinds of canvas. Design your kumiko panels accordingly. Tall and narrow for doors, square for wall panels, or continuous for screens. Think of kumiko not just as decoration but as a graphic element that interacts with negative space.

▲ A writing desk featuring kumiko panels arranged in a triptych layout. Featuring the asa-no-ha and goma (胡麻) patterns.

Material Choices: Wood as a Voice

The wood you choose affects not just appearance but tone.

- Traditional versus contemporary feel: Japanese cypress (hinoki) and basswood create a classic, pale look that lets the pattern take center stage. Walnut, white oak, or even ebonized woods offer a modern, contrasting approach.
- Texture and grain: Choose straight-grained woods for the kumiko itself. Clean grain lines prevent distraction from the geometry. For surrounding elements, use your judgment — a subtle grain like maple may offer harmony, while something bolder like zebrawood or figured cherry can introduce tension or drama.

- Color coordination: Consider whether the kumiko will match, contrast, or complement the rest of the piece. Monochromatic palettes offer unity; contrasting tones can sharpen the kumiko's lines.

Cohesion and Intent

Ask yourself: What is the purpose of this piece? What feeling should it evoke?

- Function informs design: A tea tray invites quiet elegance and tactile refinement. A wall-mounted shelf may call for stronger lines and practical proportions. Design to match the function and let kumiko enhance rather than complicate that purpose.
- Repetition versus restraint: It's easy to overuse kumiko once you get the hang of it. But restraint is often more powerful. Sometimes a single hexagon of shippo in the center of a solid panel says more than a grid of 40 repeating patterns.
- Joinery and edges: Let your joinery decisions support the aesthetic. Kumiko pairs beautifully with exposed joinery — wedged tenons, finger joints, and clean miters. Avoid bulky or visually conflicting mechanical fasteners.

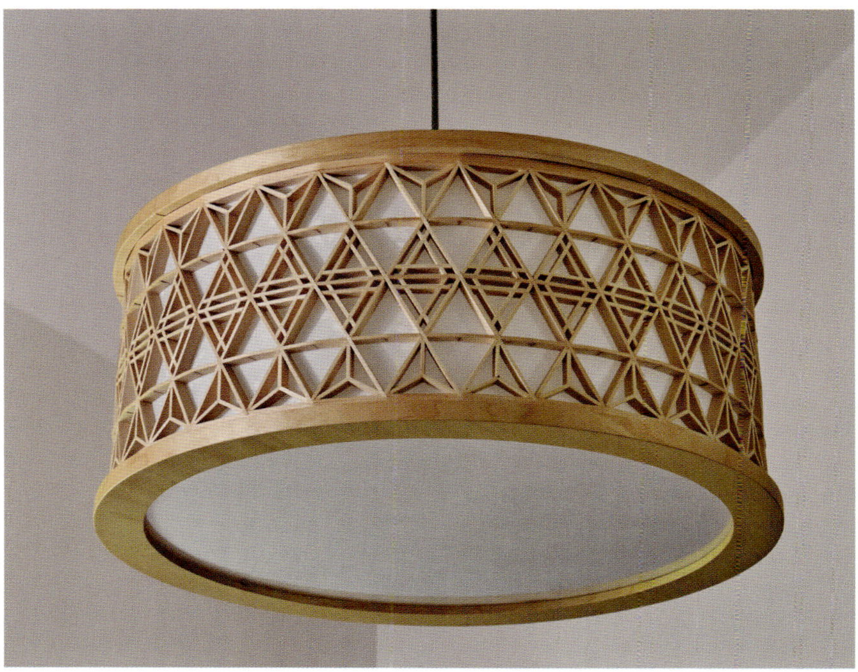

▶ Bent kumiko lamp with asa-no-ha and goma patterns.

Sketch, Mock Up, Iterate

Before committing to the full build, sketch ideas loosely. Then:

- Use tracing paper or CAD (Computer-Aided Design) to experiment with scale and layout.
- Build mini mock-ups or partial panels to test your proportions.
- Look at your design from across the room. Does the kumiko read clearly? Does the whole piece feel unified?

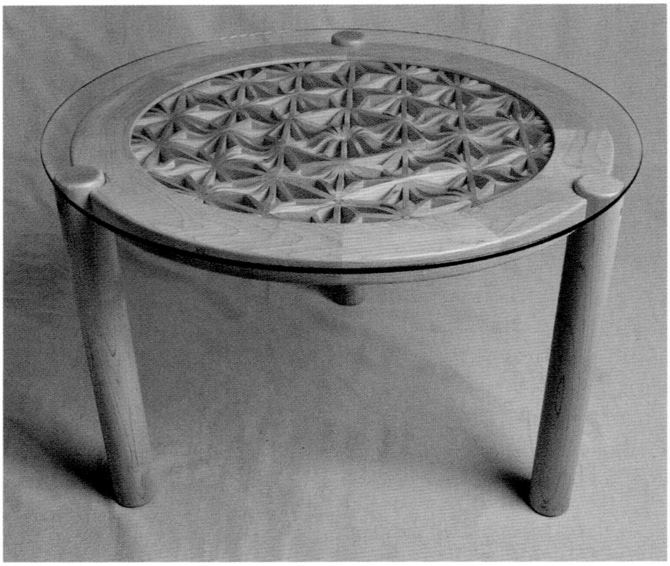

This iterative process helps ensure your final build is thoughtful and refined.

▼▶ Ripple Table. A kumiko panel is 3D carved using a CNC (Computer Numerical Control) router to create a water ripple effect on its surface.

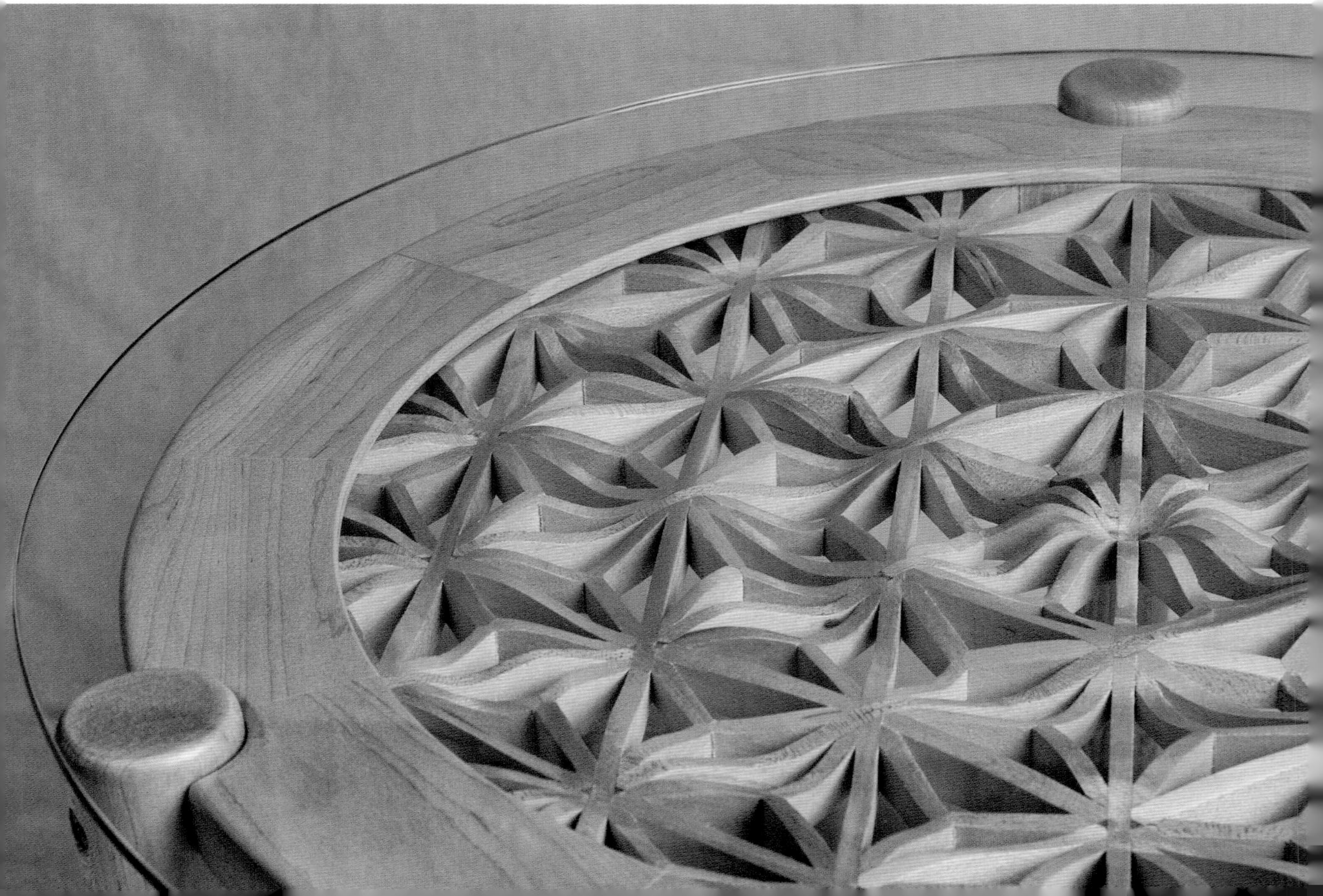

Chapter 9

Final Thoughts

Designing with kumiko is about finding harmony between pattern and frame, ornament and restraint, tradition and personal voice. Let each piece you make be a meditation on balance. With your foundational skills in place, you now have the tools to begin composing your own work, not just as a woodworker but also as an artist.

This is where the practice truly begins. As you explore beyond the patterns in these pages, you'll start to see kumiko not just as decoration, but as structure, rhythm, and language. Whether you're creating a panel for a cabinet, a light fixture, or a quiet alcove in your home, your choices of wood, scale, pattern, and proportion are acts of expression.

Don't be afraid to slow down. Allow yourself the space to experiment, to fail, and to refine. The path of the shokunin is not about chasing perfection, but about returning to the bench again and again, each time with a little more care and intention than before.

What you build will carry something of you in it, your eye, your hand, your patience. That's the quiet power of kumiko: it teaches us to notice more, to take less for granted, and to craft with meaning.

So take what you've learned, and begin your own tabi, your own journey. There's no end to where this work can take you.

Glossary

Chamfer: A beveled edge cut at an angle, typically 45°, where two faces meet. It softens sharp edges and can add a clean, intentional detail to a piece.

Fence: The straight edge that holds and aligns the workpiece at a consistent angle to the saw blade, ensuring accurate cuts.

Half lap: A joint where two pieces overlap by removing half the thickness from each at the point of intersection, so that they fit flush together.

Jig: A tool or device that guides tools or holds workpieces in place, making cuts, shapes, or assemblies more accurate, consistent, and repeatable.

Kerf: The width of material removed by a saw blade during a cut.

Pitch: The spacing between parallel strips of a kumiko grid.

Rabbet: Also spelled rebate, a recess or groove cut along the edge or end of a board.

Registration key: A fixed pin that fits into the already made cut in the workpiece, ensuring each successive cut is evenly spaced and precisely aligned.

Roundover: A rounded edge profile that replaces a sharp corner with a smooth curve. It softens the feel of a piece, improves comfort and durability, and gives edges a more finished appearance.

Spline: A thin strip of wood inserted into matching grooves cut in two adjoining pieces, adding strength, alignment, and stability to the joint.

Spline jig (DIY): A device that holds a mitered workpiece at a fixed angle while guiding it safely across the saw blade, allowing precise grooves to be cut in the corners for inserting splines that reinforce the joint.

Table saw sled: A jig that rides in the saw's miter slots and carries the workpiece through the blade on a fixed platform for accurate, stable cuts.

Appendix One

Japanese Words and Terms

Romaji	Kanji/Kana	English Translation	Notes/Context
Andon	行灯	Paper lantern	Traditional Japanese lantern, often with kumiko panels.
Asa-no-ha	麻の葉	Hemp leaf	Common kumiko motif.
Dozuki	胴付	Japanese back saw	A Japanese pull saw with a thin blade and a stiffening spine.
Gampi	雁皮	Gampi plant (*Wikstroemia sikokiana*)	Plant fiber used in making washi paper.
Goma	胡麻	Sesame	The goma motif has long been associated with youth and longevity.
Ha-ganna	葉鉋	Kumiko plane	Specialty planes used to cut the infill pieces of kumiko patterns.
Hinoki	檜	Japanese cypress (*Chamaecyparis obtusa*)	Tree native to Japan, revered for its durable, rot-resistant wood with a pale pink heartwood and white sapwood.
Jigumi	地組	Joint/grid	The basic grid or joint system in kumiko.
Kaku asa-no-ha	角麻の葉	Square hemp leaf pattern	A popular kumiko pattern based on hemp leaf shapes.
Kanna	鉋	Hand plane	Traditional Japanese woodworking plane.
Kigoroshi	木殺し	"Wood killing" (tension relief)	Technique to relieve wood tension during joinery through compression of the edges.
Kiwa kanna	際鉋	Edge or rabbet plane	A specialized Japanese wood plane used for shaving inside L-shaped corners or edges.
Kōgu bako	工具箱	Toolbox	Box used to store Japanese woodworking tools.
Kōzo	楮 or こうぞ	Paper mulberry	Plant fiber used to make washi paper.
Kumiko	組子	Assembled wood pieces / lattice work	Japanese technique of assembling thin wood strips into patterns without the need for nails or glue.

Romaji	Kanji/Kana	Translation	Notes/Context
Mitsukude	三つ組手	Three way miter joint	A joinery used to make a hexagonal kumiko grid. The basic grid work for many patterns.
Mitsumata	三椏	Mitsumata plant (*Edgeworthia chrysantha*)	Plant fiber used in making washi paper.
Monozukuri	ものづくり	Craftsmanship	The spirit of making things with care and skill by hand.
Nokogiri	鋸	Saw	Traditional Japanese saw.
Nomi	のみ	Chisel	Traditional Japanese woodworking chisel.
Nori	糊	Paste/glue	Traditional rice- or wheat-based glue used in paper arts and woodworking.
Rindo	竜胆	Japanese gentian plant	An angular pattern used since ancient times.
Sakura	桜	Cherry blossom	Iconic Japanese flower, a popular kumiko motif.
Shippo	七宝	Seven treasures pattern	A circular kumiko pattern symbolizing harmony.
Shōji	障子	Sliding paper door	Traditional Japanese doors often containing kumiko grids.
Shokunin no Tabi	職人の旅	Craftsman's journey	A metaphor for the lifelong path of skill development.
Sugi	杉	Japanese cedar (*Cryptomeria japonica*)	A conifer native to Japan.
Ume	梅	Plum blossom (*Prunus mume*)	Symbol of perseverance and renewal; kumiko motif.
Wabi-sabi	侘び 寂び	Imperfect beauty	Japanese aesthetic valuing imperfection and transience.
Yakisugi	焼杉	Charred cedar	Traditional Japanese wood preservation technique using controlled burning.
Yotsuba izutsu-tsugi	四つ葉井筒継ぎ	Four-leaf well-frame joint	A kumiko pattern featuring four leaves framed in a square-like joint structure.

Appendix Two

Conversion Table: Inches to Millimeters

Millimeter measurements throughout the book are rounded to the nearest 0.1 mm for simplicity. The values in this table show the precise conversions.

Inches = millimeters ÷ 25.4
Millimeters = inches × 25.4

Fraction (in)	Decimal (in)	Millimeter (mm)
1/16	0.0625	1.588 mm
1/8	0.125	3.175 mm
3/16	0.1875	4.763 mm
1/4	0.250	6.350 mm
5/16	0.3125	7.938 mm
3/8	0.375	9.525 mm
7/16	0.4375	11.113 mm
1/2	0.500	12.700 mm
9/16	0.5625	14.288 mm
5/8	0.625	15.875 mm
11/16	0.6875	17.463 mm
3/4	0.750	19.050 mm
13/16	0.8125	20.638 mm
7/8	0.875	22.225 mm
15/16	0.9375	23.813 mm
1	1.00	25.400 mm

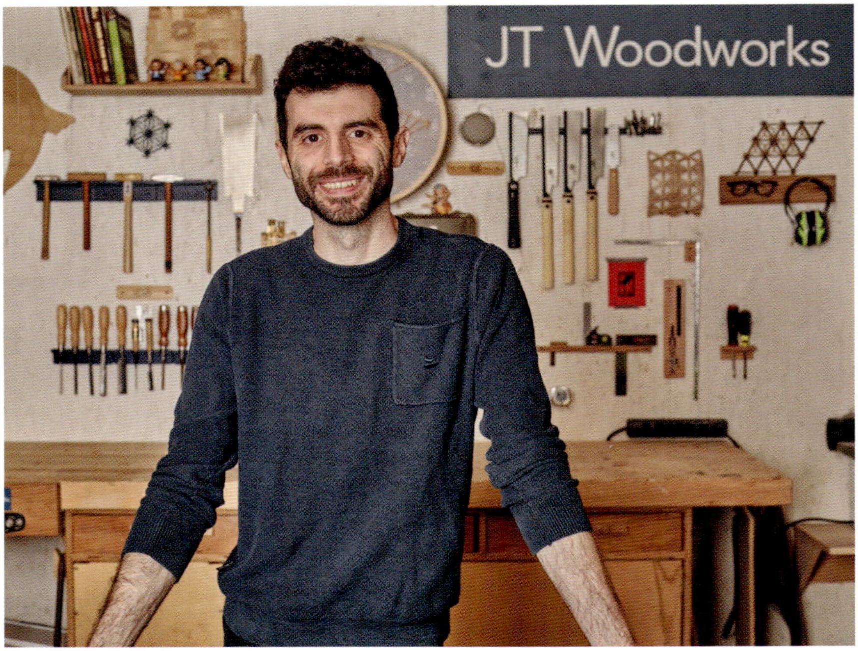

About the Author

Johnny Tromboukis is a fine woodworker and the founder of JT Woodworks, a studio dedicated to the art of kumiko. He has a deep passion for preserving the purity and authenticity of kumiko. For him, this centuries-old craft is more than just a skill, it's a way to connect with history, culture, and the timeless beauty of handmade craftsmanship.

As an educator and advocate for the woodworking community, Johnny is committed to sharing his expertise with both new and seasoned woodworkers. Through his YouTube channel, he offers step-by-step tutorials, tips, and insights into the world of kumiko, making this delicate art form accessible to all.

His work extends beyond video content, offering specialized tools and kits on his website to help woodworkers refine their skills and create their own stunning designs. Through his dedication to teaching and his commitment to preserving tradition and culture, Johnny strives to keep this beautiful craft alive, one piece of wood at a time.

To learn more, visit www.jtwoodworks.com